Published in Nashville, Tennessee, by Thomas Nelson. Thomas Nelson is a registered trademark of Thomas Nelson, Inc.

Thomas Nelson, Inc., titles may be purchased in bulk for educational, business, fund-raising, or sales promotional use. For information, please e-mail SpecialMarkets@ThomasNelson.com.

Library of Congress Control Number: 2011940099

ISBN: 978-1-59555-457-4

Printed in the United States of America

11 12 13 14 15 QGF 6 5 4 3 2 1

Dedicated to family and friends who chose to serve . . .

Family

Henry Cone: Continental Army, First Company, First Regiment, Connecticut, 1775. Served: Siege of Boston, Battle of Bunker Hill. Third Regiment, Connecticut, 1776-1783. Served: Valley Forge and the Battles of Brandywine, Monmouth, and Long Island.

William Watkins: Continental Army, Fifth Company, Third Regiment, Connecticut, 1775. Served: Siege of Boston, Battle of Bunker Hill.

Andrew Cone: Served in the War of 1812.

ARM2C Ellsworth Abbott Shirley, USN, 43-45 (KIA); Cpl. Edward Cone, USAAC, 43-45 (WWII); Seaman Gilbert Abbott, USN, (WWII); Cpl. Herbert L. Cone, USA, 46-48; PFC Ronald Lee Shirley, USMC, 46-48; Airman William Mackintosh, USAF, 49-53; RI Edward Bruce Shirley, USA, 49-51; Cpl. Fred R. Mackintosh, USAR, 52-58; Daniel Jacob, USAF, 52-54/USAFR, 54-59; F2 Louis Mackintosh, USN, 61-63; Capt. Gerald E. Eckert, MD, USAR; Seaman Kyle Richard Shirley,73-74; Spc. 4 Michael L. Cone, USA, 72-75, (Vietnam); SSgt. Ronald J. Hauer, USAF, 77–81; SSgt Tracy A. Eckert, USAR, 80-04; Pvt. Timothy Naumann, USA, 97-08; Lance Cpl. Edward Nathan Shirley USMCR, 99-05 (Iraq); Sgt. Sean Naumann, USMCR, 01-09; PV2 Ryan J. Cone, USA, 04/ USANG, 10-Present (Afghanistan); HM Andrew Abbott Shirley, USN, 07-08; Cpl. Robert G. Eckert, USA, 06-10; SPC Holly F. Eckert, USA, 06-present (Afghanistan); AFC Zachary Shirley, USAF, 09-present (Afghanistan).

Friends

Capt. Ronald Reagan, USAR, 37-42/USA 42-45; Col. Richard Snyder, USAF, 40-65 (WWII, German POW); PFC Ralph Jefferson Turner, USA, 40-45 (WWII, Japanese POW); 2LT Robert J. Dole, USA, 42-48 (WWII); LTJG George H.W. Bush, USN, 42-45 (WWII); Sgt. Franklyn Nofziger, 42-45 (WWII); HM Paul Laxalt, USA, 42-45 (WWII); MG John Singlaub, USAF, 43-77 (WWII, Korea, Vietnam); 1LT Frank Leonard, USAAC, 43-45 (WWII, German POW); ETM2C Richard Schweiker, USN, 44-46 (WWII); Seaman Stu Spencer, USN, 45-46 (WWII); Sgt. Victor Gold, USA, 50-52; Capt. John McCain, USN, 54-

81 (*Vietnam War, Vietnam POW*); PFC Richard Glen Banister, USAR, 57-62 (*Cuban Missile Crisis*); Capt. James A Baker III, USMC, 52-54/ USMCR; LCDR Frederic Johnson, USN, 55-76; Spc. 4 Fred Barnes, USA, 60-62; QM3 Robert Livingston, USN, 61-67 (*Cuban Missile Crisis*); Capt. Michael McShane, USAF, 66-72 (*Vietnam*); Cdr. Michael Phelps, USN, 66-69/MANG, 82-86; Col. Thomas A. Vaughan, USA, 68-71/ USAR 71-98 (*Vietnam*); 1LT George W. Bush, USAFNG, 68-74; Capt. Tom Finnigan, USAR, 71-81; Spc. 4 Kevin Kabanuk, USA, 72-74; Capt. Rick Perry, USAF, 72-77; Col. Robert Rowland, USMC, 73-98; LC Kyle T. Fugate, USA, 86-09 (*Afghanistan*); LCDR Frank Lavin, USNR, 87-03; Maj. Stephanie Roell Fugate, USA, 95-04; Lt. Adam Paul Laxalt, USN, 05-10; HM2 Robert Staton, USN, 07-Present; HM3 Fletcher Carson, USN, 07-Present; 1LT Joseph M. Bozell, USMC, 07-Present (*Afghanistan*).

CONTENTS

PREFACE

In 1941 a B-25 Mitchell bomber contained 107,156 rivets, each one inserted by hand. Often a woman's hand.

That year, there were as many people on the left, such as Lowell Thomas and Al Smith, who were part of the isolationist America First Committee as there were people on the right, such as Charles Lindberg and Herbert Hoover.

The U.S.O. was created in 1941, as was the comic book character, "Captain America." The first time an organ was played at a baseball game was in Chicago in 1941, and the first television commercial aired was in 1941 to tout Bulova Watches. The "Red Ryder" BB gun was also first introduced.

In 1941, the United States of America went to war with the Axis Powers including Japan, Germany, and Italy, changing America radically and forever.

Just three days before the December 7th attack, President Franklin Roosevelt received a long memorandum marked "Confidential" from the Office of Naval Intelligence, reviewing in detail all the subversive activities going on in America, including those emanating from the Japanese Embassy in Washington. "The focal point of the Japanese Espionage effort is the determination of the total strength of the United States. In anticipation of possible open conflict with this country, Japan is vigorously utilizing every available agency to secure military, naval and commercial information, paying particular attention to the West Coast, the Panama Canal and the Territory of Hawaii."[1] The 26-page document went into great detail about the coordination between

German and Japanese agents on U.S. soil. The secret paper also reviewed the attempts by the Japanese to infiltrate labor unions, Latin American groups and the National Association for the Advancement of Colored People.[2]

A second reference specifically to the Hawaiian Territory was made in the memo. "However, only the more important groups are of interest, since they are in a position to engage in espionage, sabotage and other acts inimical to the best interests of the U.S . . . . Each of these groups is at least strongly influenced if not directly controlled by similar ones in Japan."[3] The confidential document prepared for Roosevelt went into great detail regarding the Japanese civilian presence in Hawaii.

The response by the U.S. military, government, and citizenry to the events of December 7 was quick and decisive, even if it was also often bumbling and haphazard. "Everyone, I suppose, will be jotting down in a little black book somewhere the memories of Sunday, December 7—where they were, what they were doing, what they thought when they first heard of the war. Let me tell you—you don't have to make a note of those things. You'll remember them." So wrote famed sports columnist Bill Henry in his "By the Way" column in the *Los Angeles Times* on December 9.[4] This was true enough, but the entire thirty-one days of December 1941 were memorable, messy, historic, poignant, confusing, inspiring, depressing, and enduring.

After December 7, 1941, the policies towards the Japanese, Germans and Italians living in America were harsh and comprehensive but, because the government believed the Germans, and the Japanese had incredible spy and sabotage networks operating in the United States and the Hawaiian Territory, the reaction by the government at the time, they felt, was justified.

At the end of December 1941, Americans still weren't calling it "World War II" or the "Second World War," though there were hints of the standard appellations to come. Even three weeks after America's entry into the global crisis, Americans were still calling it the "national emergency" or "the war." I didn't learn many of these and thousands of other things just from researching books during the development stages of *December 1941*; I learned many of these facts from the newspapers, magazines and other publications of the era as well.

Washington Post publisher Phil Graham once said, newspapers were "the first rough draft of history." The phrase had been attributed to others before Graham, but he gets the credit for it.[5] So much of the sourcing for this book comes from hundreds of newspapers and thousands upon thousands of newspaper and magazine articles around the country and wire service bulletins and radio dispatches and short-wave intercepts sifted through to build the following account. But private diaries, personal papers, and confidential and classified materials were also heavily relied upon for this story.

There never had been a book solely devoted to the month of December 1941, surely one of the most important and decisive and nation-altering thirty-one days in the history of the American Republic. There have been days such as July 4, 1776; October 19, 1781; September 17, 1787; and April 15, 1861, that rank with December 7, but one is hard-pressed to think of another month as startling, compelling, interesting, critical, and inspiring as December 1941.

There have been many outstanding books written on World War II and the events leading up to Pearl Harbor, but never has there been a book about the days in America prior to December 7, 1941, and what happened to the country in the hours, days, and weeks after the attack. Suffice it to say, the country was radically changed forever.

Never before or since has America been so unified. There were virtually no Americans against their country getting into World War II after the unprovoked attack by the Japanese at Pearl Harbor. One of the few was Congresswoman Jeannette Rankin, Republican of Montana. She voted against declaring war on Japan and would only vote "present" when FDR asked Congress for a declaration of war against Germany and Italy—after they had declared war on America. Someday someone will write a book about Ms. Rankin, exploring her reasons for not voting for war. They were principled, nuanced, and commendable. She was mistaken but she wasn't wrong.[6]

The goal here is to make the reader feel as if they are experiencing the day to day events as they unfolded. Some historians don't like to go into the arduous tasks of going through thousand of newspapers preferring instead to rely on those bits and pieces of news reporting they may glean from other books. I did, and consequently the reader will find stories and information from the month of December 1941 they have never heard before. It makes for what I hope will be a fascinating book.

Of my previous writings, many said they gave the reader a "you-are-there feeling," while another said I wrote like a sports writer, which I took as one of the best compliments I've ever received. The goal here was to impart new information while making the reading enjoyable. I wanted to do a story of America, to allow the reader to see the country through the eyes of the 130 million citizens who lived in the forty-eight states in that remarkable month of December, 1941.

The goal was to write a book so that the reader could read and feel what their parents and grandparents and great-grandparents were reading and hearing and feeling and talking about at the time. About a time of war and peace and service and sacrifice and losing and winning and unity.

President Roosevelt, Prime Minister Winston Churchill, General George C. Marshall, Admiral Chester Nimitz, General Douglas MacArthur, and many others in both the Allied and the Axis Powers are here. Prominent Americans including political leaders, actors, and athletes are here. Yet they are all merely supporting cast members in this drama.

The central and most important actor in *December 1941* is the United States of America.

Craig Shirley
Lancaster, Virginia

CHAPTER 1

THE FIRST OF DECEMBER

"U.S. and Jap Negotiations Continue"
Fitchburg Sentinel

"Britain Puts All Far East Areas on War Basis"
Tucson Daily Citizen

"Nazis See Fall of Moscow Near"
Idaho Times

"'Wise Statesmanship' Might Save Situation, Japs Tell Reporters"
Bismarck Tribune

America's 1,974 daily newspapers[1] were crammed with war news: Russian, German, British, Japanese, Italian, Free China, Vichy France, Netherland East Indies, and Serbian. Reports were thick with hostilities in the North Atlantic and the South Pacific, in Northwest Africa and Southeast Asia, in Western Europe and on the Eastern Front.

The Third Reich and the British Empire were engaged in massive tank battles along Africa's Mediterranean coastline. Marshal Henri Philippe Petain, the puppet head of the Vichy French government, was reportedly in meetings with Adolf Hitler as a final step toward including France as part of the Axis powers'"New Order."[2] Several months earlier, in a bold military campaign that would have pleased the founder of the "First Reich," the Prussian king Frederick the Great, hundreds of thousands of German troops invaded Russia. Stalin cowered, and the maneuver looked like another brilliant offensive operation by Chancellor Hitler.

Maps of Asia, Africa, and Europe were frequently in the newspapers and magazines, showing American readers German thrusts and surges across Europe, along with counterattacks by Britain and the Russians. Other drawings showed new incursions by the Japanese into China and Indochina, their designs on Thailand and the Burma Road. Giant arrows slashed across continents.

In Shanghai and Hong Kong, the British were eyeing fresh movements by Japanese troops. British troops in Hong Kong were ordered to return to their barracks, and a state of emergency was declared in Singapore. The Philippines also watched the Japanese with concern.

War was raging on the high seas. German "Wolf packs" preyed upon helpless civilian vessels with shoot-on-sight orders from Adolf Hitler himself, and thousands of tons of hardened steel had already been sent to the bottom of the Atlantic. Berlin was also making plans to take Surinam, a strategically important outpost on the Atlantic side of South America. "Bundles" were dispatched to Britain, and Greek war relief funds were raised courtesy of American charity for those besieged countries.

To slow the inevitable German advance on Moscow, the Red Army burned the homes of Russian peasants by the thousands in hopes of denying Nazi forces any resources they might find in them. As a result, untold thousands of Russian citizens were left homeless in the blinding white cold.

It was all just one more day in a new world war that had already been a fully involved inferno for over two years. And yet there was much more to come.

But there was no American war news. No Americans were fighting anywhere in the world, at least not under their forty-eight-star flag. Americans didn't want any part of this rest-of-the-world mess. They'd been through that thankless hell once before, in a previous global struggle that was supposed to make the world safe for democracy. Memories were still fresh of American doughboys fighting and dying in the trenches of European battlefields, only to result in the rise of distinctly undemocratic societies a generation later.

An entire world was truly at war, but the United States was sitting this one out.

On December 1, 1941, Americans simply referred to the unfolding hostilities as "the emergency" and went about their business, walled off from the clamor by two giant oceans. Christmas was coming, and the economy was showing signs of life for the first time in years. For over a decade, the country had staggered through the dark valley of the Great Depression, and it could finally see some sunlight. Americans planned to enjoy an uneasy peace and a modicum of prosperity.

The only place American troops could be found "fighting" was South Carolina in war games supervised by one-star Gen. George S. Patton Jr. Because of severe budget restrictions, the troops used fake ammo. The brass wanted to conclude these maneuvers quickly so they and 300,000 participating troops could make it home in time for Christmas. But the faux battle was described as a "sham" with fistfights breaking out as parachutists landed, while "on to the field," as *Time* reported in the language of the era, "charged grease-monkeys and Negro engineers" armed with "rifles and clubs."[3] The army guaranteed they'd use real ammo for maneuvers scheduled in 1942.[4]

The navy's materiel situation was just a bit more promising. Rolling off production lines in Maine and San Francisco were new destroyers, the *Aaron*, *Buchanan*, and *Fahrenholt*. Battleships in the works were the *Indiana*, *Alabama*, *Iowa*, *New Jersey*, *Missouri*, and the *Wisconsin*. They were bigger, armed with more powerful guns than the fifteen battleships already in the fleet. "Meanwhile, Navy men find a particular comfort in their completed plans: as far as they know, the Japanese are planning nothing like them." The plan was for a two-ocean navy, an overall addition of 17 new battlewagons, along with "eleven more carriers, 54 cruisers, 192 destroyers, 73 submarines."[5] Also under development in Boston was a relatively small and light torpedo vessel known as a PT boat. Its development was "a military secret," but pictures and all the specifications were printed in detail in *Time* magazine complete with speed, armaments, length and construction, which was a plywood hull.[6]

The weather across the country was cloudy that day, from Abilene to Washington, D.C., and so was America's clarity about the threat from the East.

"Americans do not even seem worried by the prospect of war with Japan," *Life* magazine reported.[7] The reigning assumption was that if there was any action by the Japanese in the Pacific theatre, it would be directed against Great Britain and the empire's outposts there. As a result, the British were beefing up their naval presence in the region, having recently dispatched large warships including the *Prince of Wales*.[8] The British in Hong Kong ordered their garrison there to move into an "advanced state of readiness,"[9] and their troops in Singapore and Rangoon had also been so warned. As a precaution, the U.S. Army and Navy in the area were "ordered on the alert."[10] News photos of "Swarthy Punjabi sepoys"[11]—Singapore soldiers manning 40-milimeter guns—appeared in some American papers. Some 75 percent of the tin imported by the United States came from Singapore, so Washington had at least a passing interest.[12]

The American navy had been quietly moving munitions out of Honolulu and the tiny island of Palmyra to the British-held Fiji Islands and the Free French island of Caledonia to assist against possible Japanese strikes there.[13] The Americans had strengthened their military operations on Samoa, but the Japanese government made clear they too had parochial interests in the Pacific and vowed to keep the shipping lanes between their home islands and South America open. For the average American, though, when they gave the Pacific a passing thought, it was only about palm trees and sandy beaches. The very word *pacific* meant tranquility, a peaceful nature.

Consequently, few in America paid any attention to an item buried deep in a United Press International story from the evening of December 1, dateline Manila: "Sixteen Japanese heavy cruisers and aircraft carriers were reported by Manila to have swung southward. . . . Japanese reinforcements were reported landing in Indochina where there already were an estimated 100,000 troops."[14] Another unnoticed story, this one from INS news service, reported on the "precarious positions of the Philippines . . . under command of Lieutenant Gen. Douglas MacArthur" who was being "subjected to a horseshoe encirclement by Japan."[15] However, according to respected military analyst Dewitt MacKenzie, recent setbacks by the Nazis in Russia and Africa had led the Japanese to pull up because, he said, "Tokyo is anxious to evade conflict with America."[16] Indeed, representatives of the Japanese and American governments were in ongoing peace talks to gain clarity and iron out their differences.

Numerous newspaper reports and columns speculated on the intent of the Japanese government, and nearly all came to the conclusion that they had neither the will nor the industrial plant to move forward with any serious naval action in the Pacific. Furthermore, the Japanese navy was seemingly so weak the Nazis had deployed some of their ships to the Pacific to buttress their Axis ally. The Allies had lost track of a good portion of the Nazi navy—they couldn't find many of their ships.[17]

When it came to the American ships, the conventional knowledge was that "[t]he Pacific fleet . . . has a decided superiority over the Japanese. . . . The Japanese would be hard put to it to replace their losses because of the lack of raw materials which they obtained from the United States and other western democracies." Few in America worried about the Japanese navy, though there were signs they should. Chillingly, buried at the end of a piece, respected British correspondent Constantine Brown reported, "The Japanese have hinted . . . that they do have some juicy surprises if we decide to accept their challenge in the Pacific."[18]

Part of the source of the irritation between Tokyo and Washington stemmed from the Japanese invasion of Free China. The Japanese had invaded China in 1937 and proceeded to conduct genocidal activities on the Mainland. The Chinese had a strong lobby in Washington and America, as well as many sympathetic supporters.

In retaliation, the Americans slapped a boycott on products headed for Japan, including precious scrap metal. For the boycott to be lifted, the State Department set out four conditions to the Japanese. First, they had to withdraw as a member of the Axis powers. Second, they had to withdraw their forces from French Indochina and the Mainland. Third, they had to renounce aggression, and fourth, they had "observe the principle of equal trade opportunity in the Pacific." Cordell Hull, the secretary of state, also offered the Japanese government $100 million if they would agree to switch from a wartime economy to a peacetime economy, but also sell war material to Russia in order to help Stalin fight Hitler.[19]

While talks continued with Japan, most eyes in America were fixed on Europe and the North Atlantic, not Asia or the Pacific.

The night before, the Germans had downed eight British bombers on a mission over Hamburg.[20] Over the previous weekend, the American merchant ship *MacBeth* was reported missing in the North Atlantic, presumed torpedoed.[21] U.S. ambassador to the USSR Laurence Steinhardt paid a worried visit to the White House to discuss the war in Europe with FDR;[22] and Nazi propaganda minister Paul Joseph Goebbels gave a talk at Berlin University in which he predicted that it was too late for the United States to do anything to prevent England's eventual defeat.[23] The plane of an American general, George H. Brett, head of the Army Air Corps, was shot at by Axis naval vessels as it crossed the Mediterranean.[24] Privately, Franklin Roosevelt had been telling aides since 1939 he believed the Nazis were bent on "world dominance."[25]

Not that America was ready for it.

Since dissolving its forces after 1919, there was little American military to speak of. The Army Air Corps had only 51,000 trained flyers as of June of 1940. On the other hand, the Royal Air Force had 500,000 pilots, and the German Luftwaffe had a million pilots. Both countries were far smaller than America in terms of population, and the U.S. planes were inferior to boot. American Curtiss P-40s were out-gunned and out-accelerated by the English Spitfires and the German Messerschmitts, and the P-40s couldn't achieve their altitude either.[26] Still, the American military was quite proud that their tiny air force operated out of what they called "dispersion fields," meaning their geographically scattered planes would not be subjected to mass destruction as a result of aerial bombardment.[27] They were also proud of their new glider schools.[28]

Lt. Gen. Leslie J. McNair observed that against Germany, the U.S. Army could "fight effectively but losses would be unduly heavy." And he lamented about the poorly equipped troops.[29] An army draft continued in America, but 1,400 American "boys" refused to report, declaring themselves as "conscientious objectors." They were sentenced to Civilian Conservation Corps work camps around the country, where they picked up trash, planted trees, and served their time, at least a year and in some cases, more. Most were religious pacifists, including Mennonites.[30]

The army was also forcing 1,800 uniformed soldiers of the 29th Division out of service. All in excess of twenty-eight years old, they were deemed "overage." Maj. Gen. Milton A. Reckord protested that it would take "weeks to build the division back to its peak."[31]

The navy was undermanned as well. Enlistments were so poor that Secretary of War Frank Knox mused publicly that he might have to impose a draft for the blue-water service, something that had never been done before. The admirals thought the deficiency could be made up with better newspaper advertising campaigns and by "relaxation of health standards."[32] That might have explained why the navy called back seventy-seven-year-old Jesse "Pop" Warner as a chief boatswain's mate in San Diego. Warner had already served fifty-seven years in the navy, had a recent physical, and with the exception of upper and lower dental plates, was pronounced "fit for sea duty." He had originally enlisted in 1884.[33]

Americans were understandably gloomy or indifferent about world affairs, but things were bothersome at home too. The country was still feeling the effects of the Great Depression, and after the economy had made a gentle comeback several years earlier, it had slid back and had only recently perked up again. Unemployment hovered around 10 percent, though war production had begun to stabilize the economy.[34]

Despite their vow to stay out of "it," a war effort had been underway for a while now—allegedly only to aid the Allied powers. The "Arsenal of Democracy"[35] was reserved exclusively for friends of America, but there was some promising if slightly ironic upside to the early efforts. Just as Germany had pulled itself out of its own depression with a military buildup, so too was the United States. In California, for instance, industrial factories supporting the war effort numbered over 2,000 as of December, and wages were as high as $193 per week, although many employees were still scraping by on less than $40.[36]

It was a shaky and uncertain recovery. The stock market on December 1 was mixed, and Wall Street was mildly surprised that investors had not reacted more favorably to news of the Russian counteroffensive and of the Japanese desire to continue talks with Washington to try to effect a political solution to their disagreements. The market was at its lowest point since 1938, but there was no market averaging yet.[37] Stocks were broken down between railroads and industrials. In 1926, railroad stocks had been trading at over $102 per share, but by 1941, they were at $23 per share.[38]

Senator Sheridan Downey of California proclaimed that the 2 percent payroll tax was enough to fund the Social Security retirement system, which in 1941 provided a pensioner at age sixty with $36 per month for the rest of his life. With the tax scheduled to go to 4 percent in 1943, the trust fund would have more than enough to pay for the retirement of all Americans over retirement age. But, Downey told a congressional committee, rather than depositing the taxes collected into Treasury bonds, it would be "more humane" to provide pensions for those elderly who were "slowly decaying and starving" on welfare rolls.[39]

A majority thought the Depression could last another ten years, and only 37 percent thought "that their sons' opportunities will be better than their own."[40] A majority also thought the New Deal would expand and exert ever-more control over the American economy; that same majority also deemed it a good thing. But after thirteen years, the "new normal" of 1941 was to expect that nearly one out of five Americans would be perpetually unemployed, despite the best intentions of the New Deal.

The Roosevelt administration had pretty much run out of ideas and the alphabet content to simply keep throwing money at the problem and hyper-managing the economy through a weed patch of bureaus and administrative departments. No New Deal legislation had been proposed in Congress for over two years. As far back as "the winter of 1938–39, Roosevelt knew, but was not yet willing to say, that the New Deal, as a social and political revolution, was dead."[41] Washington was a bureaucratic mess and no one seemed to know what agency or department was responsible—or irresponsible—

for what. The Office of Production Management was fighting with the War Department over metals, as the allotment slated for farm equipment was being sucked up and sent to Great Britain.

The Rooseveltians ran roughshod over business. "For the first time during this emergency, the U.S. government forced the removal of a corporation executive from his own company," reported *Life* magazine. It seems that one F. Leroy Hill, president of Air Associates, a maker of airplane parts, "had been at odds with the National Defense Mediation Board." The army "fired" Hill from his own company, without ever appearing before a judge or jury. "When it finds a man that it likes, the Army plans to give the plant back to its owners."[42] The "mighty music" of America—as written by North Carolina's Thomas Wolfe—had been silent for over ten years.[43]

With all the news coverage of the war and the buildup at home, military and civilian culture mixed easily. The print ads in the nation's weekly and daily newspapers had broad military themes. The topic of national unity was deep throughout many, even in Parker Pen print ads, which depicted men in uniform right alongside civilians.[44]

The Ethyl Gasoline Corporation's ad told the story of an anonymous delivery man. "He's been delivering the goods for you and the folks next door for years. The lumber, stone, metal, glass of which homes are built. . . . Today, he's got an even bigger job to do—delivering the goods for Uncle Sam."[45] B.F. Goodrich pushed their rubber products via a heavy military thesis.[46] So did the automotive business. Plymouth was running ads for their 1942 model but also made it clear that the Chrysler Corporation manufactured "Army tanks, Anti-Aircraft Cannons, Army Trucks . . . shells and projectiles."[47] Chevy did the same thing. In fact, whether it was an Oldsmobile, a Ford, a De Soto, a Packard, a Nash, or a Buick, all their advertising had a martial theme, detailing how each manufacturer was contributing to the war effort.

Even bicycle manufacturers got in on the act. Columbia was promoting the idea of parachuting "leathernecks of the Marine Corps" along with bicycles that folded up and could "hit the silk," which upon landing "are assembled and ready to speed away on a lightning-fast maneuver."[48] Other manufacturers like Schwinn were just pushing bicycles for the Christmas season.[49]

But the combination of the war effort and the growth of federal power raised ominous flags as well. The Office of Price Administration warned that cars made after 1942 might be severely curtailed. A generic "Victory" model car was envisioned that would eliminate "double-bar bumpers" and would feature the "substitution of wool and rubber floor mats in favor of linoleum . . . elimination of all unnecessary gadgets such as clocks, cigar lighters, radios, dual tail lights . . . reduction in number of colors and the number of coats of paint." The OPM had already ordered a 50 percent reduction in the number of cars made for 1942 over 1941 because demand had gone up. It was contemplating prioritization of the civilian population to see who government would allow to own a new car and who did not *need* to own a new car.[50]

Despite the rough economic times—or more likely because of them—American citizens went regularly to the movie theaters to escape. In every city, hamlet, and town moviegoers saw their favorite actors and actresses in edifices such as the Strand, Paramount, RKO Keith, the Uptown, the Biograph, the Palace, and of course, the Bijou. Many theaters were truly palaces, elaborately designed, with heavy wood, brass railings, spit and shine ushers, dramatically large curtains, and colorful lighting. Uniformed boys and young men complete with caps and epaulettes opened doors, helped customers find seats, and pleasantly greeted all patrons as they entered. These theaters were designed for maximum comfort in order to make those attending feel special. Some were even equipped with the new-fangled air conditioning. By and large, kids went to the same movies as adults, and all forked over the 10 cents to see a movie; a double feature cost from 17 to 21 cents more. Saturday matinees for children usually ran a nickel.[51]

Americans dressed up in suits and ties and dresses to go to the movies. Everyone wore hats, and they always put on their "Sunday Best" to go to church, out to dinner, to take a train or an airplane. The whole idea was to make people think better of you as an individual. Good grooming permeated the culture, as did helpful advice and tips on landing a bride or groom.

Personal hygiene was also important, as consumers could purchase a "pro-phylactic tooth brush" and "tooth powder" for 47 cents.[52] Hair tonics such as Vitalis promised to keep men's hair in place, reduce dandruff, and "prevent excessive falling hair."[53]

Men did not go out unshaven, and only old men or psychiatrists had beards—though pencil moustaches, such as those sported by Clark Gable, Errol Flynn, William Powell, and Ronald Colman, were popular with movie actors and those who emulated their style. Women's role models were slim, chic actresses such as Barbara Stanwyck, Myrna Loy, and Greer Garson. Hem lengths were just below the knee, and women wore makeup, heels, girdles, and stockings before even thinking about going out in public.

The most popular movies in 1941 were *Sergeant York*, *The Maltese Falcon*, *Meet John Doe*, *Dumbo*, and the acclaimed masterpiece *Citizen Kane*. Along with *The Maltese Falcon*, *Citizen Kane* gave Americans one of its first tastes of film noir in which morality was ambiguous, human nature base, and all char-acters worthy of suspicion. These movies foreshadowed a post-World War II disillusionment, when in the late 1940s and early 1950s the traumatic memo-ries of battle and the haunting meaninglessness of the Holocaust provided plenty of fuel for dark and apprehensive films. But for now, such thoughts were only small gray clouds on an otherwise red-white-and-blue American horizon. Indeed many movies in 1941 depicted unadulterated patriotism: for instance, *A Yank in the RAF*, *War Front*, *They Died with Their Boots On*, *Dive Bomber*, and *Buck Privates* starring comedy duo Bud Abbott and Lou Costello.

As with most other years of the era, Hollywood churned out movie after movie, and the average American went to the theater twice a week. While at the theater, moviegoers could also watch serials such as the *Adventures of Captain Marvel*, *Dick Tracy*, *The Green Hornet*, and *Jungle Girl*.

Radio was also important to Americans, particularly the AM dial. Americans woke to farm reports and the weather, listened throughout the day to music and local programming often involving local children in contests, and settled into the evening with nationally broadcast adventure and comedy shows, such as *The Battling Bickersons*, the exploits of Jack Benny, and *Fibber McGee and Molly*. Up-and-comer Bob Hope made mil-lions of Americans laugh, while liberal columnist Drew Pearson and con-servative columnist Walter Winchell made them think or simply get angry with their commentaries. Hollywood reporters like Hedda Hopper and Louella Parsons satisfied a taste for gossip, while others tuned their ears to the strains of Tommy Dorsey, Jimmy Dorsey, Harry James, Glenn Miller, Duke Ellington, Dinah Shore, Peggy Lee, Frank Sinatra, Harriet Nelson, Bing Crosby, and the great "Satchmo," Louis Armstrong. FM radio was not unheard of in 1941, just very expensive; an FM radio in 1941 could cost as much as $390, more than most people's wages in one month.[54]

CBS had inaugurated a new radio show just a year earlier, *Report to the Nation*. It was created in response to "the problem of allocating radio time to the numerous Government agencies that wanted it." Though the hour-long show covered Washington and the events there, it used "actors and actresses . . . about two-thirds are daytime Government employees" for its usual all-news and commentary format.[55]

Everybody smoked cigarettes in 1941, and everybody smoked cigarettes everywhere. In the movie theaters, in restaurants, on airplanes, in trains, at sporting events, at the office, even in classrooms, Americans smoked 'em if they had 'em. Favorite brands were Camels, Lucky Strike, and Chesterfield. Smoking had increased in America despite some then-obscure reports linking the activity with a shortened lifespan. The average American in 1940 consumed 2,558 cigarettes, double that of ten years earlier.[56] Ads pitched Camels as great Christmas gifts because their packaging was "so gay and colorful." They also contained "28 percent less nicotine."[57] Old Gold made it clear in their ads that smoking helped women lose weight.[58]

Technically, one had to be of an ambiguous legal age to purchase and smoke cigarettes, but it wasn't unusual to see young teenagers smoking cigarettes, and cigarette ads screamed out from every publication and billboard in America. Someone often really was calling for "Phillip Morris," as the bellhop in the ad in every publication was. Smoking Phillip Morris was important, as "eminent doctors" said it was easier on the throat than other "leading brands" because "all smokers sometimes inhale."[59]

Many ads also made clear the importance of a "good purge," which seemed very important in 1941. In one magazine ad for Kellogg's All-Bran cereal, the figure of a grey uniformed Civil War vet encouraged readers to "join the 'regulars' with Kellogg's."[60]

Sports fans had a lot to talk about. Football was in full swing, and fans were looking forward to the coming college bowl season with Duke pitted against Oregon State in the Rose Bowl and Fordham versus Missouri in the Sugar Bowl. "As always, the selections stirred a few dissents."[61] The Yankee Clipper, Joe DiMaggio, had a newborn son, Joe D. III, with his wife, actress Dorothy Arnold.[62] And the "hot stove league" was hot with rumors that the great Jimmie Foxx was about to leave the Boston Red Sox and rejoin his old boss, Connie Mack, owner and manager of the Philadelphia Athletics.[63]

Other news of the day included a sixty-two-year-old North Carolinian mountaineer, Joe Downs, who wed fifteen-year-old Estelle Pruitt.[64] The photo of the scowling elderly man and his bucktoothed bride was published in hundreds of newspapers. In New York City, parents protested in front of Mayor Fiorello LaGuardia's home against the rising crime wave in the city's parks.[65] Six members of the Ku Klux Klan were convicted in Atlanta for conducting a widespread campaign of "flogging" people there—seizing people from their homes and whipping them. Despite pressure, Georgia governor Eugene Talmadge refused to pardon them.[66] He told them he'd once "helped flog a Negro himself" and then had the audacity to compare himself to the apostle Paul. "The Apostle Paul was a flogger in his life, then confessed, reformed and became one of the greatest powers of the Christian Church." *Life* magazine noted that Talmadge "frankly and deliberately stirs up racial hatreds."[67]

And 1940 GOP nominee Wendell Willkie decided to defend in the Supreme Court a self-admitted communist who had had his citizenship invalidated as a result of his political affiliations.[68]

The women's pages of the nation's newspapers were filled with articles on fashion, wedding announcements, landing a husband, and the proper conduct in the workplace. *Life* magazine detailed how the Latin American women preferred wearing black and now it was taking over American women's fashions. "Black hats, black shorts, black slacks, black bathing suits, black skirts ..." had all been inspired when a fashion designer saw "barefoot peasants of inland Mexico" attired in black.[69]

All newspapers had event-filled "Social Calendars."[70] A cartoon in the *Greeley Daily Tribune* women's page depicted a beat-up young woman, one eye blackened, head bandaged, and sporting a broken arm as she cheerily told three friends, "My boyfriend always starts a little spat just before Christmas."[71] But dozens of tamer cartoon strips were enjoyed by American parents and children. "Li'l Abner," about a hayseed in Dog Patch; "Alley Oop," a cave man in present times; "Blondie," a ditsy wife and her equally ditsy husband, Dagwood; "Prince Valiant," a knight of the Round Table; and "Bringing Up Father," about Jiggs and Maggie, two socialites seemingly caught in the time warp of 1922. Meanwhile, "Little Orphan Annie" was battling German spies in her comic strip and seemed to have a better plan for dealing with them than the U.S. government did.

Of course Annie didn't have to worry about politics, and war is nothing if not political.

In May 1941, German U-boats sunk an unarmed American freighter, the *Robin Moor*, and yet there was no great push to get America into another European war.[72] Few wanted war, and few believed it was coming to America.

Later in the year, Adolf Hitler upped the ante by ordering U-boats to fire on American naval ships. In turn, FDR ordered American vessels to defend themselves. On October 31, the Germans sank the *Reuben James*, an American destroyer, leaving a few dozen survivors. Earlier in October, German U-boats also torpedoed the USS *Kearny*, though she did not go down.[73] The *Kearny* had responded to the mayday call of a Canadian convoy, which U-boats were sinking at will.[74] The *Kearny* dropped depth charges, though it was not known if the American vessel sank any Wolf Pack subs. The sea battle lasted three hours with ten killed on the tough little American destroyer after being struck by a torpedo.[75] American freighter ships operating in the Atlantic began to outfit with fixed guns, and seven Americans serving in the British merchant marines were killed by enemy fire.[76]

Despite this Nazi aggression, there was no real groundswell for war with Germany, and no one in the country really thought war was imminent. That's not to say that there were not strong opinions about it. The political factions were pretty clear-cut on this one. America had those, like Henry Luce, head of a powerful media empire that included *Time* and *Life*, who wanted to jump into the European mess with both feet. Others, like Ambassador Joe Kennedy, thought England was finished as a country and unworthy of support.

Kennedy's public utterances were increasingly construed as isolationist, even pro-Nazi. Though he sported a patina of Brahmin respectability, the Harvard-educated Kennedy made his fortune as a stock swindler, bootlegger, and movie mogul. In what would prove to be a lasting Kennedy hallmark, Joe cultivated powerful alliances with the press, particularly the newspaper baron William Randolph Hearst, who throughout the 1930s would dutifully print sycophantic stories about Kennedy's successes. The Kennedy paterfamilias would later abhor the liberalism of his sons, but in 1941 Joe was an archconservative and apologist for Hitler. FDR neither trusted nor liked the brash and ruthless Irishman and privately excoriated him. Kennedy became such an embarrassment to FDR that he was recalled as America's representative to Great Britain.

And yet, many Americans shared Kennedy's anti-interventionist view. Of this new war Americans would typically shrug their shoulders and say, "Well, I hope Roosevelt doesn't get us into it," or "Let's hope it doesn't come over here." All through the 1930s Congress passed—and Roosevelt signed as a nod to rural and Southern constituencies—various Neutrality Acts that banned certain forms of trade with Europe, particularly sales of military equipment. Other laws passed in the 1930s prevented U.S. troops from leaving North America.

The largest and most vocal opponent of joining the war was the America First Committee, which had widespread and significant support, including famed transatlantic pilot Charles A. Lindbergh. The America First movement had sprung up after the German invasion of Poland in September of 1939, heralding the beginning of the new World War in Europe. They possessed such influence over the foreign policy debate that FDR pledged to the nation's "mothers and fathers" during his 1940 reelection bid "your boys are not going to be sent into any foreign wars."[77] Even as Hitler stormed across the European continent and England was fighting to the last, Americans were unmoved to get into it.

But by early 1941, FDR had craftily shifted the debate. The advent of Lend-Lease, a program to supply arms and equipment to American allies while staying otherwise uninvolved in the war itself, allowed America to avoid intervention as well as isolation. The old Neutrality Acts were abrogated, and Lend-Lease passed in March 1941.

It was originally pitched as a plan for Great Britain to operate on a "cash and carry" basis. But as Winston Churchill's government ran low on funds, the plan was radically altered so the English could "borrow" old American battleships and other war materiel and pay the U.S. government later. Many editorialists squawked. So, too, did the America Firsters.

FDR, the old master, had sold his argument to Congress and the American people with the rather tenuous allegory that if your neighbor's house was on fire, you wouldn't refuse him your garden hose, because his house fire threatened your house. You wouldn't sell him the hose; you'd loan it and get it back when he was done. Of course no one expected battleships and other war materiel to come back in the same shape as which it had been lent. As Senator Bob Taft wryly observed, there were two things people did not return: used military equipment and used chewing gum. But that unappetizing comparison didn't stop FDR from carrying the day.

The morning of December 1, 1941, Americans still believed they would be able to avoid any of the conflict, but by that afternoon, things had noticeably changed. The morning papers carried headlines saying the Japanese wanted to continue talks. By the afternoon, many were reporting of a worsening situation, especially after a 10:00 a.m. meeting between U.S. secretary of state Cordell Hull and the Japanese envoys that took just over an hour. They had also met the day before, on Sunday, in an extraordinary and top-secret meeting.[78]

Hull had also met in secret with British ambassador Lord Halifax, where Halifax briefed Hull on British and Japanese developments in the Far East.[79] A reporter asked Kichisaburo Nomura if the Americans and the Japanese could reach some sort of accord, and the ambassador replied ominously, "I believe there must be wise statesmanship to save the situation."[80] And "Japan voiced a preference today for further negotiations with the United States for peace in the Pacific in place of war." This was despite "great differences in the viewpoints of the two governments."[81]

In a previous meeting, Special Envoy Saburo Kurusu gave some odd comfort to Hull, telling him, "You are on Hitler's list before us." The accepted wisdom was that the Japanese were "subservient" to Hitler and would not make a move without his approval, and that if things turned bad for Hitler on the Russian front, the Empire of the Rising Sun would shrink from any military actions against the British or the Free French in the Far East.[82]

The combustible premier of Japan, Hideki Tojo, was less sanguine. He'd just issued a statement announcing that "Japan will have to do everything to wipe out with a vengeance British and American exploitation in the Far East." He also used the word *purged* in reference to the Americans and Brits presence in the Far East.[83] Noncombatants in Shanghai and Thailand were warned by their governments to evacuate soon, including Americans.[84] The British were readying their forces to defend the Burma Road.[85]

Nomura was also asked about Tojo's over-the-top remarks and replied that the premier had been "'badly misquoted' in news dispatches." He was also asked about resuming negotiations with Secretary Hull and he replied, "They have never been broken off."[86] Most indications were that both parties wanted to continue negotiations to forestall any further problems in the Pacific. Indeed, it was reported that Japan wanted to continue negotiations for another two weeks, to reach a solution to the impasse.[87] The Japanese cabinet "had decided to continue negotiations despite great differences in the viewpoints of the two governments" after meeting in a "special cabinet session." This communiqué came from Domei, a Japanese government-run news agency.[88] Hull also met with the Chinese ambassador, Dr. Hu Shih, Australian minister Richard Casey, and Netherlands minister Dr. A. Louden.[89]

Just a few days earlier, President Roosevelt had journeyed south to Warm Springs, Georgia, where he had availed himself of the hot mineral waters for years, in a vain attempt to cure his polio. He bought a house nearby that was nicknamed the "Little White House" by the press corps.[90] He was photographed carving a turkey for the patients at the Warm Springs Foundation, where together they were celebrating a "delayed Thanksgiving."[91] At a cocktail party in his honor, FDR downed several of his favorite cocktails, an old fashioned, saw his former longtime secretary Marguerite "Missy" LeHand, now herself a victim of "acute neuritis" and a patient at Warm Springs, and ate heartily of the postponed Thanksgiving feast. FDR always had a big appetite and had several helpings of turkey, "gingered fresh fruit in cider ... oyster-corn stuffing [and] pumpkin pie."[92]

The president had looked forward to spending an extended time in Georgia, until he took a confidential call over the weekend from Secretary of State Hull. Hull advised FDR that things in the Pacific had suddenly taken a turn, possibly for the worse.[93] Hull was in ongoing tense discussions with Special Envoy Saburo Kurusu and Ambassador Kichisaboro Nomura. Kurusu's wife was the former Alice Little, formerly of Chicago, Illinois. The men were photographed in America's newspapers, smiling, polite,[94] although it was also reported they had emerged from one meeting with Hull looking "grave."[95] All told, FDR was in Warm Springs for about twenty-six hours, only got in a short swim and departed for Washington looking "grave."[96] Roosevelt's hurried departure on his special train, the *Ferdinand Magellan*, was "without the usual gay hand-waving to the crowds of back-country farmers, out to see the caravan whoosh past." He arrived at the White House at 11:30 the morning of the First.

By the afternoon of Sunday, December 1, Americans knew about the call between Hull and FDR the previous evening and the president's speedy return to Washington as result. Roosevelt was spotted looking "grim," an affliction that was apparently spreading. " The *New York Times* reported that if negotiations broke down, "the American fleet in the Pacific . . . had instructions for . . . what to do if hostilities start."[97] It was later reported that FDR had met in secret with the chief of Naval Operations, Admiral Harold R. Stark.

Just the night before in Georgia, he'd given a startling speech in which he altered course, radically, saying, "It is always possible that our boys may actually be fighting for the defense of these American institutions of ours." within the year.[98] It was the first reference to the possibility of American boys dying on another continent.

White House reporters knew of the president's return by the sudden appearance of his beloved Scottie, Fala. The dog trotted into a room full of reporters, barking and wagging his tail. "Ah, the President's home," said Mrs.

Roosevelt when she saw the dog.[99] The White House refused to say exactly why FDR had cut short his trip to Warm Springs.

Upon his return, FDR met in private with Hull in the Oval Office, after the secretary's meeting with the Japanese representatives. Several days earlier, Hull had given the Japanese envoys a response in writing, stating the Americans would not cease their embargo until and unless the Japanese withdrew their forces from China.[100] The Japanese made it clear they had no intentions of slowing their drive down the Asian continent, rejecting the U.S. position as "fantastic."[101]

Waiting on FDR's desk the morning of the first was a confidential memo from his "real world" eyes and ears, John Franklin Carter. The memo detailed the Japanese population along the Mexican border around Corpus Christi and Galveston. In summary, there were very few Japanese in the south of Texas in late 1941. "Everything very quiet along the border. There seems to be more anti-Japanese prejudice in Texas than in California, also more suspicion."[102] Most who saw him thought he looked good and healthy, even if he did not have the suntan he was usually known for, because of extra-long hours of work in the Oval Office.

The National Industrial Conference Board estimated that the "economic blockade" of Japan by the United States, Great Britain, and the Netherland Indies had "cut off 75 per cent of her normal imports."[103] Japan had a population in 1941 of 73 million occupying a land mass smaller than California.[104] The embargo was hurting the empire of Japan and her people, but it was also hurting American exporters.

An AP report clacked, "Whether the Japanese decision is a step toward a final settlement which conceivably might take Tokyo out of the Axis camp or a mere temporizing in the hope of a more propitious day for hard talk with the United States remains to be seen."[105]

FDR, after meeting with cabinet members about the Far East developments, saw his doctor that evening at 7:15 and then dined alone in his study at 7:30 before retiring at 11:00 p.m.[106]

Some afternoon papers reported the situation as "grave" and that no more talks between the Americans and the Japanese were contemplated[107] while other reports said they wanted to continue them for "at least two weeks."[108] The headline of the *Panama City News-Herald* said, "Nazi Reversals Cause Japs to Ask More Time."[109]

Newspaper reports were often contradictory. But Americans also read of private meetings in the Philippines between Gen. Douglas MacArthur and Adm. Thomas C. Hart to discuss "emergency steps."[110]

CHAPTER 2

THE SECOND OF DECEMBER

"Japan Renews Talks, but Capital Is Skeptical"
New York Times

"U.S. Asks Japan to Explain Troop Moves"
Washington Evening Star

"All America Must Pull Together, Lecturer Warns"
Birmingham News

As the Christmas season grew closer, over 800,000 furloughs had been granted to America's fighting men, all of whom now would have to find a way home. A flight on Delta Airlines from Birmingham to Dallas was $32.[1] On American Airlines, a round trip flight between New York and Washington was $21.90.[2] These were considerable sums at the time, so for most men traveling commercial air was out of the question.

What about the train? Because of Washington bungling and unpredicted requisitions by the military, there was a shortage of railroad passenger cars. And the ride in some locales would be inhospitable. In New York, for instance, the Board of Transportation was to begin enforcing regulations prohibiting "smoking or spitting in stations, platforms and cars."[3] With no planes and few trains, soldiers had to either fight for a seat on a Greyhound Bus or depend upon the generosity of private citizens with automobiles.

Because of regulations, military personnel were prohibited from hitch-hiking. A campaign in the Golden State was organized by the California Automobile Association to help soldiers and sailors avoid trouble. Motorists who volunteered could place on their windshield a sticker issued by the group that would tell young men in uniform that the driver was participating in the "Give Them a Lift" effort.[4]

Travel was on the mind of many. On the West Coast, residents of four counties in California and one in Oregon attempted to create the forty-ninth state of "Jefferson."[5] They were apparently upset about poor thoroughfare conditions and declared they wanted to secede "only on Thursdays to impress on their present States the seriousness of their petitions for improved roads and aid in development of resources."[6] Armed civilians stopped cars passing through their counties to hand them pamphlets.

Fortunately, the cars forced to sit and idle had plenty of gasoline, as did all Americans. This was true even though use was up sharply—11 percent—over the previous years, despite the admonitions by the government for Americans to use less. Total gas consumption for 1941 was projected to rise by 2.5 billion gallons from the previous year. But there were also, according to estimates, 2.5 million more cars on the road.[7]

The Traffic Subcommittee of the U.S. House released a report on the state of automobile traffic in Washington. The document said in no uncertain terms that "making recommendations for relief of the traffic problem in Washington properly emphasizes the need for long-range remedies rather than temporary palliatives if there is to be any reasonably permanent and effective cure of the city's parking and traffic ills."[8] The immediate construction of a subway was discussed as a cure.

Police in Kansas City were concerned with more mundane questions. They assembled a group of fifteen drivers and plied them with shots of whiskey each half hour "to determine at what stage of drunkenness a driver is at his worst." Of the fifteen, "one dropped out after a phone call to his wife, one fell asleep, three appeared still sober after seven drinks." Another complained he was a Scotch, not a bourbon drinker. "Most of the men lost their driving judgment. But one improved for a time. His explanation: he was so nervous from being around cops that the liquor steadied him." Having reached no definite conclusions, the police packed the more or less drunk men into squad cars and drove them home.[9]

Worried about inflation settling in the auto industry, the Office of Price Administration fired a shot across the hood of auto manufacturers by announcing it would set a ceiling price on the cost of new cars. Said the head of the automobile section of the OPA, Cyrus McCormick, "The Government had the power to regiment the automobile industry to the nth degree."[10] Despite expressing personal concerns about such actions, his division went ahead with a complicated formula to regulate costs and production in Detroit that was even stricter than had been previously imposed.

Americans were keen on avoiding war and were for the most part unaware that it was coming their way. In the Philippines—relatively close to Indochina where hundreds of thousands of Japanese troops were amassing—the Army Air Corps fighter planes under Gen. Douglas MacArthur's command were still lined up wingtip to wingtip at Clark Field. It was the same at Hickam Field in Honolulu, where hundreds of army and navy planes were also lined up in such a tight fashion.

Gen. Walter Short, in command of the army garrison in the Hawaiian Islands, was more worried about saboteurs than about aerial bombardment. *Sabotage* is derived from *sabo*, the French word for shoe. In an earlier era, when French factory workers were unhappy with their working conditions, they threw their shoes into the machinery. Short was more concerned about the thousands of Japanese workers on the Islands throwing something at the military planes there on the ground than something hurling at them from the air.[11]

Also lined up—neat as you please—along "Battleship Row" in Pearl Harbor were American battleships, considered by most of the brass as the backbone of the navy. Battleships since the time of Stephen Decatur and John Paul Jones had borne the brunt of battles on the high seas. Most of the admirals in December 1941 were elderly men who viewed aircraft carriers as a passing fancy and not an important part of their operations. Serious navy men put their faith in battlewagons and not flattops.

Even so, Congress approved an additional $7 billion for new tanks, armaments, and other munitions, but the outlays would go to help Russia, China, and Britain.[12] Helping to foot the bill was the ever-present American taxpayer, purchasing Defense Stamps[13] from the government that could later be cashed in with interest.

The War Department and Washington were at the time teeming with corruption. Senator Harry Truman of Missouri, himself a product of the corrupt Tom Pendergast political machine in that state, was heading an investigation into the waste and fraud in the defense industry. Truman chaired an investigation of corporate suppliers to the U.S. military, spotlighting war profiteering and shoddy materials. His relentless inquiry ruffled feathers, but he didn't care, exposing one dirty and corrupt project after another. One construction venture for the army was supposed to cost $20 million, but five months later, cost overruns had shot the price tag up to $51 million. Dozens of contractors, including Ferguson-Oman and Taylor-Hale, overbilled and under-delivered, costing the taxpayer untold millions. The government was paying rent on equipment that wasn't worth the cost of the rental charge; other equipment was rented to the government and then hidden. It went on and on and on. One witness testified before the Truman Commission, "It seems to me all Ferguson-Oman officials and employees are organized to cost the Government every dollar they can."[14] As a result, Congress tightened military contracting practices.

Two other congressional committees were investigating a magazine that purported to have close ties to the Democratic Party and thus was strong-arming defense contractors into purchasing ads in the Democratic National Press. One knowledgeable source said their methods "would make Al Capone blush with envy."[15] It later turned out the publication had nothing to do with the party.

Yet another congressional investigation uncovered an apparently penniless man who somehow received a $200,000 defense contract for unspecified purposes and was using the money to entertain politicians and defense contractors in Washington at "championship prize fights."

"Investigators . . . have dug up considerable information about 'middle men,' 'brokers,' and 'go-betweens' who have neither manufacturing facilities . . . nor any legitimate connection with Government agencies. Yet they are said to haunt Washington hotels and ante-rooms in large numbers, seeking commissions on the basis of their alleged influence."[16]

Public monies were also appropriated for tens of thousands of houses on growing military bases, courtesy of the Public Buildings Administration. Thoughtfully, the PBA also hired a consultant for interior decorating, Miss Gladys Miller, but it wasn't made clear if she would personally redecorate every one of the forty thousand houses in the works. "She recommended . . . the purchase of furniture to scale with the rooms . . . gay, vivid colors to lend a cheery note; elimination of unnecessary objects." In addition to being paid by the U.S. taxpayer for her sage advice on paints, furniture, and spacing, she was also conveniently on the staff at New York University.[17]

The NFL title game was set for December 21, between the New York Giants and either the Green Bay Packers or the Chicago Bears, who still had one game left to play and were tied for the Western division championship. Depending on the winner, the game would be held either in Green Bay or the Windy City because of their superior records.[18] The American Professional Football League was considering expanding in order to compete with the National Football League. Washington could have used a new franchise after a dismal loss, which marked their worst record since 1935. They were scheduled to get a second pro team, which many thought the city needed given the sad sack Redskins, often derided as the "Deadskins".[19]

In Manhattan, Tommy Manville, age forty-seven, a scion of the twenties era of "Wonderful Nonsense," professional inheritor, and reminder of why so many hated the rich, took a wife—his fifth—Bonita Francine Edwards, twenty-two, heiress to a Chicago lumber fortune. Meeting only four days before their betrothal, Manville said, "[L]ong engagements may be out of style," and Edwards confessed, "I'm not in love with Tommy—I'm just infatuated. I hope to fall in love with him after a while."[20] F. Scott Fitzgerald was right about the rich, and Manhattan was still ruled by the Vanderbilts, Warburgs, and Astors, for whom the rules seldom applied because the rich were different—or at least always assumed as much about themselves.

On the other side of the rules spectrum, the first inductee under the new Selective Service act, buck private John Edward Lawton, said after a year as a dogface, "Army life is alright . . . but I don't think I'm exactly cut out for it."[21] Senator Henry Cabot Lodge told Republicans in Massachusetts that the United States needed a standing army of no less than 750,000 men, but if the country went to war, it might need on the order of 5 million men in uniform.[22]

At Jordan Marsh, a high-end department store in Boston, women's shoes were going for $7.50.[23] Customers looking for something a bit more affordable could turn to R.H. White's "bargain basement" where they could be purchased for $1.95.[24] Stockings at Jordan Marsh went for $1.15 a pair—the "philmy" kind—but "conditions may soon mean that silk top-to-toe stockings will be a luxury-memory."[25] "Health girdles" were squeezing American women for $7.00 apiece at Conrad's store in Boston.[26] In Washington, another expensive department store, Woodward & Lothrop, was touting men's dinner jackets for $75 for the "holiday season."[27]

The Office of Price Administration called on consumers to limit the wrapping on Christmas packaging. The call was issued by Lessing J. Rosenwald, director of the OPM's Industrial Conservation Bureau.[28]

But in her press conference, Eleanor Roosevelt suggested that Americans not be "too practical" in their gift buying. Gifts, she said, "should include those traditionally dispensed by Santa Claus." Mrs. Roosevelt revealed that the White House Christmas tree in the East Room would be "all white . . . and the White House will be decked out in holly, mistletoe and poinsettias. There'll be presents for the White House staff. . . . Just as on eight other Christmas Eves, the President and Mrs. Roosevelt will hang up their stockings at the big mantle in the chief executive's bedroom. There will be a sock, too, for Fala, just as there was last year when the President's Scottie got his first rubber bone." She told the reporters all of her shopping was nearly done.[29]

A delegation of Washington State Indians went to Washington to complain about government regulations that prevented them from purchasing liquor. A headline in the *Washington Post* read, "Indians Here to Demand Fire Water."[30]

William Henry Murray, a philosopher of sorts known as "Wild Bill," advised city folk to burn their paper money, "move to the country, can fruit and vegetables, and bury them in the ground to 'have something to eat when the trouble comes.'"[31]

Meanwhile, actress Tallulah Bankhead was hospitalized with the flu in Philadelphia, but it was reported that she was "much better after a day in an oxygen tent." Actor John Barrymore was also hospitalized, reportedly for an intestinal flu.[32] Though not reported, it was known they both drank deeply from the wrong bottle and often, although Bankhead's tastes sometimes ran more to cocaine and other drugs. She once quipped about cocaine not being habit forming—"I ought to know, I've been using it for years."[33] Her father, William Brockman Bankhead, had been Speaker of the U.S. House from 1936 to 1940 until his untimely death, and she was frequently in Washington, partying from Anacostia to Bethesda, shocking women and delighting men.

In California, the first of the paper drives was announced, as there was a shortage of wood pulp in the country according to the government. The Boy Scouts and the Salvation Army joined forces to collect old paper.

Federal taxes were scheduled to rise in 1942, but so too were many state and local taxes. For some in the higher brackets, they would only get one seventh of any raise while the Federal government would take the other six-sevenths.[34]

FDR officially signed legislation repealing portions of the Neutrality Act while also calling for the passage of legislation that curtailed strikes by unions in war-related industries.[35] But almost anything could fall under that designation, from agriculture to steel to newspapers. Yet another strike was threatened, this one by railroad workers. A deadline by the railroad union was set for December 7.

Meanwhile, a Japanese "expert" on America offered his assessment to his government on why America would be no competition for them in a war. "The national debt, a 'spoiled child' mentality, low national morale at the first defeat [Robert] Taft, [Gerald] Nye and [Charles] Lindberg will lead a revolt, Roosevelt is a 'buffoon,' hesitancy, Americans excite easily and cool easily, disunity—with 20,000,000 Negroes, 10,000,000 unemployed, 5,000,000 trade unionists, inflation."[36] Taft, Nye, and Lindberg were all leaders in the isolationist movement.

Many headlines referred to "Japs" or "Nips" (for "Nipponese"), and virtually every political cartoon of the era depicted the Japanese in the worst possible racial stereotype: short, squinty eyes, large glasses, buck teeth, in a menacing military uniform.

America and Great Britain considered and finally—after much haggling over fishing rights, fish oil, and wheat—aided Iceland under Lend-Lease, and troops from both countries were sent there, "all with a healthy taste for blondes." Iceland was the oldest democracy in the world, with a Parliament dating over one thousand years, the *Althing*. Despite rampant inflation, the Icelandic government "rejected price control-plans as smacking of State Socialism."[37]

While not the case in Iceland, America's and England's economies were heavily regulated and rationed. A black market thrived in the midst of the rationing, and in Britain a person could get everything from eggs, perfume, and lipstick to fruits, silk stockings, and clothes. Politicians' wives seemed to have no difficulty purchasing consumer items, including fur coats. Silk stockings were highly prized. Oranges—supposedly only for children— were consumed by all. With paper in short supply, the government ordered a "no-wrapping" rule, but this simply made it easier for thieves to identify what they wanted to steal. Shoplifting was rampant. False identity cards were sold by the thousands, allowing British subjects to register at multiple stores in order to purchase double or triple their allowed quotas of milk and other food stuffs.[38] The British experiment at managing the economy was an incomplete success.

Still, the Brits were facing the war, depravations, and bombings with a very proper stiff upper lip. The Royal Air Force had considered the stress young pilots must being going through before, during the Battle of Britain and after, and set up psychiatric hospitals and counseling centers for the flyers, but no one partook. The facilities stood idle and were eventually converted to other uses. Understandably, one British pilot who crashed six times "went berserk."[39]

A British psychiatrist said that the lower classes handled stress better than the upper classes, as did children even more so than before the war and those who did exhibit psychiatric problems were from broken homes and were not suffering as a result of the bombings. They even took to playing "air-raid games." Women too showed less signs of neuroses than before the war, it was felt, because the war gave them a new set of priorities and "pivotal values." "In London department stores, during heavy bombardment, the absence rate was lower than before."[40]

The American economy—especially outside of the industrial effort to support Great Britain and Russia—continued to suffer, and government agencies were created to help the small businessman. A premium was placed on advertising, as with the Hotel Pennsylvania in New York City, which offered "sterilized glasses in your bathroom" and the loan of "pajamas . . . a typewriter," or a "non allergic pillow!" The ads were specifically targeted to businessmen traveling for the war effort, and a single room went for $3.85 per night and $5.50 per night for two. "The lobby, public rooms and restaurants are gay with new decorations." Glenn Miller was performing in the hotel's club room.[41]

The economy of the South was showing improvement as demand for cotton for military uniforms had jacked up the cost sky high. The price had reached a twelve-year peak, and farm income across the South was up substantially since the advent of Lend-Lease in early 1941.

On Capitol Hill, the House passed legislation regulating the importation of sugar from outside the country, while favoring and expanding quotas for domestic cane and beet sugar growers. The State Department opposed the action, seeing it as antagonistic toward potential war allies, but the Department of Agriculture supported it, seeing it as favoring domestic allies.[42]

For some there was no Great Depression. The Andrews Sisters—LaVerne, Patty, and Maxine—sold their eight-millionth record, for which Decca Records paid them the princessly sum of 2 cents per. They were harmoniously making on average $5,000 per week, before taxes.[43]

For American amateur and professional painters, it was another scene. Because so many of their canvases and brushes were imported from Ireland,

Belgium, and Russia (there, brushes were made from Russian squirrels) they faced a shortage, and because so many of their paints contained precious metals such as zinc and cadmium—rare earth metals possibly needed for the war effort—they faced a possible confiscation of the metals by the government. "Manhattan's American Artists' Professional League recently petitioned Washington for cooperation in keeping artists supplied with their annual ration of paint (about a gallon apiece.)"[44]

America's parents and educators worried about the low reading proficiency of pupils. There were "16,000,000 illiterates in the United States— they cannot read beyond the fourth grade reading level." Of all places, Harvard found that incoming freshmen had low reading acumen, and the school was forced to "start a course in reading fundamentals." Professor Reed Smith, sixty, of the University of South Carolina thought he knew the problem. "The old principle . . . that you can't sharpen an ax on a velvet grindstone has given place to the view that if the pupils don't like it, they shouldn't be required to do it . . . the underlying assumption seems to be . . . that students will write clearly and correctly by some sort of blessed intuition if only the teacher does not depress them with such inconvenient and unprofitable matters as spelling, paragraphing, punctuation, sentence structure, grammar and the choice and order of words."[45]

On American campuses, there was growing agitation for war with Germany. At the University of Chicago, Professor Bernadette Schmitt said that "western civilization would not be safe until the German people were crushed on their own soil." She made her comments at the twenty-first annual meeting of the National Council for the Social Studies, gathering in Indianapolis.[46]

FDR had passed through Atlanta on his way to Warm Springs, but did not get off the train, though he did have his window open so he could be seen. On the way back to Washington, the curtains to his private car were closed. Had he stayed there, he might have tuned in to WGST to hear *Aunt Hattie* or *Man I Married*. The station was turned on at 6:00 a.m. and turned off at midnight. On 750AM, WSB, he might have heard the *Dixie Farm Hour*, or later, the soap opera *Guiding Light*, or later still, *Fred Waring*, a popular band leader. Like WGST, the station WSB also came on at 6:00 a.m. and "signed off" at midnight.[47]

One region where the economy—at least for the "nobility" there—was doing well was Hollywood. It was raking in millions each week, mostly for the top four studios: Metro-Goldwyn-Mayer, 20th Century Fox, and Warner Bros. Fifty-four actors made over $100,000 per year, but 50 percent of all the actors there had never made more than $10,500 per year. Indeed, the average annual income for over seven thousand extras "was $350.00."

Two-thirds of the producers in Hollywood made over $150,000, including the shy and retiring Orson Welles, for whom it was said, "There but for the grace of God, goes God." The "colony" was described as "*nouveau riche*, thriving . . . lacks lineage and decorum" whose power players "came from vaudeville, flea circuses, petty trade, other shabby zones of enterprise."[48] Hollywood did have to make some concessions to the world situation, including canceling the banquet at which the 1942 Academy Awards would be presented. Also, Los Angeles proclaimed "Medical Aid to Russia" day to raise money for Mother Russia and "Uncle Joe" Stalin.[49]

Welles's *Citizen Kane*'s release was bitterly fought by the subject of the movie, William Randolph Hearst, and many movie houses in America did not show it for months—or show it at all. Hearst controlled a vast media empire and with it, enormous power. Deeply offended by Orson Welles's critical portrait of him, Hearst even made a brazen offer to the movie studio that produced the film, RKO: he would buy the film from RKO, at a price that guaranteed a small profit, if in return he had the right to destroy the print. Thankfully, RKO turned him down, and the movie that is consistently voted by critics as the Best American Film Ever Made lived on for posterity, to be endlessly explicated by intellectuals and studied in film class ever after.

Citizen Kane debuted—"long-awaited" and "Nothing Censored!" said the *Birmingham News*—at the Empire theater in Birmingham, Alabama, yet a local column panned not the movie but Welles himself, comparing him to Hitler. "Certainly he has applied almost Hitlerian policies in his approach to fame."[50] Admission was 30 cents. Another racy movie airing was *Honky Tonk*, starring Lana Turner and Clark Gable.

The power of movies in 1941 could not be underestimated. They enthralled all in America, were affordable, and theaters across the country were often the hub of social activity for families, boys and girls, children, social clubs, and fan clubs. One of the biggest stars of the era, Gable, took off his shirt in the movie *It Happened One Night* to reveal his bare and masculine chest. Unlike most men in America, he did not wear a T-shirt and as a result, T-shirt sales dropped 40 to 50 percent in one year. The power of movies was such that Pope Pius XI devoted "a special papal encyclical to it." When classic novels such as *David Copperfield* and *Wuthering Heights* were made into movies, copies of the books flew off the shelves at public libraries and bookstores.[51]

Hitler remained a fascinating (if also feared, loathed, and later hated figure) for many Americans, and one of the most popular books of the time was *Total Espionage*, published by Putnam. The book detailed the rise of the Third Reich and the men behind it and especially about how they had perfected the art of spying and intelligence gathering.[52] But Americans were also reading novels such as *Grim Grow the Lilacs*, *Forty Whacks*, and *Prescription for Murder*.[53]

News reports said the British had mounted a counteroffensive using American-made army tanks against the Germans in North Africa and that Russia was pushing back the German advance on Moscow, aided by the harsh Russian winter, just as it had aided Russia once before against Napoleon. But many of the news reports of Russian successes came from the Soviets own state-controlled news agencies including the Soviet Information Bureau, so it was difficult to know fact from fiction.

Double-talk from the Russians was the rule, rather than the exception. As they were claiming their hold on the port city of Rostov; it was reported that German troops had secured the town. The Russians had evacuated because of "unnecessary losses," but the Germans had taken "more favorable positions to meet the Russian assaults."[54] Of course, when it came to disinformation, the Germans were no pikers, and they matched the Russians lie for lie in describing the Russian Front. A spokesman claimed German troops could see Moscow "with the aid of good field glasses."[55] All in all, reports from the winter battle were a mishmash of lies, distortions, half-truths, and prevarications. It was clear, though, that both sides had suffered horrific losses of men, many simply due to the bitterly cold weather, especially the Germans, who were underprepared for the Russian winter.

The battle could be heard in London, live, via radio. "The guns never cease. . . . The battle is fierce. The Germans are continually throwing in new troops," said an announcer on the scene.[56]

Meanwhile Roosevelt spoke before the State Chairmen of Birthday Ball Committees, who were planning festive celebrations in each state for FDR's birthday in January, when he would turn sixty on the 30th.[57]

The birthday was celebrated in part to raise money for the March of Dimes, whose purpose was to cure infantile paralysis, and while nobody mentioned the president's affliction, many knew about it.

At home the debate continued over the America First Committee and its stances. Most of the debate focused on their high profile members, especially Charles Lindbergh, but the membership also included former president Herbert Hoover, retired gen. Robert E. Wood, and 1936 GOP nominee Alf Landon, as well as Norman Thomas, a nationally known leader of socialism in America. Other prominent members included Walt Disney, Alice Roosevelt Longworth, and famed writers and liberals Sinclair Lewis and E. E. Cummings.

The GOP's 1940 nominee, Wendell Willkie, was a vicious opponent of the "Firsters." Only formed one year earlier, the organization had gained national prominence because if its mission and the people involved. Wood was a highly decorated veteran of the Great War and by 1941 was the chairman of the Sears & Roebuck Co.

The East and West Coast papers were generally more internationalist, while the periodicals down the center of the country generally opposed any U.S. involvement in the European war. As a result, America First was more popular in middle and rural America, less so in the metropolises of New York, Washington, Los Angeles, and San Francisco.

The America Firsters announced their intention to have as much influence over the 1942 off-year elections as possible by supporting candidates who "have kept faith with the people's mandate to avoid participation in the war." They would support any Republican or Democrat who opposed entry into the European war.[58]

If Henry Luce's *Life* and *Time* magazines could be reasonably described as pro-FDR and pro-intervention, the weekly magazine *Look* was a downright "pap" sheet for FDR, the Democrats, and the New Deal while ripping Republicans and anybody who stood in the way of the sophisticates of Washington and New York.

As with the Luce publications, nary a woman was found in the masthead of *Look* magazine, though women were often the most enthusiastic readers. The magazine was loaded with ads for Ipana Tooth Paste, Kleenex, Sal Hepatica (yet another laxative), movies such as *The Men in Her Life* starring Loretta Young, Listerine Tooth Paste, General Electric clocks, Chevrolet trucks (with the "Load-Master" engine), Colgate Dental Crème ("Scientific tests prove conclusively that in 7 out of 10 cases, Colgate Dental Crème instantly stops oral bad breath.")[59] Zenith radios, Pond's Vanishing Cream, Sanka Coffee, Ovaltine, General Electric vacuum cleaners, the U.S. Army Recruiting Service, and of course, cigarettes. Chesterfield cigarettes featured the beautiful actress Maureen O'Hara pitching them in the obliging carton size, which displayed photos of handsome young men in navy and army uniforms. The copy helpfully suggested, "[D]on't forget to mail them to the boys in the Service."[60] She was also found in the newspapers hawking Lux soap.[61]

One feature story in *Look* magazine was written by a "friendly critic of the New Deal" who nudged Roosevelt for not doing more to ramp up Americans' fears to help push them into the war as soon as possible.[62] Another was a profile of the many "dollar a year men" who had gone to Washington to man the New Deal. A survey was made, and some "288 Men, 1 Woman" were listed in the "dollar-a-year class."[63] Having made millions in other lines of work, they now stepped forward to "donate" their administrative and leadership skills to help Roosevelt implement the New Deal. This article was about Floyd

Odlum, who'd made millions on Wall Street, cashing out before the crash in 1929. He made his fortune by "pyramiding." The article said he cashed out because he'd been "expecting a crash."[64]

The ubiquitous celebrity story, this time covering the "Café Society" of New York socialites, appeared in *Look* with plenty of pictures of both the hoity-toity and the hoi polloi. Radio personalities such as Bob Hope and Jack Benny, showgirls such as Patricia Lee, gossip columnists, publicists, debutantes, leftist columnist Walter Winchell, Betty Grable, and actor George Raft all made appearances in the fawning story.[65] It was harmless, but far more dangerous was an article that could only be labeled as propaganda, disinformation, and half-truths.

Under the appalling headline "Meet the Men and Women of Russia Whom Hitler Will Never Enslave," the article mentioned not one of the purges of the 1930s in which "Uncle Joe" Stalin put millions to death. It contained some of the most dreadful lies ever to appear in an American publication. "Russians Don't Like Slavery," said one subheading. The article claimed instead, "Only two decades ago they fought one of the bloodiest civil wars in history to free themselves from slavery to the Czar. They have not grown so used to the joys and dignities of freedom as to surrender them with apathy." And, "There are only 2,000,000 Communists in Russia." And, "These are people who have been living in a new world—suddenly given . . . a voice in their government."[66] It was atrocious.

Another article berated conservatives in England, containing one self-serving and arrogant quote after another attacking the conservatives, but never with attribution. The "article" was clearly made up out of whole cloth by Samuel Spewack, a dramatist.[67] He and his wife, Bella, were successful as Hollywood playwrights, but their politics were hopelessly leftist.

More disinformation was forthcoming from *Look* when they did a long feature on how women now preferred cotton stockings to silk stockings. Because of the war effort, silk was in short supply. Silk was needed for parachutes and was regulated by the Supply Priorities and Allocations Board.[68] Cotton stockings were being churned out by experimental mills with the Department of Agriculture. To buttress the point of the article, actresses Rita Hayworth, Ann Sheridan, Dorothy Lamour, and Linda Darnell sported their "gams" in the hideous cotton covering for the benefit of photographers.

Of course, these women's legs were so beautiful, they could have been wearing cow hides and their legs still would have looked gorgeous. Unfortunately, also showing his legs for the article was Vice President Henry Wallace, who should have worn cow hide for the photograph.

In Washington, the chairman of the House Committee on Un-American Activities, Martin Dies of Texas, a Democrat, charged that "Communists and Criminals" had infiltrated the leadership of the American labor movement, specifically the Congress of Industrial Organizations, the principal umbrella group for organized labor.[69] The labor movement and the Roosevelt administration hated Dies. But railroad workers at the last minute gained huge concessions from the railroad companies, courtesy of a "compromise" hammered out by the government. The strike that had been set for December 7 was averted.

However, the army did discover a plot involving at least eighteen members of the Socialist Workers Party who were conspiring "to create insubordination in the armed forces of the Government." They were convicted in a trial in Minneapolis and faced up to ten years in prison. These were the first ever "convictions under the Smith amendment to the Sedition Act of 1861,"[70] which made it against the law to advocate overthrowing the government.

In the Mediterranean, the British government announced it had sunk three Italian naval ships headed for Libya where the Axis powers were fighting a furious tank battle with the British. The British ships suffered no damage or casualties in the battle.[71] Still, the Germans won a major victory in North Africa by cutting through British forces and "joining their two panzer divisions," and in the process the Brits were compelled to retreat from Rezegh and Bir El Hamed. The British forces, as a result of the maneuver, were encircled, with their backs to the sea. "A British spokesman . . . said the joining of the 15th and 21st Panzer Divisions had not in any way impaired British confidence." He said, "It could be termed a local German success."[72] The Germans accomplished this even as two Italian tank divisions fled the fight. Hitler's favorite general, Erwin Rommel, had engineered the counter-offensive. An embedded American journalist with the *Boston Globe* traveled for ten days with the British forces in Libya, noting that he had to get by on only two cups of tea per day, like everybody else, but "no other liquid."[73] The journalist Matthew Halton captured well the dangers and deprivations of war in the desert. It was not pretty or desirable. Roosevelt had already received several worried memos from the British ambassador Lord Halifax—Edward Wood—apprising him on the bleak situation in North Africa.[74]

With British forces spread across the world, Winston Churchill proposed an expanded draft of civilian men. Now, men from the ages of "18½ to 50" would be drafted for military service, but the British government hinted that men as old as sixty might soon be drafted. Previously, the draft had been of men from nineteen to forty-one years of age. The prime minister called it a "crisis of man power and woman power." The plan was also to draft unmarried women between the ages of twenty and thirty. The prime minister, what's more, warned of a possible invasion by the Nazis.[75]

On December 2, much of the public concern of the afternoon before over war with Japan had waned a bit. Maybe cooler heads were thinking. But some in Washington were mulling over the explosive statement by the Japanese: "The United States does not understand the real situation in East Asia. It is trying to forcibly apply to East Asiatic countries fantastic principles and rules not adapted to the actual situation in the world and thereby tending to obstruct the construction of the New Order. This is extremely regrettable."[76]

Franklin Roosevelt "politely asked" the Japanese government for an explanation on its intentions in Southeast Asia, specifically on new troop movements into Indochina and whether this was a prelude to an invasion of Thailand.[77] There were also reports that the Japanese army was practicing drills using parachutes in Kwangtung.[78] Furthermore, Japan was seizing private ships to use for their navy, and there were worries that if they seized Thailand, Japan could cut of the trade routes to the Indian Ocean.[79]

FDR's request was given to the Japanese consulate in Washington via Undersecretary of State Sumner Wells, who was filling in for Cordell Hull, whom the *New York Times* said was "indisposed."[80] As Wells entered the room for their thirty-five-minute meeting, Ambassador Nomura blurted out, "Nobody wants war." Wells later told reporters he could not disclose anything that had been discussed, but Nomura did. He said he told Wells, "War would not settle the issues anyway. Issues that cannot be settled by diplomacy cannot be settled by war."[81] Yet a huge chasm divided the two countries, and not just over their policies of talking to reporters. Some speculated that FDR was about to take control of the negotiations, personally.[82] The meeting with Wells was inconclusive, as they had not yet answered the president's question. But the *Washington Post* reported that FDR "assumed direct command of diplomatic and military moves relating to Japan and the lights of peace flickered low in the Orient."[83] "Mr. Roosevelt recalled that this Government had been somewhat surprised in June when Japan had sent troops into Indo-China, while discussions were going on here in an effort to reach an understanding for a permanent peace in the Pacific area."[84] As of December, the Japanese already had amassed a huge army, navy, and air force in the region, but was still adding to it. Roosevelt met with Henry Stimson, his secretary of war, and Frank Knox, the secretary of the navy. In a separate meeting, he met with Adm. Harold Stark, the chief of Naval Operations, and Hull in the second floor oval study of the private residence in the White House at noon, to discuss yet again the situation in Thailand. These meetings had not previously been disclosed to the press, with whom he met at 4:00 p.m.[85]

Roosevelt's alter ego, Harry Hopkins, who had been hospitalized for weeks at the "Naval Hospital," left his bed and met with the president over lunch on December 1, according to reports.[86] A Japanese official said they wanted to "make the United States reconsider Pacific problems."[87] The media—especially the Japanese press—began referring to the "A, B, C, D" coalition (America, Britain, China, and Dutch East Indies) and how they were conspiring against the Japanese. The administration also began referring to the State Department's document given to the Japanese as "principles for peace in the Pacific."[88]

Analysts argued that if Japan went ahead and invaded Thailand, they would gain an advantage in a final assault on the Burma Road, a vital thoroughfare used to supply the Free Chinese. If the Japanese seized the Burma

Road, it would put them in better stead to attack the British and Dutch, it would allow Japan to further interdict tin, rubber, and other resources going to America, and it would be more evidence that the Axis powers really did want to rule the world. Some speculation intimated that Germany was over-extended in North Africa and on the Eastern Front, so would be of little aid to Japan in their drive south and deeper into China.[89] But news reports continued that the Japanese cabinet wanted to proceed with peace efforts.

At his press conference, Roosevelt expressed hope for a speedy response from Tokyo, but said that it would be "silly" to set a deadline for a reply.[90] News reports said the Japanese could not get back to Roosevelt for "three days or more" because they were seeking "'clarification' of various points in Secretary of State Cordell Hull's statement on the American position."[91] Newspapers in Tokyo suggested that with the new British ships arriving in the South Pacific by order of the Admiralty and because of the heightened state of alert by the British, American, and Dutch forces, it was they who were agitating for a war and accused the British of planning to invade Thailand.[92] Japanese news agencies also flooded the airwaves with accusations against Australia and America.[93]

In fact, it was revealed that the navy had evacuated all 750 marines in Shanghai and they'd been redeployed in the Philippines, out of harm's way. They had crossed the China Sea—along with remaining American civilians—in two ships, the *President Madison* and the *President Harrison*.[94]

Americans worried that if Japan invaded Thailand, "it would enable Japan to menace American sources of tin, rubber and other raw materials essential for defense production, and, by giving Japan a firm hold in the South Pacific, jeopardize the future security of the Philippines."[95]

On the other hand, other government experts were reassured. "If the Japanese want to start something . . . we can bomb Japanese cities and war objectives from the Philippines easier than they can come this way in the air, since we have longer range, faster planes—the flying fortresses." The U.S. government was reportedly sending more armaments to the Philippines to rebuff the Japanese if they attempted an invasion. "The highest Army and Navy authorities here expect a Pacific war to be a series of quick and heavy air blasts, like tornados over Japan, the Philippines, Indo-China and Malaya," reported via radio journalist Royal Arch Gunnison for the Newspaper Alliance.[96]

The Japanese newspaper, *Yomiuri*, compared their circumstances with America's in 1776.[97]

Expenditures by the federal government in 1941—ending with the fiscal year in November—revealed that the government was only collecting in taxes one out of every three dollars it was spending. The government had brought in taxes from June to October just under $3 billion, but had spent almost $9 billion. Government officials were not worried about the massive borrowing, however, because new taxes would go into effect in 1942 and discussions were underway for even greater taxing of the American people. In that five-month period, 70 percent of federal spending had gone to defense.[98]

Like all bureaucracies, the navy was often engaged in fights large and small. As they watched earth-shattering developments around the world, a fierce turf battle broke out over who would "operate the cafeteria in the Navy Department Building."[99]

The Navy Cafeteria Association operated the dining hall, but Secretary Knox wanted the Public Buildings Administration to take things over. The association bitterly fought the secretary. "Officers of the Cafeteria Association insist that the cafeteria, which has been under their operation since 1937, provides better food, larger portions and better service." The facility provided for twelve thousand meals per day, and to break the impasse, the matter was turned over to the sage council of the Judge Advocate General.[100]

Several days later, FDR received a memo from an aide about a "Mr. Davies" who was complaining that the navy had commandeered his yacht, but it was not seeing any action. "The Auxiliary Vessels Board . . . which indicates that if acquired, she will later be restored and returned to her owner in the condition in which received by the Navy—if still afloat at that time."[101] He also received a more serious memo on the horrible conditions the Polish prisoners were subjected to by the Soviets. "As penalties food rations are reduced to 300 grams of bread and 200 grams of thin soup every twenty-four hours and [the Poles were] imprisoned in cold, wet dungeons."[102]

Secretary of War Knox seemed not to worry about the abilities of the U.S. Navy. He'd just written an article for *American Magazine* saying the navy "is ready for any emergency in the Atlantic or Pacific."[103] But it was noted in another publication that "units of the Japanese fleet have been reported maneuvering north of British Borneo."[104] No one paid attention.

The shooting war on the water continued unabated, and Germany had the upper hand over the Allies. It was disclosed that the British aircraft carrier, *Ark Royal*, had been sunk by U-boats in the Mediterranean, with a number of planes appallingly still strapped on her decks.[105] German ships had also sunk a number of Australian ships, both military and civilian.[106] Berlin exulted that in a matter of weeks, they had sent to the bottom forty-eight merchant ships and eleven naval craft while damaging thirty-nine others. All told, the Germans had sunk 231,870 tons in November alone.[107]

America was starting to churn out "Liberty" ships, which would become the backbone of the merchant marines. In Baltimore, six of these workhorse boats were shortly launched, including one christened the *Roger B. Taney*.[108] Taney, a son of Maryland, had been chief justice of the U. S. Supreme Court less than a century earlier and was famous for delivering the majority opinion in the *Dred Scott* decision, which in essence codified slavery in America, saying that slaves were not people but property and thus could not sue in federal courts.

No American war or discussion of war would be complete without its politicization, and syndicated columnist Walter Lippmann did the trick. "A failure on the part of the Republican party to give the national policy wholehearted support, which, of course, includes outspoken criticism of incompetence, unwisdom and inefficiency, will have to be construed as meaning only one thing: that the party is gambling on the defeat of the United States and that it is staking its political future on a national disaster. If the Republican party in Congress merely sulks and opposes, waiting for trouble, and appearing to hope for trouble . . . the Republican party will have placed itself in the intolerable position of have a vested interest in the humiliation and defeat of the United States."[109]

Yet another columnist, Westbrook Pegler, took dead aim at Congress, calling members there a "miserable, fumbling, timid aggregation of political trimmers and panhandlers" that bowed down before organized labor. Members were incensed, including Clare Hoffman of Michigan, who said, "Oh, we can lick Mr. Hitler all right but he's 2,000 miles away. But Pegler's right here at home." Hoffman called for a congressional investigation of Pegler.[110]

Pegler also became a shrill critic of a young up-and-coming singer, Frank Sinatra. In a preview of later cultural phenoms such as Elvis Presley, the skinny kid from Hoboken, dubbed "The Voice," was making teenage bobby-soxers swoon at the Paramount Theater in New York City. Social conservatives such as Pegler saw Sinatra as a threat to decent society; it didn't help that Sinatra was Italian, a flagrant philanderer, and an outspoken liberal. Pegler referred to the singer in his columns as a "New Deal Crooner"[111] and a "Commie Playboy."[112]

In 1941, newspaper columnists wielded enormous power. Pegler and many other ink-stained wretches of the day delighted in taking potshots at the earnest do-gooder Sinatra, suggesting that he was a reprobate at best and a communist at worst. Sinatra's vicious and unfair treatment at the hands of the press in the early 1940s helped explain his lifelong animosity toward the Fourth Estate, especially in his later years when the political outlook of Ol' Blue Eyes grew decidedly more conservative.

While Pegler decried the self-absorption of Sinatra's screeching teenage fans, the self-absorption of Capitol Hill was long and legendary. Members were squawking about parking fees on the Hill, and Congressman Everett Dirksen, a Republican from Illinois, proposed price controls. He complained that while downtown garages charged 60 cents for eight hours, lots and garages on Capitol Hill charged at much as 25 cents for the first hour, 10 cents for the second hour, 5 cents per hour after that, a whole 5 cents more for eight hours.[113]

Washington was still hopeful for a workable solution to the crisis with Japan. Meetings took place and an exchange of documents continued between the Japanese embassy and the State Department, and the diplomats continued talking. Some publications took a decidedly "wait and see this will all blow over" posture on developments in the Pacific. Others, like the *Baltimore Sun*, were more breathless. "A single additional act of aggression by Japan may be sufficient to provoke instant large-scale retaliation by British forces—with the United States taking an active supporting role," greeted readers in Charm City the morning of December 2.[114]

Roosevelt had had a light schedule that day, seeing now more than half a dozen people over the course of the day. He dined that evening with his personal secretary, Grace Tully, from 7:30 p.m. until twenty minutes after midnight. He then turned in at 12:35 a.m.[115]

In a fashion, tensions seemed to have diminished in twenty-four hours, and while coverage of the situation in the Far East continued by the nation's newspapers, it faded somewhat against the backdrop of the ongoing war in Europe. A columnist wrote, "If there is to be war, it will start under strange auspices. The American people have no hate in their hearts for the Japanese. For generations a mutual admiration has been developing between the two countries and, despite the differences in language and customs, some warm friendships have sprung up."[116]

CHAPTER 3

THE THIRD OF DECEMBER

"British Rush Troops to Libya"
Sun

"Nazis Rush Reinforcements"
Tucson Daily Citizen

"Tokyo Must Explain Actions"
Washington Post

"Airport Coffee Shop Refuses to Serve Colored Quartet"
Washington Evening Star

Winston Churchill, along with influential Jewish leaders in Great Britain, America, and Palestine, called for the creation of a separate "army of Jews" to fight in the war. Thousands of young men from Palestine, America, and other countries stepped forward to volunteer for the unique fighting force. "What people, what group have more at stake?" said Emanuel Neumann, an American Jewish leader. "Hitler has openly proclaimed the annihilation of European Jewry as one of his war aims." Henry Stimson, secretary of war, voiced his support. Ultimately, "entrenched bureaucrats" inside the British government threw enough monkey wrenches into the works and the concept withered. One London bureaucrat smarmily said that the British government was fighting both the Nazis and "Zionism."[1]

Newspaper stories and editorials on the situation in the Pacific waned somewhat, as their attention was diverted to the Russian Front, the Atlantic, the Mediterranean, and North Africa, where the real fighting was going on. The situation there was simply more pressing.

More and more American correspondents were becoming embedded with Allied forces, especially with the British in North Africa, and poignant stories of heroism, humor, and sacrifice were appearing in American publications. One popular columnist, John Barry, sent back regular dispatches via his "War Diary" column.[2] Photos and their captions of the African war zone had to be approved by the British before being released for publication in the West.[3]

So it was with a good deal of news coverage that President Roosevelt publicly announced on December 3 that Lend-Lease aid would be extended to Turkey. In actuality, the U.S government had been covertly aiding the strategically important country for some time, as it was a target for takeover by Germany. Roosevelt said, "The defense of Turkey [is] vital to the defense of the United States."[4] Billions under Lend-Lease had already gone to Great Britain, Russia, Free French operations, and other allies in the war against the Axis powers. Allegations arose that Washington was playing favorites with its lending and leasing policies, putting Great Britain ahead of the Soviets, but Roosevelt's spokesman, Stephen Early, dismissed them. Congress had just allocated $78 million more for Russia.[5] It was later revealed that under Lend-Lease, FDR was also aiding India.[6]

When it came to a president's ability to make war, the *Baltimore Sun* editorialized in no uncertain terms, "We know from the experiences of other countries that Fascism results when the legislative branch of the Government surrenders to one man its powers to make decisions for the people. In the face of this same trend toward Fascism in America the immediate duty of the American people is to return to Congress only those representatives who faithfully execute the people's trust."[7]

Meanwhile, Edward R. Murrow of CBS, already a journalistic legend, was the guest of honor at a dinner at the Waldorf-Astoria and in front of over one thousand celebrants said that "unless the United States enters this war Britain may perish." The establishment was out in full force to honor a charter member of the establishment; telegrams were read from FDR, the British ambassador Lord Halifax, Secretary of State Cordell Hull, and Brendan Bracken, the British minister of information. Murrow went on to say the war would be decided along the "banks of the Potomac" and not in North Africa or on the Russian Front.[8] By now, Halifax was sending daily confidential memos to Roosevelt, advising him on British advances and defeats.[9]

The Philippines government first issued a confusing statement from President Quezon as to where it stood in the Pacific mess; it was blamed on a medical condition for which he received a complete checkup. He then issued a loyalty oath to FDR—and to the United States.[10]

To checkmate German designs on Greenland, from where their subs and ships could more easily continue their now unrestricted warfare against American and British ships, the American military was contemplating its own bases along the east coast of Greenland, including the island of Jan Mayen, in an area that had been discovered by Henry Hudson in 1607. Germany had already conquered Norway, and its sights on Greenland were simply an extension of its plans to dominate the North Atlantic and, eventually, the world.[11]

Russia, a large beneficiary of Lend-Lease, claimed anew to have successfully pushed back the German advance on Moscow and that their troops "were finding the frozen bodies of Germans wrapped in flimsy blankets; huddled in roadside ditches."[12] Russian troops also reported recapturing some towns first taken by the invading German army. Still, the information came from the state-owned media of the Soviet Union, and other news reports were less glowing about the Red Army's successes. A news report from the Associated Press said that German troops had broken through the Soviet lines and were advancing once again on Moscow.[13]

The British meanwhile were "reorganizing" in Libya,[14] mounting an effort at a counteroffensive against Gen. Erwin Rommel and his 16th Panzer Division and the rest of the German "Afrika Korps" as reported by Edward Kennedy, an "Associated Press War Correspondent."[15]

Consternation was running high in America over Europe and to what extent Congress and America would allow FDR to set national policy. Secretary of State Cordell Hull emphasized the disagreements with other countries including "the basic doctrines of law, justice, morals and equality of treatment among nations—especially in trade—and settlement of controversies by peaceful negotiation rather than by force."[16] Hull, in private, was not confident about a favorable outcome in the Far East.[17] The issue of Japan, which had ebbed and flowed over the past several days, was beginning to flow again.

More bluntly, the senator from Montana, Burton K. Wheeler, Democrat and first among America Firsters, acidly said, "The President's foreign policy meant the plowing under of every fourth American boy. The only time the administration has intimated that we should go to war with Japan is when the British Empire is threatened."[18] Everybody in the Roosevelt White House hated Wheeler. Wheeler had already announced he would investigate "interventionists" in Hollywood.[19] Just a year earlier, in 1940, John L. Lewis, head of the mine workers union and another isolationist and Roosevelt-basher, had tried to convince Wheeler to run for president.[20]

In truth, Hollywood in 1941 was reluctant to take on the subject of fascism overseas and whether America should intervene in Europe's troubles. Germany was a huge and profitable market for American films, and the movie moguls were reluctant to alienate the cultural gatekeepers in Berlin. At the end of the day, Hollywood was first and foremost a business. When Charlie Chaplin's *The Great Dictator* was released in late 1940, many critics panned his satire of Hitler as left-wing propaganda, earning Chaplin the lasting enmity (and surveillance) of FBI director J. Edgar Hoover. It was only after America entered the war that suddenly Chaplin's film was seen as a courageous masterpiece.

For fifteen years, Sergeant Major Robert Smith, stationed in San Diego, had been a technical advisor to Hollywood on movies about the military. Smith observed that all inductees were essentially klutzes, both the real kind and the reel kind. He singled out actors Randolph Scott and John Payne as leading men who were "all thumbs."[21]

Nevertheless, the winds in 1941 were slowly starting to shift the weathervane of American opinion, as reflected by the drubbing that the America First Committee was taking from the commentariat. One columnist went so far as to suggest that the America Firsters were in league with Berlin. "It has begun blackmailing our Representatives and Senators with the threat that they will not be re-elected unless at this moment they play the Axis game. They are threatening the country . . . which would . . . lose us the war and lose us the peace. In the whole diplomatic game, the America First Committee has been the only ace in the whole for the Axis."[22]

On Capitol Hill, a much debated bill on curbing strikes in war industries, passed the House, 252–136. If it passed the Senate and FDR signed it, the measure would mandate a "60 day 'cooling off' period" before a union could undertake any strike in an industry that supported the war effort, and it could be argued that all industries somehow supported the war effort.[23] In San Diego, the U.S. Navy was concerned about a strike among shipyard workers. Some referred to union strikes as "sabotage."[24] Unsurprisingly, according to Gallup, large majorities of Americans opposed strikes in defense industries.[25] A ban on aid from the government to unions that affiliated or employed "members of the Communist party, the Young Communist League, and the German-American Bund" was also being discussed in the halls of Congress.[26] The Los Angeles Times editorially supported the measure, saying there was no "right to strike." "What about the right of self defense and self-preservation which, though the first law of nature, these unioneers call it their right to deny and to imperil?" the paper stormed.[27]

The American labor movement had additional problems. Congressman Martin Dies said the Congress of Industrial Organizations (which later merged with the American Federation of Labor to become the AFL-CIO) was "marked by a coalition of communism and criminality." High officials had been charged or convicted of "petty larceny, grand larceny, burglary, grand theft, carrying concealed weapons, assault and battery, robbery, white slavery, holdups, conspiracy, attempted arson, receiving stolen property, felonious assault, extortion and forgery."[28]

It wasn't just the unions that were seen as hotbeds of communist agitation. New York City was also concerned with the "red menace" in their very own high schools, according to a report prepared by the New York state senate. "Communist students in the New York City colleges and high schools are taught to lie, cheat and create disturbances in the classroom and on the campus. . . . Young Communist League branches are found in four colleges, nine high schools, teachers groups and the Navy Yard in Brooklyn." Teachers, students, and staff were suspended or fired as a result of the report and hundreds openly claimed membership.[29]

On December 3, the *Birmingham News* had a different take on New York: "The gay side of war—laughing soldiers, sailors and mariners promenading the streets, many with girlfriends clinging admiringly to their arms—is showing itself increasingly as the volume of American preparedness grows."[30] But the numbers weren't growing fast enough.

Roosevelt criticized the Selective Service for being too selective. Over 20 percent—nearly 200,000—of men rejected were because of "defective teeth." After the president intervened, the decision was to enlist the men into the army and then turn them over to the dental division for repairs.[31] A headline in the *Hartford Courant* said, "5 Negros Among 197 Given Tests" in a story about the draft in Connecticut. It also noted that "such things as fever, sore throats and certain correctible defects are reasons for temporary rejections."[32] In New Hampshire, the *Portsmouth Herald* announced that thirty inductees were being called and they published the names of all thirty in the newspaper.[33]

In Georgia, 707 men received "greetings" from Uncle Sam. One of these was a man convicted for failing to keep his local "draft board advised of his address."[34] He was sent up for three years for draft evasion, but he pleaded that he'd tried to enlist a number of times. In court, the prisoner, Horace Woodrow Hampton, who had also been convicted twice of automobile theft, was advised that under a federal statue, inmates could be released if they went into the military.[35]

Mexicans who crossed the border and did not declare their intention to become U.S. citizens were exempt from military service. They could continue to live in Mexico and work in America, commuting each day.[36] But because defense contractors required most workers to have a birth certificate and the military required all personnel to have such documents, it created a land office business with the state agencies that handled legal documents.[37] Prior to 1941, birth certificates had not been much of an issue and people took prospective employees at their word as to where and when they were born.

There was a news report that covert Nazi agents were operating in Mexico City to recruit young Mexican boys—members of the "Mexican Sinarchists" to the Fascist cause and then send them overseas to join the Nazi cause. "A new pamphlet entitled, 'Mexico in 1960' contains a historical review indicating Sinarchist hostility to the United States," complaining about lands taken in 1847.[38]

Bad behavior did occasionally take place in America, as some men discovered it was easier to panhandle wearing a uniform. Some donned uniforms of the Royal Air Force and stood outside clubs and restaurants in New York, claiming they lost their wallets; kind-hearted civilians often bailed them out.[39] It also wasn't unusual for inductees to be found with syphilis.

Some men, especially farm boys wanting to get off the farm, enlisted rather than wait to be drafted, as enlistees got better treatment and a chance to learn a trade. One twenty-year-old who had just finished a three-year hitch signed up for another and said he liked the army and planned on being in it when he was fifty. "I don't know how to act around people," he told the *Los Angeles Times*.[40]

The U.S. government announced that the hulls for twenty-four "escort vessels" ordered by the navy would be built in Denver, Colorado—1,300 miles from the nearest ocean port. The initial budget was $55 million.[41] Part of the largess of the war effort also went to America's prisons. In Atlanta, a penitentiary received a bonus check from the government for the "outstanding work" by inmates there. The check was presented in person by the attorney general, Francis Biddle.[42]

Congress continued its investigations into corruption in defense contracting and discovered a "sub-subcontractor" who was taking kickbacks of nearly one-third of the contract he'd brought Remington Arms Co. of Connecticut and its subcontracted maker of "shell dies." The treasurer for the company said the sub-subcontractor, Leon K. Shanak, had performed "no service" and that the subcontractor, Trans-Continental, had provided nothing for the federal government.[43]

Washington "disqualified" 560 individuals for work because they failed to pass loyalty oaths to the U.S. government. This was out of a pool of 40,000 seeking jobs in defense industries. Arthur Flemming, a commissioner with the Civil Service, speculated, "Does [this] give evidence to you of some fifth column activities in the Government?" He answered his own query, "Certainly, if one studies our records, he would get some indication of that." Another 2,400 failed to pass "character investigations."[44] In London, a pacifist member of the House of Lords, the Duke of Bedford, was seated only after taking that country's loyalty oath to the king. The duke said he was only doing so to help some friends, who had been picked up by the government for violating "regulation 18B," which allowed the home secretary "to hold without trial anyone he regards as dangerous to the war effort."[45]

At the other end of the spectrum, Lady Astor—née Nancy Witcher Langhorne of Virginia—criticized Churchill for not including more women in the war effort. In a speech in the House of Commons, she said the prime minister should go "further in proposals to conscript women . . . If you don't conscript married women there will be great discontent."[46] Lady Astor had been born in the United States and like Churchill, she was nobody's fool. Like Churchill, she was a Tory, but unlike Churchill, she was beautiful. She was also the first woman to sit in Parliament, having succeeded her husband, Waldorf Astor.

Later, a poll of British subjects demonstrated wide support—55 percent to 35—for the conscription of women into the military; however, the vast majority—65 percent over 26—disapproved of women in combat. There were already a few women who were serving in harm's way, some "wo-manning" antiaircraft emplacements. "It is reported that women have been found to excel men in the handling of complicated mechanical instruments and range finders."[47]

Americans were more chivalrous on the subject. In a *Los Angeles Times* poll, nearly 60 percent opposed drafting women into the military.[48] Of course the nation's attitude about the sexes was hardly modern, as evidenced by syndicated columnist Dorothy Dix, who advised divorced women to buck up and accept the fact it was probably their fault that their husbands had left them.

"The discarded wife always poses as martyr and calls upon her friends and acquaintances to shed tears of pity over her. They look upon marriage as a graft in which the husband must give all while they give nothing."[49]

As a result of the Allied embargo of Japan, 75 percent of her imports had been cut, but that was only the beginning of her economic strain. Because of the shift in the Japanese economy to a war footing, billions of yen were being devoted to armaments, and annual rice production fell from 400 million bushels to 297 million because of the cutoff of fertilizers for farmers.[50]

The Japanese had still not answered President Roosevelt's question from the day before: what were their intentions in Thailand? The Thai government felt certain it knew the answer and issued an open invitation for help, assuming a likely and imminent attack. But diplomacy is a complicated art. "It is no secret here that the discussions have been severely hampered by the Japanese proclivity for combining peaceful words with warlike actions," reported the Associated Press from Washington.[51]

FDR "made clear that the objective which was sought meant that no additional territory should be taken by anyone," reported the *Los Angeles Times*.[52] But Roosevelt said his query "did not constitute an ultimatum."[53] He also complained that the Japanese people were not being made aware of Washington's position when it came to the Pacific and that the press there was only telling citizens of British military actions in the region. "The Chief Executive termed Japan a friendly power with which the United States was at peace."[54]

But the situation was dicier than a word like *peace* would indicate. The White House let it out that the administration might "abandon talks if good faith is not shown."[55] Yet there were still hopes for an "armed truce,"[56] though some of the striped pants set said the "crisis may come to [a] head within [a] few days."[57] Another group of diplomats said that FDR "placed Japan in a position where she must withdraw forces recently sent to and in transit to Indo-China and continue negotiations . . . or face . . . a possible war" with America.[58] Meanwhile, Japanese officials said Premier Tojo had been "misquoted" when he said that Americans and British had to be "purged"[59] from the Far East, and that a "subordinate official . . . did a clumsy job" of translating Tojo.[60] Later, the Japanese government denied outright that Tojo had ever said the word *purge*.[61]

An assistant secretary for the navy, Ralph A. Bard, said the situation in the Pacific was "a tinder box . . . waiting for a spark that will explode all over the eastern quarter of the globe."[62] But he also stated, like everybody else in the navy, that they do not "underestimate Japan's power" and "in the regrettable event of trouble in the Pacific, that trouble will not be a minor one."[63]

Despite FDR's assurance of a non-ultimatum, the *Washington Post* ran a story with a dire lede, dateline Washington, that appeared to blame Tokyo. "The issue of peace or war in the Pacific . . . may turn on Japan's reply."[64] The headline said, "Tokyo Must Explain Actions,"[65] And the story detailed how FDR was waiting, how his question amounted to an ultimatum, even as he said in his press conference it did not. It also reported that Washington had set a deadline of December 15 as "zero hour." That was when the rice fields in Thailand were no longer flooded and the ground would be firm enough for mechanized vehicles.[66]

The paper ran a story, the same day, with an ominous headline dateline Tokyo, that appeared to blame Washington. "The uncompromising attitude of Washington undoubtedly has dimmed any chance for success of the United States-Japanese negotiations, but Japan is determined that all avenues of a peaceful settlement be exhausted . . . informed sources said." The headline said, "Japan to Exhaust All Peace Avenues."[67]

As many times as FDR waved off speculation that any invasion of Thailand would lead to war, the *Post* speculated just as many times that an invasion would lead to "undeclared hostilities . . . general war in the Pacific." FDR also told reporters that "some progress" was being made in the peace negotiations and that it was his understanding the Japanese "would take no additional steps while the negotiations were underway."[68]

However his query was interpreted, by Tokyo or American newspapers, Roosevelt had good reason to be concerned. While the talks continued, one report came in saying, "A sizable Japanese naval force also is reported in Indo-China waters. . . ."[69] New reports coming from Saigon said the Japanese continued to amass extraordinary numbers of troops and supplies in Indo-China, along the Thai border. "The docks" in Saigon "are piled with drums of gasoline, trucks, guns and other equipment. Troops and supplies are arriving daily by ship and train at Saigon." Military experts thought the islands of the Dutch Indies would be the first target of Tokyo.[70]

FDR that day received a confidential memo from the Office of Naval Intelligence informing him on developments in the Far East, including troop movements into China and south, possibly as a prelude to invading Thailand.[71]

The British government was telling reporters that if Japan attacked their Far East outposts, America would jump into the fray, but this was wishful thinking as Churchill had been agitating for months for direct involvement by America.[72] As much as the Japanese were provoking America, England was cajoling America. But it was also reported that the Dutch were pressuring London to go into Thailand to keep it from going to the Japanese, should they invade, much as FDR did with Surinam, taking it before the Germans could. The report out of Manila said a source close to the administration suggested that even if talks broke down between Washington and Tokyo, this would not presage a war between the two countries. "Washington sees no spark for an immediate Japanese-American war."[73] Even so, Americans were still evacuating Asia, many headed for the Philippines.

The *Chicago Tribune* was continuing to taunt FDR, contrasting his words of 1940: "I give you one more assurance your boys are not going to be sent into any foreign wars" with his words of just a few days earlier: "It is always possible that our boys in the military and naval academies may be fighting for the defense of these American institutions of ours."[74] The paper stated its platform on the editorial page in one simple phrase: "Save Our Republic."[75]

Some former government officials seemed to be agitating for war with Japan. The former ambassador to Thailand, Hugh Grant, told the *New York Times*, "If the Japanese really want war, now is the time to let them have it. I believe we could smash them within a period of a few months with our superior air and naval forces."[76]

Another civilian, Senator Tom Connally, Democrat of Texas, gave a speech in Florida in which he thundered that the U.S. Navy "in the Pacific . . .

can shoot and shoot straight. That is my answer to the Japanese Premier." Connally threw some other choice barbs at Tokyo. FDR also sent a message to the United States Saving and Loan League, to whom Connally gave his incendiary remarks, but it was simply to praise them for their work in constructing "defense housing."[77]

After upbraiding FDR over his war-making powers, the *Baltimore Sun* then turned on a dime and taunted the Japanese. "By deciding to go on with the negotiations the Japanese statesmen are serving their own nation well. In ships, in planes, in all the stuff with which to make war, the United States grows stronger week by week. Both relatively and absolutely Japan grows weaker. The longer we can keep the Japanese talking, the greater the chance that they will finally understand that war with this country would be an undiluted disaster for them."[78]

The Japanese representatives in Washington, Ambassador Kichisaburo Nomura and "special envoy" Saburo Kurusu, told the Roosevelt administration they had transmitted the president's request for an answer on the Thailand question. Washington was suspicious of Kurusu, though. He'd only joined the Japanese embassy in Washington two weeks earlier and had been the representative of the empire of Japan in Berlin to sign the Tripartite Pact in September of 1940.

Maps in the nation's papers depicted the Far East with Japanese troop and ship emplacements, complete with the mileage by air from Tokyo to Singapore, Manila, and a newly mentioned potential target, Guam, an American territory. It was 1,600 miles from Tokyo to the tiny island in the Pacific.[79]

At Saks Fifth Avenue, Christmas ads were hawking lingerie for women, saying, "There is no shortage of pure silk."[80] Men in uniform were more pedestrian in their gift choices for Christmas. A poll conducted of soldiers said their preferences were "[m]oney, cigarettes, stamps, subscriptions to home-town newspapers, cookies and candy." Also shirts—but families were warned not to send striped or polka dot shirts as they were banned by the military, even when off duty.[81]

Macy's department store helpfully listed dozens of military posts and dates by which gifts had to be shipped to be there in time for Christmas. The store had its own "post exchange" to help family and friends get gifts headed for all forty-eight states.[82]

Another popular item for Christmas was a radio, and many houses had more than one. Emerson, Philco, and General Electric all touted AM radios that were as cheap as $16.95.[83] On WMAL in Washington, residents could listen to *Orphans of Divorce*, *Honeymoon Hill*, and *Quiz Kids*. On WRC, they could tune into *Guiding Light*, *Stella Dallas*, and at night listen to Eddie Cantor.[84] Shirley Temple was heard on stations across the country.[85]

In order to stay warm in December, many homes in the Washington area still used the relatively safe coal as opposed to natural gas. There was hardly a day that went by that the newspapers did not report on a home death via a natural gas explosion or poisoning. A ton of good Blue Ridge bituminous coal—delivered—was $10, but if you wanted the small, "egg"-sized chunks for the stove, it was $10.50. The Blue Ridge Co. also delivered a full cord of firewood, stacked, for $7.50.[86]

The men in uniform were facing a traveling maelstrom to get home for the holidays, provided they were granted leave. It was expected that December of 1941 would be the heaviest travel month in years. Not enough planes were flying to accommodate everybody, railroads were scrounging to come up with extra cars, and an estimated 100,000 troops were expected to pass through Washington's Union Station over the Yuletide. The furloughs came in waves, staggered out over the month of December, beginning on the 12th and extending to the 29th. Most of the GIs were looking forward to a two-week vacation.[87] Print ads suggested, "If he can't get home for Christmas—send a carton of Camels."[88]

One soldier (whose name was not revealed) who had taken his furlough a bit too casually years earlier tried to come back; having received a ten-day pass in May of 1919, he did not return to post for twenty-two years. While away, he got married, saw the country, and started his own business, but decided to return to Fort McPhearson to clear his record and serve his country as a mechanic. In truth, he tried to come back in 1919. After his pass was up, he returned to his duty station, but the army said they could not find his records proving he was a soldier in the U.S. Army. He was kicked out of the camp. Still, his conscience bothered him and, two decades later, he attempted to clear the matter up. He'd originally enlisted in 1915 and served under Gen. John J. Pershing in Mexico.[89]

The bureaucrats of Washington were in a quandary. A federal tax of $5 per car in America was costing the government more to enforce than it generated in revenue. Few wanted to repeal it, but no one could figure out how to distribute millions of windshield stickers, collect the tax, and still have money left over. Some suggested that additional revenues be raised so the Treasury Department could collect the tax. "If the Treasury is not given the money it needs to finance the collection . . . it cannot collect."[90]

Senator Walter George, Democrat of Georgia, fussed publicly that federal taxes on the American people had reached their limit, and the new borrowing to finance the New Deal and the war effort could mean pushing off repaying the debt, which would then "have to be amortized over the life of the present, the next and maybe the third generation." He projected that at the current rate the national debt could reach somewhere between $110 and $150 billion. Any future taxes could "tremendously [weaken] our whole economy."[91] But administration officials were already floating the notion of an additional tax of nearly $5 billion.[92]

Other congressional representatives were concerned that the huge outlays from Washington were only going to large corporations and that small businesses were missing in the equation, including getting the raw materials they needed to operate. The Office of Production Management said it was working on it. They had, they said, "10 different methods" and these "would be ready in four to five weeks." The navy said it was interested in helping small businesses, "but not at the expense of the defense effort."[93]

Nazi Germany's expensive war machine was also costly to their national economy, with two-thirds supported by tax revenue and one-third financed with borrowing, according to the Tax Institute at the University of Pennsylvania.

Economists noted, however, the indebtedness, borrowing, taxation, and spending were all controlled by the government in Berlin, and no amount of fiscal or financial Keynesian excessiveness could stop a country from going to war if the country truly wanted to go to war. "On the whole, the methods of German war finance have neither been very radical nor have they been very different from other countries. They contain very little of specific Nazi elements. Like all other countries, Germany is financing the war on sound methods, mainly by taxing much more heavily now than in the First World War."[94] Moreover, Hitler had the firm backing of Germany's industrialists, notably the aristocratic Thyssen and Krupp families, who perhaps privately viewed the former corporal from Vienna as a clown but also as a useful expedient for ridding the country of unions, communists, and other undesirables. Germany's industrial might was open at full throttle, for all-out war.

Because of the trouble obtaining precious metals from the Far East, the United States began procuring these materials from Chile, and an agreement between Washington and Santiago was established.[95] One congressman had a novel solution to the metal shortage; he suggested melting down all the statues in the country, all ninety thousand of them.[96] Not even scarcity could improve government efficiencies. A huge pile of scrap aluminum collected by citizens at the urging of the government was sitting unattended in San Francisco, "oxidizing under early winter rains on the lot where the metal was dumped." An official with American Smelting and Refining Co. explained, "We're awaiting orders from the government."[97]

The navy announced their $300 million effort at island building on Puerto Rico had come for naught. The plan for years had been to turn the island into an American outpost, complete with a thriving economy, English-speaking citizens, clean living, and a modern military capability. The locals thought otherwise. Indeed, "the headaches"[98] had been going on since 1898, when the U.S. government took over the island. "Filth, some of the slimiest slums of the New World, poverty, disease and a potent brand of Latin politics are still here," reported the *Washington Evening Star*. The appointed governor general, Dr. Rexford Guy Tugwell, one of FDR's "original New Deal 'brain truster,'" was

at his wits end and contemplated imposing a very un-good-neighborly martial law. Concerns about the "native population" birth and death rate were also
heard.[99] It would not be the first time America had failed at nation building.

Farther south, the navy was finding Brazil to be a more hospitable part-
ner, at least when it came to joint operations. With the blessing of the country, American ships patrolled the three thousand-mile-long coastline of the
country, running at night under blackout conditions, watching for German
ships and U-boats. The Brazilian government was also mobilizing their army,
fearful of a German invasion.[100]

Ireland was officially neutral, but its hatred for Great Britain caused
some of its citizens to cheer the Germans. Still, the Nazis attacked four Irish
commercial ships, including passenger ships.[101] The German Luftwaffe also
blasted and sank a British refrigeration ship, the *Meriones*, 7,557 tons, as it
was stranded on the high seas. They also destroyed another British ship, the
Jessmore, 4,099 tons.[102]

In the face of what was happening to Ireland and Britain, Navy secretary
Knox coyly told reporters that the sinking of American vessels in the Atlantic
had recently slackened, but without giving any reason why. When pressed
by the scribes, he evasively said, "Make your own guess about that. There's
a good story in it if you dig it up." But "the Secretary refused to say whether
the Atlantic patrol of the United States Navy was being made more vigilant
or whether repeal of the Neutrality Act had anything to do with the drop
in the number of sinkings." He refused to say anything else about the ticklish situation in the Pacific or much else, except that he'd placed orders "for
5,334 vessels, costing $7,351,497,905 since January 1, 1940" or that "[n]early
$1,000,000,000 has been spent for expanding shipbuilding facilities in that
time," or that "27 combatant ships have been commissioned, 41 launched and
the keels laid for 128."[103]

Loose lips indeed.

If enemy spies in the United States had missed anything, the last information hole was filled by Assistant Secretary for the Navy Lewis Compton who
said America was launching "a boat a day and the schedule will be stepped
up to two a day by July. . . . He also revealed that Navy launchings are well
ahead of schedule."[104] The *New York Times* joined in the fun, reporting on
new battleships being launched and their locations, such as the *Indiana* and

the cruiser *Cleveland*.[105] Indeed, the *Los Angeles Times* had a large regular section in the paper, "Shipping News," in which construction, status, and launch information was all carefully and completely reported, along with "activities at Los Angeles Harbor." It also helpfully reported on "vessel arrivals and departures," including ships compliments, destinations, and estimated arrival times in other ports of call.[106] The Air Mail Schedule was also reported in detail.[107]

Mel Ott was named "playing manager" of the New York Giants, replacing Bill Terry, who was kicked upstairs to oversee the team's farm operations.[108] It was big news in the sports world. Less covered, Lou Boudreau was named player-manager of the Cleveland Indians.[109] Boudreau was part-Jewish,[110] and for many Americans, this was meaningful, especially at this time in the world. Being only twenty-four, Boudreau's announcement was duly noted, though he was an outstanding infielder and was already a part of history, helping to stop Joe DiMaggio's fifty-six–game hitting streak.

That year was an exceptional one for baseball, as not only "Yankee Clipper" DiMaggio set a record for the next century, so, too, did Boston's Ted Williams, the last man to hit over .400 for a season. Baseball in 1941 was not only the "national pastime"[111] it was the national obsession, and coverage of trades, drafts, and standings were often on the front pages of American newspapers, following the exploits of Bob "Rocket Robert" or "Rapid Robert" Feller, a young sensational pitcher, both players with the Indians. In Washington, a journeyman front office worker from the minor leagues, Calvin Griffith, was named as the traveling secretary for the Senators.[112] In Atlanta, fans had no major league team to root for, but minor league baseball was as popular as it was in other secondary cities around the nation. Atlanta's fans rooted for the Crackers.

Football was still gaining a toehold, but the college game was more popular than professional football, who some regarded with suspicion. Considerable attention was focused on the "Negro college football championship," with the title game to be played before a sellout crowd at Memorial Stadium in Atlanta. The game would pit undefeated Morris Brown, located in Atlanta, against North Carolina State of Durham, also undefeated, though they had tied one game. The North Carolina squad was the champion of the "Colored Intercollegiate Athletic Conference."[113]

A one hundred-year-old man, Joseph Punch, was making plans to wed a child bride, Minnie E. Smith, age sixty-six. Punch was born in 1841 in Mississippi. Punch said his father had been a slave but gave no indication as to his own status in a Southern state twenty years before the Civil War.[114]

Progress in civil rights was slow at best in the North and had gone into reverse in the South. At Washington's National Airport, "The Southern Airs, a well-known National Broadcasting Co. colored quartet . . . were refused table service at the coffee shop . . . because of a Virginia segregation law." The singers had driven to National from Williamsburg to catch a flight to Cincinnati, but it was canceled due to weather. The airport manager, John Groves, hid behind his little bureaucracy, claiming he did not know who had jurisdiction over the airport: the private owners of the coffee shop and restaurant, the Commonwealth of Virginia, or the District of Columbia. Waitresses had refused to serve the foursome. Representatives of the NAACP came to the airport to confer with the musicians and finally, accommodations were offered in the cafeteria "which has permanent facilities for serving colored guests" but not in main dining room of the airport or the coffee shop.[115] Refusing, the Southern Airs departed, their dignity intact.

Yet contrary to what many people in the North thought, not everybody in the South was a racist. In Georgia, a prison camp warden, C. A. Jacobson, a white man, was sentenced to three years in the state penitentiary for the involuntary manslaughter of a black inmate, Louis Gordon, whom Jacobsen had placed in a "sweat box." The jury deliberated for only forty minutes before convicting Jacobson.[116] And yet, lynching was prevalent in the South—a tragic fact about American society that Adolf Hitler delighted in pointing out to the world.

In Florida, in a war game exercise, a group of "Negro troops" successfully "captured" MacDill Field. "Shortly before 10 o'clock the invaders 'landed' from the bay, pushed through a gas barrage and smoke screen in utter darkness and had infiltrated the field before they were discovered."[117]

Military leaders in Japan were naturally calling for the United States to stop aiding Gen. Chiang Kai-shek's forces in China, to give up any presence or designs in the Far East, and to "retire, strategically and politically, to the Western Hemisphere." And in Washington, attention was fixed on the upcoming conference between President Roosevelt with Japanese ambassador Kichisaburo Nomura and special envoy Saburo Kurusu.[118] References to an old "Nine-Power Treaty," were thrown around diplomatic circles, but the Japanese said recent events had rendered it null and void.

Halfway around the world at another conference, five Nazi operatives in the Far East met in Shanghai, "anxious to patch up an understanding so that Japan's resources in men and weapons may be turned elsewhere against Germany's enemies."[119]

CHAPTER 4

THE FOURTH OF DECEMBER

"Defense Units Study Means to Protect Girls Hired by U.S."

Washington Evening Star

"Jap Evacuation Ship Sails after Mail Is Ordered Taken Off"

Tucson Daily Citizen

"America–Firsters Japan's Ace in Hole"

Atlanta Constitution

"Jap Press Hurls Bolts at Allied Powers in Crisis"

Birmingham News

An explosive twenty-six-page memo marked "CONFIDENTIAL" arrived at the White House from the Office of Naval Intelligence, analyzing "JAPANESE INTELLIGENCE AND PROPAGANDA IN THE UNITED STATES" and under the heading marked, "Methods of Operation and Points of Attack," it read, "The focal point of the Japanese Espionage effort is the determination of the total strength of the United States. In anticipation of possible open conflict with this country, Japan is vigorously utilizing every available agency to secure military, naval and commercial information, paying particular attention to the West Coast, the Panama Canal and the Territory of Hawaii." [1]

It also went into great detail about the subversive Japanese elements in the Hawaiian Islands. All the Japanese consulates on the West Coast were busily gathering information on the U.S. Navy, especially in the Pacific. One passage was underlined—perhaps by Roosevelt himself: "Recently it was brought to the attention of the Office of Naval Intelligence that out of a total of 198 postal employees in Honolulu, 51 have dual citizenship and that the foreman in the registry section, Ernest Hirokawa, is an alien Japanese. As a result of this discovery that registered mail for the fleet stationed in Hawaiian waters is not routed directly to the Pearl Harbor Navy Yard as a security measure." Chillingly, ". . . the [Japanese] Naval Inspector's Office . . . was primarily interested in obtaining detailed technical information which could be used to advantage by the Japanese Navy." [2]

Washington, D.C., was experiencing growing pains. The nation's capital was filling up so quickly with new bureaucrats and new bureaucracies that Senator Jennings Randolph of West Virginia, no stranger to political opportunism, proposed moving all agencies out of Washington that were not directly related to national defense. Naturally, he had in mind moving large chunks of the government to his home state and produced the mayor of Elkins, West Virginia, John C. Freeland, to attest to how his town was ready to handle thousands of new residents. "The delegation traveled 200 miles, mostly over fogbound mountains, this morning to attend [Randolph's] hearing," as one report informed.[3] The word *decentralization* was introduced into the political lexicon. Suddenly, members of Congress had all sorts of ideas about moving around the bureaucracy and coincidentally, all these suggestions were in their home states.

A great big new part of that bureaucracy was the massive building being assembled just across the Potomac to house the War Department. Five-sided, many storied, many ringed, and with roads going everywhere, it was already named the War Department Building. The site was a giant mess, but it was envisioned to become the largest building in the world when completed. The traffic in the area had already been chaotic at best, and the gigantic construction endeavor only added to drivers' and commuters' headaches. To ameliorate the complaints of local residents, the military announced it would hold a briefing for the public on the building, its construction, and the new road system being built "at a meeting . . . at 12:30 p.m. at the Harrington Hotel." There, representatives of the Public Roads Administration, the Office of the Quartermaster General, architects, planning engineers, and top military brass explained the building, its workings, and answered all questions.[4] No one was satisfied.

The army also announced with great fanfare the purchase of almost thirty-nine thousand acres in rural Virginia to add to the existing Ft. A.P. Hill facility. The cost was $1,206,000.[5] Additional housing for nurses at Ft. Belvoir post, also in the Commonwealth, was announced, as well as expansion plans in other parts of the state.

Back across the river, the District of Columbia began to mandate fingerprints for business licenses, including "operators of massage, bowling, billiard . . . establishments, solicitors, private detectives, fortune tellers, clairvoyants and mediums . . . boxing promoters and applicants for liquor licenses."[6] The Young Democrats were planning to descend on Washington December 12 and 13, but they probably would not be fingerprinted.

Along with all the bureaucrats, Washington was filling up with women, as ever-more numbers of young ladies flooded into the nation's capital in search of employment with the national government on account of the war effort. The Consumer and Welfare Committee and the District Defense Committee of the city of Washington announced plans to form groups to meet them at the train and bus stations "in an attempt to keep girls . . . away from questionable rooming houses." Their stated goal was to call "attention to the bad character of some of the establishments encountered."[7] In simpler language, they wanted to keep these impressionable young girls—some literally just off the farm—from falling into prostitution. And the best way to promote clean living, it was thought, was by associating with decent people in decent parts of town with decent housing.

These were not "Rosie the Riveter" blue-collar laborers but instead "Tessie the Typist"—sprightly young girls in search of white-collar employment in steno pools, as clerk typists, filing clerks, secretaries, and certainly as "Girl Fridays," though undoubtedly there were more than a few men in Washington who wanted them for "Girl Friday Nights."

Problem was there was little good housing to speak of in Washington, which despite its status as the nation's capital was a dirty and humid backwater. Indeed, there has been little decent housing since its founding as the federal city—especially since the residents of the better neighborhoods fought the city's Zoning Commission when it planned to allow for rooming houses in their neighborhoods with zoning variances.

After a protracted fight and over objections from civic groups, the Zoning Commission shoved through the desired changes in the law and announced a new plan to allow up to four tenants to rent rooms in residential homes. It would only be "abandoned at the end of the national emergency proclaimed by President Roosevelt or by December 31, 1945, whichever date is reached first."[8] The lead editorial in the *Washington Evening Star* the next day was not about the war in Europe or the situation in the Pacific, but the decision of the Zoning Commission and the newspaper's concern about the new regulations.[9]

The state of affairs was worse in New York and other defense "boom towns" for young women. Though money was flowing out of Washington to defense contractors and as many as 1.5 million people had relocated to take jobs in national defense, "for the average woman and girl employee it's a story of inflated living costs and inadequate rates of pay." A study was issued by the U.S.O. and the Y.W.C.A. saying, "No one takes responsibility for their welfare, and girls, many of them never having held jobs before and drawn by the thousands into these boom towns, have found their wages, averaging from $18 to $20 a week, almost entirely consumed by board and high rentals, with little or no money left over for clothing and recreation . . . Involved is a pay rate of 40 cents an hour, 45 cents on night shifts with . . . facilities often so poor that the 'morale' service had put up tents with cots and equipment for doing laundry. . . . Girls are sharing not only rooms, but beds, with native commuters resenting intruders as 'trailer trash' and refusing to house single girls because they are waitresses or munitions workers."[10]

One could not help notice the change in Washington and across the country with the growing number of working women, and not just in the war effort. So many women now had jobs that department stores began having "Night Sales" to accommodate women who could not get out of the office for daytime sales. To keep the girls from being taken advantage of by renters, the city instituted rent control and appointed a "Rent Czar."[11] A number of profile stories were devoted to some of the young women who had streamed into Washington. They worked long days, socialized in the evenings, and did charity work, such as volunteering for "Bundles for Bluejackets," where they learned to knit windbreakers and sweaters for American sailors operating in the cold north Atlantic.[12]

Sumner Wells, the undersecretary of state, and his wife offered to the American Women's Voluntary Service the use of their stables on Massachusetts Avenue, but they were rejected as they could only accommodate around two hundred girls, said Miss Anita Phipps, chairman of the A.W.V.S. On the morning of December 3, on the front page of the *Washington Post*, "an attractive girl . . . Miss Lila Quick, a 19-year-old Veterans Administration worker" was reported missing. Miss Quick had only arrived in the nation's capital several months earlier from Birmingham, Alabama.[13] The city also announced its "first woman air raid warden, Miss Mary Mason." She worked for the National Broadcasting Company as well as serving as a member of the Home Economics Association.[14]

The *Birmingham News* ran an entertaining regular feature on the front page entitled "No Man's Land in Washington; Lulu Tells Betty What's Going On." In the guise of a letter, it opened, "Dear Betty, I have been too busy with defense work to write you lately. Let us make a New Year resolution ahead of time to write more often in the future. Speaking of the future, in some ways it looks brighter, in others more depressing. From all I hear, the 'peace emissary' from Tokyo, Suburo Kuruso, came to Washington just to stall for time. There are few persons here who believe his intentions were ever honorable. If all negotiations fail between Tokyo and Washington, then look out for trouble P.D.Q."[15]

Traffic fatalities had skyrocketed in Washington over just one year, possibly because more drivers were speeding, certainly because there were more drivers, and possibly because of the growing sense of crisis in the city. It was not unusual for a child, alighting from a school bus, to be mowed down by a car.

Perhaps some drivers had become impatient, as some most surely had when a convoy of two thousand cars "containing infantry and mechanizedtroops" rolled through Washington on a weekday "en route from the Carolina maneuvers to Camp Edwards, Mass. Washington traffic police routed the division over Key Bridge, Canal Road, Foxhall Road, Nebraska and Wisconsin Avenues to the District line." And later that afternoon, an additional 350 army vehicles were expected to make the approximate same route through Washington.[16]

In California, it was just the opposite. Drivers were pulled over for driving too slowly because of troop convoys or because their cars were "jallopies" that could not maintain a rate of speed.[17]

It didn't help matters when Washington and all of the East Coast were enveloped in the worst fog in years. The gleaming new National Airport, built near the banks of the Potomac River in 1941, was closed, as were airports from New York to Atlanta, but also west to Pittsburg and Kansas City. The fog and "low lying smoke from defense-busy factories caused semi-blackouts." Ferryboats collided in Norfolk, five ocean-going passenger ships had to layup in the Chesapeake, and traffic ground to a halt for the day.[18] In Boston, the R.C.A. Company picked the foggy night to test out its new air-raid siren, and the moist air contributed to a weird sound that pierced Beantown. Across the region, people called the local police and fire departments asking what was going on.[19]

A senator from New York, James Mead, complained that men in uniform were being ill-treated in the District. On the floor of the Senate, Mead said that some Washington establishments "discriminated" against the military. A bill had been introduced earlier in the year that would "make it unlawful for any restaurant, hotel or other place of public assembly to bar men in uniform from its facilities or service."[20] A move was also afoot in Congress "to continue the fight for legislation giving residents of the District the privilege of voting...."[21] As it was the cold and flu season, the District Health Department and the

Pneumonia Control Committee asked sick people to stay home. As of 1940 in Washington, 80 out of every 100,000 individuals died of pneumonia.[22]

Congress was making plans to quit Washington sine die on December 20, giving members from long distances just enough time to get home to their districts, especially those traveling by rail, car, or bus. But before the Senate could depart, they would have to take up the bill regulating strikes in war industries, as labor unions were beginning to mount a lobbying campaign to defeat the controversial bill. Many were aghast it had so easily passed the House, with its overwhelming control by the Democrats, long aligned with the labor movement. But the unions found themselves on the wrong side of the patriotism argument. Industrial America saw the temporary advantage and they exploited it, pledging to put "patriotism above personal gain," and even William Knudsen, a high official with the Office of Production Management, said, "Let's, by the Almighty God, see to it that the boys, if they have to go, go with guns in their hands and not with a broom handle."[23] The War Department issued press releases claiming strikes had cost "7,000,000 man-hours."[24]

Henry Ford's plants in Detroit had already been partially converted to manufacturing to support the war effort. Ford himself was supportive. "[O]ut of the present conflict in Europe I see emerging a world federation, a union of all peoples in which there will be no customs, monetary or economic barriers," he said.[25] The Ford Motor Company was already churning out tanks and planes, but the old man was, as always, a visionary, quoting Tennyson's "Locksley Hall" speech of one hundred years prior.

At Union Station, where members of Congress and Washingtonians could catch trains leaving town, it was disclosed that government officials under the Wage-Hour Division were trailing Red Caps porters around to see if they were disclosing all their tips for tax purposes. "The checkers would dog the steps of the porters and compel them to disclose the amount of the tips they received. Arthur Brown, negro porter at the Camden Street Station . . . in Baltimore testified that the check system was a 'nuisance' which annoyed customers and Red Caps alike. He stated that Red Caps would do as well without any check system or guaranteed minimum wage." At the time, Red Caps could keep everything over 10 cents per customer to help with their luggage.[26]

The Washington social scene was in full swing in the early days of December, and the newspapers were filled with stories about this cocktail party, that black tie dinner, and hoity-toity embassy parties. "Delightful Parties Held" and "Air Attaché and Mrs. Kenny Honored at Informal Party Given by Canadian Minister" were some of the headlines.[27] One party honoring "Senhor Paulo Bettencourt" and "Senhora de Bettencourt" was hosted by Nelson Rockefeller and "Mrs. Rockefeller."[28]

But one Georgetown socialite was having trouble with the help, according to the *Post*. "A popular Georgetown hostess tells this story on herself. Seems that along with a number of other Capitalites, she has had her share of servant trouble lately. A couple of days ago, however, she interviewed a colored maid whose qualifications appeared to be ideal. Arriving with the domestic for the interview was her brother." At the conclusion of the tour, the hostess welcomed the maid, telling her "you will feel like home here. She ought to," put in the brother with a wide smile. "She was bawned in this very room."[29]

In December of 1941, newspapers in America often published the impending military transfer of army personnel. In long columns, the names of men being assigned to the Medical Corps, the Infantry, the Coast Artillery, the Air Corps, the Ordinance Department, the Quartermaster Corps, the Dental Corps, the Field Artillery, the Veterinary Corps, and the Sanitary Corps were all right there in black and white along with the location of their new assignments. Anybody could read it, including jealous girlfriends, old enemies, collection agencies, and Japanese and Nazi spies.[30] The notion that anyone could enlist in the military, pack up their troubles, and get a fresh start was absurd.

The newspapers also thoughtfully listed shortwave radio broadcasts, including war news and broadcasts from London, Berlin, and "Tokio."[31] Also right there in black and white were details about how the navy's newest dive-bomber, the "HELL-DIVERr," was being made in Columbus, Ohio, at a newly dedicated twenty-six acre facility. The plane, to be manufactured by the Curtiss-Wright Corporation, was a continuation of American pioneering in the new art of naval dive-bombing. The plant was opened by Rear Admiral John B. Towers, who helpfully told reporters, "Germany copied its dive bombing technique from the Unites States Navy. Ernst Udet witnessed a demonstration of Navy dive bombing in this country eight years ago and took the idea back to Germany."[32]

The war continued its steady spread across the globe. In Lebanon, "war widows and orphans" of men who died fighting were receiving Red Cross aid.[33] President Fulgencio Batista of Cuba wanted his national legislature to grant him emergency powers to act in the event of hostilities. "He also declared that Cuba must be ready to carry out her commitment to the United States, with which the island's policy is linked."[34] The Argentine government was looking to clear up a previous misunderstanding with Washington, so as to gain access to its funds and pay for its own army.[35] Great Britain was moving ahead with declarations of war against "Finland, Rumania and Hungary." Churchill's policy was that "any man or state who marches with Hitler is our foe."[36] Finland had attacked Russia, an English ally.

The famed war correspondent Royal Arch Cunnison was in the Far East documenting, "Here in the Philippines the United States Army and Navy and the Filipino troops are on a 'war alert' 24 hours a day" and that the daily activities by America to strengthen its position in the region might dissuade Tokyo from military action." He was not hopeful, though, that the Emperor would put a halt to his country's militarists. "It is not logic that will govern the Japanese. If they were logical, there would be no war."[37] Others in Washington's diplomatic circles were convinced that the Germans' complications in North Africa and the Russian Front would give the Japanese pause; that maybe there was a chance Hitler might not win the war, especially after two Italian divisions had surrendered to the Russians. Moscow issued a statement proclaiming that Josef Stalin was personally directing the Russian defense as "supreme commander in chief of the Red Army." The statement also claimed the Red Army had "severely defeated the Adolph Hitler Elite Guard."[38]

But Senator Claude Pepper of Florida, a staunch supporter of FDR in general and of Lend-Lease in particular, publicly predicted that the Vichy French government and the Japanese would engage in a "pincer" move into Thailand and toward the Burma Road.[39] Meanwhile, the Vichy French would support pinning down the British in Libya, thus reducing the armaments they could send to the Far East to strengthen their garrisons. But there were also rumors in Washington that the Japanese navy—thought to be a moderating force in Tokyo—was squabbling with the militarist elements inside the government. "[T]he conservative element struggles with the military group to prevent aggravation of the Pacific crisis to the point of war against the United States."[40]

This slim reed was grasped by many, that internal discord and food riots among the populace would prevent Japan from going to war. "If there is a ray of hope that a solution other than general war in the orient will be found, it rests on the uncertain attitude of the Japanese naval high command. . . . Reports to the State Department declare that" riots, provoked by unemployment and shortages of rice and fish, the main staples of the Japanese diet, are rapidly spreading over the country."[41]

"Finally, Japan is confronted in the present situation with overwhelming naval and air supremacy of her potential enemies. An American fleet, bigger than her own, is poised at Pearl Harbor in the mid-Pacific."[42]

Suffice it to say, opinions as to Japanese intentions were sharply divided.

On December 3, The *Tatuta Mara*, a Japanese passenger ship, was stopped from departing San Francisco for Japan until sixty tons of U.S. mail destined for that country had been removed, though there was no mention of this being for security reasons. Because of the American embargo against Japan, longshoremen went aboard and off-loaded "a huge shipment of electric refrigerators, binoculars and electrical equipment." The ship also contained a large number of bankrupt businessmen who were going home to Japan after FDR had ordered a freeze of credit for Japanese in America. "One of the passengers was Jiuji G Kassai, member of the Japanese Diet, who warned the United States against going to war with the Japanese in a speech last week to the Commercial club."[43]

In Mexico City, it was reported that Japanese diplomats and their families, including the Japanese minister, were making hurried preparations to leave the country and head back to Japan. "In diplomatic circles, it was reported their decision was prompted by the arrival of a courier bringing from Washington confidential reports of the progress of United States-Japanese negotiations. A number of Japanese residents were reported to be trying to dispose quickly of their property preliminary to leaving."[44]

Japan also revealed that they had a response to the American position, though they did not indicate if they were responding to Secretary Hull's "principles for peace in the Pacific" of late November or the president's question on Japanese intentions when it came to Thailand of two days earlier. Whichever they were responding to, they let it leak out that Washington would not be happy with Tokyo's response.[45]

Thailand—renamed from Siam in 1939—was a prized possession for either side. The new name meant "Land of the Free" but the Japanese were thinking otherwise. It remained the only independent nation on the Asiatic Peninsula. "The nation's extensive mineral wealth includes tin, gold and silver, coal, tungsten, lead, antimony, copper, manganese, some iron and precious stones. Rubber production has been of increasing importance in southern and eastern Thailand."[46]

The mystery was cleared up when Tokyo rejected the Hull proposal, calling it "unacceptable" and saying that it could not serve as the foundation for "negotiations henceforth." It also did not address Roosevelt's question about Thailand. The Japanese news agencies, including Domei, let loose with a verbal blast against Washington. The newspaper *Asahi* claimed the Hull initiative was "'evident' that the United States was becoming 'more and more undisguised in her hostile activities against Japan.'"[47] After Hull said the two countries were at a near-breakdown in negotiations, the United Press called it "the strongest verbal whiplashing yet administered [at the] Tokyo government by an American official."[48]

The Japanese then floated the argument that they were amassing soldiers in Indochina as a security precaution to quell internal disturbances. "There have been no evidences of internal disorders . . . to warrant such extraordinary military and naval maneuvers," replied the *Washington Star*. The Vichy government had already signed over the former French colony to Tokyo. "Indo-China was taken over so easily that Tokio [sic] undoubtedly was encouraged to look upon further aggressive steps."[49] Still, the Japanese sent diplomats to Indochina to give the whole situation a veneer of officialdom, rather than a blatant military incursion. Tokyo even produced a "neutrality" treaty between the Japanese and then-Silan signed in 1606.[50]

The Japanese government also broadcast over a radio in Hanoi that it would send no more troops into Indochina and further, the troops there would not be used to attack either Thailand or the Burma Road. They also disputed the number of soldiers FDR claimed were there.[51]

Before receiving the Japanese delegation in Washington, Hull met once again with FDR. Roosevelt then met with congressional leaders about the crisis in the Far East. Attending the meeting were Vice President Henry Wallace, House Speaker Sam Rayburn, and others. "Mr. Roosevelt told how the Japanese army twice had deliberately sabotaged peace negotiations with the United States just when these seemed to be going favorably." Hull echoed FDR's pessimism.[52] He had concluded that the Japanese had fully embraced "Nazi doctrine in tactics in the Far East." Also discussed was FDR's Lend-Lease announcement for Turkey.[53] The Germans were none too happy about Lend-Lease being extended to Turkey, storming, "[T]he last words have not been spoken in Defense Zone expansion" matters.[54] The Germans had designs on Turkey as a port on the Mediterranean.

Also in attendance was Senator Elbert Thomas, Democrat of Utah and chairman of the Senate Armed Services Committee. He had a kinder and gentler view of the Japanese, later predicting that shortly, the two powers would begin to cooperate against Germany and Italy. "Japan's Axis alliance is so unnatural and she is lonesome." Thomas made his remarks at a dinner in New York honoring a Soviet diplomat.[55]

A similar high-level meeting to the one convened by FDR at the White House took place in Tokyo, lasting two and a half hours and conducted by the "Privy Council, highest advisory organ of the empire to which Premier Gen. Hideki Tojo and Foreign Minister Shigenori Togo report in detail." The Privy Council in turn gave its advice to Emperor Hirohito. Pessimism filled the air in all the meetings and counsels in both Washington and Tokyo.[56] Meanwhile, Japan was working on creating a sham agreement with French Indochina, as it was ostensibly under Vichy control, which was under Berlin's control, but Indochina was already overrun with Japanese troops.

"Hull, in his press conference, specifically declared that Japanese policy is based on the doctrine of force and that this force is being wielded Nazi-fashion to attain political, economical, moral and social domination of the territory belonging to other sovereign nations."[57] The normally placid man was near to throwing up his hands, so frustrated was he with Tokyo. He was working to create a solution, but whatever he offered, the Japanese rejected and then blamed Washington for the continued stalemate.

A Japanese newspaper piled on. "If anything ruptures in the Pacific, the Anglo-American powers should take the responsibility."[58] Hull was a proud, successful, and patient man, but the Japanese intransigence had about beaten him.

British and Dutch commercial shipping in the Western Pacific effectively came to a standstill, in part because Nazi ships operating there were raiding them. British battleships had arrived in Singapore "but censorship cloaked that fact."[59] The Australians announced the loss of the cruiser, *Sydney*, after being shelled by the German boat *Steiermark* in the Indian Ocean. The German boat had been "disguised as a merchantman" and opened fire on the Aussie boat. It was of little consequence that the German boat was sunk by the *Sydney* before she too went down.[60]

The Atlantic was no better than the Pacific.

By now, hope had faded for the recovery of most of the seventy-plus seamen who went down on the *Reuben James* in the North Atlantic, the greatest loss of naval personnel since the *Maine* went down in Cuba in 1898. A survivor, George Beasley, twenty-two, of Tulsa recounted, "We were swimming about 30 yards away . . . when she went down. Just as she slipped under, the depth charges went off. The ocean was thrown up in great wave, our raft was overturned and I was pulled under. About half of the men on the raft were drowned." Beasley was anxious to get back to sea.[61]

A month earlier, the U.S. government told the German government it would accept $3 million, cash on the barrelhead, for the previous sinking of the *Robin Moore*, which would settle all claims. The Germans then sunk the American cargo carrier *Lehigh*, off the coast of Africa.[62]

Over the previous month, Germans had lost more ships than the British, but the British had lost more planes than the Germans. London reported it had lost three bombers over France while "German planes bombed a port on the British southwest coast."[63]

December 4 was a bad day in California for military flyers, as several became lost in fog and perished. Out of the sky in Dublin appeared a German soldier, floating down in a parachute. The police arrested and booked him.[64] Winston Churchill's nephew, Pilot Officer Esmond Romilly, was declared missing in action after oversees air operations in the North Sea, flying for the Canadian Air Force. At twenty-two, he'd already been a bartender in Florida, lived in Alexandria, Virginia, with his wife, Jessica, a prominent London socialite, had been active in Socialist politics in England, and had fought on the Republican side in the Spanish Civil War.[65] Romilly was later declared dead.

America launched two more destroyers, the *Aaron Ward* and the *Buchanan*, in New Jersey, which was covered by all the newspapers, including ship compliments and armaments.[66] A wire photograph of an unusual view of the stocks and flukes of a giant anchor in the Pearl Harbor navy yard went out on all the wires, published in many papers. Again, photographers and reporters had unalloyed access to American military installations and information.

The navy vessel *Salinas* was fired upon in the North Atlantic just a month earlier by German subs and the ship managed to limp into port, but not before returning fire on the subs, damaging one.[67] It was the first time the U.S. Navy had successfully fired upon and damaged a German naval vessel. American naval vessels were under orders directly from FDR to defend themselves and had been for some time. The naval battle was heavily covered in all the newspapers. But if anyone really needed more detail on American vessels, all they had to do was pick up a copy of the publication *Jane's Fighting Ships*, easily available. "The publication . . . credits the *Salinas* with two 5-inch guns and three 3-inch anti-aircraft guns. Whether the latter could be depressed sufficiently for fire on a submarine would depend on whether they are of a late model."[68]

Photos of an unidentified British freighter being torpedoed in the Atlantic by a U-boat ran in newspapers on December 4. In Chungking, Chinese sources spotted forty Japanese warships in Camranh Bay. This fleet included at least one aircraft carrier and "45 planes aboard. The Japanese were hastily building an air base in Western Indochina near the Gulf of Siam (Thailand) having impressed 5,000 native workers for the job." *Impressed* was a polite word left over from an earlier era that in fact meant "slavery."[69]

At the same time Seigo Nakano, a "pro-Axis political leader, was demanding the sinking of United States ships unless aid to China ceases."[70] The Maritime Commission urged the speedup of the production of Liberty ships, which were needed for transporting goods and war materiel. At the time, ships were "splashing" at the rate of one every seven months, but the goal was to streamline the process so that one could be launched every four months.[71]

In Nazi-occupied Belgrade, Serb guerillas were making the occupying German army's life miserable. "The Serbs were . . . harassing German patrols, cutting German communications and looting German supply trains." An initial report said the Serbs had inflicted six hundred casualties on the Germans. The Serbs, numbering around eighty thousand, led by Gen. Draja Mihailovic, "were locked in battle in the Yugoslav Valley of the Western Morava." The Germans were determined to wipe out every Serb as punishment for reprisals. The ragtag Serbs were fighting and winning against five Nazi divisions, heavily armed, with superior firepower.[72] The Nazis eventually lost four of five divisions before withdrawing.

Also, in a week's period of time, four German passenger planes between Belgrade and Ankara, Turkey, had crashed, and while some blamed the cold weather for causing engine failure, others blamed Serb saboteurs for the planes' demise.[73] Moscow also claimed credit for killing four thousand German troops, and the British claimed that Nazi planes accidentally killed or wounded sixty German prisoners who were being transported in freight cars to a camp in the Nile Valley.[74]

When it came to security, the American government wasn't completely feckless. "The United States yesterday added 189 names to its blacklist of individuals and firms in South and Central America alleged to be acting for the benefit of Germany or Italy."[75] The government had already assembled a list of two thousand persons of interest thought to be aligned with Italy and Germany. But apparently no Japanese interests were listed, even though

America was not at war with any of the three principle countries of the Axis powers.[76] Many papers referred to it as a "Black List."[77]

In Paris, the German Gestapo set a deadline for those guilty of "terroristic acts against German soldiers." In recent days, a German doctor had been shot and a bomb had been detonated, killing two artillerymen. "The Germans have dealt sternly with previous attacks on soldiers. Fifty hostages were executed by German firing squads at Nantes for the assassination of the commander of that city and fifty others were executed at Bordeaux for the assassination of a German military lawyer."[78] In the occupied countries of Europe, it was not unusual for the Nazis to shoot one hundred civilians as reprisals for every action taken against a German national.

In the time since Nazi occupation of Paris, the city's population had sharply declined, from over 2.6 million in 1936 to just over 1 million as of the spring 1941. It was estimated that 1.5 million French had been deported to "German oflags and stalags."[79]

It turned out the House Military Affairs Subcommittee had only begun to scratch the surface when it came to Leon Shanack, the so-called "defense broker" whose exploits the papers had covered avidly the day before. It was subsequently revealed that Shanack was no piker when it came to bilking the American taxpayer and, in fact, had so far pocketed $97,959 and stood to collect another $91,990 in "brokerage fees" from Remington Arms for services rendered as a go-between with the Greenwich Machine and Tool Company of New York. It was later discovered that Shanack received even more fees from additional companies for other defense contractors.[80]

The economy wasn't in completely bad shape, even with a minimum wage of 30 cents an hour.[81] The newspapers abounded with bank ads for car loans and home loans, and pitched opening savings accounts with each, insured up to $5,000 by the government.[82] At the People's Bank in Atlanta, they were paying 4 percent on a passbook savings account.[83]

Flush with defense dollars, New York was a downright party town. The Rainbow Room, a swank restaurant and nightclub with a revolving dance floor and live big band, located on the sixty-fifth floor of the Rockefeller Center, was the scene of lavish parties given by Manhattan's elite. "This is NBC, coming to you from the Rainbow Room" was a frequent phrase heard on national radio, causing a frisson of wistful yearning among ordinary Americans in the listening audience not privileged enough to be dancing there in formal attire to the strains of jazz kings like Tommy Dorsey or Harry James.

An astonishing story was reported at length in the *Chicago Tribune*, owned by Col. Robert McCormick, an isolationist whose Republican leanings were well-known, as was his opposition to FDR. Because of this, the paper's news gathering—which was often superb—was sometimes discounted by the more New Deal supplicant newspapers.

In an exclusive, lengthy, and detailed story, the paper reported that a secret "War Plans Division" was laying out how the United States government was preparing to create a massive armed forces—over 5 million men— and would make a "supreme offensive effort" to enter the war on July 1, 1943. The document was called "Blueprint for War." A highly confidential letter was produced for the article from Roosevelt to Henry Stimson, secretary of war, urging he coordinate with Henry Knox, secretary of the navy, to formulate a grand plan for America's entry into the war. The main objective was the absolute defeat of Nazi Germany. "I wish you would explore the munitions and mechanical equipment of all types, which, in your opinion, would be required to exceed by an appropriate amount that which is available to our potential enemies," FDR ostensibly wrote the secretary of war.[84]

Just as astonishing, FDR's secretary, Stephen T. Early, did not dismiss the explosive story out of hand, but simply said, "I am in no position to confirm or deny the truth of this story" and that there would be "an investigation." The War Department could only say, "No comment."[85] In Washington, at all times, "no comment" was a surefire confirmation that the allegation was true, as was any call for an investigation. Early went even further, defending the notion that FDR should be preparing for war. "An unlimited national emergency has been declared. If these divisions lacked plans to meet this emergency or any phase of it, they would be guilty of inefficiency."[86]

What rankled so many people was their perception of FDR's autocratic and secretive approach to governance and presumed preparations for war with Germany. Indeed, it came to light that he'd been arming Turkey for six months prior to announcing the extension of Lend-Lease to the beleaguered country, a promise he'd made to Churchill months earlier, even though there were forces in Ankara attempting an alliance with the Axis powers. Senator Robert Taft, Republican of Ohio, did not object, though. "I would much rather give aid to them than to Russia."[87]

Analysis in the Stimson document was cold and accurate. "By themselves, however, naval and air forces seldom, if ever, win important wars. It should be recognized as an almost invariable rule that only land armies can likely win wars."[88] It did recognize the political realities of December 4, 1941, when the document said, "It is out of the question to expect the United States . . . to undertake a substantial and successful" effort to enter the World War.[89] Astonishingly, war with Japan was only referred to as an aside, barely considered by the war planners.

Harold Ickes, secretary of the Interior, outlined his own view of America foreign policy in a speech before the Jewish Community Council. "I know of no one, except the Nazis and the self-acclaimed but misnamed American Firsters, who is suggesting a negotiated peace, or who is likely to ask for a negotiated peace. I know the only way to prevent a war epidemic is through the establishing of democracy at the sources of war."[90]

On the East Coast, it was open season on the America First Committee, and syndicated columnist Dorothy Thompson said the group was "Japan's Ace in [the] Hole." The grassroots movement, she said, "creates in Tokyo the false impression that Japan can risk war with us."[91]

For good girls and boys expecting gifts from Santa (and with some assist from Mom and Dad) a "Slingin' Sammy Baugh" football made by Spalding was selling at the Plaza Sports Shop for $1.95, a Spalding "Babe Ruth" fielder's glove was $3.50, and boys' and girls' skates were selling for $6.95, available in either black or white.[92]

In Washington, in an era when downtowns were still vibrant and big department stores dominated shopping, men could shop at Frederick's for "nationally known Men's wear." For women, "Lysol for feminine hygiene" was being advertised under the heading, "Her Husband Was a Stranger." The dreadful ad copy continued, "His coolness was hard to bear. She blamed it on everything but the real cause—her 'ONE NEGLECT'—carelessness about feminine hygiene. You can prevent this threat to your romance. Do as modern women do. Use Lysol for your intimate personal care. Endorsed by many doctors." The ad was accompanied by the photo of an understandably stricken woman.[93]

For evening entertainment in Washington, patrons could enjoy the sounds of the Don Carper Four in the Café Caprice at the Roger Smith Hotel. "Dance to the enchanting rhythm . . . nightly at 10. . . . Tremendous Cocktails."[94] The hotel was located at Pennsylvania and 18th streets, just two blocks away from the White House. Also open for business was the Pall Mall Room at the Hotel Raleigh, "with music by Bert Bernath and his Sidney Orchestra."[95] The Lounge Rivera, with dancing from "9 to 2" and music performed by Pete Macia's famous orchestra was also a popular hangout.[96] For those whose dancing skills were suspect, they could always learn or brush up at any one of dozens of Arthur Murray Dance Schools around the nation.

There was also a great deal of cheer in South Carolina, where army troops finally finished two months of maneuvers. Some headed back to their bases, others to their homes for Christmas. "While music boxes blared in the smoke-filled cafes and taverns, long lines of soldiers impatiently stood on the sidewalks awaiting their turn to eat." The restaurants were so filled that many men ate standing up as "perspiring waitresses staggered under trays of food. . . . Last night was a barber's nightmare." Many of the soldiers had gone for over a month without a haircut but now "enjoyed the luxury of shaves and shampoos in warm water. Many waited three to four hours before getting a chair."[97]

A new and wholly ugly car was rolled off the assembly lines, the Crosley. "For Maximum Defense Economy, it costs 2/3 less to buy . . . up to 50 miles on a gallon . . . up to 40,000 miles on tires." The car sold for $447 but could be driven off the lot for just $149 down. It was being sold in Washington by the Manhattan Auto and Radio Co.[98] The car looked like it was made out of paper mâché.

A new cereal was unveiled, and to help boost sales they were selling two for one. The advertising claims suggested it did everything except cure the heartbreak of psoriasis. And it "sticks to your ribs!" too. What was this wonder food? "Shaped like cute little doughnuts . . . they stay crisp in milk." Its name was Cheerioats. Breakfast cereals were often marketed as edible medicine cabinets—to wit Kellogg's All-Bran: "The better way to treat constipation due to lack of proper 'bulk' in the diet is to correct the cause of the trouble with a delicious cereal . . . eat it every day and drink plenty of water."[99] The brainchild of Will Keith Kellogg, prepackaged cereals such as All-Bran and Toasted Corn Flakes were considered nutritional innovations.

Virtually every newspaper of the era pitched a miracle cure for baldness. "More than a quarter million persons have retained or regained good heads of hair by the reliable, proven Thomas method."[100] If Christmas cheer got to be too excessive, Americans could always turn to Phillips Milk of Magnesia, so they could "wake up clear headed after too much smoking, drinking, late eating." Apparently "alkalizing" one's "overindulgence" was the ticket.[101]

The scrap paper drive initiated in Washington just a day before and implemented mostly by children was a huge success. The tykes brought in tons of paper to recycling centers with the proceeds to go to local schools and PTAs.

In New York, the heavyweight champion of the world, Joe Louis, was looking forward to a title defense fight with Buddy Baer, brother of Max Baer, whom Louis had defeated several years earlier.[102] Both Louis and Baer had something to prove, Louis, the African American and Baer, the Jewish American.

The *Atlanta Constitution* announced as part of the Christmas celebration it would serialize the Charles Dickens manuscript *The Life of Our Lord*. Dickens had written it for his children and read it to them each Christmas, but asked that the book not be published until the last of his children had died. In 1933, the last of his children, Sir Henry Fielding Dickens, had passed away after a long and successful life.[103]

In Bogata, Colombia, the offices of the "anti-Nazi committee" were burglarized, and money was stolen that had been "collected during Anti-Hitler Week."[104]

In North Africa, British tank commanders still talked confidently of defeating Rommel, the "Desert Rat," but they would first have to involve Rommel in their plan, as he'd been pushing them all over North Africa and they were retreating right along the coast all the way to Egypt. Time may have been against Rommel however, as the British navy's goal was total control of the Mediterranean so they could interdict German supply ships with impunity. The Germans were rushing supplies via plane and ship. Daily reports of the tank battles in North Africa often contradicted themselves, but both sides agreed that Rommel had crushed the New Zealand tank division aiding Great Britain.

Military service could be downright hazardous for the enlistee or draftee, but it could also be dangerous for the members of the Selective Service Board. In Athens, Georgia, former Major League pitcher William Austin "Cy" Moore struck the chairman of the local draft board when he questioned whether Moore's parents had given false documents as to their dependency on their son.[105] It could also be dangerous for the loved ones of potential inductees. In Los Angeles, a twenty-three-year-old carhop shot and seriously injured herself, greatly distraught that her boyfriend might be drafted.[106]

As with other newspapers around the country, the Boston Daily Globe reported on new assignments by troops and war equipment. "The newly organized Tank Destroyer Tactical and Firing Center has been stationed temporarily at Ft. George C. Meade, Md. according to a War Department announcement."[107] One G.I. from up north was so pleased with southern hospitality in Farmville, Virginia, he exclaimed, "If anybody mistakes us for southerners now, it will be ok."[108] Army chaplains were in short supply and a call went out for more men of the cloth to put on khaki and camouflage.

New York mayor Fiorello LaGuardia dedicated a new building in his city designed to house military personnel. He said that America was not "bluffing," that it may have been fooled in the "last World War" but would not be again. "We do not know what will happen tomorrow, next week or next month, but the United States Navy stands ready."[109]

The Globe also reported on new military construction with great fanfare. "The United States submarine Halibut, 40th undersea boat to be built at the

Portsmouth Navy Yard, was launched today. . . . Today's launching was the sixth of the year and establishes a new record for submarine construction. In 1940, there were four launchings. As soon as the ways were clear today, workmen began laying another keel in Uncle Sam's defense program." The story also detailed all the military brass in attendance at the yard in New Hampshire.[110] Yet another story detailed again how America expected to meet its goal of fifty thousand airplanes produced in 1942.[111] The military budget, it was announced, was almost $68 billion.[112]

When it came to telling America's enemies everything about the military, the *Los Angeles Times* was no slacker. A story went into great depth about "air raid defense exercises" planned for the area in mid-December. It would involve hundreds of planes, as well as ground personnel and spotters. The planned drill was "similar to those in New York and other eastern cities during the last few months." . . ."[113]

"Taking part in the aerial portion of the tactical problem will be scores of planes from the 20th Pursuit Group, Hamilton Field, using P-40s and the 17th Bomber Group, McChord Field, Washington, in B-25s. The planes, it was learned, will fly as theoretical enemies as well as interceptors. Across a huge, kidney-shaped filter board, 120 women, plotters and tellers, will filter the information and pass it on to the information room."[114]

On tour was the typing champion of America, "a plump, brown eyed girl" who could rattle off 150 words per minute, setting a per-hour record that had never been broken. "Miss Margaret Hamma" of Brooklyn was on a publicity tour to promote the new IBM electric typewriter.[115]

Actor Joseph Cotton reported that his car was stolen. Forty-eight hours later, it was discovered at the bottom of his pool. He'd failed to set the brake and it rolled backward, unnoticed.[116] The *Los Angeles Times* was celebrating its sixtieth anniversary.[117] The paper had seen much, and by 1940, the population of the city was just over 1.5 million citizens, and in 1939, water began to arrive at the city via the new Colorado River Aqueduct. That same year a heat wave kept the city hot under the collar, as the daytime temperature averaged "around 107 degrees for days and days."[118] The paper also reported on the

"Latin American Queen" picked for the Rose Tournament Parade: Juanita Estela Lopez, "olive-skinned and dimpled . . ."[119]

In San Jose, a frustrated husband filed for divorce because his wife would not stop listening to the radio. His wife "Eva wouldn't clean the house, care for the children, cook my meals or talk to me," complained Max Barrott. Judge John D. Foley "awarded Barrott the divorce and his wife the radio."[120]

Knowledgeable observers tried to make some sense of Japan's actions. London had made it clear that any incursion into Thailand meant war with the British and that meant war with America as well. It would mean fighting a multifront war with countries that had more industrial capacity than Japan did.

"Japan is facing international economic siege and she is very vulnerable. If there was ever a country that needed to live on terms of peaceful trade with the rest of the world, it is Japan. Japan Proper has a population of 73,000,000 packed into an area less than that of California and far less rich in its material resources. Scarcely able to sustain herself in foodstuffs, she is heavily dependent upon imports of other raw materials. For such industrial and military necessities as petroleum, iron, steel, aluminum, lead, zinc, copper, tin, machine tools, wool and cotton she relied chiefly upon the United States, the British Empire and the Netherland Dutch Indies, nations which are now enforcing against her a rigid economic blockade." Imports from the United States had shriveled to nothing, from $18 million in September of 1940 to $500 in September of 1941. The country was also cut off from U.S. credit and the country lived and died by trade.[121]

"Japan, in the grip of her militarists, has chosen to seek the will-o'-the-wisp of economic self-sufficiency by the path of military aggression. Now, after four years of exhausting war, she finds her economic and industrial life strangling. She has made the tragic error of following a course of military aggression irreconcilably opposed to that kind of world. She can expect relief only when her national policies again permit peace-loving nations to do business with her, without risk to themselves, and in good conscience."[122]

Because of her own policies and myriad mistakes, Japan was now desperate. Washington was openly talking about a naval blockade of Japan, in cooperation with the British. "In that case . . . the Roosevelt Administration would be disposed to ask Congress for an outright declaration of war, rather than to wage an undeclared fight."[123]

The peripatetic First Lady, tireless champion of social causes, was out and about as usual, appearing on national radio shows of her own including a "Town Hall Meeting of the Air" broadcast over NBC. Her cohost was the famous photographer Margaret Bourke-White. The topic they addressed was "What Must We Do to Improve Health and Welfare of the American People?"[124]

While giving a speech in New York at a "symposium on 'Recent Immigrants and National Defense,'" Eleanor Roosevelt assured the audience that if war came, "aliens with good records . . . need have no anxiety about being placed in United States concentration camps should this country declare war against their homelands."[125] Italian, German, and Japanese Americans were relieved.

CHAPTER 5

THE FIFTH OF DECEMBER

"U.S. Proposals Downed by Japs"

Nevada State Journal

"Japanese See Talks Continue"

Standard Examiner

*"Tokyo Envoy to Mexico Ordered Home
as U.S.-Japan Crisis Grows"*

The Sun

Scientists discovered in December of 1941 that the sun was 100,000 miles farther away from the earth than previously thought. Rather than the formerly believed 92,897,416 miles, Dr. H. Spencer Jones, astronomer royal at the Greenwich Observatory in Great Britain just outside of London, calculated *Sol* was actually 93,003,000 miles from *Terra Firma*. Dr. Jones also made some discoveries about asteroids, which other scientists referred to as "the lice of the heavens."[1] Astronomers also enlarged their knowledge about sunspots.

During this time, astrophysical research was gathering momentum in an intriguing area: black holes. In a new line of exploration that was dismissed by the scientific old guard as erroneous and fanciful, more imaginative scientists were theorizing that when a star collapsed after a supernova, it created a sufficiently dense mass from which even light couldn't escape, deforming the fabric of space and time.

Despite the war, German and British astronomers continued to exchange information.[2] The world may have been on the brink of annihilation, but it was also on the brink of exciting new discoveries with enormous, lasting implications.

Science was advancing in others areas as well. In Los Angeles, an amateur "ham" radio operator, Karl E. Pierson, said he had developed important technology to quiet the static heard over broadcast receivers. Pierson had gained fame previously when he had been one of the last to hear transmissions from the lost aviatrix, Amelia Earhart, "on her fateful around-the-world flight in 1937." He also claimed to have received transmissions from Earhart after her plane went down.[3]

Because of the aluminum shortage in America, a new, strong, and flexible material was being perfected: plastics. Some scientists predicted a bright future for the revolutionary new synthetic product and for young men going into the business of polymer and acetate development. "Someday . . . bathtubs, caskets, automobiles and airplane sections may be made of plastic."[4] Plastic automobile bodies were also envisioned, but at the time, the material was mostly dedicated to the war effort.

Scientific advancement also extended to diet. Nutritionists in England, for instance, discovered that Rose hips were "20 times richer in vitamin c— the anti-infective vitamin—than orange juice, now scarce because of the war." The Ministry of Health initiated a "harvest of the hedgerows . . . to garner 500 tons of the rose fruit to be converted into a tasty health-giving syrup."[5] And scientists in Australia were working to perfect powdered beef and in one instance, a six year old can of powdered meat came out in a perfect condition.

Dr. Karl Menninger, head of the American Psychoanalytical Association, produced a report explaining that man sought war because it was "a way to gratify subconscious desires to destroy and kill." Elaborating, Dr. Menninger said, "War appeals to people for the same reasons that the Fascist philosophy appeals to people. It stimulates the wish to exert power over other people, to be aggressive, dominant commanding, possessive."[6]

Science was also unfortunately improving man's ability to make war in the air, on the high seas, and over land. The American military announced the development of a fantastic new gun that could shoot down "anything that can fly and that is expected to prove a major factor in the war against Hitlerism." The announcement was made by Brigadier Gen. G. M. Barnes before a meeting of the American Society of Mechanical Engineers in the Hotel Astor in New York City. "Quantity production . . . will begin next month. The new weapon has a caliber of 4.7 inches or 120 millimeters. The characteristics of the gun are a carefully guarded military secret, but General Barnes discussed its history," reported the New York Times. Barnes elaborated, "Reports from abroad indicate that 90 per cent of the bombing over England and Germany has been carried out at altitudes not exceeding 12,000 feet" and the new gun would be effective "at higher altitudes, using a heavier and more effective projectile." So as to leave no doubt, Barnes went into even further detail for the benefit of casual readers and not so casual readers such as Nazi and Japanese spies. Then General Barnes turned it over to Colonel L. B. Lent, chief engineer of the National Inventors Council, who "told the meeting that some 'revolutionary' new weapons submitted to the council were under test and development and 'someday soon may be heard from in tones not pleasant to the Axis powers.'"[7]

Unfortunately, a 70-ton "flying boat" built for the government by the Glenn L. Martin Co. caught fire and then ran aground in Baltimore harbor while conducting sea and air trials. A propeller flew off and hit the fuselage, causing the mishap, and the plane was badly damaged as other parts of it caught fire. The plane had been named Mars.[8]

For the first time in months, Washington was drenched by a really good gully washer, and a strange rainbow shone over the city for a brief time. The temperature on December 5 was unusually warm for the season—it was in the sixties.[9]

Because of better sanitation, including treated water and the improved methods of handling sewage and trash, American life spans had rocketed up in just a few short years. At the turn of the century, the average life expectancy for an American was around forty-four years of age, but by 1941, it had gone up to sixty-six years for women and sixty-three years for men.[10] And yet, Americans diet was still questionable, as 50 percent of draftees were rejected, mostly due to poor nutrition, which was attributed to substandard household income. A Gallup poll found that four in ten American families were bringing in less that $25 per week and, as such, could not afford enough food. The residents of 12million households went to bed hungry every night.[11]

There was still too little work to go around.

Many eyes were now on Thailand and war seemed to move closer. "To most Americans, Thailand is still Siam. The name conjures pictures of white elephants, temple dancers and pagodas, rather than clashing empires. England declared months ago that Japanese invasion of Thailand would produce immediate collision with the armed forces of the British Crown." Japan propagandists continued their drumbeat that Thailand was threatened by outside forces. It was much the same argument Hitler made before invading Poland, Denmark, Norway, and Czechoslovakia, declaring he would be subjugating them for their own good.[12] The Japanese also claimed the number of troops they were sending into Indochina had been grossly exaggerated and besides, they claimed, Thailand was a Buddhist country and thus anti-Chinese, and they, the Japanese, were there to protect Thailand.[13]

Syndicated columnist Walter Lippmann declared, "For the first time, the country is now on the verge of actual, all out war." Lippmann was the de facto voice of the "reasonable" establishment; his word carried clout. He saw another war coming for America not because of Lend-Lease or because of FDR's order to naval ships to fight back in the Atlantic, but because a fight with Japan would provoke America into jumping into the whole shooting match. In this, his was a voice both accurate and rare. He excoriated the isolationists and America First Committee for misunderstanding the situation in the Far East while focusing all their arguments on Europe.[14] Others saw Lippmann as little more than a shill for the Roosevelt administration when it came to intervention.

A large school of thought in American foreign policy also believed that Japan's society was overtaxed, having failed in four years to completely subjugate China. Large amounts of men and resources were being devoted to fighting a war without resolution and because of this, Tokyo could not seriously consider expanding the war any farther south.[15]

Yet other writers and observers saw the arrival of new British battleships in Singapore as another deterrent to Japanese actions against Thailand. "Political observers here say the arrival of the British fleet brought powerful new pressure on the Japanese in connection with the Washington negotiations and believe it may be decisive in forcing Japan to drop her plans for new aggressions and to begin a general retreat."[16]

A seesaw battle of public relations and war continued on the Russian Front, with the Germans claiming their big guns were raining shells on Moscow while the Soviets claimed the guns had been "silenced."[17] Temperatures on the Russian Front had reached 13 degrees below zero.[18] The British claimed to have repulsed two surges by the Germans in North Africa, though they conceded that Axis forces had "reoccupied the important Gambut supply base which the British captured in the early days of the Libyan campaign."[19]

Public relations battles were also raging in Washington with isolationist Democrats and Republicans fighting with internationalist Democrats and Republicans. On the floor of the Senate, a sharp exchange took place between Senator Charles McNary of Oregon, a Republican, and Claude Pepper of Florida, a Democrat. Pepper charged his honorable colleague with being a "laggard in supporting the President's defense program."[20]

A grand jury had convened to investigate Nazi propaganda in the United States, and a star witness was Republican congressman Hamilton Fish of New York, an isolationist, whose chief aide had been indicted for perjury.[21] Fish represented a grand legacy as his family boasted over one hundred years of political involvement.

Henry Stimson, the respected secretary of war, declared a war of his own against the *Chicago Tribune* for publishing the leaked documents on covert military planning by the U.S. government the prior day. Stimson did not deny their veracity and calmly said all contingencies were being explored, but he questioned the "wanting in loyalty and patriotism" of the newspaper for printing the story. Roosevelt had been asked about the report, but threw it into Stimson's lap to handle. Stimson did so, reading a long statement, lecturing the paper on proprieties in wartime and said his department was conducting an investigation. Capitol Hill erupted into a donnybrook over the *Tribune* story, while some charged that FDR was planning to give a "blank check" to Winston Churchill.[22]

Japanese propagandists and newspapers had a field day with the account. "Secret United States plans against Japan and Germany are exposed," blared a headline in the *Chugai Shogyo Journal*; yet other Japanese newspapers said the story demonstrated that America was not ready for war and that Secretary Hull was pursuing "dollar diplomacy." Japanese radio was little better, bashing America, spreading disinformation, playing the race and regionalism cards.[23]

A controversy over uniformed men and Washington's nightclubs had not died down, as both a general and a senator claimed their sons, both army privates, had been turned away and were told to go and change into civilian clothes before being admitted. Not to say there weren't plenty of other organized activities for soldiers and sailors.[24] The local newspapers listed dozens of locations of Service Clubs and U.S.O. clubs in Washington. At the Soldiers, Sailors, and Marines Club on L Street in the nation's capital, enlisted men found a "library, writing desks, table tennis, pool, radios, pianos, canteen, showers." The club was open twenty-four hours a day, seven days a week.[25] At many clubs, young single women put up Christmas trees, and if a homesick soldier or sailor had trouble finding a room in Washington, they could go to the hospitality committee in the District Building for help.[26]

Both Catholic and Jewish groups operated clubs for young servicemen as well. Over at the Bureau of Printing and Engraving, the Women's Battalion was sponsoring a dance. There were also dances at the Y.M.C.A., sightseeing tours of the area, teas, and lectures. There were also plenty of "Activities for Colored Service Men" in Washington, including an open house at the Phyllis Wheatley Y.W.C.A., religious services at various institutions, lodging at the Y.M.C.A. in Anacostia, and dances.[27] The *Washington Evening Star* referred to the minority clubs as for "colored," while the *Washington Post* referred to them as for "Negro."[28] Many political leaders, including no less a luminary than Eleanor Roosevelt, lobbied for greater civil rights for blacks. But those gains were to come much later. For now, Washington was still a part of the

South, a region where segregationist Jim Crow laws would continue to hold sway for the time being.

Despite his complaints about leaked documents, Secretary of War Stimson nonetheless "disclosed" in great detail army plans for training ten thousand new bombardier-navigators. He also announced plans for "52 'tank destroyer' battalions, and the conversion of two additional regular Army triangular divisions into fully motorized units. The infantry divisions to be motorized are the 8th, at Ft. Leonard Wood, Mo., and the 9th at Ft. Bragg, N.C. The action will double the number of such divisions on wheels, the 4th and the 7th already having been motorized."[29]

Military planners and civilians living and working in the areas of Arlington and Alexandria, Virginia, were still battling over the mishmash of new roads being proposed for the new $31 million War Department. When completed, "some 20,000 Government employees" were expected to work there, but "[i]t is estimated that more than 85,000 vehicles now pass the area of the new building daily."[30] The plan was for the entire building to be outfitted with air conditioning, which most federal buildings still lacked.

In New York, two shipping companies were indicted by a federal grand jury, "charging each with conspiracy to violate the Neutrality act by shipping abroad . . . material that might have been used by Axis powers."[31]

The presidents of the various South American countries were not lagging in their concern about a possible conflict between the United States and Japan. An "extraordinary meeting" was planned in Buenos Aires by the leaders of Brazil, Chile, Peru, and Argentina to discuss the matter.[32]

The District Court of Washington upheld "[t]he validity of covenants under which white owners agree not to sell land in Washington to colored persons . . . was voided when the Home Owners' Loan Corp. became owner of the property in question." A white family had "conveyed" property to a black family, but the white neighbors objected and brought a complaint to the city government. In simpler language, racism was still a protected institution in Washington, D.C.[33]

Ugly free speech was upheld in New Jersey, as the State Supreme Court voided a "race hatred law" aimed at the German-American Bund actively operating there, including holding rallies. Nine men "accused of making or promoting anti-Jewish speeches" were found to be innocent as the state law "conflicted with constitutional guarantees of free speech." "The State's race-hatred law made it a misdemeanor to make utterances in the presence of two or more persons of 'hatred, abuse, violence or hostility' against any race, color or creed." The anti-Semites had been convicted, fined, and some sentenced to jail time before the upper court's ruling. "To denounce one's fellows or advocate hostility to them . . . is as revolting to any fair-minded man . . . yet . . . his utterances must be such as to create a clear and present danger that will bring about the substantial evils to society that the state has a right to prevent," wrote Chief Justice Thomas J. Brogan.[34] An appeal was under consideration.

The spirit of Christmas wisped thin in some places. A draft dodger of the World War, Grover Cleveland Bergdoll, was denied parole by the War Department to be with his family for the holidays. He'd lived in Germany for many years, later coming home in 1939 with a wife, Berta, and six children in tow. Bergdoll "was convicted of desertion, escape and draft evasion during the World War" and was sentenced to seven and a half years at Ft. Leavenworth.[35]

The Vichy government was charitable when it announced that Americans located there could broadcast a twenty word Christmas message to "10 friends in America provided the messages contain no politics or military information."[36] Meanwhile, the French Resistance, underground opposition to Nazi control in their homeland, continued to undermine the Axis powers in Paris. Another Nazi officer was shot "in the Rue de Seine Latin quarter of Paris" by a bicyclist who quickly fled the scene.[37] It meant fresh reprisals against Parisians, but the Resistance pushed on.

The Serbs continued to give the Nazis fits even as "seven Nazi divisions . . . at least 100,000 men had been dispatched in an attempt to wipe out armed opposition to the Axis occupation." The dateline for the story was Jerusalem.[38] There were only sixteen shopping days left until the birthday of the celebrated son of Joseph and Mary who had been born there, 1,941 years earlier.

An underground movement in Nazi-occupied Romania was also taking shape, with an unusual leader—none other than King Michael, a mere sapling of nineteen years, but a brave one at that. Together with his sweetheart, Irina Malaxa, they were actively arming, aiding, abetting, and plotting with the anti-Nazi guerillas growing in the country.[39]

The British government took to the airwaves and called for a "V for Victory" army of civilians in the occupied countries—estimated at 200 million—to switch over from "passive to active resistance. The time has come . . . over the B.B.C. for the army to form in small platoons . . . factory workers lose their tools and that office workers muddle and miscalculate."[40]

The Japanese government finally responded to President Roosevelt's question via the State Department about their intentions for Thailand. Brushing aside reporters and photographers, it was formally presented to Secretary of State Cordell Hull by Ambassador Nomura and Special Envoy Kurusu in a twenty-five-minute meeting "and after their departure, it was rushed immediately to Mr. Roosevelt's desk. The President also met Secretary Hull at a luncheon for a personal discussion of the document."[41] Hull was exhausted, but FDR was anything but. He was looking spiffy in a new, green tweed suit except for the black mourning armband he was wearing for the death of his mother three months earlier. When Hull walked in, FDR airily said, "What's cooking?"[42] Over the course of the day, FDR also met with various members of Congress, his staff, and the cabinet, but also with a young congressman from Texas, Lyndon Johnson, who huddled with the president to discuss his running once again for the senate in Texas. Johnson was described by the *Post* as the "fair haired boy of the Administration." FDR later met again with Hull for an hour and a half.[43]

In a long and sugary communiqué, Japan claimed their actions in Indochina had been because of Chinese troop movement—nothing more. The rambling text said "[t]hat no measure has been taken on the part of the Japanese government that may transgress the stipulations of the protocol of joint defense between Japan and [Vichy] France. Reference is made to your inquiry about the intention of the Japanese government with regard to reported movements of Japanese troops in French Indo-China. . . . As Chinese troops have recently shown frequent signs of movements along the northern frontier of French Indo-China bordering on China. Japanese troops with the object of mainly taking precautionary measures, have been reinforced to a certain extent in the northern part of French Indo-China. . . . As a natural sequence of this step, certain movements have been made among the troops stationed in the southern part of said territory. It seems that an exaggerated report has been made of these movements."[44] The Japanese had now formally offered yet another reason for their actions, and the missive was so reasonable, many thought something was up.

Following the message, a spokesman for Tokyo, Tomokazu Hori, also raised again the chances for peace in the region, saying that America and Japan would "continue with sincerity to try to find a common formula for a peaceful situation in the Pacific." He added, that the administration had "misunderstood our fundamental policy" and that Washington and Hull "seem[ed] to allege that we are following a policy of force and conquest in establishing military despotism." Chillingly, he concluded, "If there is no sincerity then there is no need to continue the conversations."[45]

The U.S. government had no initial response, but rumors swept Australia that America and Japan were near to breaking off diplomatic relations, even as the U.S. government was attempting to allay fears that relations were in danger of imminently breaking down. Nomura tried his best too, saying, "[A]s far as we are concerned, we are always willing to talk—after all, we are a friendly nation." A news report further said, "Japan desired no precipitate action."[46] But in fact, a military skirmish had broken out in Manchukuo, China, near Vladivostok, between Russian and Japanese military forces. The Japanese dismissed them as "Soviet armed agitators."[47] The Japanese media then reported on a second incident involving Russian troops supposedly violating the border, and to many, it seemed a pretext, just as Hitler had done several years earlier in justifying his invasion of the Sudetenland area of Czechoslovakia.

A Japanese passenger ship was dispatched from Yokohama to Panama and Los Angeles to bring home its citizens as soon as possible. "Repatriation of Japanese nationals from strategic areas in and along the Pacific gained ominous pace today amid signs of deteriorating relations with the United States and associated powers." . . ."[48]

After the polite official response from Tokyo came the "unofficial" response from the Japanese news agency Domei. This time, the response was more dire, in snapping tones. "Japan cannot accept" Hull's proposal for peace in the Pacific.[49] "Such a document cannot serve as a basic datum in Japanese-American negotiations henceforth. Japanese-American conversations have taken place twice since the United States handed over to Japan the document in question . . . but there is no tangible evidence of progress of the negotiations."[50] The news agency then astonishingly quoted government officials saying that Hull's "unilateral disclosure . . . of details of the negotiations has made the situation still graver." Japan was accusing Hull of leaking their statements, which they had already released publicly.[51]

Piling on, they then accused the United States of "scheming to impose on Japan the provisions of old, obsolete principles which are incompatible with even the actual Far Eastern conditions of bygone days."[52] In short order, the Japanese had accused Washington of colonialism, plotting to invade Thailand, being too militant, not being militarily prepared, being too soft, being too hard, disinformation, of plotting to encircle Japan, and leaking to the media.

The initial move by the Japanese into French Indochina by citing a mutual defense arrangement was a charade. The Japanese had gone in because Hitler told the French to let them send in troops, but it was all cloaked in diplomaticese.

Hull vowed not to respond but then did so, saying, "[A] general settlement in the Pacific still depended on Japan's acceptance of non-aggression policies outlined to the Japanese envoys last week." He also "described the months of . . . talks since April as a period of confusion arising from actions and statements at variance with the principles under discussions."[53] In short, Hull accused the Japanese of dissembling and prevaricating.

The First Lord of the British Admiralty, A. V. Alexander, offered up his two cents on the ticklish situation in the Pacific, warning the Japanese that "even at this late hour, aggression . . . will not pay. I had hoped that wiser counsels in Japan would prevail over those who appear to be leading her people into a new war of aggression. The threat has not abated and aggression may be imminent."[54]

In a marked change from only days prior, observers in diplomatic circles were now giving odds on war in the Pacific with war occurring as a huge favorite, 100–1. Only a fool would bet on peace now, or at the very least ignore the warning signs. Even so, there was no national will to go to war. Yet some naïve residents of Capitol Hill believed it when administration officials told them, in confidence, that "war with Japan is not expected. The White House had privately told congressional kibitzers not to get too excited about the poker game with Tokyo. War was apparently not expected by the top-most authority."[55]

Of the 17 million men registered for the draft in America, approximately 10 percent had been classified as 1-A, and there were only 1.6 million men in uniform, barely enough to handle all the new operations the War Department had planned, what with all its announced new equipment and programs. To make matters worse, some 200,000 were scheduled to be discharged some-time in December because they were over twenty-eight years of age or had dependents.[56]

Oliver Wendell Holmes never said FDR had a "second class mind, but a first class temperament." He said that instead about FDR's cousin, Teddy Roosevelt.[57] Whether Franklin Roosevelt had a second-class intellect was arguable, but he was indisputably a man of immense charm and persuasion. As Winston Churchill said of his friend FDR: "Meeting Franklin Roosevelt was like opening your first bottle of champagne."[58] FDR also had a very fine and enthusiastic mind when it came to details, especially about the navy, which he dearly loved and once helped run as assistant secretary of the navy under Woodrow Wilson.

At a press conference, FDR discussed in great specificity a recent fight on the high seas between the U.S. ship *Salinas* and German U-boats. This was a commander in chief with a firm grasp of operational detail: "Mr. Roosevelt said that during the World War the navy greatly overestimated the number of submarines it had sunk. He said he kept a set of figures on the reported sinkings and these totaled 725 German submariners at the end of the war.

Mr. Roosevelt added that it is silly to say a submarine has been sunk unless the person making the statement actually saw it sink."[59] Still, from the standpoint of Washington, the most important fighting going on was in the North Atlantic, after FDR had instituted Lend-Lease, after Hitler ordered his U-boats to sink "every ship with or without convoy that approaches Britain," after FDR issued his "shoot-on-sight" order to the American fleet.[60] However, he was not very forthcoming—by design—with the disappointed press corps.

The newspapers began keeping charts of ships lost and how much tonnage, like box scores of a baseball game.

A one-page memo marked "Confidential" was sent to Roosevelt disputing a rumor that Adolf Hitler had been shot. A garbled communication had previously said, "Big Chief shot down," but it was later disproven. (The memo was almost completely redacted.)[61] Also, the ever-present seemingly daily memo from "there is more here than you realize" John Franklin Carter went into a recent unpleasant meeting with "Mr. Astor" (that would be Vincent) over recruitment of civilians in the New York City area. The memo was so circumspect, so guarded, wary, and inscrutable, one could be excused if they thought Carter was referring to underworld figures. "We . . . agreed as to future lines of cooperation and I arranged immediately to establish contact between him and the man who really heads my work in his area."[62]

On the same day, Roosevelt also signed a bill awarding $830 to a man who three years earlier had suffered personal injuries when "his right foot was crushed between a subway car and a loading platform" in the U.S. Capitol. FDR agreed that the government should pay the damages on the advice of the architect of the Capitol.[63]

That night, Eleanor Roosevelt entertained a Christmas party at the White House with 112 guests, but the president did not attend, preferring to have his supper on a tray in the private residence of the White House while working the phones.

To help reinforce the American army garrison in Manila, FDR ordered the 970 Marine Corps officers and enlisted men who had been stationed in Peking to leave immediately. That meant a big financial hit for these Americans; in

China, a dollar purchased about $18 in goods and services. Marines had been stationed in China for almost one hundred years, but FDR wanted them out before they became engaged in fighting the Japanese in China rather in the Philippines, where it was presumed they would be safer.[64]

Even with Chiang Kai-shek holding power and doing his best to hold off the invading Japanese, over the years, the American marines had quarreled and fought with Chinese nationals. However, some three hundred American pilots continued to fly with the Chinese nationals, having been encouraged by Washington to "resign" from the Army Air Corps citing "arthritis" and "lumbago" but being told their rank would be waiting for them anytime their maladies cleared up.[65]

The Japanese had denied they had 80,000 to 100,000 troops in Indochina and they were right.[66] The number was more like 125,000, with another 150,000 in transit. "This force is composed of Japan's best divisions, veterans of the Chinese war, picked guards regiments from the islands, and some of the Kwantung army 'toughs.'"[67] People often forget that Tojo and Hitler were soldiers in arms, bent on world conquest, and that if Hitler was capable of duplicity—then so too was Tojo. The Tripartite Pact bound them together in that mutual quest for world power. Some also foolishly thought that to fight one was not to fight both; but in fact, a fight with one was a fight with all the Axis powers.

Meanwhile, in Tokyo, the American ambassador, the skillful and experienced Joseph C. Grew, was just as frustrated as Cordell Hull. The Japanese were also violating the rule governing the treatment afforded diplomatic representatives. Grew found "himself in a complete diplomatic back-out. For several days he has not been able to transmit to the State Department other information than the official statements carried in the Tokyo press."[68]

The famed Karl Decker "ace correspondent for William Randolph Hearst during the Spanish-American War" died at the age of seventy-three.[69] He was the reporter depicted in the movie *Citizen Kane* who sent a telegram to Charles Foster Kane informing him there was no war in Cuba, to which Kane replied, "You provide the prose poems, I'll provide the war." Indeed, the Hearst newspapers beat the explosion of the USS *Maine* like a toy drum, drumming America into the war. Over the years, some had suspected the *Maine* exploded because of a faulty boiler and not because of a nefarious bombing plot by the Spanish, but Hearst whipped up public opinion anyway. Decker had gallivanted the world as an intrepid journalist, and his kind would soon become a dying breed.

Since 1932 and the rise of the New Deal, the Republican Party struggled for relevancy. For nine years, they had simply not been a part of the national debate, save a few leaders like Senator Robert Taft and 1940 presidential nominee Wendell Willkie, who between them agreed on very little. The Young Republicans met in Kansas, one of only a handful of states Willkie had taken in the 1940 election. People in Republican circles look back on the campaign and claimed it was close, but that was a relative concept. It was closer than 1936, when Roosevelt wiped the floor with Alf Landon, winning over 98 percent of the electoral vote, but the truth was he also skunked Willkie in 1940, taking 449 electoral votes to the Republican nominees 82 and winning the popular vote by 10 percent.

At the GOP gathering in Topeka, Alf Landon and Joe Martin, minority leader in the House, exhorted the Republicans, but most simply claimed they were relevant when all evidence was to the contrary. Martin disputed that the GOP was not "a strong, virile, vigorous party destined to come back into power." He warned, "Wait till the people get their tax bills next March and in March, '43." This was the era before withholding; Americans could keep all their earnings until March, when they would receive a tax bill from the federal government for what was owed on April 15. Landon complained about government corruption, especially in national defense and that the "administration controls the radio" and eviscerated "one-man government."[70]

The majority Roosevelt Democrats were unconcerned about the minority Republicans. Indeed, there may have been people more in the Roosevelt family

than there were in the Republican party, as Eleanor Roosevelt purchased "bedroom slippers for 22 children" in her family, including both children and grand-
children.[71] She was also busy with Christmas entertaining in the White House,
including those visitors from many of the foreign embassies in Washington
such as "young ladies from the Central and South American republics."[72]

Booze flowed freely across the country and in the White House for the
season, and every publication was studded with ads for hard liquors, wines,
and beer. One of FDR's first acts had been the repeal of the controversial
Eighteenth Amendment, which attempted to prohibit alcohol in America.
Many regarded it as one of FDR's greatest accomplishments, but the bitter
enders of the Women's Christian Temperance Union hadn't given up. They
issued a report saying that since 1933, Americans had consumed over $23
billion worth of booze or, 13,924,871,297 gallons of adult beverages.[73] Many
Americans simply lifted their glasses at parties and toasted the president for
his sagacity. At those parties, chocolate was plentiful and popular, going for
19 cents per pound. And for the next morning after too much drinking and
eating, a tin of Anacin tablets sold for 14 cents.[74]

Along with the Republicans, the National Association of Manufacturers
was struggling for relevance. Business, especially big business, had been a dirty
word since 1929. Nonetheless, the N.A.M. at their annual meeting came up
with some radical ideas for government that included: "Make investments
attractive by allowing both business and individuals who risk their money to
keep enough earnings to make the venture worthwhile." They also suggested,
"Have tax policies which encourage, not penalize, reserves, and savings." They
embraced radical ideas about government spending and regulations.[75]

By now, nearly everything was politicized or colored by the war. "Hitler's propaganda department went to some trouble recently to prove that Mozart was
really a German and in that case it was all right for the citizens of the Reich
to hear and enjoy the compositions of the great master." In fact, Mozart "was
born in Austria in 1756."[76] In New York, a concert celebrating the composer's
150th anniversary of his death was held and conducted by Bruno Walter, a
Jew who had fled Germany where he was born Bruno Schlesinger.

Walter had been in Austria during the Anschluss, and though he was born in Berlin, he renounced his citizenship and sought asylum and citizenship in America, even after the Germans asked him to become an "honorary French citizen." Having conducted orchestras in Boston, Berlin, Vienna, Munich, London, and with the Detroit Symphony, Walter considered himself a citizen of the world, and an opinionated one at that. He hated jazz music, saying it was "like looking at Rembrandt through a distorted mirror." The inspiration of the Salzburg Music Festival, he recommended listening to the works of Wagner, even though his music had become the unofficial music of the Third Reich. Walter said, "We are making war against the Nazis, not against the composers." He also called the war a fight "between the forces of good and evil."[77]

The same politicization applied to American movies and Hollywood. Nathan Golden, the motion picture consultant at the Commerce Department, reported that American films remained popular in Europe, even as some were not being shown because "the Nazis exercise a rigid censorship over the films shown in the conquered areas." Still, of those American movies that did air in Great Britain and other unoccupied countries, "export markets react unfavorably to pictures that play up scenes of sordid wretchedness, reckless lawbreaking, alleged social injustice, or any phase of squalid, shiftless life."[78]

Some things escaped the tar of war. Newspapers featured daily columns out of Hollywood, authored by Hedda Hopper, her hated rival, Louella Parsons, and Harold Heffernan. In these columns, Americans delighted to read about a lunch between Bob Hope and Rita Hayworth, or "Are Hollywood's 'name' ladies in the midst of a crackup epidemic?" According to Heffernan, Loretta Young, Irene Dunne, and Joan Fontaine were all showing the stress of movie making and all had been hospitalized or taken to bed for "protracted rest spells."[79]

Plenty of guidance columns filled the newspapers with advice for the lovelorn and information about personal hygiene, exercising, cooking, and FDR's dog, Fala. And Mrs. Roosevelt's "My Day" was popular as it was light on politics and heavy on her life as a wife, mother, and grandmother. When she did slip into politics, she made clear her opposition to women in combat, but was most definitely in favor of saving excess wrapping paper and string.[80]

"Animal interest" stories delighted readers, and one, about a dog named Sport, should have been shown to Fala so he could know how lucky he was. Sport was first run over by a train and lost an eye. Then he was run over by a car, but survived. Barely. Then Sport was run over by another car and lived long enough to be accidentally backed over by his owner's wife. Just as the dog's owner, Grover Lee, was digging a hole to bury the dog, Sport sprang to life and was seen later out hunting quail with his master in Georgia.[81] In New Jersey, a cat named Whitey fell forty-five feet into a dried up well, survived the fall, and went three days without food or water before finally being rescued.[82]

On Friday, December 5, radio programming was light on news, heavy on the soaps, comedians, serials, and specials, such as Kate Smith's *All-American Football Team* and *The Lone Ranger*, although at 9:15 on WOL in Washington was a special, *What Price Defense?* featuring an interview with Emory S. Land, head of the U.S. Maritime Commission.[83] A new show was also debuting across the nation, *Shirley Temple Time*.[84]

Georgians were stunned to learn that ten state colleges in the university system were academically decertified because of "political interference" by the governor, Eugene Talmadge. A virulent racist, he charged the schools with "teaching of whites and Negros in the same schools." He attempted to take pro-integration members of the Board of Regents off and replace them with political cronies who would do his bidding. In retaliation, the Southern Association of Colleges and Secondary Schools stripped ten of eleven Georgia schools of their academic status and thousands of undergraduates were left high and dry. It was a huge issue in the state and indeed the entire South for days.[85]

Farmers were getting better prices for their crops than in previous years and at Christmas time were delighted to find they, for once, had some "folding money" in their pockets. Employment—mostly because of the war effort—was up over the prior year, as was real income, and the Commerce Department forecast heavier outlays for the Christmas of '41 than the previous year. However, the cost of living for the average American had also gone up 11 percent over the last twelve months.[86] The government urged consumers to control their spending, issuing guidelines and admonishing Americans to be careful with their money, while at the same time Washington was engaging in a massive bond drive, urging Americans to spend lavishly and buy as many defense savings bonds as possible, so the government could spend more on the war effort. Keynesian economics taught on the first day of class that government spending did not produce inflation, but consumer spending did.

Initial reports from the Treasury Department said the bond sales were strong, and the government was generating over $1 billion.[87] Preorders showed the danger of a possible oversubscription, but it also fit in with the new normal of America, circa 1941. The Great Depression was still a part of America's economic life, and few had escaped its terrors without being scarred for life. For every banker or Wall Street broker who jumped (no doubt cheered on by thousands), there were tens of thousands who lost their homes, their jobs, and their dignity, who scrapped and struggled just to get a decent meal into their children once a day.

As money and hope flowed from the New Deal and the alphabet soup of agencies and bureaus created by FDR's "Brain Trust," the country stabilized, but the economy did not expand and the days of "wonderful nonsense" of the 1920s were over. People who did have jobs saved their money, living on a "cash basis," and that included purchasing government bonds, many thinking that it would help stabilize their government. But because of government programs and the new frugality, there was not much in the way of consumer borrowing, which also hampered economic growth. No one wanted to be caught with too much debt and too little cash ever again. And it was a simple and direct act of patriotism for liberals to support FDR and for conservatives to support their constitutional government.

The privately held Alabama Power Company took out newspaper ads to announce that the power restrictions had been lifted and its customers were invited to "unrestricted use of electricity service."[88] The company clearly was attempting to encourage customers to use more electricity as a means of generating additional profits. The order came down from Washington's Office of Production Management, which seemed to have its hands in everything. Georgia Power also ran identical ads announcing "Blackout lifted."[89] Again, the national government was sending conflicting signals.

Even so, a spiffy double-breasted suit for a boy was retailing for $9.88 while "Longies" were going for $2.98 a piece.[90] All the department stores in the country touted long, "leisure hour" robes for women, in the style made famous by Rita Hayworth and other Hollywood actresses. The hemline of skirts and dresses had already moved up to just below the knee. Also, long hair was very much in style for women, especially younger women. Hair was up for evening and formal occasions but curled and quaffed and about the shoulders during the day. Of course, no stylish woman went out in public without a hat. Neither did men. American women's hair styles were only regulated by popular fashion, unlike in Japan, where the government only allowed four approved hair styles for women.

At Rogers Jewelers store in Boston, a five-tube countertop radio—a Superheterodyne—could be purchased for $9.95 or just 50 cents down and 50 cents per week.[91] General Electric lightbulbs, the 40, 50, and 60 watt versions, were going for 13 cents apiece while the 75 and 100 watt bulbs were going for 15 cents per.[92] In Philadelphia, bags of mail stolen nearly ninety years earlier—long before the Civil War—were found in an attic of a home. All the envelopes had been opened in an obvious search for money, but the real value now was the stamps.[93] Philatelists like FDR drooled at the thought of pouring over the thousands of cancelled envelopes.

Tens of thousands of American GIs were traversing the country, the lucky ones on their way home in time for Christmas. It was not unusual to see convoys of hundreds of trucks and thousands of uniformed men heading for their home base before heading home. For most, home was priority, war a distant thought.

But news dispatches on December 5 said the American flyers fighting with the Chinese were just "itching" to get after Japanese pilots. Also the story noted that the Japanese had not yet taken the Burma Road using airplanes for aerial bombardment campaigns because they hadn't thought of that "vital overlooked method of attack. . . ."[94]

And the *Los Angeles Times*, in an editorial on the whole matter of Japan and the United States, wrote on Friday morning that while war could be imminent, it appeared "that nothing decisive will be forthcoming till next week, if then."[95]

At week's end, the editorial pages of America's newspapers were filled with speculations and analysis of the preceding several days. Nearly all concluded that the country was moving closer to war with Japan. All the pieces speculated on Thailand, Indochina, the Philippines, Singapore, and other locales in the Far East. With the exception of some internal documents generated by the navy, including ones from Adm. Husband Edward Kimmel, newly installed head of the Pacific Fleet based on Pearl Harbor, no one else was speculating on whether the Japanese might strike elsewhere.

Japan's consulate in Mexico City was being hurriedly evacuated, and the staff had at first requested visas from the U.S. government to leave for Japan via Los Angeles, but they were then advised by their government that they would depart from Mexico, via the port at Manzanillo. The Japanese minister to Mexico, Yoshiaki Miura, worriedly held, "Only God knows how this crisis will be resolved."[96]

CHAPTER 6

THE SIXTH OF DECEMBER

*"Joint U.S.-Japan Commission
Is Proposed to End Deadlock"*

Atlanta Constitution

"Japanese Plea of Self-Defense Coldly Received"

Washington Post

*"Britain Takes Up Battle Posts in Far East as Crisis Grows;
Tokyo Reply Keeps Door Open"*

Christian Science Monitor

"Far East Makes Ready for War"

Fairbanks Daily News–Miner

Bob Feller, standout pitcher for the Cleveland Indians, made his major league debut in 1936 at the age of seventeen, but after a meeting with Lt. Commander Gene Tunney, now the director of the navy's physical conditioning program, he announced that he was planning on enlisting early in the U.S. military reserves. Back home at his father's farm in Van Meter, Iowa, "Rapid Robert" reasoned that because he expected to be classified 1-A in February of 1942 anyway, he might as well beat the crowd. Feller was intrigued by the idea of being a reservist while still pitching for the

Indians on his days off from the military. He paid a visit to the Air Corps at W Field in Ohio, as he was interested in flying planes, having already taken lessons and soloed.[1] Both the army and the navy had pursued Feller "concerning his plans for entertaining" their troops.[2]

British actor Captain David Niven was just as patriotic. He had it written in his contract that wherever he was making a movie, he had to be allowed to leave if he was called up to join his regiment.[3]

The USS *Arizona* was the pride of the American navy. At 31,400 tons, she was larger than many other battleships in the American fleet. She was older too, having had her keel originally laid in 1916 at the Brooklyn Navy Yard. Her early days were spent close to home, patrolling the waters off the Atlantic coast, her shakedown cruise a quick jaunt to the Caribbean. The *Arizona*'s home port was Norfolk, Virginia, until 1921, when she was transferred to Southern California, sometimes making the journey to Hawaii and back. In 1929, she went back to Virginia to be reoutfitted and modernized, which took two years. In August of 1931, she returned to the West Coast and from there was ordered to reposition to Pearl Harbor in 1940, on direct orders of the president.

The navy had seventeen battleships all told, some launched as long ago as 1912, as the *New York* and the *Texas* were. The *Arkansas* had been launched in 1911. In fact, the fleet was very old, with only the *North Carolina* and the *Washington* splashed in the previous year. Virtually all the battleships had been built during or just after the Great War. The Japanese had five less battlewagons, but they tended to be newer and of heavier tonnage. The United States' seven aircraft carriers were newer than the battleships, but the *Lexington* and the *Saratoga* were both launched in 1925. The *Enterprise* and *Yorktown* were built in 1936 and the *Wasp* in 1939. Japan also had seven carriers, but again, they tended to be bigger and lighter and thus faster than their American counterparts.[4] The United States had more heavy cruisers than Tokyo, eighteen to twelve, but overlooked was the fact that Japan only had one ocean to worry about. The United States had two—or more—to concern itself with.

On December 6, there were dozens of large and small ships along with four subs moored at Pearl Harbor: eight battleships, two heavy cruisers, six light cruisers, and twenty-nine destroyers, as well as a handful of PT boats, ocean-going tugs, minesweepers, minelayers, seaplane tenders, repair ships, and two general store ships along with one hospital ship, the *Solace*. A destroyer, the *Helm*, was underway at sea; another, the *Ward*, was patrolling the entrance to the harbor at Pearl.[5]

Three carriers had also been stationed at Pearl Harbor: the *Enterprise*, under the command of Captain George D. Murray; the *Lexington*, under the command of Captain Frederick C. Sherman; and the *Saratoga*, with Captain Archibald H. Douglas at the helm.[6]

Less than two weeks earlier, on November 28, Adm. Husband E. Kimmel sent Halsey and the *Enterprise* on an errand to deliver Marine Corps fighter planes to Wake Island.[7] On December 5, Kimmel ordered the Lexington to transport twenty-five scout bombers to Midway Island.[8] The *Saratoga* had also left Pearl Harbor for repairs at San Diego[9]

The "carriers versus battleships" debate continued unabated and unresolved within the American navy. The Japanese had pretty much decided that the airplane was the weapon of the future, while the navy was pushing ahead with plans to build eighteen carriers—by 1945.

The foreign correspondent for the *Sun* newspaper of Baltimore, Marc T. Greene, submitted a story "by mail," from Manila, which reviewed the American military situation in the Pacific, especially with regard to the airplane. "The rapid expansion of American air strength . . . in the southern and central Pacific area is giving immense satisfaction. . . . The recent acquisition of such islands as Palmyra and Johnston, in easy touch with our Hawaiian bases constitute the most recent evidence of that."[10] Readers were reassured of American air dominance in the Pacific.

The secretary of war, Henry Stimson, one of the cooler and more respected heads in Washington, nonetheless found himself in a fog, though not yet of war. He was on a military plane headed to Washington from New York, but the fog that had enveloped the city the day before was still too thick, so the flight was diverted to Richmond; upon landing he found he had no way to get back to the nation's capital. Stimson, seventy-four years of age, did what any resourceful person would do; the cabinet official on whose shoulders would fall the burden of the surely coming war stuck out his thumb and hitched a ride back to Washington.[11]

Another form of debate was the soapbox kind, taking place on the street corners of America, including Fifth Avenue in New York. There, proselytizers and preachers, orators and lecturers, along with just plain cranks, attempted to convince small crowds of the curious to either be pro-intervention, anti-intervention, and, depending on which side the soapbox, either denouncing FDR or praising him, denouncing Stalin or praising him, denouncing Charles Lindberg and the America First Committee or praising them. Law enforcement tolerated them as long as no violence broke out and nobody tried to sell anything without a license.[12]

On December 6—as with every Saturday—many newspapers ran quotes in advance from the sermons that priests, pastors, ministers, and reverends would give the following day. Nearly all dealt harshly with Adolf Hitler, war, and realistically about the human condition and the eternal struggle of free men against tyranny. Though they followed the teaching of a martyr, they did not preach martyrdom for their flocks but instead exhorted them to fight. Said the Reverend Louis St. Clair Allen of the Brooklyn Methodist Church: "The cross has not departed out of human affairs. If an enemy persists in destroying us, our only recourse is slavish submission, death or defense of liberty. I do not choose death or submission. I believe we must give ourselves for our liberties."[13]

Little had changed as far as America was concerned by Saturday, December 6. Diplomats and political observers were still kicking the embers and reading the tea leaves of the conflicting messages sent by the Japanese over the previous few days. Yet another Nipponese source accused America of trying to "pass the buck" in the Far East, whatever that meant.[14] President Roosevelt had convened his weekly meeting with the cabinet on Friday, and afterward the White House said it would have no further comment on a new 150-word official Japanese communiqué.[15]

So reporters went to Cordell Hull, who said he had nothing to say and referred them back to the White House. Official Washington, for once anyway, had nothing to say on a grave matter, including in the editorial pages of most newspapers, which had no new take on the grim matter in the Pacific. The *New York Times* did take a hard line, urging FDR to stand by the government of the pro-American Chiang Kai-shek forces in China. But even spokesmen for the Third Reich had no comment regarding matters in the Far East. The *Christian Science Monitor* said the situation was "momentarily in suspense."[16] The *Monitor*, based in Boston, occasionally ran editorials in German, as there was a heavy Germanic population in the area.[17]

Another editorial took the U.S. government to task, though, for not being frank and transparent in announcing the military buildup during the emergency. In fact, back in October, FDR had prohibited any more announcements on the production of new airplanes, but publications kept announcing them anyway. The *Monitor* concluded, "[T]hose in the opposition camp argue that a full exposé of America's skyrocketing production might have persuaded the Japanese to forgo further aggression in the Far East."[18]

The Japanese were sticking to their guns, though, saying the troops sent to Indochina were to protect Thai security and that they had the permission of the Vichy French government to move troops into Indochina because of Chinese troop movement in the region. They also introduced a new argument, their own version of a "Monroe Doctrine": the affairs of the Far East were of no concern to Washington.[19]

Tokyo conveniently overlooked—or expected America to overlook—the fact that Vichy France was a wholly owned subsidiary of Adolf Hitler, including all French possessions and military hardware, or that America's Monroe Doctrine said nothing about the United States abusing or invading her neighbors.

The British had been supplying Chinese forces along the Burma Road, and more and more analysts thought invading Thailand to then cut the strategically important venue was the real goal of the Japanese.[20]

Some of the Saturday newspapers reviewed the impasse, hashing it over. "An uneasy peace hung over the Pacific today as the United States waited for Japan to makes its choice between conciliation or further attempts at conquest in the Far East."[21] Negotiations that had started seven months earlier had made no progress whatsoever, but both sides acknowledged they were learning more about the negotiations from the newspapers than from the actual meetings and documents.

Suddenly out of Tokyo came a new proposal, courtesy of a member of the influential Privy Council. Count Kentaro Kaneko suggested a "Japanese-American Commission to iron out the Pacific deadlock." Kaneko, eighty-eight years old, was respected and a student of American culture. He suggested officials from various walks of life be appointed to the commission. The *New York Times* saw hope in the proposal, writing, "[A]n impression prevailed in diplomatic circles that something approaching a status quo may have been reached temporarily that might permit the exploratory conversations to continue with less disturbance."[22]

However, Japanese nationals were being hurriedly withdrawn from Panama, British North Borneo, Malaya, India, Ceylon, and other countries, just as they had already begun withdrawing diplomats from Mexico.[23] Also, the Japan Institute in New York announced abruptly it would close and the director and his immediate staff would depart for home while another "132 Japanese nationals . . . applied for passage back to Japan." However, approximately two thousand Japanese nationals in the greater New York area had no plans to repatriate as far as anybody knew.[24]

A government spokesman in Tokyo, Tomokazu Hori, held a press conference and said it was all just one "big misunderstanding on the part of the United States government regarding our policy in the Far East." Washington "seems to allege that we are following a policy of force and conquest in establishing a military despotism."[25]

Australia had some reason to believe that about the Japanese and hastily reconvened their War Cabinet as a result because the "Pacific crisis had reached a new and graver stage." All Christmas leaves were canceled for Aussie troops, "a million gas masks for the civilian population" were ordered, and their naval ships were being convoyed to the Pacific, though an official said all the precautions did not "'mean that war is inevitable' with Japan." But there was internal debate in Australia over the government's power to conscript men of fighting age and whether Australians should fight for England, just as there had been during the Great War. The Aussie Labor Party opposed the draft, declaring "a volunteer army is always more effective."[26] War measures were also taking place in Thailand, "the most directly menaced," as well as the Netherland East Indies.[27]

The Churchill government implemented its own emergency measures in the Far East including "recalling all fighting men to their posts" in Singapore and prepared for a "state of readiness." The British referred to Singapore as their "Gibraltar of the Orient." It was announced the sale of gasoline would be suspended in Shanghai, which had become a virtual ghost town, as commercial shipping had slowed to nothingness over the past several months. Those not of British ancestry were forbidden from leaving British Malaya, and rumors swirled that Manila would soon be evacuated of noncombatants. The Associated Press also reported, "Without explanation, Japan recalled two attachés of the Japanese government in Washington. (The German radio identified them as military attaches, Col. Tadamuri and Lt. Col. Ariuo Uehida.)"[28]

In character, the Australian government issued a blunt statement: "We are fully alive to the Japanese threat and are not afraid of it."[29] The pro-West Chinese government of Chiang Kai-shek also issued a statement, predictably leveling Tokyo, calling its response to FDR "an insult to the intelligence of the American people."[30]

Many in the West felt that the combined military forces of the "ABCD" powers, as Tokyo called them—American, British, China, Dutch—were more than a match for the Japanese should they press on with their invasion and consolidation of the Far East. In the Philippines alone there were "a dozen divisions, one American and 11 Filipino, several hundred planes, two heavy cruisers, several destroyers and 18 submarines."[31]

Douglas MacArthur was confident his forces would repel any Japanese attack on the Philippines and that he was "well-prepared . . . to meet land onslaughts from the Japanese in the event that military folly leads Japan to war with the United States. . . . The air arm of America is a long one. From the Philippines it can sweep to and over Japan with ease, and back to its insular bases."[32] But Japanese air officials brushed off MacArthur's swagger, authoritatively pointing out that the B-17 planes under his command were of the older "B and C type with a range of 2200 miles which is insufficient to Japan, from Manila, and return."[33]

Some, however, were worried instead about the power of the Japanese fleet and counseled a more aggressive posture by the American navy. The notion was floated of moving the American fleet stationed at Pearl Harbor to the Philippines to help MacArthur stave off an invasion but "this could not be brought to the Philippines without great danger, because the cruising range of the fleet is only 2500 miles, and it would be necessary to make one jump of more than that distance without refueling. . . . This would be a risky operation for it would require the use of the whole American battle fleet and would leave the West Coast open to Japanese raiders. It probably will not be tried."[34]

A new $8 billion defense bill had passed the House 309–5 and was headed for the Senate, where its passage was all but assured.[35] America Firsters or no America Firsters, no one on either side of the aisle was going to allow themselves to be accused of being unpatriotic, or miss out on federal contract goodies for their states.

The funding bill could not have come along at a better time, as a new report out by the U.S. Senate scored the army for pitiable recreational facilities at bases across the country. With the exception of Ft. Mead, all had extremely poor sporting facilities. Camp David in North Carolina had eighteen basketballs but no basketball courts. Pine Camp in New York had plenty of baseballs and bats, but no baseball fields. Camp Blanding in Florida, with a compliment of fifty thousand men, had "no basketball courts, no football fields, no handball courts, no gymnasium—but 25 chapels." A congressman called the situation "ridiculous."[36]

The navy did a far better job taking care of their personnel, especially their officers, than did the army. The navy's air base in Miami looked like a "superswank country club." It had tennis courts, bars, squash courts, a movie theatre, and swimming pools (one for officers and cadets and the other for enlistees) for the pilots to enjoy when not in training.[37] The competition between the army and the navy, and the Marine Corps and the navy, was not without basis, as the other two branches thought the navy elevated themselves to be the royalty of the American military. But navy pilots could also be dangerous and foolish. Two pilots were released from a navy prison after an investigation in which they had clearly been hot dogging in Alabama, when they flew too low over a turnip field in Alabama and decapitated a woman with the wing of their plane, according to news reports.[38]

The navy was also building dozens of temporary structures on the Mall between the Lincoln Memorial and the U.S. Capitol. Always referred to as "temporary," the Public Buildings Administration said they could be torn down faster than they were built and the plan was to do just that after the "emergency."[39]

For the first time in FDR's nine years in office unemployment was slowly tracking downward, after years of joblessness in the high teens and low 20s. The economy had perked up considerably as a result of the war effort, with the government plowing billons into defense contractors. Yet, as corporations began to finally show a profit after long years of languishing, Washington began talking up a new tax on corporate dividends, cutting into investors' profits.[40] Congressman Carl Vinson of Georgia was touting legislation that would cap corporate profits, with the excess turned over to Washington, even as Wall Street had been dwindling down since September.[41] But the guns versus butter versus success issue seemed settled to the Brain Trusters of the New Deal. Government would dispense and control all.

Regardless, a profound shift was occurring in the administration's priorities that met sharp resistance from the eternally crusading First Lady and her allies among the more liberal New Dealers, such as Vice President Henry Wallace. Funding for social programs was increasingly subordinated to ramped-up preparation for what seemed like inevitable war. The more conservative advisers and cabinet members in FDR's orbit, always ambivalent about the New Deal anyway, were starting to win the day, as the president shifted his attention from domestic concerns to the existential threat posed by geopolitical crises abroad. By 1941, the pendulum was swinging away from butter, and inexorably to guns. Ironically, the transition to rearmament also provided a Keynesian spending boost that helped ameliorate unemployment. A lasting structural change to the American economy was unfolding.

That said, doubts at the time persisted about the viability of capitalism. Even owners and operators of private business, such as C. M. Chester, chairman of General Foods and a high official in the National Association of Manufacturers, told their annual gathering that the "free market must prove itself." The redoubtable *Wall Street Journal* was crammed with stories specifying how government was regulating businesses, pressuring them, harassing them, but also contracting with them. On Friday the fifth alone, dozens of government contracts were announced, many of them with clothing companies such as the D. & D. Shirt Co. of Pennsylvania for 50,000 flannel shirts for $24,500; or 10,000 khaki shirts from the Philadelphia QM Depot for $5,345; $2,250 to the Marine Tobacco Co. for "Tobacco, cigarettes and cigars"; and $34,510 to the Gillette Safety Razor Co. of Boston for 2,285,250 safety razors.[42]

The American ambassador to Great Britain, John C. Winant, had no doubts (and no understanding) about Moscow's commitment to the free market. He ludicrously told a prominent Jewish leader, Rabbi Morris S. Lazaron, "that Russia has turned her back on Communism in respect to the work of the individual, religious liberty and the employment of the talents of man."[43]

Audaciously, the Third Reich announced that because of the "black list" of pro-German business in the Americas produced by Washington, they would ask for reparations from the U.S. government to pay for business "losses . . . after the Reich wins the war."[44] An authoritative new book, *The Structure of Nazi Economy*, authored by Maxine T. Sweezy and published by the Harvard University Press, was released to favorable reviews. "As a critical study it should be of considerable interest to students of economic affairs, who will find Miss Sweezy's discussion of Nazi policy in terms of Keynesian theory particularly rewarding," wrote a reviewer in the *Christian Science Monitor*.[45] The book took no political position but was simply an exhaustive look at the German economy under Hitler.

Up on Capitol Hill, a House committee was continuing their investigation into Nazi propaganda in America and was uncovering an astonishing amount of material as well as the fact that both Italy and Nazi Germany were sending a tremendous amount of money to America to fund anti-interventionist movements including the "Citizens No Foreign War Coalition."[46] Led by Martin Dies, a Democrat from Texas, the House Committee on Un-American Activities had discovered so many German agents operating in America and so much activity, he was actually worried about the formation of a Fascist political party in America.[47]

One of the organizations being investigated by the Dies Committee was the America First Committee itself, worried that it was a front group for the German Bund. It was estimated that "twenty-five percent of America First membership were Nazi sympathizers." The rest were simply "honest American isolationists."[48] What's more, "It is understood that the committee also has amassed a considerable amount of information about Japanese activities in the United States. This, however, has been withheld in view of the delicate situation." Dies was further investigating "365,000 persons ostensibly Communist sympathizers."[49] Dies was heavily investigating labor unions, which his fellow Democrats—including more than a few at the White House—found grating.

A suspected pro-Soviet group, Fight for Freedom, was under investigation by HCUA for its ties to Moscow. Another group, the Washington Youth Council, was also decidedly pro-interventionist. They heard from Senator Claude Pepper of Florida, who brought down the house when he shouted, "Adolf Hitler is a devil from hell! You had just as well try to make peace with the devil!" Pepper warned against Hitler gaining a "foothold in South America." Other speakers included representatives of England and China.[50]

What Dies and his committee did not know was the Japanese consulate in Honolulu was just a few blocks from the harbor, had a magnificent view of the fleet, and was a beehive of espionage, with detailed reports going daily to Tokyo, via radio, telegram, telephone, and the U.S. mail.[51] Nor did he know that the United States was hip deep in Japanese agents and sympathizers.

Because of their poor recruiting numbers, the navy announced that enlistment into the reserves would be cut from a minimum four-year obligation to a two-, three-, or four-year obligation. Joining the navy and seeing the world was not the cup of tea most young American men dreamed of. That could have something to do with German submarines, though not all Wolf Pack U-boats were skippered by courageous men either. The British Admiralty released the story of a U-boat that was forced to the surface as a result of repeated depth charges dropped. The commander jumped into the water before his sub was sunk by the British; some of the crew were lost. This particular German commander had no interest in going down with his ship.

German policy toward Jewish Germans was even more cowardly than the sub's captain. Yet another harsh edict was issued in Berlin. Jews could no longer sell their own property without "official permission" from the state. The reason given by the Nazis was that Jews were selling their possessions in a manner "that is threatening to upset existing market regulations for their respective articles."[52] "This statement . . . refers to the sale of furniture, clothing, china, rugs and similar articles by Jews who have been expecting their turn to be expelled from the Reich capital."[53]

Curiously, American Jews were not nearly unified in their approach or attitude toward Hitler, internationalism, or Roosevelt. In 1941, a considerable number of Jewish Americans were financial supporters of the America First Committee or simply pacifists that blanched at the idea of getting involved in the European conflict. A leading Jewish intellectual and member of the Roosevelt administration, Jerome Frank, published a book in 1938 titled *Save America First*. In his book, Frank spoke for many, calling for "100 percent American—Western Hemispheric—isolation as the only safe way to save America. . . . It by no means [argued] for pacifism, but it warned against the propaganda of American Anglo-philes, Communists and sentimental internationalists."[54]

Frank later admitted that he and others did not see Hitler for the evil monster he was in the early days and that, in fact, many Jews had at first supported Benito Mussolini. "We thought Hitler was a paranoiac buffoon with mad bad dreams of world conquest which could never come true and he was no menace to the United States. We deplored as needlessly provocative the speeches of Secretary [Harold] Ickes criticizing Hitler."

Franks was not alone, as he recounted other Jewish members of the administration embracing isolationism. One of the biggest proponents of the America First Committee was Lessing Rosenwald, one of the richest Jews in America. Frank wrote all this in a long and provocative article in the *Saturday Evening Post*. "Strangely enough, there is a group of wealthy Fascist Jews in America—a group not large in number and who have escaped public attention for the most part. Hitler is alright, they believe, except for his anti-Jewish 'mistake.' Even this, they half forgive because, they say, too many Jews had participated in the German democratic government established after [the] World War . . . or the German Communist movement."[55]

Frank also identified another troublesome group in America, the Christian Mobilizers, a virulently anti-Semitic group that passed out "Buy Christian" signs for window display. From the right, lecturers warned darkly about the "fifth columnists" inside the U.S. government, pro-communist forces bent on a marriage between Washington and Moscow.[56]

In his piece, Frank also covered an even far more dangerous group, the German Bund. "It will help . . . to consider the Americans who are classified as German Americans. There is, unfortunately, a small percentage of such citizens who are merely Germans in America. They are hyphenates. They part their American citizenship in the middle. Their wholehearted loyalties are not given to the United States. Some of them . . . would like to see this country dominated by the Nazis."[57]

Of the many controversial members of the Roosevelt cabinet, Interior Secretary Harold Ickes was at the top of the list. His official responsibilities were the natural resources of the country, but he expanded his portfolio to include foreign policy, trade, Jewish affairs, immigration, gas rationing, whatever caught his attention. Widely regarded as effective and brilliant and a marvelous public speaker, he was just as effective at rubbing others the wrong way. Claire Boothe Luce once caustically said of Ickes that he had "the mind of a commissar and the soul of a meat axe."[58]

Ominously, the very first American concentration camp was opened for business on Long Island. Named Camp Upton, it had extremely high fences topped with barbed wire, machine gun nests, and was built to house up to seven hundred "aliens."[59] Meanwhile, the British began rounding up aliens of every stripe, from Finns to Romanians and Hungarians, all countries with governments allied with Nazi Germany, all countries on which England had declared war. In the initial sweep, Scotland Yard arrested two hundred suspects.[60]

The East Coast was still recovering from an oil shortage that dated back to the summer of 1941, when some tankers were diverted to England to help fuel the British military effort. Fingers had been pointed at Interior Secretary Ickes, who some thought unnecessarily alarmed Americans along the Eastern Seaboard by exaggerating the situation and arbitrarily closing gas stations when he should have been calming fears.[61] There had been a brief congressional investigation, but before it really got under way, the "crisis" had passed.[62]

Making matters worse was the government's order for the gasoline companies to reduce the lead content in ethyl gasoline for the war effort. All sacrifices, it seemed, were made for the "emergency" or the "war effort." Lead had been added to gasoline for years, as it reduced engine knocking while improving engine efficiency. With the reduced lead content, drivers would have to use more gas, which was going for as much as 20 cents per gallon.[63]

The war effort permeated nearly all advertising content, as with General Motors Trucks, billed as "Partners in Power for the nation's defense."[64] And if the male reader wasn't sure about how to enlist in the war effort, the U.S. Army was running ads everywhere for recruiting purposes, claiming over 100,000 vacancies for "picked young men" and listing various recruiting offices in Boston, Baltimore, Atlanta, and other locations. Young men who signed up right away could expect as a private to make up to $105 per month, "plus uniforms, board, lodging and medical care."[65]

American G.I.s could always count on enjoying a good bowl of Campbell's Chicken Noodle Soup or any of the other twenty-one soups available in a can, including Asparagus, Consommé Madrilène, or the good old standby, Tomato.[66] Campbell's had been an American institution since a few years after the Civil War, when the company was launched.

A new cigarette was being marketed. Spud menthol Imperials, which helped relieve a sore throat, a dry throat, a hoarse voice, or a "thick taste in the morning."[67] At Landsburgh's jewelry store in Washington, "lovely monogrammed 10-piece cigarette sets" were going for $1.79. Their suggested gift for men was a cigarette box and nine ashtrays.[68] As a suggestion for Christmas gifts, Kelly Kar Co, in Los Angeles, offered five hundred used automobiles, the prices ranging from $25 to $1,500.[69] But most everybody in the West was making sacrifices.

Canada was shipping huge amounts of food stuffs to Great Britain to help feed the troops and civilian population. They were shipping so much cheese to England, Canadians were experiencing their own shortage.[70] America was sending massive amounts of food stuffs to Great Britain and Russia as well as other participants in Lend-Lease. So much so, the U.S. government was calling on American farmers to increase their output by 15 percent in 1942. "Reports from England state that cheese, dried milk, evaporated milk, dried eggs, fruit and tomato juices, poultry, meat, bacon, lard and pork products are most urgently needed." Corrugated paper boxes, "cellophane," tin foil, and other packaging materials were in short supply in America because so much had been shipped overseas.[71]

There were only fifteen shopping days left until Christmas, and Americans were making many of their purchases at the growing number of chain department stores. Sears & Roebuck had been around for years, but others that also dotted the cities and towns of America included F. W. Woolworth, Montgomery Ward, The S.S. Kresge Co., and the Ben Franklin Five and Dime.

In a story earning a minor headline in the *Washington Evening Star*, the works of a "colored artist," William Smith, went on display in the Library of Congress as announced by the librarian there, Archibald McLeish. Smith had been near homeless, living in the basement of a theater, subsisting on potatoes, when he got some help up from the Karamu House, a "negro cultural and art center."[72]

As with most Saturday evenings, Americans were either going to the movies or listening to the radio. Nationally syndicated shows included *Quiz Kids*, Bill Stern's sports show, Guy Lombardo's Orchestra, and a top favorite, *Your Hit Parade*, which featured all the top songs of the week. Also heard on many stations around the country on Saturday the sixth was the show *Hawaii Calls*, which featured native Hawaiian music broadcast live from the Moana Hotel on Waikiki Beach, hosted by local personality Webley Edwards.[73]

Late in the evening of December 5, over Italian radio and later picked up by NBC, it was broadcast that large numbers of Japanese ships were sighted north of Luzon and "south of Formosa."

Meanwhile in Honduras it was revealed by the government that Nazi provocateurs had been attempting to destabilize their government as well as other Central American countries "to fight against the United States."[74]

Hitler, though, was greatly occupied with the Russian Front, and went on radio in Berlin to announce he was throwing 1.5 million fresh troops, as well as one thousand big guns and eight thousand tanks, into the fight against Stalin. "It now appears that the Red capital now faces its hour of greatest peril."[75] The tenacity of Germany led Senator Burton Wheeler of Montana to predict that FDR would send at least a "token army" to England, "if the war lasts."[76]

The Russian winter had now registered 31 degrees below zero, even as the Third Reich was marching once again toward Moscow, though the Russians were heavily bombing German truck columns. Hitler was caught in the very pincer he wanted to avoid, with British bombers walloping Berlin every night from the West and a protracted struggle against the Russians in the East. Still, the predicament did not stop Germany from sinking five British ships—including a submarine—in the first few days of December just off the coast of England.[77]

Hitler was frankly hoping his Japanese allies would push their invasion of China harder and cross through to Russia, creating a two-front war for Stalin. Nazi Germany had already taken 600,000 Russian troops prisoners of war, and had moved them to camps inside of Germany, where they were treated poorly, at least as compared to the treatment afforded British POWs. Germany claimed they had, all told, taken 3 million Russian troops prisoner.[78]

The Germans and Russians traded charges of atrocities committed against their soldiers by the other side.[79] The *New York Times* reported of "cannibalism" among the Soviet prisoners, according to the International Red Cross.[80] The Third Reich put many of their prisoners to work in their war industry. "In the great armament plants in Saxony opened for a glimpse to the foreign press, thousands of non-Germans [labor] . . . over roaring abrasive machines . . . then trudge off to their barracks quarters, within the confines of the factory. Besides the silent Poles wearing a purple and yellow letter 'P' on their chests, sit those other former British allies, Croats of former Yugoslavia."[81]

Churchill's government had to imprison one of their own, Adm. Sir Barry Domvile and his wife, Lady Domvile, accused Nazi sympathizers. Lady Margaret Domvile was a German national and her husband had, in 1937, journeyed to the Third Reich as a hunting guest of Heinrich Himmler, head of the odious Secret Police. Though retired, the admiral had once headed the office of British Naval Intelligence. The couple were both active in "the Link," an Anglo-German group. Domvile had twice been a guest of Hitler's, including a visit to Salzburg, just one month before the war began. Admiral Domvile was incarcerated in Brixton Prison, along with his son, and Lady Domvile was held in Holloway Prison.[82]

As a new professional football league was contemplated, the NFL's regular season was scheduled to end December 7. The Washington Redskins, 1941 also-rans and patsies to the Bears in the 1940 Championship game, losing 73–0, the most lopsided game in league history, were scheduled to play a meaningless game at Griffiths Field at 1:00 p.m. against the Philadelphia Eagles.[83]

Starting at quarterback for the Eagles was Jack Banta, a college star whom the Redskins had drafted and then treated badly, and now Banta was aiming for revenge.[84] Redskins fans were in no way fanatical about their team. The town was simply too transient; the owner, George Preston Marshall, too odious; the team too spotty; but it was a pleasant way to pass a Sunday afternoon for the high and mighty of Washington, including government officials, military brass, and the like.

Also a bit undependable was the forty-seven-year-old ditzy socialite Tommy Manville of New York City, who just days after marrying twenty-two-year-old (asbestos) heiress Bonita Edwards found himself divorcing his fifth wife. For his troubles, Manville agreed to pay his wife a $200,000 settlement, not including alimony for their two-week marriage.[85] Just as their May-December marriage had been covered in all the papers, so was their May-December divorce.

Rita Hayworth, dubbed "The Love Goddess" by drooling newspaper columnists, was the top of the heap, flavor of the month, toast of the town actress and celebrity in December of 1941. Her photos and articles appeared everywhere, and readers of family newspapers learned all there was to learn, including her weight, which was 118 lbs.; her height, which was 5'6"; and her measurements, which were 35-25-35.[86]

Charles J. Pietsch of the Gideons met with the chaplain of the navy, Robert D. Workman, in Washington to present him with a Bible to give to the president. Pietsch was the Gideons' representative from Hawaii.[87]

The weather across the East Coast, which had been unseasonably warm, all of a sudden turned much chillier, especially in Washington, where administration officials also braced for the worst in the Far East. "Certain extremely well-informed American officials are ... convinced that Japan will start a fight in the near future."[88] Golfers had been on the links well into winter in the East because of the mild temperatures, but now they retreated to their favorite 19th hole.

A correspondent for the *New York Herald Tribune*, Wilfred Fleisher, who had spent several years in Japan, bluntly told a group in Washington that the United States and Japan were "at the end of negotiations."[89] Indeed, most headlines across the country said war between Great Britain and Japan was imminent in the Pacific.

But the "World Golden Rule Foundation" called for a week of "Self-Denial and Generosity" and designated the next seven days for seven occupied countries, beginning on the seventh, which had been proclaimed to be "Chinese Day."[90]

A more authoritative source, a Chinese diplomat, Dr. Wel Tao-Ming, said Japan was running a "bluff."[91] Dr. Tao-Ming said Japan's expansionist policies had reached the end of their supply lines, and while the island nation had harbored dreams of controlling access to natural resources it did not possess, they had pursued their course out of weakness and not strength. "My personal opinion . . . is that the Tojo Cabinet is a bluff. . . . In our struggle of more than four years, we have drained them, both militarily and economically, to such an extent that they have neither war materials nor man power left to launch into an adventure on a grand scale in other zones."[92]

Japan had hundreds of daily newspapers, most of which strongly reflected the policies of the government of Gen. Hideki Tojo. Of the deteriorating situation in the Far East one Japanese paper said, "Japan might be forced to abandon her peaceful endeavors." With all the arrogance he could muster, a member of the Tojo Cabinet declaimed, "We watch tensely to see whether Mr. Roosevelt or Mr. Churchill will commit on an epochal crime and further extend the world upheaval."[93]

CHAPTER 7

THE SEVENTH OF DECEMBER

"Extra! War!"

San Francisco Chronicle

"Japs Attack Manila, Far East Crisis Explodes"

Marysville Daily Forum—Extra!

"War! Oahu Bombed by Japanese Planes"

Honolulu Star-Bulletin 1st Extra

"U.S. at War! Japan Bombs Hawaii, Manila"

Washington Post Extra

"Navy Is Superior to Any Says Knox"

New York Times

S unday in America was a day for relaxing whether you followed the fourth commandment or not. It was a day for church, for family meals, for reading the newspapers, listening to the radio, going for long walks, for afternoon naps, for working in the yard and visiting with neighbors.

Sunday, December 7 was different.

Ten days earlier, on November 27, Chief of Naval Operations Adm. Harold R. Stark and Chief of Staff of the U.S. Army Gen. George C. Marshall authored a two-page memo stamped "Secret" for their commander in chief, "Subject: Far Eastern Situation."[1]

"If the current negotiations end without agreement," they wrote, "Japan may attack: the Burma Road; Thailand; Malaya; the Netherlands East Indies; the Philippines; the Russian Maritime Provinces." The memo then went on to discount why the Japanese would attack most of the cited strategic locations. "There is little probability of an immediate Japanese attack on the Maritime Provinces.... The magnitude of the effort required will militate against direct attack against Malaya and the Netherlands East Indies until the threat exercised by United States forces in Luzon is removed. Attack on the Burma Road would, however, be difficult and might fail. Occupation of Thailand gains a limited strategic advantage as a preliminary to operations against Malaya or the Netherlands East Indies, might relieve internal political pressure, and to a lesser extent, external economic pressure. The most essential thing now, from the United States viewpoint, was to gain time. Considerable Navy and Army reinforcements have been rushed to the Philippines but the desirable strength has not yet been reached. Of great and immediate concern is the safety of the Army convoy now near Guam, and the Marine Corps' convoy just leaving Shanghai. Ground forces to a total of 21,000 are due to sail from the United States by December 8, 1941, and it is important that this troop reinforcement reach the Philippines before hostilities commence."[2]

"Precipitance of military action on our part should be avoided so long as consistent with national policy. The longer the delay, the more positive becomes the assurance of retention of these Islands as a naval and air base. Japanese action to the south of Formosa will be hindered and perhaps seriously blocked as long as we hold the Philippine Islands."[3]

"After consultation with each other, United States, British, and Dutch military authorities in the Far East agreed that joint military counteraction against Japan should be undertaken only in case Japan attacks or directly threatens the territory or mandated territory of the United States...."[4]

"It is recommended that: prior to the completion of the Philippine reinforcement, military, counter-action be considered only if Japan attacks or directly threatens United States, British, or Dutch territory . . . in case of a

Japanese advance into Thailand, Japan be warned by the United States ... that advance beyond the lines indicated may lead to war; prior to such warning no joint military opposition be undertaken."[5]

Significantly, no mention was made by Stark or Marshall of any other American military installation in the Pacific region, including Hawaii.

Adm. Husband E. Kimmel, newly installed commander of the Pacific Fleet in Hawaii, had obsessed for months about a Japanese naval attack on the American fleet at Pearl Harbor located on the south side of the island of Oahu, up a narrow and well-protected channel.[6]

A navy report had been given to him detailing how the Japanese could pull off such an attack on the base. The report said the Japanese would attack on a weekend and would not declare war first. Outside of those in the "war gaming" sections of the military, no one in or outside of government had given the notion of an audacious daytime bombing on a weekend even a passing thought. There had been only one blackout drill on Oahu in May the year before to simulate response in an attack.[7]

An extraordinary Sunday meeting was requested by the Japanese embassy in Washington with Secretary of State Cordell Hull. The meeting was set for 1:00 p.m. (EST). It would be 7:30 a.m. in Honolulu. In 1941, Hawaii was in its own "half time zone." Tokyo had already reassigned some of their Washington envoys back to Japan.

Just one day before, Hull had told reporters that he anticipated no further meetings with his Japanese counterparts.[8] Privately, Hull had already told Henry Stimson, "I have washed my hands of it and now it is in the hands of you and [Frank] Knox—the Army and the Navy."[9]

Most American newspapers Sunday morning were by and large quiet when it came to the Pacific crisis. The *Honolulu Advertiser* was covering local news involving housing issues, a display by the Shriners, and the typical international war news coming from Russia, Germany, and England.[10] There was also a special feature on where children could see Santa Claus—from 11:00 a.m. to 5:00 p.m. that day—in front of a fake fireplace in the lobby of the newspaper.[11] Another front-page story reported on the newly formed

"Razor Blades for Britain Committee in Hawaii," which was taking up a collection because blades could no longer be purchased in England as all steel was being devoted to their war effort. "All razor blade donations . . . must be new," the story cautioned.[12]

Inside, stories and features favorably reviewed the movie *A Yank in the R.A.F.*; announced clipper tours between Hawaii, the West Coast, Midway, Wake Island, and the Philippines; and detailed the ongoing prostitution problems in Hawaii. On page seven was a feature, "Week's War Review." The column opened saying, "A critical week of war news was highlighted by heightening tension in the Pacific, but no new developments towards war."[13]

In the *Washington Star*, only one story was devoted to the Far East while the rest of the war and foreign news was about the Russian Front, North Africa, and the North Atlantic. The other news of the day covered sports, the weather, traffic reports, human-interest stories, metro articles, editorials, and columns. The most human of human-interest stories ran across the wires on Sunday morning about the death of a ninety-seven-year-old man, "Ray Fritman, who had spent a lifetime seeking his true identity. . . . He became lost during a parade in New York in 1852 and never saw his parents again." He got his name from an orphanage in New York, fought in the Civil War, and later taught school in Indiana.[14]

When there was news in some papers about the crisis with Japan, it was tucked between all sorts of other stories. However, buried on page three of the *New York Times* was an ominous piece dateline "Tokyo, Sunday, Dec. 7." The headline read, "Japanese Herald 'Supreme Crisis.'" The account was on the United Press wire. "Japan indicated early today that she was on the verge of abandoning efforts to achieve a settlement of Pacific issues by diplomatic negotiation [in] Washington." The story further detailed Tokyo's anger over Russia's apparent decision to throw in her lot with the "ABCD" powers of America, Britain, China, and the Dutch and oppose Japan in the Far East. But also a Japanese government official said, "[T]he time for alteration of the Thai Government's neutrality is believed at hand."[15]

The Thai government announced a state of emergency, and despite the claims of Tokyo, the Thais said they were not worried about the British. However, the British were worried about the Japanese. Civilians throughout the Far East had been told to evacuate and all British troops had been recalled, some picked up in bars and clubs in Singapore and taken back to their respective bases and ships. Twenty Japanese nationals had been taken off of a ship headed for Bangkok and detained by the British.[16]

England's military commanders planned an "all hands on deck" meeting for December 8 to game out the dire situation.[17] One fact was becoming increasingly clear: Britain was now incapable of defending its Far Eastern prizes—especially oil, the greatest prize of all. To defend its empire against the resource-hungry Japanese, the British desperately needed the assistance of its rich cousins across the Atlantic, something President Roosevelt well understood.

On Saturday evening, December 6, FDR sent a message directly to Emperor Hirohito, "an unprecedented action—as disturbing reports reached the State Department that two large and heavily escorted convoys were seen yesterday morning steaming into the Gulf of Siam, which washes the shores of Thailand."[18] The contents of the president's message to the emperor were not revealed at the time. Later it became known and was utterly respectful and solicitous of the emperor. Words such as "friendship" and "virtue" and "wisdom" littered the missive, but also words like "fear" and "concern."[19]

"Only in situations of extraordinary importance to our two countries need I address to Your Majesty messages on matters of state. I feel I should now so address you because of the deep and far-reaching emergency which appears to be in formation. Developments are occurring in the Pacific area which threaten to deprive each of our nations and all humanity of the beneficial influence of the long peace between our two countries. These developments contain tragic possibilities." Roosevelt politely raised the subject of China *and* Indo-China and expressed concern over Japan's military incursions in those two countries. "During the past few weeks it has become clear . . . that Japanese military, naval and air forces have been sent to Southern Indo-China in such large numbers as to create a reasonable doubt on the part of other nations that this continuing concentration in Indo-China is not defensive in its character." Roosevelt reviewed other matters in the area including the Philippines, the East Indies, and Malaya and the apparent Japanese designs on these countries as well. "I am sure that Your Majesty will understand that the fear of all these people is a legitimate fear in as much as it involves their peace and their national existence. I am sure that Your Majesty will understand why the people of the United States in such large numbers look askance at the establishment of military . . . bases manned and equipped so greatly as to constitute armed forces capable of measures of offense." He assured Hirohito that the United States and the other countries of the region had no warlike designs on Japan.[20]

Roosevelt closed with a plea. "I address myself to Your Majesty at this moment in the fervent hope that Your Majesty may, as I am doing, give thought in this definite emergency to ways of dispelling the dark clouds. I am confident that both of us, for the sake of the peoples not only of our own great countries but for the sake of humanity in neighboring territories, have a sacred duty to restore traditional amity and prevent further death and destruction in the world."[21] The telegram was sent at 6:00 p.m. Washington time on the sixth, but there was no evidence Hirohito ever saw it.

Even with the details of the message then unknown to the public, it was clear to most that the Roosevelt administration felt some sort of breakthrough was still possible in the Far East that might relieve the pressure cooker it had become. "The dispatch of the President's message was announced after a day in which appeared some slight hopes that the crisis with Japan would subside and that conversations could be resumed . . . on some satisfactory lines."[22]

Only once before, on December 13, 1937, had Roosevelt communicated with Hirohito. That was when the Japanese had bombed an American ship, the gunboat *Panay*, while she sailed in Chinese waters. That message was delivered orally to the Japanese ambassador in Washington and "it produced results, and the United States received satisfaction for the *Panay* attack."[23] The new Roosevelt initiative was interpreted to reflect his dissatisfaction with Tokyo's military maneuvers in the Far East and as a last ditch effort to restart the talks.

Following FDR's plea observers agreed, "The next step, it was felt, is wholly up to Japan . . ."[24]

"The message also was viewed as possibly a step of last resort to avert an open break with Japan since it was considered unlikely that Mr. Roosevelt would communicate directly with the Emperor unless virtually all hope had been abandoned of a satisfactory adjustment of Japanese-American difficulties through the usual diplomatic channels."[25]

While coverage might have otherwise been slight, every radio newspaper in America covered in detail Roosevelt's olive branch to Japan the morning of December 8, though not all reported on the "two large and heavily escorted Japanese convoys . . . steaming toward the Gulf of Siam (Thailand) this morning."[26] Another large convoy featuring six aircraft carriers heading southeast from Japan and briefly reported on six days earlier had not been seen or heard from since. Kimmel had received a notice on December 2 that this Japanese task force, moving at flank speed, around 24 knots per hour, had been lost to American trackers.[27]

The American military policy in the Far East had never been completely clear, and Roosevelt never articulated specifically that if Japan went ahead and invaded Thailand the United States would get into a shooting war with Tokyo. But everybody assumed Thailand was the line in the sand, especially since the British had made clear their intention to attack Japan if Thailand were invaded.[28]

The Japanese press meanwhile continued to pound the United States, accusing Washington of stalling and "insincerity," though without elaborating.[29] Domei, the government-owned news agency, announced that the Japanese government, from Premier General Hideki Tojo to the foreign minister to the navy minister Vice Adm. Shigetaro Shimada "'would speak the whole truth about the current international situation as well as the Japanese-American talks' in speeches Monday."[30]

The Japanese, having invaded China, incredibly called for "self-determination" for the Chinese and had used this as yet another reason to tell Washington to butt out of the affairs of the Far East.[31] They also blasted the "sensationalism" of American "press and radio," but that was nothing new. American politicians had complained of this for years.[32] The War Department had done a little saber-rattling of its own and called attention to new bases it was building in the Aleutian Islands, a potential threat to Japan.[33]

Yet another Japanese spokesman, Dr. Morinosuki Kashima, unsurprisingly blasted the United States and its "offensive attitude diplomatically, politically and strategically." News reports confirmed that "certain attaches of the Japanese Embassy in Washington had been shifted, but reasons for the move were not specified." Other unexplained actions by the Japanese were reported, including the recall of the heads of steamship offices in Bombay and Singapore.[34]

Australia was actively preparing for war and ordered "nonessential" civilians to leave the Philippines immediately and that an evacuation might be necessary.[35] The British were still furiously evacuating Singapore, sending trucks around the city to pick up soldiers and sailors.[36]

On the other side of the world, Great Britain declared war against Finland, which had become an "ally" of the Third Reich. "Each of the German satellite states had refused ultimatums that they halt hostilities against Russia, Britain's ally." Immediately, the British government arrested 150 Finns "who will be removed later to concentration camps," while "[n]ewly designated 'enemy diplomats' prepared to leave London."[37]

In concert with the British declaration of war, FDR put Finnish ships in American ports in New York, Philadelphia, Boston, and Baltimore under "protective custody."[38] Finland's president Risto Ryti received "a telegram of independence day congratulations from Adolf Hitler."[39] In the Mediterranean, another German ally, the Vichy government of France, activated its fleet there to assist the Nazis and Italians against "British piracy."[40]

The British scored some heavy air wins over Libya, due to the new American plane, the Tomahawk fighter, obtained under Lend-Lease.[41] Also under Lend-Lease—and because of the wheat surplus in America—a large shipment was headed for Russia that Moscow had purchased using American credit.[42]

But the relentless German counteroffensive on Moscow was scoring results, in spite of the claims from the Soviet-controlled state media. "Moscow appeared tonight to be in her direst peril . . . the Russian capital had become the target for 1,500,000 advancing troops, 8,000 tanks and 1,000 guns."[43] The Nazi panzer groups were a mere forty miles from the Soviet capital; the huddled residents of the besieged city could hear the Germans' heavy guns in the near distance. For the Russians, all appeared lost—until temperatures plummeted and the historical military asset that some refer to as "General Winter" emerged from his slumber. The "iron willpower" of the

German Supermen, ill-protected in lightweight uniforms, was about to face the supreme test.

The day before, navy secretary Frank Knox released a report he'd prepared for FDR that stated America's fleet was "superior to any" in the world and that it had recently been "placed on a war footing with full personnel manning the ships of three fleets," including the Pacific fleet in Hawaii. "I am proud to report that the American people may feel fully confident in their Navy." It is, he said, "without superior. On any comparable basis, the United States Navy is second to none." Knox concluded, "In the Pacific, the strategic importance . . . with development of the islands guarding the approach to the Navy's defense in the Hawaiian area with the resultant safety of the Pacific Coast, are obvious."[44]

It was good PR, but there were problems, particularly with enlistments. Because of the ongoing recruiting difficulties of the navy, it was announced that physical standards would be reduced and young men heretofore disqualified for "varicocele, hydrocele, hernia, nasal deformity, seasonal hay fever not accompanied by asthma, and undernourishment," would now be admitted. The navy had already lowered the standards for bad teeth.[45] A December 2 memo from Knox spelled out the problem. In one month, the net gain for navy personnel from October to November of 1941 had gone up by only 6,921 men, from 280,184 to 287,105. His report to FDR was signed, "Very Respectfully."[46]

Badly needed by the navy were men with radio experience, and a public plea was issued. "Men experienced either as amateurs or professionals in operation and maintenance of radio equipment are urgently needed by the navy and will be given ratings upon enlistment as radiomen, second class." The navy had an immediate opening for one thousand enlistees, as long as they were high school graduates or "actively engaged in radio repair or service work . . ."[47]

The army, too, was having difficulty meeting its announced goal of 2 million men in uniform and a "new class of 21-year-old youths will be called up for possible military service at least by July 1 of next year." The army was experiencing a "shortage of man-power . . . many local [draft] boards throughout the country are rapidly drawing to the end of their lists of potential Class 1-A registrants." Class II-A and Class II-B men might be reclassified as 1-A. In Washington, over four thousand healthy young men were classified as II-A or II-B.[48]

Captain Dickinson S. Pepper of Walter Reed Hospital berated young doctors who, while in medical school, received deferments and were then "shirking" their duty. "I cannot believe that the medical student of today appreciates the crisis that confronts our Nation," he said.[49]

The nation's women were not shirking. In full-page ads, Revlon Nail Enamel and the Beauty Salons of America featured actress Joan Crawford doing her bit for the war effort. "Morale is a woman's business. The way you look affects so many people around you. . . . To them, a woman's beauty stands for courage, serenity, a gallant heart . . . all the things that men need so desperately these days. So the time spent in your favorite beauty salon every week isn't selfish or frivolous. It's part of your job of morale."[50]

At 3:42 a.m., the Condor, on patrol outside the entrance to Pearl Harbor, spotted an unidentified and unauthorized midget submarine. Later that morning at 6:45 a.m. the Ward fired on and hit yet another mysterious midget submarine. The young captain with the perfectly nautical name of William Outerbridge ordered his number three deck gun to fire on the unknown submarine. Outerbridge reported, "We have attacked, fired upon, and dropped depth charges on sub operating in our defensive zone."[51] A report was made to naval authorities at Pearl, but no action was taken.

Scout planes from the Enterprise, some two hundred miles out and heading back to Pearl after making her delivery, spotted Japanese bombers and escort planes over the Pacific at 6:15 a.m., heading southeast. Radio confusion between a scout plane and the "Big E" prevented it from taking any action.[52] Adm. Bill Halsey and his aircraft carrier had been due back at Pearl Harbor the morning of December 7, but a storm had waylaid them, and they would now not arrive until the afternoon.

At St. Agnes Episcopal Church in Washington, sitting in a pew alone and deep in prayer was Viscount Halifax, the British ambassador to the United States. As "Father DuBois reached that part of the service where he prayed 'for guidance for all Christian rulers,' Viscount Halifax was visibly and deeply moved."[53]

In the predawn of December 7, the first wave of planes from six aircraft carriers had become airborne and headed for the island of Oahu. Their code several days before if diplomacy failed was "Climb Mt. Niitaka."

At Opana Point Radar Station, set on the highest point on the island of Oahu, two young army privates, Joseph L. Lockard and George Elliot, noticed what looked to be a huge grouping of planes headed for the island. A call was placed around 7:00 a.m. to Lt. Kermit Tyler, who was the morning duty officer, informing him of "many planes." Tyler, thinking the two were seeing a squadron of American B-17s due in that morning, told them to forget about it. They turned off the radar and went to breakfast. An earlier radar "blip" had also been ignored.[54]

A private pilot was up for a quiet and leisurely flight over Honolulu early that morning. Ray Buduick, a lawyer, expected to have the airspace all to himself and his seventeen-year-old son, Martin.[55] Shortly after takeoff, he realized that his expectations were wrong. All of a sudden, the skies over the island were filled with hundreds of airplanes. "A private plane owner reported he was given a salute of machine-gun bullets by the Japanese planes. His craft was damaged but he managed to land."[56]

A female flight instructor, Cornelia Fort, in her early 20s, was also aloft, giving a lesson, when she was overwhelmed with hundreds of planes bearing a red flaming ball.

A squadron of Japanese fighter planes, being faster than the bombers, arrived at Oahu at 7:30 and orbited the island for twenty-five minutes while they waited for the slower planes to catch up.[57]

On a beach in Santa Monica, a group of sun worshipers was out early playing volleyball when one of them heard something over the radio and tried to catch the attention of the others who were disinterested at the moment in anything other than the outcome of their morning match.[58]

The first wave of 183 planes, including dive bombers and torpedo planes on approach to Oahu, continued unmolested and basically undetected. They'd been transported in secret since November 26, at 0900, having departed their home waters of Tankan Bay. The six carriers, *Akagi, Kaga, Soryu, Hiryu, Shokaku,* and *Zuikaku* could deploy hundreds of war planes. They were under the orders of the fleet commander, Isoroku Yamamoto, and the command of Chuichi Nagumo. The massive fleet halted in mid-ocean to refuel on December 3. The standing order was radio silence and, if not recalled by Tokyo, to attack.

As they flew over the island, on their approach from the north, over the sugarcane and pineapple fields, they saw no puffs of antiaircraft black smoke in the sky, no airplanes rising to meet their challenge. Realizing they had succeeded in their audacious sneak attack on the American fleet, the code indicating their achievement was transmitted: "Tiger! Tiger! Tiger!"[59]

"Tora! Tora! Tora!"

Along the Waikiki beach, some early morning fishermen were out. "Downtown nothing stirred save an occasional bus." Then came the Japanese planes. "They whined over Waikiki, over the candy pink bulk of the Royal Hawaiian Hotel."[60]

A commercial liner just making port from San Francisco slipped into the harbor at Honolulu. Thinking themselves lucky to be witnessing naval war games, what with the planes diving overhead and all the puffs of black and white smoke, "[s]cores of delighted passengers crowding the deck remarked that it was mighty fine of the United States Navy, timing it so nicely with [their] arrival."[61]

Initial reports out of Hawaii were light. The first bulletin went out over the local airwaves, garbled, not from a military source or official government spokesman, but from a broadcast personality, Webley Edwards, who hosted the popular radio show *Hawaii Calls* on CBS, which was heard all over the mainland.[62]

"Attention. This is no exercise. The Japanese are attacking Pearl Harbor. All Army, Navy and Marine personnel are to report to duty."[63] Shortly thereafter, a government-ordered blackout was secured on Hawaii, but long-distance phone calls, telegrams, or messages from ham radio operators continued.[64] The phone lines eventually became jammed as the navy was frantically using them.

But this didn't stop anybody from hearing about the attack all across the mainland. It went out over the airwaves, repeatedly, with regular programming interrupted, on every radio station in America. News spread by word of mouth, from neighbor to neighbor, parents to kids. The words *Pearl Harbor* were questioningly and angrily on everybody's lips. In the living rooms of America, people huddled around Philco or General Electric radios, listening to war news that for the first time directly involved the American people. On the sidewalks, people huddled around car radios, listening to the flash bulletins.[65]

The headlines of the morning newspapers of December 7, 1941, contained no news about the surprise attack on Pearl Harbor as they had gone to bed hours before the attack. Plus, there was a five-and-a-half-hour difference between the East Coast and Hawaii. But by that afternoon, hurriedly rushed "Extra!" editions of newspapers were printed in large-point type by the droves, nationwide.

At the meaningless football game at Griffith Stadium in Washington between the Redskins and the Philadelphia Eagles, twenty-seven thousand attendees—including many military personnel and journalists—"were the last to know anything about the world-stirring events."[66] Throughout the game there was no announcement whatsoever through the loudspeakers, although radio broadcasters in the booths continually were breaking into their accounts of the game with war bulletins. Listening on the radio, fans heard, "Japs bombed Pearl Harbor—Japs make direct hit, killing hundreds." People in the bleachers heard none of this. The famed sports reporter Shirley Povich of the *Washington Post* recalled that a colleague had received a private message from his newspaper. "The Japanese have kicked off. War now!"[67]

In the interval after the first half, it became evident to the football fans that something extraordinary was in progress. Throughout the intermission and the second half there were constant calls over the public address system for various newspapermen, believed to be at the game, to get in touch with their offices immediately and for high-ranking army and navy officers to call their departments. "Important persons were being paged, too many important persons to make it a coincidence." In the first half, the chief of the Bureau of Ordnance with the navy was paged. So, too, was a high official with the Philippine government. Of the flock of cameramen there to cover the game, by the second half only one lone photographer stood vigil, the others sent to the Japanese embassy and others now to more interesting and important locations.[68]

As the rumor of war spread, the seats emptied. One enterprising wife sent her husband, who was attending the game, a telegram. "Deliver to Section P, Top Row, Seat 27, opposite 25-yard line, East side, Griffith Stadium: War with Japan Get to office." The Redskins ownership later said using the PA to announce the war news was against its management's policy.[69]

It was reported initially that the Japanese had struck at 7:35 Hawaiian time, 1:05 (EST).[70] According to *A Battle History of the Imperial Japanese Navy*, the time was 7:55 a.m., local time.[71] Because Hawaii had gone into a news broadcasting blackout, it is likely that there were many in the scattered Hawaiian Islands who did not know about the attack until nearly everybody in the world knew about it.

In all, some 353 Japanese fighters and bombers descended on Oahu, more than 3,500 miles from their homeland.[72] "An NBC broadcast said Japanese planes—estimated as high as 150 in the opening assault—struck at Ford Island in Pearl Harbor."[73] Initial reports said the planes appeared over the harbor out of the south coming over Diamond Head. Civilian locations were also bombed and strafed. One of the first to die in the attack may have been a ten-year-old Portuguese girl.[74]

A reporter for the International News Service, Richard Haller, filed this report:

Japanese warplanes brought sudden death and undisclosed destruction to the beautiful Hawaiian Islands in their sudden raid this morning. A flotilla of planes bearing the Rising Sun of Japan on their wingtips appeared out of the south while most of the city was sleeping. The planes dove immediately to the attack on Pearl Harbor and Hickam field, the giant air base lying nearby. . . . Three battleships were struck as they lay at anchor in the naval base. One . . . was reportedly set afire. Another . . . we hear has been sunk along with another warship. There was no confirmation of the sinkings by officers of the Fourteenth naval district. . . . I wasn't able to confirm reports that Japanese paratroopers had landed. But the report spread through Honolulu like wild fire. There were rumors that a number of prisoners were taken. From the rooftop of The Honolulu Advertiser building I saw a thick pall of smoke rising from the Pearl Harbor and Hickam field areas. Three separate fires were raging there. A staggering series of explosions came shortly after 10 o'clock when the attack was already two hours old. Army authorities later reported that a direct torpedo bomb hit had been made on the Hickam field barracks. The army said it was feared that 350 men had been killed. A few minutes later the Japanese planes, flying at an immense altitude returned over Honolulu. . . . Waikiki, the world famous resort beach, was also subjected to sudden attack as the raiders tried to silence the big guns of Fort DeRussy, guarding the entrance to Honolulu Harbor. . . . The raiders fantailed over the residential districts and dropped what appeared to be incendiary bombs over Pacific Heights and Dowsett highlands. Some fires were ignited.[75]

Associated Press reporters in New York could clearly hear over the phone the bombing in the background, as an unidentified local NBC reporter standing on the roof of a building, microphone in hand, "radioed direct from the scene." He noted that although two local broadcast stations had reported on the raid, local citizens did not heed the warning to take cover until the sound of bombs was heard.[76] Some did not go home but instead to the hills over the harbor, to get a good look at the ensuing battle.[77]

The reporter from the local NBC affiliate then said, "We have witnessed this morning the attack of Pearl Harbor and a severe bombing of Pearl Harbor by army planes, undoubtedly Japanese. The city of Honolulu has also been attacked and considerable damage done. This battle has been going on for nearly three hours. One of the bombs dropped within fifty feet of the KGU tower. . . . It is no joke; it is a real war," he said, before his connection died.[78]

A few minutes later he began broadcasting again. "We have no statement as to how much damage has been done, but it has been a very severe attack. The army and navy, it appears, now have the air and sea under control." Then his line went dead, this time for good.[79] John Daly of CBS also broadcast early reports from the scene for a time.[80]

Right in the middle of the attack, a squadron of B-17s making a refueling stop on their way to the Philippines from San Francisco arrived as Japanese war planes buzzed around them. The squadron was commanded by Major Truman Landon, who remarked, "Hell of a way to fly into a war! Unarmed and out of fuel!"[81] Radio station KGU in Hawaii had kept broadcasting all night so the B-17s could use their radio locators.

The Japanese planes did likewise.

FDR and the War Department were hampered by misinformation coming out of the Pacific. Nearly all initial reports were sketchy, incomplete, and often woefully false. One news report said that the *Oklahoma* and the *West Virginia* battleships were engaged in sea action against the Japanese.[82] Another said Japanese planes had glided in over Pearl Harbor so as to escape detection.[83]

Wild speculation was one thing; the lack of full information and detail was another. One of the first "Extra" editions out was the *Maryville Daily*

Forum based in Missouri. Over the top one-third of the broadsheet read in huge, old Western-style wanted-poster type face, "Japs Attack Manila"[84] with the subheads "Reports Stagger London"[85] and "Far East Crisis Explodes!"[86] Another said, "Little information is immediately available regarding the strength of the Japanese air attacks."[87]

An Associated Press wire story with the dateline of Honolulu carried the headline "Two Japanese Bombers Appear over Honolulu; Unverified Report Says a Foreign Warship Appears Off Pearl Harbor." The excited reporter filed his story via the transpacific telephone cable as the battle was actually taking place. The story noted that no bombs had apparently been dropped on Honolulu and that civilians were being taken off the streets by military personnel. The initial report noted there were no casualties yet known.[88]

Within minutes, the AP story made its way around the world, with reactions from Berlin, New York, and Washington. America's great and loyal ally, Russia, was quiet on the attack. The Third Reich had no comment initially, and the story out of the nation's capital announced that President Roosevelt had called for an "extraordinary meeting of the cabinet for 8:30 p.m. tonight and to have congressional leaders of both parties join the conference at 9 p.m."[89]

Another local report was filed, this one by Frank Tremaine via the United Press: "Flash—Pearl Harbor under aerial attack. Tremaine." His initial dispatch was sent via cable to UP offices in San Francisco and Manila. Subsequently, he filed additional reports as his wife, Kay, sent them along.[90]

A newlywed couple, Wallace Holman and Rosalie Shimek, had been married the day before in Baltimore and spent their honeymoon in New York City at the Roosevelt Hotel where that evening they listened to Guy Lombardo perform at the hotel. The next day they were strolling along a street in New York, startled as furious shopkeepers began throwing out anything that bore the brand "Made in Japan." No one knew where Pearl Harbor was, including the couple, and one merchant told them it was "off New Jersey."[91] But all knew America had been attacked by Japan. A little boy, Gerald Eckert, in Rochester, New York, heard about an attack on Pearl, but wondered why the Japanese were attacking the old lady down the street whose name was Pearl.[92]

Rumors mixed easily with reports. One said the Japanese fleet, having blasted the navy out of the water at Pearl Harbor, was now steaming north to the Aleutian Islands to attack military outposts there. Yet another said that American ships were in hot pursuit of the Japanese fleet now heading for its home waters.

In Washington, the formerly sleepy town quickly began to take on a war atmosphere, as pedestrians huddled around cars to listen to the radio, citizens called newspaper offices, hungry for details, and others called to inquire about the location of air-raid shelters. "The shrill voices of newsboys calling war extras broke the ordinary Sabbath evening calm."[93] In bold type, the *Washington Post*'s Extra edition boomed, "U.S. AT WAR! JAPAN BOMBS HAWAII, MANILA."[94]

As soon as Roosevelt had been notified by Secretary of the Navy Frank Knox, he summoned his press secretary, Stephen T. Early, who then called together the White House press corps to make an official announcement at 2:22 p.m., Eastern time.[95] "The Japanese have attacked Pearl Harbor from the air and all naval and military activities on the Island of Oahu, principal American base in the Hawaiian Islands," said Early, reading from a statement given to him by the president. Early responded to the first question, "So far as we know, they came without warning."[96]

Some 150 tense reporters were in attendance then, and throughout the day. The White House became the country's hub for information on unfolding events. Roosevelt remained in his private library in the second-floor residence, taking reports and meeting with staff, including his "two secretaries, Marvin McIntyre and Maj. Gen. Edwin S. Watson."[97] The president "ordered war bulletins released at the White House as rapidly as they were received. A sentence or two was added to the story of the surprise attack every few minutes for several hours."[98]

Early called press conferences all throughout the afternoon, and reporters ran back and forth from their cubbyholes to the press secretary's office, writing fresh copy or issuing radio broadcasts with each new announcement.[99] As each new development was ready to be announced, a secret Service man would stroll across the hall and remark, 'Press Conference!' setting off a stampede for Early's desk."[100] Telegraph boys rushed about.

At each press conference, Early would attempt to elaborate on the coordinated and unfolding attacks by the Japanese throughout the Pacific. In case no one missed the duplicity by the Japanese, he said,

> So far as is known, the attacks on Hawaii and Manila were made wholly without warning when both nations were at peace, and were delivered within an hour or so of the time that the Japanese ambassador and the special envoy, Kurusu, had gone to the State Department and handed to the Secretary of State Japan's reply to the Secretary's memorandum of November 26. As soon as the information of the attacks . . . was received by the War and Navy Departments it was flashed immediately to the President at the White House. Thereupon and immediately the President directed the Army and Navy to execute all previously prepared orders looking to the defense of the United States. The President is now with the Secretary of War and the Secretary of the Navy. Steps are being taken to advise the congressional leaders.[101]

At 3:18 p.m. Early's personal secretary told the reporters the attacks were apparently still under way. Halfway through the afternoon, Early appeared to retract the story that Manila had been bombed but later retracted the retraction.[102]

Unfortunately, there was no plan for the defense of the United States. The navy in the Pacific was either obliterated or scattered, and the Army Air Corps in Oahu had simply been annihilated. A second wave of 171 planes then hit Hawaii. And then another round of news came, this time confirming the worst fears: "Admiral C. Bloch, commandant in Hawaii had reported 'heavy damage' to the islands, with 'heavy loss of life.'"[103]

As the second wave continued the attack on Pearl Harbor, the governor of Hawaii John Poindexter, was on the phone with Roosevelt.[104] A bomb went off in front of the governor's mansion at Washington Place, killing a man. Another detonated close to the offices of the *Honolulu Advertiser*. A woman was killed when the Waikiki section of Honolulu was bombed.[105] Poindexter had been appointed territorial governor by FDR, but within a few months, he would be replaced by a military government in Hawaii.

Early or his secretary, Miss Ruthjane Rumelt, held press conferences at 2:22, 3:18, 3:22, 3:33, 3:57, 4:45, 6:00, 6:08, and 6:24. It was 3:33 when he announced that a Japanese sub seven hundred miles off of California had fired on a transport, crippling it. It was 3:57 when he announced the emergency meeting with the cabinet and congressional leaders. At 6:00 p.m., he announced that another over-flight of Japanese planes was preparing yet again to hit Pearl Harbor. He later had to retract it, saying that the White House and the War Department were attempting to separate fact from rumor, but because they had not been able to reach the commanders of the navy and army in Hawaii, "[t]he President is, therefore, disposed to believe, and is rather hopeful that the . . . report is erroneous." At 6:08, he reported that unidentified planes had been spotted over Guam. At 6:24, he announced Guam had been attacked.[106]

While the news buzzed, other issues needed to be addressed. One of the first people FDR met with after his phone call from Knox was Charles Fahy, solicitor general of the United States. The two met "to discuss what steps were to be taken against Japanese aliens in the United States."[107] The same question was being considered and answered in other quarters as well. According to one story datelined Norfolk, Virginia, the director of public safety there, Col. Charles B. Borland, "immediately ordered the arrest of all Japanese nationals in this strategic naval center" as soon as he'd heard of the attack.[108]

On the streets of America, strangers were talking to strangers, and some compared the atmosphere of hotel and movie lobbies, restaurants and clubs to that of London during the German blitz two years earlier. "Something of the strange psychological phenomenon . . . Folks wanted to be together. A sense of comradeship . . . was apparent."[109] Americans across the country attending Sunday movie matinees were surprised to see the film stopped, the managers walk out on stage, and news reports read to them of the bombing of Pearl Harbor.

Pedestrians lined Pennsylvania Avenue and the streets on both sides of the White House, including West Executive Avenue between the State Department and the Executive Mansion, but Secret Service agents and police officers later closed the perimeter around the area. As night fell, the crowd moved across the street to Lafayette Park. "Some stood on the running boards of the cars. Some climbed the stone abutments of the iron fences. Some stood in the middle of the thoroughfare. Some held their children on their shoulders. But all kept quiet and all looked at the lighted windows, with no eyes for anything else." A visitor from Colorado, Dorothy Quine, was in the crowd. "I can't understand it when Kurusu is here talking about peace," she said.[110]

At the Soldiers, Sailors, and Marines Service Club in Washington, a sign was posted: "All Servicemen Are Due in Camp at Reveille Tomorrow. Signed, Secretary of War." The servicemen, like everybody else, were stunned at the attacks and yet cocky too. "The men at the club last night were generally grim and confident of a quick American victory."[111]

The military ordered all personnel into uniform, immediately. Many military men had been working in "civvies" instead of their uniforms at their defense jobs for years to avoid making the town look "militaristic." That would all change.

Then an oddly worded paragraph appeared in an AP story: "There was a disposition in some quarters here to wonder whether the attacks had not been ordered by the Japanese military authorities because they feared the President's direct negotiations with the Emperor might lead to an about-face in Japanese policy and the consequent loss of face by the present ruling factions in Japan."[112] The reporter and their source(s) seemed to be trying to pin the blame for the surprise attack on President Roosevelt because he reached out to Hirohito the night before.

Vice President Henry Wallace was in New York, but he caught the first available plane back to Washington and he arrived at 6:00 p.m. that evening. Wallace went directly to the White House where he and the cabinet met alone with FDR, beginning at 6:40 p.m. Wallace then attended the second meeting that included members of Congress. He still had time to make his near daily visit to the White House physician at 5:50 and was, according to records, there for over an hour.[113]

Earlier, he'd met alone with the Solicitor General of the United States, Charley Fahey. Fahey's capacity was to act as the lead attorney for the country, and presumably FDR wanted to discuss the legalities of declaring war against another nation.[114]

As members of Congress and the cabinet arrived that night at the White House, the crowds outside cheered. The first to arrive was a now former isolationist, Senator Hiram Johnson of California, smoking a cigar, saying nothing.[115] Longtime internationalists gloated, if under their breaths. "What a sight. The great isolationist . . . All the ghosts of isolationism stalk with him, all the beliefs that the United States could stay out of war if it made no attack," penned Richard Strout, famed writer for the *Christian Science Monitor*.[116]

Roosevelt had been in meetings off and on for a reported ten hours from the time the White House had first learned of the attack. It was in these meetings that he received a report from Gen. Douglas MacArthur that Japanese planes were also over Luzon and that they had bombed several American airfields in the Philippines.[117] "Upon being advised of the attack on Pearl Harbor, Hawaii, Lieut. Gen. Douglas MacArthur . . . placed his entire command on the alert."[118] But the planes at Clark Field remained parked wingtip to wingtip, and many were easily destroyed by the Japanese.

MacArthur told reporters there would be no censorship in the Philippines, as was instituted in Hawaii, and announced he would hold press conferences every half hour. He told reporters that his commanders were already making preparations for the internment of Japanese nationals and captured Japanese soldiers. "We are calm and confident," the general said.[119]

During the Japanese attack on Manila, Don Bell broadcast live from a bunker crammed with army personnel. Calmly, Bell said, "Perhaps ladies and gentlemen, you can hear the sound of those Japanese bombers again. Apparently the raid is not over yet."[120]

In meetings with FDR were Henry Stimson, Cordell Hull, other members of the cabinet and Congress, as well as Army Chief of Staff George C. Marshall. "The president reviewed for them all information received . . . and gave them also other information not yet verified and which at the time had to be classified as rumor. The President told them of doubtless very heavy losses sustained by the Navy and also large losses sustained by the Army on the Island of Oahu."[121] At 9:15, the navy issued a press release, announcing it had no information on casualties in the Pacific.[122]

Roosevelt took a break from the afternoon meetings and began dictating his remarks to Grace Tully, his personal secretary, to deliver to Congress the next day.

In his landmark book *White House Ghosts*, Robert Schlesinger described the scene. "Shortly before 5 pm . . . Roosevelt summoned Grace Tully to his study. Reports had been coming in from a smoldering Pearl Harbor all afternoon and the president finally had a moment to reflect on the speech he would give the next day to Congress and the nation. Tully found him behind his desk. Two or three piles of notes were neatly stacked in front of him and he was lighting a cigarette. 'Sit down Grace. I'm going before Congress tomorrow. I'd like to dictate my message. It will be short.' He took a long drag from his cigarette."[123]

The president had dinner at around 7:30 that evening.[124] His son, James, dined with him. At 8:30, he met once again with high government officials "in the second-floor red-room study"[125] and gave it to them right between the eyes. "FDR told the Cabinet and congressional leaders the full scope of the disaster—battleships sunk, planes destroyed. . . . He said it would be very difficult to mount a retaliatory attack on Japan and that the way ahead was long. He said it was very unpleasant to be a war president, according to a diary account of the meeting written that evening by Agriculture Secretary Claude Wickard."[126] Wickard noted, "The Secretary of the Navy has lost his air of bravado. Secretary Stimson was very sober." FDR also indicated that while he did want to speak to Congress the next day, he was not sure he would ask for a declaration of war. At one point, Senator Tom Connally "exploded," storming, "Where were our forces—asleep?"[127] When they departed, FDR took a nap and then awoke to work again on his remarks. Then, "in the small hours, he went to bed, slept for five hours."[128] As the officials left the White House, Richard Strout said, "They won't talk. They went in grim, they came out glum."

It was announced that evening the president would speak to a joint session of Congress and the American people the next day, the eighth, at 12:30 (EST). Eleanor Roosevelt was surprised at how "serene" her husband was. "I think it was steadying to know finally that the die had been cast."[129]

One of the last persons to see Roosevelt that evening was William "Wild Bill" Donovan, who led the Office of Strategic Services. He'd become a late and trusted advisor to the president, and not part of the original "Brain Trust" around Roosevelt. Donovan was respected, in part, for having won the Congressional Medal of Honor in the Great War.[130] Roosevelt also saw Edward R. Murrow late that evening, shortly after midnight before he retired for the evening at 12:30 a.m.[131]

The lights of the Navy Department glared all night, burning the midnight oil, and one officer said the reports on the commercial airwaves were "surprisingly close" to the official reports. Like other military men, naval officers had not worked in uniform for a long time, preferring to blend into the culture of Washington by dressing like ordinary civilians. Now, one quipped of uniforms coming out of storage, "There'll be the worst smell of mothballs around here tomorrow."[132]

Cots were brought into the Munitions Building, where the army was also working all night, including Secretary of War Stimson. They, too, were deluged with phone calls asking about loved ones in Hawaii and around the Pacific. The army, like everyone else in the government, had no answers to give them. The Munitions Building was surrounded by machine guns.

The crowd in Lafayette Park remained late into the night of December 7 and began singing "God Bless America."[133] Wickard memorialized how calm FDR was and how impressed he was of the president. "As I drive home, I could not refrain from wondering at the fates that caused me to be present at one of the most important conferences in the history of this nation."[134]

Japanese prime minister Hideki Tojo went on state radio and told the Japanese people, "I hereby promise you that Japan will win final victory" and reminded them that in 2,600 years, they had never lost a war.[135] On the other hand, they had never actually declared war on an enemy before engaging in an attack on them either.

The Japanese propaganda agency, Domei, announced at 6:00 a.m., Tokyo time, that "naval operations are progressing off Hawaii, with at least one Japanese aircraft carrier in action against Pearl Harbor."[136]

Tojo met with the Japanese cabinet one hour later, and after that short meeting, U.S. ambassador Joseph Grew and British ambassador Sir Robert Leslie Craigie were "summoned" to an audience with the foreign minister, Shigenori, to give them Japan's formal reply to Cordell Hull's missive of November 26. The reply rejected Hull's four points for peace in the Pacific.[137]

Over at the Japanese embassy at 2514 Massachusetts Avenue NW in Washington, reporters and curious onlookers watched the bonfire on the back lawn, as diplomats and officials burned thousands of documents. "Members of the Embassy staff . . . burned their code books in an outside fire behind the Embassy. . . . Newspaper men watched while the Japanese secrets were fed into the crackling flames."[138]

A crowd of about a thousand watched from the sidewalk, occasionally booing or taunting Japanese officials as they entered the compound, but no violence took place as some in the White House feared. Several young men yelled, "That's democracy for you! They kill us and we protect them." Another screamed, "We ought to kill them instead of guarding them."[139]

Several deliverymen knocked on the door in vain. Finally, a note was posted on the door to the embassy, though it was in Japanese. It said, "If you have business here, please use the side entrance."[140] But no one was allowed to leave, including the Irish maid, who wept to police that she had six children and a husband at home to feed. "With a noticeable brogue," she implored the Secret Service agents to let her go, but to no avail.[141]

"Police were assigned to guard the Japanese, German and Italian Embassies," but the Japanese had already taken precautions and hired "30 private detectives for the same job."[142] The State Department was already making plans for the safe passage of Japanese embassy officials to Tokyo, but it was not clear yet if the Japanese government was making the same provisions for their American counterparts.

Nomura and Kurusu glumly watched the blaze from inside the legation. All reports said they were truly shocked over the attack on Pearl Harbor. "If several sources of information can be believed, they knew nothing of what their army and navy were preparing while they were conducting diplomatic negotiations."[143]

Embassy Row was a hubbub of activity with all the tourists, cars, reporters, police, Secret Service, and a few actual residents of the palatial buildings that lined the northwest end of Massachusetts Avenue. Lord Halifax was working in his library at the British embassy when he learned of the attack. He immediately called Churchill by radio-telephone, and this was how the British learned of the attack on them by the Japanese.[144] The British prime minister had already given a stirring speech to the Parliament. Prior, he and

FDR spoke by transatlantic phone. "They discussed a synchronized declaration of war on Japan."[145]

The FBI straightaway arrested a Japanese national, the first of many, Kiyoshi K. Kawakami, at his home on 3729 Morrison Street NW. "Officials later declined to reveal what had become of him." The provost marshal general of the West Coast, Alaska, the Canal Zone, and Hawaii, Allen Gullion, ordered "a general roundup of all 'previously known suspicious aliens.'"[146] But this was only the start.

In Baltimore, a group of boys hung "an effigy of a Japanese bearing the sign, 'This Jap Tried to Invade the U.S.'"[147] Sometime during Sunday, a Clipper plane coming in from San Francisco with twenty-eight passengers and eleven crew members landed safely "at an unnamed airport in the Hawaiian Islands." Still unknown was the status of a Japanese ocean liner in the middle of the Pacific with many Americans on board.[148]

No one expected war like this. On December 7, Gen. H. H. "Hap" Arnold, chief of the Air Corps, was quail hunting in California, accompanied by Donald Douglas, president of Douglas Aircraft. The pair was so remote that a local sheriff had planes drop notes on the two men, alerting them to the new war.[149]

If Arnold was caught unawares, so was the beautiful city of Honolulu. "Honolulu isn't built for war," wrote Elizabeth Henney in the *Washington Post*. "White, gleaming, tropical buildings in the heart of the city (perfect targets) give an impression that joy and beauty are important, even more so than business." Sure, the harbor was right there, but the locals also celebrated "Boat Day," and when employers were informed that someone was coming in via a liner or a Clipper plane, Henney said, "One is given time off to meet them and welcome them with fresh flowers leis. Friendship is that important. There are no ragged beggars on the streets of Honolulu, but there are flower venders, selling leis, gardenia ones with two dozen or more blossoms for a quarter. And now, when the great black drops hurtle from the sky, ripping the gay red and blue tiles from the buildings, stilling songs and laughter, blasting soft bodies to shreds, what is the answer to Honolulu's question: 'Why this to us?' We have welcomed the Japanese race with the others that came. Our creed has been that of friendship."[150]

The Japanese attacked the Philippines. They attacked Wake Island. They attacked Thailand. They attacked Hong Kong. They attacked Malaya and British troops in Singapore. They attacked U.S. Marines stationed in China. They attacked Guam. They attacked Midway Island. They attacked Shanghai. They attacked Pearl Harbor.

"The purpose of the Japanese in striking at Pearl Harbor is obvious. The vast area of the naval base, 1,735 acres, with 250 buildings and 15,000 linear feet of berthing space, is a natural target, as it is the most complete naval base owned by this country, the center of Pacific Fleet operations, and possesses many vulnerable features which are well and easily recognized."[151] It was all so obvious as the day closed. But no one saw it coming the day before.

A White House memo had been quickly prepared for FDR telling him what he already knew about the attack, but this memo had some with inaccuracies. "At least two aircraft were known to have a swastika sign on them."[152] On balance, though, the memorandum was pretty accurate. Another fascinating memo was a transcription of a conversation at 6:40 p.m. between the president and Henry Morganthau. Morganthau routinely had all his phone conversations transcribed, and though FDR had prohibited him from doing so with their phone calls, he did record on this day, memorialized for history. The secretary of the treasury informed Roosevelt that he'd frozen all Japanese funds, had secured the border, and had doubled the guard at the White House while closing off adjoining streets. "We are not going to let any Japanese leave the country or to carry out any communications," Morganthau said and FDR only said, "I see" to that.[153] FDR got a bit heated about making the White House look like an armed camp.

As Admiral Kimmel watched from a window in his office which overlooked the harbor, the horrific butchery of the men and ships of the navy, a round of ammunition came crashing through the window and exhausted itself after tearing a hole in his white dress uniform.

Kimmel muttered, "It would have been merciful had it killed me."[154]

CHAPTER 8

THE EIGHTH OF DECEMBER

"U.S. Declares War on Japan"

Birmingham News

"Japan Wars on U.S. and Britain;
Makes Sudden Attack on Hawaii;
Heavy Fighting at Sea Reported"

New York Times

"Japanese Aliens' Roundup Starts"

Los Angeles Times

On the morning of December 7, isolationist America was at peace, desperately trying to stay out of the conflict. By the morning of December 8, internationalist America was at war and became forever an altered country.

From coast to coast and beyond, army and navy forces went on a "wartime footing."[1] That was just the beginning. "Censorship was established on all messages leaving the United States by cable and radio."[2] Christmas leaves were canceled for the military. Borders closed. Roadblocks erected. Armed guards posted everywhere. Blackouts ordered. Japanese nationals rounded up. All radio communication from and to Hawaii was suspended indefinitely.

The Coast Guard stepped up guarding, well, the coast. And governors were "asked" to call up the Home Guard.

America was about to formally enter its Second World War, and yet as of the 8th, no one was actually referring to the new conflagration as such. "Tonight the war becomes a World War in grim earnest," opined the *Los Angeles Times*.[3] The *Sun* of Baltimore got closer, writing, "Japan's declaration . . . puts the United States into this second and most terrible war of the nations."[4]

In the moments after the Japanese attack on Pearl Harbor, some Americans, mindful of the Orson Welles nationally broadcasted ruse of 1938, when he turned H. G. Wells's book *War of the Worlds* into a seemingly real-life invasion by Martians, thought this was another hoax. "That was the reaction of civilians and military men alike as the news of Japan's attack . . . became public. It was a study in human refusal to believe harsh truth."[5]

On the front page of the *Los Angeles Times* on the morning of December 8 was a box notice from Brigadier Gen. William O. Ryan, commander of the Fourth Interceptor Command. "Air Guards Attention! To chief observers: All observation posts: A.W.S. (Aircraft Warning System). You are directed to activate your observation posts immediately and to see that the post is fully manned at all times."[6] The West Coast of the United States was over 2,500 miles from Hawaii and thousands more from Japan, but with so little hard information coming out of the Pacific, the military wasn't leaving anything to chance. On the morning of December 7, the American military was asleep, rhetorically and behaviorally. Twenty-four hours later, everybody was at or headed for their battle stations.

Initial news reports of the massive and unprovoked attacks by the Japanese throughout the Pacific were all over the place, and many news stories, short on accuracy or facts, were full of speculation, half-truths, and outright guesses. Others only scratched the surface. An observer said publicly it was nuts to have lined up airplanes wingtip to wingtip. But then criticism of the U.S. Army stopped.[7]

One thing *was* for sure, though: the Japanese had been planning and practicing precision bombing for months, the evidence being the carnage they'd inflicted all over the Pacific and especially Pearl Harbor. They knew their targets cold. In those few Japanese planes shot down in Hawaii was detailed information on the location of the various ships, armaments, crew complements, and other important specifics.[8] "The Japanese radio reported that Nipponese warships had surrounded Guam and said all big buildings on the island were ablaze."[9] It also claimed the Pan Am Airways base on the island had been destroyed, its gasoline stores aflame.[10]

"Japanese bombers, following up earlier successes in the two-day Battle of the Pacific, raided Manila in the darkness of night, dispatches from the Philippine Capital disclosed this afternoon. The heavy attack opened shortly after midnight Tuesday, Manila time (11:00 a.m., Washington time). Dispatches telling of the raid followed acknowledgment earlier in the day at the White House that the Japanese raid on Pearl Harbor yesterday had resulted in the sinking of 'one old battleship' and serious damage to other war craft. There were casualties of 3,000 on the Island of Oahu, the White House said, and nearly half are dead."[11]

This story in the December 8 afternoon edition of the *Evening Star* in Washington did not even touch on the real story of the bloodbath wreaked by the empire of Japan; at Pearl Harbor, Hickam Field, Ford Island, various other locations on the island of Oahu, and a half-dozen additional strategic locations in the Pacific. Hickam had cost $22 million to build.[12] Although the report did near accuracy in saying, "Blood was spilled heavily in a war which Tokyo did not declare until three hours after Japanese raiders struck soon after dawn yesterday."[13] General Tojo went on the radio and blamed the Americans for provoking the Japanese into attacking the Americans. Audaciously, he said, "Japan has done her utmost to prevent this war."[14]

Fully twenty-four hours after the attack, White House press aide Stephen Early understatedly told reporters, "The damage caused to our forces in Oahu in yesterday's attack appears more serious than at first believed."[15] Early was the first White House official called by FDR,[16] after the president had been told by Secretary of the Navy Frank Knox of the attack at 1:40 p.m.[17] Eleanor Roosevelt had been hosting a private luncheon, and FDR was in his Oval Study having lunch with friend and confident, Harry Hopkins,[18] who was living for a time in the private residence of the White House along with his motherless daughter.[19] Hopkins doubted the initial report. FDR did not.[20] The appalling message via radio to Knox from Rear Adm. Patrick Bellinger was "Air Raid Pearl Harbor. This is no drill."[21]

Along about the same time, Ed Chlapowski, only in the navy a year, stationed at Pearl, also sent a message. "This is no drill. Pearl Harbor is being attacked by the Japanese. This is no drill."[22]

Congress had passed a law in 1798 that was later amended and called the Espionage Act of 1918. "All information relative to strength, location, designation, composition and movement of United States troops or Army transports outside the continental limits of the United States are designated by the War Department as secret and will be so considered under the law."[23] The U.S. government announced that violations of the Espionage Act carried the death penalty.[24]

The War Department issued an order to all three military branches to institute strict censorship in the Canal Zone and Hawaii, as well as the Southern Pacific coastal region covering Southern California.[25] Additionally, all outgoing mail and other communication by men in uniform would be heavily checked so as to not reveal any sensitive information to people outside the military. The American media were asked "to cooperate in observing the restrictions against publication of secret information."[26]

Roads were cleared in California by the State Police to allow antiaircraft guns to get to their destinations. On the West Coast, "special patrols [were] set up in Japanese sections." The military police were ordered to "arrest all persons 'previously designated' as suspicious characters."[27] The president's personal bodyguard, Tom Qualters, tracked down and found the Japanese correspondents for Domei and took away their White House Correspondents Association press passes.[28]

Another order was issued from the government ordering all companies engaged in manufacturing munitions to go on a twenty-four hour production schedule.[29] Round-the-clock armed military guards were posted all over government and war manufacturing facilities. In Washington, police leaves and vacations were canceled.[30]

America was at war with Japan, although a formal declaration had not yet been offered to Congress by the president of the United States, who was scheduled to address the members at precisely 12:30 eastern standard time at their invitation.[31] The president had not formally told Congress he would ask for such, but few doubted he would and some speculated that a declaration should also be made against Italy and the Third Reich.

Roosevelt awoke at first light, "examined latest war dispatches, conferred with military and naval leaders, completed his draft of the message to Congress . . . conferred with Mayor La Guardia on civilian defense on the Pacific Coast."[32] FDR, as a political payoff had appointed Fiorello La Guardia as head of Washington's Office of Civilian Defense.[33]

Winston Churchill beat FDR to the punch; the British government declared war on Japan several hours before America did, as they, too, had been underhandedly attacked. Churchill and Roosevelt had spoken by transatlantic phone Sunday night. The next morning the prime minister went before Parliament, war was declared, and by 7:00 a.m. Washington time, "a note was handed to the Japanese Charge d' Affaires . . . [in London] 'stating that in view of Japan's wanton acts of unprovoked aggression the British government informed . . . that a state of war existed between the two countries.'"[34] The prime minister had pledged to declare war on Japan "within the hour" if the empire attacked the United States, and he was off by only a few.[35]

Costa Rica and the Netherlands Indies also declared war on Japan before the United States. In Costa Rica, the government began arresting Japanese workers laboring in cotton and rice fields and "seized on suspicion of espionage" a Japanese fishing boat.[36] China also declared war on Japan but threw in Italy and Germany for good measure.[37] Australia also declared war on Japan before the United States did.[38] Nicaragua's president general Anastasio Somoza announced his country would also declare hostilities on Japan.[39] Canada threw in with America's lot.[40] Local Number 1,442 of the United Brotherhood of Carpenters, located in Chattanooga, Tennessee, issued a statement that they, too, were declaring war on Japan.[41] The secretary of the union, Roy E. Hayes, said, "With the power vested in my office . . . a state of war does exist between this union, 1,442, and the present Japanese government."[42]

Because of the news blackout clamped on Hawaii, the extent of the devastation was still not generally known, nor did anyone know where the Japanese might strike next; this only added to the surreal sense and abject fear. Nothing was getting out of the Pacific by the afternoon of December 7. Some in America were openly speculating that the Japanese might capture one or more of the Hawaiian Islands, including Hilo, which according to sources had no defenses whatsoever.

Twenty-four hours earlier, no one thought it possible that a massive Japanese convoy featuring six of their first line aircraft carriers could cross an ocean—stopping to be refueled along the way—traveling thousands of miles, undetected, to Hawaii. Now everybody was contemplating the prospect that Japan could and would strike the West Coast of the United States. The distance from Tokyo to Honolulu was 3,860 miles, but from Hawaii to San Francisco, it was only 2,397 miles.

Unsubstantiated stories and rumors were rampant, including that the Japanese had attempted to also invade British Borneo,[43] that the battleship *West Virginia* had been sunk, that the *Oklahoma* was ablaze and subsequently sunk, that a civilian ship, the *President Harrison*, had been seized by the Japanese while in Chinese waters, that a U.S. transport, the *General Hugh Scott*, had been sunk, and that another transport carrying lumber was sunk just a little over a thousand miles off of San Francisco.[44] A different report said the Japanese were parachuting into Hawaii and that saboteurs were running amuck there.[45]

Roosevelt received yet another memo from the ubiquitous John Franklin Carter clearly generated several days before the attack going into great detail about the racial composition on Hawaii, the number of Japanese, and where their loyalties lay. "There will be, undoubtedly, planted Japanese and agents who are there for the purpose of sabotage. The danger of espionage is considerable. This is especially the case as many Navy wives are over-garrulous with regard to their husbands' departures and where they are going." A reference was made speculating about "the Japanese fleet appear[ing] off the Hawaiian Islands."[46]

The *Washington Post* reported that the attacking planes had been "land-and-sea-based" and that the planes had taken off from the Marshall and Caroline Islands, which had been turned over to the Japanese by the Germans at the conclusion of the last war.[47] The Associated Press also reported that four engine bombers had been used in the attack, but this was no idle mistake.[48] If the Japanese already had long-range bombing capabilities, they could—at least theoretically—reach the West Coast of the United States. The *Post*, going for the same three cents as every other paper in the country cost, had a banner at the top of the fold that said, "Keep It Flying! The *Post's* suggestion: Let the Stars and Stripes fly from every building in Washington today, the symbol of America united!"[49]

Additional stories reported that the U.S. military had downed "many Jap planes" in the battle over Hawaii.[50] Others said the Japanese had parachuted into Manila and they'd used mustard gas in their invasion of Malaya.[51] Hundreds of rumors went out over the airwaves, including one that said Germany had participated in the attack on Hawaii.[52] Another said on NBC radio out of Manila that "Germany soon will follow Japan in a declaration of war on the United States."[53]

The Japanese also claimed they sunk an American carrier off the mouth of Pearl Harbor with one of their submarines and that they had captured dozens of commercial vessels. Some disinformation was coming directly from the White House, as Press Secretary Stephen Early reported that American forces had destroyed "a number of Japanese planes and submarines."[54] Another rumor was the U.S. government would hold the Japanese diplomats Kichisaburo Nomura and Saburo Kurusu in effect hostage until the government was assured that Ambassador Joseph Grew and his staff were safely out of Japan.[55]

An AP story erroneously reported, "At sea the United States Fleet apparently had engaged the enemy. Destroyers steamed full speed from Pearl Harbor, and spectators reported seeing shell splashes in the ocean. Unconfirmed reports said the attacking planes came from two enemy aircraft carriers and probably these and other enemy ships were being fought by the American ships."[56] Yet another story said that as of December 8, "American operations against the Japanese attacking force in the neighborhood of the Hawaiian Islands are still continuing."[57] Also, errant wire stories claimed that British and American forces had sunk many Japanese ships,[58] and the *New York Times* erroneously reported that "four engine dive bombers" had been used at Pearl Harbor.[59] The paper furthermore mistakenly said that "four submarines were destroyed" by the U.S. Navy.[60]

The *Sun* reported "an oil tank there was seen blazing and smoking. An unconfirmed report said one ship in the harbor was on its side and four others burning. . . . In Washington, some hours later, the War Department gave the White House a preliminary estimate that 104 were dead and more than 300 wounded."[61]

Unconfirmed reports from Panama and London said a Japanese aircraft carrier operating off Hawaii had been "sunk by United States Navy ships." The word "unconfirmed" filled hundreds of out-of-breath news stories. However, one story on the AP wire, dateline Honolulu, was accurate. "Japanese bombers, striking lightning-like aerial blows from off the Pacific, brought death and destruction . . . to this mid-Pacific island fortress and vacation paradise. Scores of men in United States uniform, as well as civilians, died under the savage blows which shattered the Sabbath morning peace and spread the European war to the vast expanse of the Pacific Ocean."[62]

Thousands of concerned citizens gathered in front of the White House on December 7 and 8, quietly peering through the wrought iron fence. Pennsylvania Avenue was jammed with cars until the police closed it. The sidewalk in front of the White House was also closed, so the curious gathered along West Executive Avenue. Thousands more were on Capitol Hill as the members, the Supreme Court justices, the guests, and the president of the United States made their way there. There was a real fear of a Japanese terrorist attack in Washington. "Her undercover agents, a suicide squad, might . . . arrange a surprise here."[63]

Berlin and Rome were surprisingly cautious in their public statements, not immediately rallying to the cause of their Axis ally, Japan. But a radio report in Rome monitored by CBS said that the two Axis powers were indeed at war with the Allies because of the actions of the Japanese.[64] But who knew? Disinformation was more plentiful than information, and the Japanese were filling the airwaves with claims both true and false. "Japanese headquarters said the United States aircraft carrier sunk was the victim of a submarine off Honolulu and that many merchant ships had been captured in the Pacific."[65]

There still had been no mention of the exact extent of the damage in Hawaii, and as far as anyone in the United States was concerned, the *Arizona* had come through unharmed.

In Tokyo, some forty-five American diplomats, led by the estimable Joseph Grew, were stranded in the middle of a war in the middle of a hostile power.[66] Grew had been ambassador to Japan since 1932, with a long career serving both Republican and Democratic presidents, including Wilson and Coolidge.

The Japanese had maintained fifteen consulates in America and the territories, including San Francisco, New York, Mobile, Seattle, Philadelphia, New Orleans, Galveston, Portland, and Pearl Harbor. All these localities had significant naval bases or manufacturing facilities, not so coincidentally. At some, including the one in New Orleans, crowds gathered to boo and hiss the Japanese until local police dispersed them.[67]

On the West Side of New York City, a Japanese national was severely beaten by some street toughs, screaming, "Why don't you go where you belong?" The Japanese man checked himself into a hotel with a fractured skull.[68] Stones were hurled through the plate glass window of the Taijo Trading Company at 121 Fifth Avenue.[69]

The Japanese had attacked with lightning speed and precision although their attempts so far to take Singapore were faring poorly; the British "cut to pieces" the invading Japanese troops while they waded through the surf.[70] Eventually, they took the strategically important area and, having planned ahead, dropped leaflets "announcing the seizure of the settlement but urged people to go about their business and remain calm."[71]

Another report said that American planes in Manila took to wing in search of Japanese targets.[72] Manila was no stranger to war. It was here in the harbor, in 1898, where Commodore George Dewey engaged the Spanish in the kickoff battle to the Spanish-American War. Since that war's conclusion, America had had a military presence there. Germany had not taken part in the Pacific attack, as some stories had it, but the Third Reich was taunting America via the airwaves.

FDR had his eye on the ball, though, as his White House claimed that

Germany "pushed" the Japanese into the attacks in the Pacific.[73] Indeed, Japan radio issued a broadcast claiming Germany would join the war within twenty-four hours.[74] In fact, Berlin had wanted the Japanese to prosecute the war in China further, march across Asia, and eventually catch Moscow between the Axis forces. But Roosevelt knew that to win the new world war, America would have to engage the Germans and Italians eventually. Still, in his speech to Congress, he refrained from mentioning the other Axis powers. He only discussed Japan, even as Germany and Italian officials offered cooing words of support for Tokyo and called FDR a "shylock."[75] The spokesman for the Third Reich backed away from an actual military commitment to Japan, though.[76]

Because of the European war and Hitler's unrestricted warfare in the North Atlantic, FDR had already declared "an unlimited state of national emergency" on May 27, 1941.[77] Three weeks later, on June 16, the U.S. government ordered the eventual closing of all German consulates on U.S. soil.[78]

Time stopped in America at 12:30 eastern standard time on December 8 as everyone tuned in to listen to the president of the United States address a joint session of Congress with an elegantly simple five-hundred-word avowal.[79]

Street commerce stopped; traffic stopped. Many schools had already closed, some fearing Japanese attacks: the public schools in Oakland, California, shut down responding to a report that a Japanese carrier lay off of San Francisco. The district attorney said he had closed the schools based on the recommendation of the Office of Civilian Defense in Washington.[80] Newspapers were already printing helpful stories on the various time zones of the east coast, the west coast, Hawaii and Tokyo, along with an explanation of the International Dateline. When it was noon in Washington, Japan was fourteen hours ahead, but Honolulu was nineteen and a half hours behind Tokyo. And Honolulu was five and half hours behind Washington. All papers had the standard "Man on the Street" reactions to the attack, but women were interviewed as well. That day the Honolulu Star-Bulletin printed three "Extra!" editions, all told 250,000 newspapers. With the radios often shut off, residents were desperate for news.[81]

First thing Monday morning, Wall Street plunged except for commodities such as beef, wool, and steel, which climbed dramatically.[82] Then the traders stopped to listen to their president.[83] Congress opened at 12:00 noon with a prayer, offered by the Senate chaplain, the Reverend ZeBarney T. Phillips, asking for national unison.[84]

A now former isolationist, GOP congressman Joseph Martin said of the new unity, "There is no politics here. There is only one party when it comes to the integrity and honor of this country."[85] FDR's remarks would be broadcast live on NBC, CBS, and Mutual Radio.[86]

"Promptly at noon the big glass doors at the White House swung open, six limousines drew up, and President Roosevelt came out."[87] He was walking, using the painful leg braces, but did not speak. "The car, bearing the White House insignia, started at once for the Capitol." In the other cars were "Mrs. Roosevelt, Mrs. Dorothy Brady, Mrs. Stephen Early, Grace Tully . . . General Edward M. Watson and Captain John Beardahl, the President's military and naval aides."[88]

FDR was attired in the familiar dark blue cape.

Silent crowds encircled the White House, watching the procession, with little doubt as to what their president was going to ask of their Congress. Telegrams of support and shock had already flooded the White House. "The messages came from Governors, Mayors, religious leaders, heads of civic movements, newspaper editors and radio broadcasters, many offering their personal services."[89]

A resolution offered at noon for a joint session of Congress was quickly approved.[90] The galleries were packed, and crowds outside were kept two blocks away from the Capitol. Even with a pass, police checked those favored every few feet. The Diplomatic Corps began to file in, except the Chinese ambassador, Hu Shih, who was detained briefly by a guard, until a senator interceded.[91] Seated together were Gen. George C. Marshall, Adm. Harold Stark, and Maj. Gen. Thomas Holcomb, commandant of the Marine Corps.

The president departed the White House at 12:10,[92] still tinkering with his remarks on the way to the House chamber where he spoke to a solemn, angry but resolute audience at 12:32. In his car, he "sat back in the deep cushions . . . adjusted his big dark Navy cape."[93]

The running boards on Roosevelt's car were draped with Secret Service agents, three on each side, and four were inside the car. "The men in the" limousine "held sawed-off riot guns. Those outside carried .38-caliber service revolvers."[94]

Soldiers guarded each doorway in the Capitol and credentials were demanded while FDR waited in the Speaker's office. The Senate marched into the House Chamber. Then the Supreme Court came. A committee, chosen by the Speaker, then escorted the president to the rostrum. They were John McCormack, the House Majority Leader; Joseph W. Martin, House Minority leader; Robert Doughton, Chairman of the House Ways and Means Committee; Alben Barkley, Senate Majority Leader; Charles McNary, Senate Minority Leader; and Senator Carter Glass of Virginia. The same man, Garrett Whiteside, a House clerk in 1917 and now a Senate clerk in 1941, who had delivered the 1917 document to President Wilson, this time typed the address for President Roosevelt.[95]

"When all are seated, the speaker announces the President of the United States. Cheers, applause, more cheers, and Franklin D. Roosevelt, with a tired and worn face, is ascending the ramp which is always provided for him. When the president took the stand, every man, woman and child, every Republican, isolationist (on Saturday), Roosevelt-haters and Democrats stood as united Americans and cheered for their president." Some in attendance discovered to their embarrassment they were crying, until they saw others around them crying as well.[96]

FDR was accompanied by his eldest son, James, to the rostrum. James, a captain in the Marine Corps, was in his blue dress uniform. "The President stood erect, his head held high. He spoke in clear, measured words to a chamber in which there was not even the sound of a deep drawn breath or the rustle of a woman's skirt."[97] He "gripped the reading clerk's stand, flipped open his black, loose-leaf schoolboy's notebook."[98]

The floor was crammed with senators and congressmen and other dignitaries as they had rushed back to Washington beginning the afternoon before, as soon as they heard about the attacks. Reporters caught up with Senator Harry Truman in St. Louis, just as he was about to board a flight for Washington the day before. "It's for the welfare of the country that we must declare war and put Japan in its place," he said. Wendell Willkie, the 1940 GOP nominee, who had attacked FDR, accusing him of wanting to send American boys into the European war, now said, "I have not the slightest doubt as to what a united America should and will do."[99]

The galleries, which could only hold five hundred people, were filled to capacity, but not with the general public, as the Capitol had been closed off to private citizens;[100] they were gathered outside on the lawn of the Capitol. Instead, only VIPs and those receiving permission and a special pass could be there to see history unfold.

The Rotunda had been closed and barriers and cable ran everywhere on Capitol Hill, cordoning off the tourists and merely curious. The crowd on Capitol Hill was larger than eleven months earlier when FDR had been inaugurated for a third time, and many had been waiting since early in the morning to see him arrive. As many as five hundred District cops and the Secret Service were crawling everywhere.[101] Seated next to Eleanor Roosevelt in the gallery, who was in a black dress that gathered at the neck and wearing her favorite silver fox furs, was Edith Wilson, the widow of Woodrow Wilson, in a maroon dress, matching hat, and white gloves.[102] Their fashions were duly noted by society writers.

Twenty-four years earlier, on April 2, 1917, she had sat in the House chamber, listening to then-President Wilson solicit Congress in a long, long speech for a declaration of war on Germany.

Seated behind Mrs. Wilson was Mrs. Hull. Also in attendance were Harry Hopkins, the cabinet, and the Diplomatic Corps, excluding the Japanese envoys. The audience rose as the cabinet and members of the Senate filed in. "The atmosphere of the Capitol was grave, but for the first time in years there were no doubts."[103]

The chaplain, Phillips, opened with a short prayer.

Since 1932, "There was in the United States a tradition of silence about the physical affliction of President Roosevelt, an implication that it would be tasteless ever to mention the misfortune that galvanized his energies, transformed his personality and therefore the subsequent history of the United States."[104] The newsreel cameras and the attending journalists never recorded that FDR had been wheeled to a side door leading to the House of

Representatives, given a chance to lock in his leg braces, and then stood before Congress of the United States, the citizens of America, and the struggling peoples of the world.

"With infinite slowness, limping from side to side, Roosevelt came up the ramp to the dais, one arm locked in his son's, the other hand feeling every inch of the long sloping rail." At the dais, he fiddled with his glasses and opened the binder of the short speech that would change the world.[105]

Then Speaker Sam Rayburn simply announced, "The President of the United States!"[106]

After a pause, Congress stood and cheered wildly and long, as FDR stood before them. "They cheered him again and again. Every space was filled. Every entrance doorway was jammed. People were standing packed into the corners of the House floor, in tiers, one row behind another, as at a parade. They were standing on chairs, on sofas, on the narrow ledge of the panels of the wall itself."[107] The ovation was unlike any the old building had ever heard before.

FDR asked for an American declaration of war against the empire of Japan. The room was deadly quiet as he began in a grim tone. His speech was broadcast live on every imaginable radio network, filmed and photographed by every imaginable news agency. His voice was sonorous, the cadence and pitch, perfect:

Yesterday, December 7, 1941—a date which will live in infamy—the United States was suddenly and deliberately attacked by naval and air forces of the Empire of Japan.

The United States was at peace with that nation and, at the solicitation of Japan, was still in conversation with its government and its Emperor looking toward the maintenance of peace in the Pacific. Indeed, one hour after Japanese air squadrons had commenced bombing the American island of Oahu, the Japanese Ambassador to the United States and his colleague delivered to our Secretary of State a formal reply to a recent American message. While this reply stated that it seemed useless to continue the existing diplomatic negotiations, it contained no threat or hint of war or armed attack.

It will be recorded that the distance of Hawaii from Japan makes it obvious that the attack was planned many days or even weeks ago. During the intervening time the Japanese government has deliberately sought to deceive the United States by false statements and expressions of hope for continued peace.

The attack yesterday on the Hawaiian Islands has caused severe damage to American naval and military forces. Very many American lives have been lost. In addition American ships have been reported torpedoed on the high seas between San Francisco and Honolulu.

Yesterday the Japanese Government also launched an attack against Malaya. Last night Japanese forces attacked Hong Kong. Last night Japanese forces attacked Guam. Last night Japanese forces attacked the Philippine Islands. Last night the Japanese attacked Wake Island. This morning the Japanese attacked Midway Island.

Japan has, therefore, undertaken a surprise offensive extending throughout the Pacific area. The facts of yesterday speak for themselves. The people of the United States have already formed their opinions and well understand the implications to the very life and safety of our nation.

As Commander-in-Chief of the Army and Navy I have directed that all measures be taken for our defense. Always will we remember the character of the onslaught against us. No matter how long it may take us to overcome this premeditated invasion, the American people in their righteous might will win through to absolute victory.

I believe I interpret the will of the Congress and of the people when I assert that we will not only defend ourselves to the uttermost but will make very certain that this form of treachery shall never endanger us again.

Hostilities exist. There is no blinking at the fact that our people, our territory and our interests are in grave danger. With confidence in our armed forces—with the unbounding determination of our people—we will gain the inevitable triumph—so help us God.

I ask that the Congress declare that since the unprovoked and dastardly attack by Japan on Sunday, December seventh, a state of war has existed between the United States and the Japanese Empire.[108]

Roosevelt's six-and-one-half minute address was interrupted several times with ovations and cheers and whistles and rebel yells from Congress and again, at the end, sustained applause was heard as he waved his hand to the members.

Roosevelt often wrote his own speeches, or at least provided substantial edits. Reading the president's original manuscript of his address revealed the sheer power of words. He initially wrote December 7, 1941, would be a day that would live in "history," but he later crossed out that word, inserted a proofreader's carrot, and scribbled "infamy."[109] As Mark Twain once said, "The difference between the almost right word and the right word is really a large matter—'tis the difference between the lightning bug and the lightning."[110] In his speech to Congress on December 8, the president had captured lightning in a bottle. Churchill, who had long lobbied for America's entry into the war, was jubilant. And the American media was breathless.

The United Press reported, "Democracy was proving its right to a place in the sun with a split second shiftover from peace to all-out war."[111] Journalist Louis M. Lyons of the *Boston Daily Globe* was on hand, one of the few privileged reporters allowed to sit in the eighty-six seats in the press gallery that five hundred other journalists were denied. Of the crowd in the House Chamber, Lyons wrote, "All rose in a mighty crash of supporting applause as he asked in one simple sentence that Congress declare a state of war exists between the United States and Japan."[112]

The war resolution (in language identical to 1917, with the exception of substituting Japan for Germany)[113] passed the Senate thirty-two minutes after FDR's speech to the joint session began and less than fifteen minutes after he concluded his impassioned remarks.[114] The refrain "Vote! Vote! Vote!" echoed throughout the chamber.[115] It passed the House twenty-two minutes after that.[116] The Senate vote was 82–0 for war with Japan. The House vote was 388–1 for war with Japan.[117] In 1917, Congress had debated for four days to go to war with Germany. This time, they did so in a little over forty minutes.[118]

There were still some in Congress now, who had been in Congress then, who had voted against war with Germany. Not this time. Even the most rabid isolationist, anti-Roosevelt Republican voted to go to war with Japan. Save one. The one dissenting vote was Jeannette Rankin from Montana. She had voted no once before, in 1917 when Congress was asked to vote on the Declaration of War. At that time she stood weakly, and said, "I want to stand by my country but I cannot vote for war." Then she broke out in tears.[119] This time there were no tears. But boos and hisses rained down on the silver-haired woman. A Democratic member could be heard saying sarcastically, "Sit down sister!"[120] Speaker Rayburn gaveled for the chamber to come to order.

Rankin had remained seated, along with Congressman Clare Hoffman, Republican of Michigan, while everyone else stood as the president entered the House. Hoffman was a vocal opponent of government-initiated fluoridation and polio immunization. Rankin was the daughter of a rancher, a Republican, a pacifist, a suffragette, and utterly principled. She'd first been elected in 1916 and in 1917 and had voted against entry into the European War. In 1918, she lost a primary bid for the U.S. Senate. She kicked around for twenty years, working on social causes, until once again elected to the House in 1940. After her vote against war with Japan, she was essentially hounded out of office and did not bother to seek reelection in 1942. Following the vote, she told reporters, "As a woman I can't go to war and I refuse to send anyone else."[121]

Both houses of Congress adjourned almost immediately after passing the war resolution. Very little discussion had taken place in either body prior to the vote. Of the thirteen senators and forty-two representatives who missed the vote due to distance or illness, all declared they would have sided with FDR to go to war. Several rushed back, only to walk onto the floor as the voting had finished.[122]

At 4:10 eastern standard time that afternoon, Roosevelt signed the declaration of war against Japan at his desk in the Oval Office. In cursive he wrote, "Approved—Dec 8th 4:10 p.m. E.S.T. Franklin Roosevelt."[123] Also signing the Declaration of War, as stipulated by the Constitution, were the vice president and Senate president Henry Wallace, at 3:23; and Sam Rayburn, Speaker of the House of Representatives, at 3:15.[124] Roosevelt was photographed surrounded by congressional leaders while he signed the document.

As the *New York Times* reported, "The United States went to war today as a great nation should—with simplicity, dignity, and unprecedented unity. The deep divisions which marked this country's entrance into the wars of 1776, 1812, 1861, 1898 and 1917 were absent. Overnight, partisan, personal and sectional differences were shelved."[125]

After the leaders departed, Roosevelt took an hour-long nap on the sofa in the Oval Office. "When he arose he checked reports again (still piled with bad news)."[126]

And then, everything changed in America.

All troops out on passes were immediately recalled to their posts. All leaves and furloughs were canceled and men ordered to return to their duty stations immediately. Military posts were closed to civilians. Nationwide, recruiting offices were flooded with applications for all three branches. "Young boys of 'teen age' and grizzled veterans of the last war—swamped Army, Navy and Marine recruiting stations here today, ready to give their lives if need be to whip Japanese. White and colored, the uneducated and professional men, joined together."[127]

The recruiting office of the navy in Washington usually had three applicants on an average morning, but this morning, two hundred young men showed up. The phones of recruiting offices across the country began ringing Sunday afternoon. The navy was accepting candidates from the ages of seventeen to fifty, the marines sixteen to thirty.[128] The first elected official to volunteer was Senator Albert "Happy" Chandler, Democrat of Kentucky, who was a veteran of the last war.[129] Recruiting offices also offered training for women in "first aid, diet and canteen ambulance corps."[130]

Boston Red Sox slugger Ted Williams had been classified 3-A, but his draft board in Minneapolis announced that he would shortly be reclassified as 1-A.[131] Every newspaper carried photos of young men gathering outside of recruiting offices. Women descended in the droves onto defense training centers in New York, asking, "What can we do?" "You can wash dishes," answered a member of the American Women's Voluntary Services. Shortly, the contributions of American women would become more substantive. "A police instructor for women air raid wardens opened his usual Monday morning meeting with the words, 'our subject for today is incendiary bombs.' His class was most attentive."[132]

While voting to declare war on Japan, Congress had also voted for supplemental funds for the war effort and a bill to "freeze" all currently enlisted men into the services "for the duration of the national emergency."[133]

After the bill signing, FDR met with the Soviet ambassador, Maxim Litvinoff; La Guardia; and the chairman of the Red Cross, Norman H. Davis.[134]

The mayor of San Francisco declared a state of emergency and ordered a halt to all strikes in his jurisdiction while calling for thousands of Civil Defense volunteers. The metropolis had an especially heavy concentration of Japanese citizens, and city fathers feared sabotage.[135] Big tuna fishing boats owned by Japanese in Monterey were ordered to stay at their berths or anchorage. The West Coast felt doubly vulnerable to sabotage and the possibility of a Japanese invasion. Blackouts were ordered up and down the coastline. A "Jap Boat" was spotted off of Laguna Beach "flashing messages to the shore from that point." The local police issued an APB to find and apprehend the vessel.[136]

Government officials began to discuss the possibility of rationing commodities such as rubber, tin, and gasoline. The government also took out ads in newspapers, calling for blacksmiths, boat builders, machinists, boilermakers, and other skilled labor for work in the Panama Canal Zone. The pay was good, too, as much as $1.66 per hour.[137] Air-raid warden schools were opened in Rhode Island. Stevedores called off their strike in New London, Connecticut.[138] Harvard hosted a debate on its role in the war, "its role in a country at war," and what the war meant to Harvard. Dean Paul Buck foresaw no "radical change" for his school. More practically, Emerson College "suspended classes" and hosted a pro-American rally. "An American history exam was cancelled while war in the Pacific made current history."[139]

Roosevelt immediately ordered the arrest of all Japanese "dangerous to the peace and security of the United States," said Attorney General Francis Biddle. At the time, ninety-three thousand Japanese had registered with the government as a result of the Alien Registration Law.[140]

The FBI was ordered to implement the arrests. Almost immediately, 738 Japanese aliens were picked up and the Bureau had another 50,000 on their watch lists.[141] The government also began rounding up Japanese "in the jurisdiction of the Fourth Army, which takes in the west coast and Alaska, and the Hawaiian and Canal Zone departments."[142]

Those arrested were placed in "immigration detention centers" and from there would be turned over to the U.S. Army. The U.S. attorney in charge of the program announced his office would remain open twenty-four hours per day until further notice. They already had in custody 1,200 Germans and Italians locked up in facilities in Montana and North Dakota.[143]

In Baltimore, a municipal judge, William Coleman, was supposed to preside over a pro forma citizenship swearing in ceremony but instead, he denied the thirty-four individuals of German, Italian, and Finnish origin their application to become U.S. citizens.[144] At the time, Japanese could not become American citizens. Over the objections of President Calvin Coolidge, Congress had passed the Asiatic Exclusion Act in 1924.[145]

A number of Japanese nationals were arrested in New York under the Enemy Alien Act and taken to Ellis Island for holding. Japanese newspapers were ordered closed.[146]

The secretary of the treasury, Henry Morgenthau, announced "the seizure of all Japanese banks and business in the United States," to be carried out by his agents.[147] He warned "that anyone hiding or destroying, or helping anybody else to hide or destroy, any of the Japanese property ordered seized would be risking ten years in prison."[148]

Morgenthau also ordered all communication with the empire of Japan banned as well as commerce under "Section 3 of the Trading with the Enemy Act."[149] The order covered all indirect commerce or communication as well. He also closed the borders of Mexico and Canada to all Japanese nationals and placed a ban on any financial transaction in America by "Japanese aliens." Those intercepted at the borders were detained and additional security was added.[150]

Additionally, Morgenthau ordered the impoundment of over $131 million in Japanese holdings in U.S. banks, and all exit visas out of the country were canceled for Japanese nationals. Customs officials were ordered to stop and detain any Japanese national from leaving the country. Morgenthau's order was complete, absolute, and harsh. "All general licenses, specific licenses and authorizations of whatever character are hereby revoked in so far as they authorize, directly or indirectly, any transaction by, on behalf of, or for the benefit of, or any national thereof." The order was not only aimed at preventing commerce with Japan; it also prevented the conduct of commerce by Japanese citizens in America or any territory controlled by the United States. The United States had $217 million in banks and holdings in Japan, and all assumed they would freeze those as well.[151] Morgenthau hinted that his actions might also apply to Germans and Italians.[152] It was unclear how the new edits from Washington would affect second generation Japanese Americans, known as "Nisei."[153]

One Japanese-American, grasping at straws, speculated that it might have been possible for the Germans to get a hold of Japanese planes to carry out the attack. Another young Japanese man, a truck driver, said, "This is it. I guess I'll join the Army.' He meant the American Army.'"[154]

Public facilities around the country immediately took on a "nation at war" cast. There was an increased military presence, and spontaneously, Americans began showing up at Red Cross stations to donate blood for the war effort. As men returned grimly to their bases, the *Los Angeles Times* noted, "There were no gay farewells in sharp contrast to the usual scene of men returning to duty."[155]

Brandishing M-1 carbines, the standard military issue, affixed with bayonets, armed marine, army, and navy guards stood at post around Washington's government buildings, including the Capitol, something that had not been seen since 1917 and before that, since 1865. They were under orders to be "strict." Carrying full field packs and wearing steel helmets, they were on guard twenty-four hours a day.[156]

The phrase *war footing* was injected into the lingo while the word *theater* took on a whole new meaning. Rather than the local movie theater, now it was used in the context of "Pacific Theater" and "European Theater."

An increased police existence was noticeable in Washington, as were increased Secret Service agents, though not as noticeable. But in other cities and towns, the reality of men and women in all sorts of uniforms and others wearing officious badges and armbands took root. The civilian guard around the Boston Navy Yard was doubled and other precautions were taken, including increasing the boats patrolling the Inner Harbor and "guarding of the different Japanese business concerns in the city proper. Guard posted at the Emperor Hirohito Club, Braddock Park, South End, headquarters for the greater Boston Japanese." Riot squads were also reconstituted in Boston, and an air-raid system was announced.[157]

The America First event scheduled for Boston Garden was up in the air for the coming Friday evening. Lindberg was slated to speak, along with other leading isolationists. Mrs. Sohler Welch, head of the Boston office, sheepishly said, "If they do go through, I imagine the plans will have to be radically altered."[158] Other America Firsters came forward and issued statements of support for FDR. Herbert Hoover, Gen. Robert Wood, and Alf Landon all came forward.[159] Senator Gerald Nye, however, accused the United States of "doing its utmost to provoke a quarrel with Japan" and said that America was being led around by the nose by Churchill and the British. He said the attack on Pearl Harbor was "just what Britain had planned for us. Britain has been getting this ready since 1938." Even knowing of the attack, Nye went forward with an America First speech in Pittsburg.[160] An antiwar rally in Baltimore, sponsored by the Keep America Out of War Congress, featuring noted socialist Norman Thomas, was also slated to go forward.[161]

The Coast Guard issued a sweeping order preventing any ship from departing Boston Harbor and all sailing permits were confiscated. The order affected several ships carrying war materiel under Lend-Lease. The FBI also ordered the Boston and Maine railroad to not sell any tickets to Japanese citizens, and conductors were instructed to notify the local police of any Japanese on board any train.[162]

In New York, ships in the harbor were put under extra guard, and police closed the Nippon Club. "Twelve Japanese who were there when the police came were escorted to their homes." The State Department ordered the halt of all ships departing from New York for foreign ports. "New York City policemen extended their visits to all Japanese restaurants in the five boroughs. They permitted diners to finish their meals, then escorted owners and their staffs to their homes. Various Japanese commercial units seemed to have had some official signal of what was to come. Many did not renew leases."[163] Government officials seized control of six Japanese banks based in New York.[164]

Adm. Adolphus Andrews, commander of the North Atlantic Coastal Frontier, was in charge of protecting New York Harbor, though he was not too concerned about an attack. Asked why, he replied nonchalantly, because "there is no Japanese Navy in the Atlantic."[165]

Those Japanese apprehended by FBI agents were told they were "prisoners of the Federal authorities" and then removed via paddy wagons and patrol cars after they were allowed to pack a suitcase. Upon arrival, their background records were checked and then they were "taken to the Barge Office at the

Battery and to Ellis Island by ferry." Many "underwent extended questioning. Federal stenographers and clerks were called in to [record] the pedigrees of the prisoners. All the prisoners were treated with every courtesy, although they were well-guarded." Many of the Japanese nationals seized by the government hadn't been to their native country in years. "Some of the Japanese were crestfallen, some were smiling, but none offered resistance."[166]

Revisions to the Draft Act were being hurriedly contemplated as the quota for January was not big enough. The pool of eligible young men needed to be expanded, especially as the first solid casualty reports were slowly coming in from Hawaii. First Lt. Hans Christiansen, a marine aviator, of Woodland, California, age twenty-one was killed. Sergeant James Guthrie of Republican Grove, Virginia, an Air Corps engineer, was killed. No age given. Private George G. Leslie of Arnold, Pennsylvania, age twenty, with the Army Air Corps, was killed. Dead American boys came from other small towns including Ravenna, Ohio; Janesville, Wisconsin; and Bloomfield, New Jersey.[167] The lists were swelling as bodies were still being recovered in Honolulu and elsewhere. Nearly all killed were little more than small town boys; no one in America yet knew the full story of the thousands of deaths of military and civilian alike. The first Hawaiian casualty may have been a civilian, Bob Tyce, who owned a civilian airport on Oahu. He was seen attempting to "hot prop" the propeller of a plane, but was strafed from the air by a Japanese fighter.[168] The Navy Department put out a statement asking reporters to stop making inquiries about the status of military personnel. The department would only respond to the inquiries of families.[169]

Nor did Americans fully understand yet that the Japanese had practically declared war on America two hours after the attack on Pearl Harbor. Curiously, Tokyo instituted complete wartime blackout measures, but Washington did not do so immediately. Bridges and important points of transportation in Maryland and Virginia were put under guard. Air raid wardens prowled the streets of Washington, yet without proper identification papers some were stopped for questioning by the police as "suspicious characters."[170]

The America First Committee began to quickly melt away, as all now previous isolationists, issued statements supporting the war and the president, and denouncing Japan. The group's inspirational leader, Charles Lindberg, in Chicago—ground zero for the isolationist movement—issued a terse (and some thought) ungracious statement. "We have been stepping closer to war for many months. Now it has come and we must meet it as united Americans regardless of our attitude in the past toward the policy our Government has followed. Whether or not that policy has been wise, our country has been attacked by force of arms and by force of arms we must retaliate. Our own defenses and our own military position have already been neglected too long. We must now turn every effort to building the greatest and most efficient Army, Navy and air force in the world." The famed aviator then took his family to Martha's Vineyard and went into seclusion, accepting neither telegrams nor phone calls.[171]

The National Committee of the Communist Party, headquartered in New York, also issued a statement supporting the United States.[172]

A Christmas charity drive for children sponsored by NBC, the *Star* newspaper, and the Warner Brothers Theaters was "suspended . . . because of the war."[173] The federal government and military installations went into lockdown mode, and only those carrying special passes could be admitted. National Airport went on a "wartime basis" as "special attention was being paid to anti-sabotage patrol."[174] Attention was also being paid to gas lines, water lines, and electrical plants to guard against sabotage. All across the country, War Emergency Committees and Regional Defense Councils and the like were hurriedly organized.[175]

At 11:00 p.m. on December 7, a partial blackout was ordered for Washington, but it looked more like a "dim out" to officials. "Residents—at least some of them—did as they were requested and snapped off lights in their homes or pulled the shades down." But much of Washington was still brightly lit, from the great chandelier in the White House to the U.S. Capitol.[176]

Mrs. Roosevelt, in her weekly Sunday evening radio broadcast, had called on American women to "rise above their fears" and support their sons in the services and help support the morale of their families. "Many of you all over this country have boys in the services who will now be called upon to go into action. You cannot escape a clutch of fear at your heart and yet I hope that the certainty of what we have to meet will make you rise above these fears."[177]

The First Lady told her listeners that she, too, had a son in harm's way. "I have a boy at sea on a destroyer. For all I know he is on his way to the Pacific." Mistakenly, she also said that the president had been meeting with the Japanese diplomats at the very time when Japan was attacking. In closing, she said, "To the young people of this nation I must speak tonight. You are going to have a great opportunity—there will be high moments in which your strength and your ability will be tested. I have faith in you! Just as though I were standing upon a rock, and that rock is my faith in my fellow citizens."[178]

General Motors declared it was putting all its plants on "full war status."[179] The United Brotherhoods of Welders, Cutters and Helpers—which had scheduled a nationwide strike for the following week—called it off.[180] The War Department issued orders to defense contractors that workers in those plants "be required to work as many additional hours as is necessary to get the day's work done. Additional overtime work and second and third shifts must be arranged. Our production must be put on a 24-hour-a-day basis."[181] The War Department also ordered all defense plants to take steps to ensure that sabotage did not befall them.

Soon, there would be plenty of work for all Americans. Pearl Harbor was the final nail in the coffin of the Great Depression; shortly, the problem wouldn't be creating enough work—it would be finding enough workers.

In Abilene, Texas, "the only Japanese soldier in the 45th Division was a prisoner in the Camp Barkeley stockade today. He is doing six months at hard labor for desertion. Headquarters said he refused to tell a court martial where he had been during two months absence."[182]

In Panama and Alaska, and at a military installment in Sacramento, blackouts were ordered. Antisubmarine netting was spread across the San Diego harbor.[183] Over one hundred Japanese civilians were picked up in the Canal Zone, in part because the canal was an inviting target for sabotage. The Japanese minister demanded their release, but it fell on deaf ears.[184]

The naval base at Puget Sound announced it would shoot down any plane flying overhead. All private aviation was canceled in the United States by the Civil Aeronautics Authority and licenses were suspended. Only commercial and military planes were allowed aloft.[185] Fishing boats in San Francisco harbor were ordered to stay at anchor, and the lights on the Golden Gate Bridge were turned off. On the Bay Bridge, cars were allowed to pass except those containing Japanese. These were stopped and questioned. The new water aqueduct in Los Angeles was put under guard. Cargo ships in Los Angeles, San Francisco, and other West Coast harbors were "bottled up."[186]

The downtown area of the city was clogged with traffic, but citizens were warned to stay at home. "Then came a reaction as truly American as apple pie." The word on the street was, "They started it—we'll finish it!"[187] Four thousand antiaircraft troops were deployed around the city, and the navy ordered a blackout of the harbors at Long Beach, San Pedro, and Wilmington. The city also ordered the darkening of street lights[188] and . . . airfields landing lights were turned off. "Black-outs, wild rumors of 'approaching aircraft'"[189]

Reeves Field was closed around 11:30 a.m. on the seventh "as word of the attack on Honolulu was received. Gates to the field were closed, all leaves were cancelled, all visitors were banned and those within the gates were subject to questioning before they were permitted to depart."[190]

A national call was issued for volunteer amateur radio operators and airplane spotters. The first request the government made of the ham radio operators was to switch off their crystal sets to clear the airwaves so Washington officials could better monitor enemy transmissions from inside the United States.[191]

The real story of the events in Washington, Tokyo, and the Pacific were only beginning to emerge by December 8 and would not be entirely unraveled for some time. In short, the Japanese military attacked unarmed civilians and unprepared and unaware military outposts without first declaring war. The time in Washington was 1:05 p.m.

Secretary of State Cordell Hull had been in conferences Sunday morning with Secretary of the Navy Frank Knox and Secretary of War Henry Stimson for three hours, beginning at 9:45 a.m. At 1:00 p.m., Japanese ambassador Nomura requested an immediate appointment with Hull.[192] The fourteenth part of the long message from Tokyo had arrived and it concluded,

"The Japanese government regrets to have to notify hereby the American government that in view of the attitude of the American government it cannot but consider that it is impossible to reach an agreement through further negotiations."[193] It could be interpreted many ways, and only one as a declaration of war. Countries had broken off negotiations in the past, had withdrawn envoys, all without going to war.

The meeting was set for 1:45, but Nomura and fellow diplomat Kurusu were fifteen minutes late. They then cooled their heels in Hull's outer office for another fifteen minutes. The meeting started at 2:15 and lasted only ten minutes. The pair presented an ultimatum from their government.[194] Just before meeting with Nomura and Kurusu, Hull learned of the attack on Pearl Harbor in a startling phone conversation with the president.[195] The meeting, suffice it to say, was short and unpleasant. *Time* magazine said the statement they'd delivered was "an incredible farrago of self-justification and abuse."[196]

The Japanese envoys departed, curiously photographed smiling, while surrounded by dozens of scowling reporters and photographers,[197] though it was not clear the diplomats knew that their country had attacked America. These photos became infamous, further inflaming the already inflamed American populace. Most people didn't follow the diplomatic interplay between the two countries, the boycotts, the invasions, or the subtle and not so subtle military moves. Then came a declaration by the emperor of Japan, Hirohito, which was picked up, translated, and then broadcast by NBC radio. Surprising no one, Hirohito told his listeners, "We by the grace of Heaven, Emperor of Japan and seated on the throne of a line unbroken for ages eternal, enjoin upon thee, our loyal and brave subjects. We hereby declare war upon the United States of America and the British Empire."[198] From there, Hirohito made his case against America and England while crafting essentially a "pep talk" for the Japanese people. Servicemen—many of them sailors—teemed Times Square and other city gathering places where they read newspapers, some anxious to go to war with Japan. "'We can whip them in no time,' was a common remark sailors made."[199] Of course, none of these young men had ever been to war, nor did they realize the Japanese population had been making sacrifices since the invasion of Manchuria in 1931, and the Japanese troops were battle-hardened from that incursion as well as the invasion of China in 1937.

The Japanese had, by best estimates, somewhere between three and five thousand fighter planes and sixty-six divisions or 1.8 million men in uniform, not including the twenty divisions occupying Eastern China as well as others in Indochina, Formosa, and other locales. Also, "the Japanese fleet [was the] world's third largest," consisting of "eleven capital ships with [others] nearly ready; eight or nine aircraft carriers plus three carriers converted from merchantmen; forty-four to forty-six cruisers . . . about 126 destroyers and sixty-nine or seventy submarines, some of them large craft of long range probably now operating in the Eastern Pacific."[200] The Japanese had a hell of a fighting force and no one was going to "whip them in no time."

Most Americans could not find Pearl Harbor on a map before December 7, 1941. One congressman lamented that Pearl Harbor should have been put in the middle of the United States rather than the middle of the Pacific. The Washington Post made reference to "Bickam Field,"[201] while the *New York Times* called it "Hickman."[202] It was Hickam Field.

But Americans did understand fair play and playing by the rules. Fair play was ingrained in Americans, as was American Exceptionalism and Manifest Destiny. Editorials across the nation freely used the adjectives "sordid," "deceitful," "consummate duplicity," "perfidy," "treachery," "unscrupulous," and others far worse.

All made it abundantly clear to their infuriated readers that Japan had declared war after attacking America. While most of the immediate information coming out of the White House was inaccurate, their initial estimate of the dead in Hawaii, three thousand was fairly correct.[203] None of the names of the American ships hit by the Japanese were released by official sources.

Roosevelt—at least outwardly—took the crisis in stride. "Deadly calm" was how Eleanor Roosevelt described him. "He was completely calm. His reaction to any event was always to be calm. If it was something that was bad, he just became almost like an iceberg, and then there was never the slightest emotion that was allowed to show."[204] Secretary Morgenthau suggested more protection for FDR, but he balked. "You've doubled the [White House] guard," said the president. "That's all you need."[205]

Editorially, every paper in the country called for American victory and denounced the Japanese in the harshest and sometimes most personal terms. The *Los Angeles Times* called the Japanese a "mad dog . . . a gangster's parody." The *Philadelphia Inquirer* called them "war-mad." The *St. Louis Globe Democrat* accused Tokyo of "international rapine."[206]

A palpable rage against the Japanese was everywhere. "Let the Japanese Ambassador go back to his masters and tell them that the United States answers Japan's challenge with steel-throated cannon and a sharp sword of retribution. We shall repay this dastardly treachery with multiplied bombs from the air and heaviest and accurate shells from the sea." The author of this "bombastic" statement was seventy-four-year-old Tom Connally of Texas, a member of that deliberative body known as the United States Senate.[207]

American boys had grown up playing cowboy, and the rule was you didn't shoot anyone in the back, even an Indian. Boys did not sucker punch other boys. You gave your opponent a chance to defend himself. American girls had grown up learning good manners and the rules of life. Dirty play and breaking the rules was frowned upon. Chivalry and good manners reigned in American culture in 1941. Men held doors for ladies. Ladies acted like ladies. Men and women abided by the rules of courtship and life. It was the America way. Now, Americans were storming mad. "We'll mop them up," said one. Another said, "I've got a brother somewhere on the Pacific. . . . I just hope he gets three or four of those yellow rats." Yet another said, "Now we've got to go get those yellow rice eaters." Mrs. A.V. B. Gilbert of Clifton Road in Atlanta said, "The Japanese are despicable people." Barney Oakes, a salesman said, "The Japs will find those were expensive warships they sank."[208] American public opinion was uniformly anti-Japanese, to say the least, and some of it quite ugly.

The Japanese had not played by the rules. They had assaulted America without provocation, without declaring war. They had deceitfully attacked America on a Sunday, and in 1941, America was for all intents and purposes a Christian country.

The lead editorial of the *Los Angeles Times* pulled no punches. "Japan has asked for it. Now she is going to get it."[209]

CHAPTER 9

THE NINTH OF DECEMBER

"New York Has Two Air Raid Alarms;
Planes Reported Near"

Birmingham News

"Frisco Drives Off Japanese Raiders"

Boston Globe

"Pacific Battle Widens; Manila Area Bombed"

New York Times

"More Planes Off Frisco, New Raid Alarm Sounded"

Sun

Two days after the attack on Pearl Harbor, America was in a panic. A war that had been oceans away now appeared to be on the country's doorstep. News stories raced across the United States of more imminent assaults, including on New York.

"The great metropolitan area of New York City was put on an air-raid alert twice within an hour shortly after noon Tuesday amid varying unconfirmed reports of an imminent attack by hostile planes," ran the Associated Press wire. "The vast stretch of Long Island from the city to Montauk Point also braced itself for the reported possible attack. A million school children in New York and thousands on Long Island were sent home. Army planes took to the air after the first alarm was sounded. . . . We have information that a squadron of planes is headed toward Long Island. Make all necessary preparations, if identified as enemy planes," heard police patrolmen on their car radios.[1]

No one seemed to know where the reports of the unidentified planes came from. Citizens were confused, not knowing what the sirens were for, and others claimed they didn't hear the sirens. But this did not stop city fathers from going into a full-fright lockdown. Many New Yorkers, however, took it in stride, ignoring the air-raid sirens, going about their business. In Times Square, people took a decidedly "so what?" attitude. It was much the same in Brooklyn, Queens, and Harlem.[2]

A policeman boarded a bus full of passengers and told them they had to get off and take shelter, but no one moved. Stymied, he said, "What was I to do? Use my gun on them?" A pretzel vendor got into an argument with another police officer who ordered him off the street, but the vendor, with hot wares to sell, won the argument, not budging.[3] "Spotters" were looking in the sky, armed with field glasses, looking in vain for enemy fighters. Cops tried to get people off the streets and into shelters, while civil defense volunteers tried to get customers in department stores and restaurants to lie down on the floor.[4] "In at least one fashionable East River apartment, women volunteer wardens . . . ran through the building, breaking up early bridge games and rousing late sleepers; soon the halls were filled with women in dressing gowns, with cold cream on their faces."[5]

Military planes at Mitchel Field took off, searching for enemy planes. Radio beams that planes "rode" into airports were shut off. The *New York Times* said planes were guarding the city for "air raids," antiaircraft guns had been deployed, and the police and fire departments were trying to figure out how to efficiently notify the eight hundred schools in the area.[6] The paper also published a special feature, "What to Do in an Air Raid."[7] New York City did not have air-raid sirens in any of the five boroughs, so a Rube Goldberg operation involving the sirens on police squad cars and fire engines, in concert, was employed.[8]

Unsubstantiated rumors continued to wash all over America. A story opened in the *Los Angeles Times*, "As battle comes close to the Pacific

Coast..."[9] Boston also went on the alert, thinking it, too, was under imminent attack. The "approach of enemy planes" was heard broadcast over the radio. "New Englanders suddenly were confronted with the possibility that the war was about to burst on them with terrible realism."[10] Sirens in Beantown wailed for over an hour.

Civilians were barred from the Boston Navy Yard. Area schools were closed and children sent home. The Coast Guard "cancelled all liberty" on reports that enemy planes were headed for Boston.[11]

In New York, guardsmen stepped up their patrol of the harbor, on the lookout for "incendiary" bombs.[12] The docks were covered with armaments and one well-placed bomb could send the whole thing up. Fourteen thousand workers at the Bethlehem Steel Company at Quincy, Massachusetts, shipyard were sent home. Antiaircraft guns were deployed along the New England coastline.[13] Teachers in the Boston schools were reported crying. "Conditions of near-panic were reported in several places ... [amid] wild rumors that the Japanese were in New York, among other rumors."[14] Cars, headed for Boston, were halted in Cambridge.[15]

The head of the Bay State's Committee on Public Safety, J. Wells Farley, said, "Remember—panic is the worst danger."[16]

On the other side of the country, in San Francisco, a woman, Marie Sayre, was shot and wounded by a member of the Home Guard when her husband failed to stop their car as ordered as he approached the Golden Gate Bridge.

In newspapers across the land, it was reported that there were "unidentified planes" over San Francisco; the planes were never identified, nor took any hostile actions. The army claimed that thirty planes had flown over the "west coast sector" and consequently an air-raid signal was sounded and the civilian population went into hiding.

Searchlights lit up the sky as the air raids sounded at 2:39 a.m., and the darkness added to the sense of panic.[17] The whole thing earned screaming headlines in American newspapers even though there was no real evidence that the planes were, in fact, the enemy. Gen. William Ryan claimed they had been turned back at the Golden Gate Bridge. Still, he did not know to whom the planes belonged. "They weren't Army planes, they weren't Navy planes, and you can be sure they weren't civilian planes."[18] No one could account for the mystery aircraft that mysteriously vanished southward.

Also on the West Coast was a persistent rumor of an enemy aircraft carrier nearby. Ryan maintained that enemy ships had been "detected . . . about 100 miles at sea."[19] Then it was reported over the radio that the military was searching for "two or three Japanese aircraft carriers and some submarines reported operating off the coast." Some supposedly saw fifteen planes flying south toward San Jose. "The lights went off in Oakland and most of her sister cities . . . and there were strange reports of planes being heard overhead but no confirmation."[20]

Military planes were sent aloft in wild goose chases looking for phantom ships and planes, but none were found. Stories also circulated that Japanese attacks on the Aleutian Islands and Canada were imminent.[21] Alaska was on full alert status.[22] Rumors begat fresh rumors. In this case, it was that the Japanese carriers in California waters were there to try to "panic" Washington "into calling [the] fleet back home,"[23] presumably to join in the search for the phantom ships and phantom planes. The country was utterly convinced that the Japanese were on the brink of attacking and possibly invading the West Coast of America, or were plotting to engage in a harassing naval action, much as the Germans had been doing in the North Atlantic for nearly a year.

Cities including San Francisco were completely blacked out at night, and many imposed curfews. In Seattle, a mob took to the streets and smashed the windows of store owners who were not complying with the blackout orders. "The crowd, urged on by shouting women," totaling one thousand people, broke the windows of some thirty shops and stores that had left some lights on.[24] Many radio stations, including those in Seattle, were ordered to stop broadcasting after 7:00 p.m., except those used to transmit official business to the worried citizenry.[25] Blackouts were ordered in nearly every city on the West Coast, along with the U.S. capital on the East Coast. In Washington, "Autoists should use only their dim lights and drive slowly, spotlighting of bridges and public buildings must cease, all theatre marquees must be turned out, all show windows must be darkened and outside advertising put out, street lights will be dimmed, although traffic lights will stay on; citizens must pull their window shades down."[26]

In Manila, a radio correspondent had to debunk a rumor that American planes had bombed the Japanese cities of Tokyo, Kobe, and the island of

Formosa, which was in Japanese hands. This was after CBS had reported that the bombing had taken place.[27] Another rumor was "Japanese planes were reported off Panama."[28] Military officials in Boston later claimed the air-raid alarm was just a "dress rehearsal" and there had been no approach of planes.[29] The civilian government had not been let in on the army plan, which had made the announcement. It was the same in New York. The "air raid" was a hoax concocted by the military.[30]

Another rumor making the rounds—fifth hand—was that the Japanese had told Adolf Hitler six days earlier that they were planning to attack. attack.[31] Another was that Germany was getting ready to declare war on the United States, and Berlin chortled that the United States was now facing a "two-front war." Another tale was that Christmas leave was still on, on schedule and as planned, for the military.[32]

The initial reports that Japanese troops had parachuted into Hawaii were now largely dismissed. More likely, it now seemed, observers saw the parachutes of Japanese pilots who had bailed out of their planes due to antiaircraft fire.

It was also whispered in Walter Winchell's column that Charles Lindbergh and Anne Morrow Lindbergh were contemplating a divorce, as she'd become fed up with his politics and his ego. The worm was turning for the once-unassailable aviator hero who had crossed the Atlantic. Winchell was enormously influential, and he both shaped and reflected public opinion. His trademark staccato voice on the radio riveted listeners throughout the nation. A supporter of FDR who morphed into a red-baiting reactionary after the war, Winchell was a feared and fearless reporter who could make or break careers. His reportage was a mix of politics, opinion, hokum, sensationalism, and celebrity dirt.

Forty-eight hours after the attack, Washington would neither openly confirm nor deny the details of the assault.

The Japanese claimed they'd sunk the *Oklahoma* and the *West Virginia*[33] while other rumors had it the *Pennsylvania*, another battleship, had been sunk. Then the Japanese upped the ante, saying they had destroyed eleven ships including "four battleships, an aircraft carrier and six cruisers . . . more than 100 American airplanes." The White House stuck to their story of only a couple of ships being badly damaged and some planes being "put out of commission," although the number of dead had been upped to 1,500.[34] "Just what the condition is of the United States Pacific fleet is at the present time has not been revealed by Washington." FDR, however, did make a reference to "severe damage" in a press conference.[35]

About the only thing the White House would say about Pearl Harbor was that an old battleship had capsized and a destroyer was lost, along with some smaller ships. They did concede the damage "appears more serious than at first believed."[36]

Stephen Early announced that FDR would take to the airwaves on December 9 at 10:00 p.m. (EST) to lay out a "more complete documentation" of the events in Hawaii the previous Sunday. Roosevelt was scheduled to speak for half an hour, and it would be carried live on all networks nationwide.[37] His day on the ninth was occupied with reviewing reports and meeting with the military brass.

During the day on the ninth, the president held a press conference in which he "outlined in general terms a broad program for intensification of military production efforts." He also discussed the attacks in general details, but did not address any specifics, begging off until more information was forthcoming. He also bristled when the reasons for the attacks were brought up. According to one report, "Mr. Roosevelt resentfully remarked that neither he nor any member of Congress knew the reasons at present for the Japanese success in surprising the American defenders of Pearl Harbor. He was even more resentful when told that rumors were spreading that an important percentage of the Navy personnel in Pearl Harbor had been given week-end leaves." Reporters also pressed him on releasing war information.[38]

Within hours of the attack, hundreds of volunteer-staffed "Defense Centers" opened around the country. More popularly known as "canteens," they operated as a resting area for troops on their way to their posts.[39] Magazines and newspapers were available to peruse. Mostly women worked at these, serving coffee and doughnuts, giving out writing papers to the young G.I.s so they could write home. It was this way all over the country. In Atlanta, "hundreds of women of all ages, gray-haired grandmothers and young high school girls, swarmed into the American Women's Voluntary service headquarters."[40]

Meanwhile, the White House continued the drumbeat against Germany, claiming Berlin had "pushed" Tokyo into the attack as a way of cutting off Lend-Lease. FDR and Winston Churchill issued a joint statement saying the "Anti-Axis world" would prevail in the global conflict.[41] Churchill had just received word that ten RAF planes had been shot down over France, and renewed Nazi bombs rained down again on his war-torn island. German planes also sunk four commercial ships off the coast of Scotland.[42]

Washington was confronting the very real prospect of having to foot the bill for a worldwide war. Since early 1941, the country had been subsidizing the British, the Russians, the Free Chinese, the Free French, the Turks, and other anti-Axis powers under Lend-Lease. But now, the newest price tags were coming in and estimates as high as $150 billion to pay for the whole war were being floated. The cost of the final year of the "first World War" was approximately $18 billion as reported in the *Birmingham News*. This may have been the first public reference to the Great War as the "first,"[43] the implication being that America had just entered the second.

But the country was already paying for a new war and with heavy interest too. The first official casualty list from the Pacific was released from the War Department. The list of thirty-seven names included officers and enlisted men. The very first name released was Second Lieutenant Robert H. Markley. His nearest living kin was his father, Arthur H. Markley, of Nardin, Oklahoma. The first enlisted man was "Private Robert G. Allen. Nearest relative, Mrs. Sarah T. Allen, mother, Sims, Ind."[44] Ages were not given. They were all men, and nearly all came from the small towns and villages of America. Another casualty was Private Dean Cebert of Galesburg, Illinois. Also lost was a navy chaplain, Robert Carl Cornelius, of Buffalo, New York.[45] Of the thirty-seven initially announced dead, "six were commissioned officers, four of the Air Force and two of the infantry. All 31 enlisted men were of the Air Force."[46] The very same reporter for the Associated Press, Horace A. Lowe, who had the same sad job of reporting the initial casualties of the Great War now reported on the new American losses.[47]

Condolences from the government to the next of kin began arriving in mailboxes throughout the United States. The letters were personally signed, long, individually typed. "The adjutant general of the Army, in each case, notified the next of kin of the deep regret of the Secretary of War at the death of this soldier in the defense of his country."[48] Only later, with so many young boys killed and or missing in action, would Uncle Sam resort to Western Union telegrams, with hundreds of thousands of saddened parents and family members reading, "We deeply regret to inform you that your son . . ."

Elected officials also debated the duration and cost of the war, with some saying it could take up to six years. Senator Robert Taft said it might also cost the lives of 2 million young American boys. The Selective Service, with the permission of Congress, altered the draft laws to allow the military to keep in uniform all men for the duration of the war and for six months thereafter. No more two-year hitches.[49]

Everywhere, efforts to get Americans to purchase war bonds were stepped up. Eventually, they would become a part of the fabric of the society, appearing in movies and newsreels, endorsed by Hollywood celebrities, sports heroes, and other noteworthy Americans. Appeals screamed from posters on every bus and lamp post, in the lobbies of movie theatres, and from magazines and newspapers and on the radio. The U.S. Treasury pleaded with Americans to buy more defense bonds and stamps. "War needs money. It will cost money to defeat Japan. Buy defense bonds or stamps today. Buy them every day if you can."[50]

Everybody, it seemed, wanted to pitch into the war effort. In Texas, the senior class at Baird High School decided to forgo a planned class picnic and use the $37.50 instead to purchase bonds.[51] In New York, the Society of Composers, Authors and Publishers made an appeal to its membership to come up with patriotic songs of the kind heard during the Great War.[52] The government also announced plans to recruit private pilots to form a civil air patrol.[61]

On the byways of America, it was impossible for a man in uniform to wait for more than a few minutes while hitchhiking, even though hitchhiking was prohibited by the military. Volunteers poured forth from American Legion halls and from Boy Scout troops. The navy asked women to come forward and knit socks, turtlenecks, and watch caps. Sewing needles at the ready, they turned out by the thousands.

In Birmingham alone, over 600 men showed up to volunteer for military service in just a few hours, but officials estimated that less than 150 would qualify, because many were too young or too old, had dependents, had infirmities, or did not qualify because of the results of the findings of "mental tests." Those under twenty-one would have to get parental approval before they could join. The navy's recruiting offices nationwide were open twenty-four hours a day, seven days a week. Meanwhile, "veterans of the first World War and Spanish-American War insisted that they weren't too old."[54]

Men were attempting to enlist in large numbers all over the country. Boston's recruiting offices were overrun with cheering young men, and a thousand showed up at the navy's Federal Building offices. It was the same with the marines, the army, and the Coast Guard. Many waited for hours in line, "laughing, joking, discussing each new war bulletin," while tickets for food were handed out and women, from the Boston Red Cross, supplied the young men with coffee and doughnuts.[55]

City boys, who had once turned their noses up at military service, were clamoring for the chance to serve. LA was officially put on a war footing, and ironically, the Lindbergh Beacon atop City Hall was turned off, though not because the aviator was associated with anti-Roosevelt policies, but because the light would be an easy target and signal for enemy planes.[56] In Syracuse, New York, Chapman W. Schanandoah, thirty-five, "an Onondaga Indian, whose tribe, as one of the Six Nations of the Iroquois Confederacy, opposed the Selective Service Act, was among the naval volunteers."[57]

Detroit Tigers star Hank Greenberg, an army reservist, was expecting to be called up, as was heavyweight champ Joe Louis. Indeed, a day later Greenberg announced, "I'm going back in. We are in trouble and there is only one thing to do—return to the service." In doing so, he would be giving up a reported annual salary of $50,000.[58] Greenberg was a class act. So, too, was Louis, who was honored by Count Basie and Paul Robeson with his own song, "King Joe."[59]

In London, thousands of young American men who had joined the RAF or the British army were champing at the bit to get out of the English military and join in the fight against the Japanese. "The American Embassy was besieged with inquiries from Americans eager to get back home and fight in an American uniform."[60]

Farmers were now urged by the Department of Agriculture to plant "fence-post to fencepost" in order to feed and clothe a hungry army and navy and much of a hungry world. A premium was also put on cotton. Because of lost tax revenue, the government asked merchants—focusing on Alabama—to notify officials of excessive sales of sugar to the makers of down-home adult beverages. Joe Rollins, head of the U.S. Alcohol Unit, "announced . . . a plan to obtain cooperation of merchants in reporting sugar sales to moonshiners."[61] Officials also worried about shortages of dairy products in America because so much butter, eggs, and milk was being shipped to England under Lend-Lease.[62]

The AFL and the CIO pledged to do their utmost to put a halt to all wildcat strikes during the emergency.[63] A walkout in lumber yards around San Diego was canceled. Even John L. Lewis, head of the Mineworkers, a Roosevelt-basher and a Republican, offered his support to the war effort.[64] In Minneapolis, a dozen members of the Socialist Workers' Party were sentenced to sixteen months and one day in prison for advocating the overthrow of the U.S. government. They had promoted using violence in doing so.[65]

Some aggressive internationalists were arguing that the United States ought to go ahead and declare war on Germany and Italy. Syndicated columnist Dorothy Thompson penned, "We have got to dispose our common forces in a world war. Therefore, the only logical answer to Japan's declaration of war against us is to reply with a declaration of war against the Axis, for Japan's war is an Axis war."[66]

Indeed, buried in Henry Stimson's private papers donated to Yale University was a draft of a declaration of war against all three Axis powers and not just Japan.[67] Clearly, it had been hotly debated, but in the end, Roosevelt decided to declare war only on Japan, even as Winston Churchill had been nagging him about Europe and North Africa as well. FDR was being well served, however, by men like Cordell Hull and Stimson. He even got a fan telegram from an obscure New England newspaper publisher, William Loeb.[68] Another concluded his letter to Stimson saying, "V for Victory, and also for Veng[e]ance!"[69]

Henry Stimson had been secretary of war as a young man under

President William Howard Taft and again as an old man under President Franklin Delano Roosevelt. In between he'd been secretary of state under President Herbert Hoover. Handsome, distinguished, and mustachioed, Stimson had been a soldier and a statesman, serving both Republican and Democratic presidents. At one point, he'd even had a doctrine named after him. In 1936, he wrote a prophetically titled book, *The Far Eastern Crisis.*[70] He was born to wealth, attended Harvard and Yale, was Phi Beta Kappa, and could have lived the leisurely life of Jay Gatsby but instead devoted his life to public service. His wife, Mabel, was the granddaughter of Founding Father Roger Sherman, but Stimson himself could not father children, as a case of the mumps as an adult left him sterile.[71] Stimson loved his country and would come to be known as one of the greatest public servants in its history along with Ben Franklin, John Hay, Colonel Edward House, George Kennan, and John Foster Dulles.

Buried in the *New York Times* was a curious story, headlined "Anti-Japanese Society Aide Claims He Warned Stimson." It said, "Evidence that Japan was planning [the] thrust at the United States as long ago as late August was disclosed today by Kilsoo K. Haan, Washington representative of the Sino-Korean People's League, a volunteer anti-Japanese society. Mr. Haan released to *The New York Times* a copy of a letter he said he had sent to Secretary of War Henry L. Stimson on Oct. 28, in which Koki Hirota, former Foreign minister, was reported to have given members of the Black Dragon Society a rather accurate forecast of the hostilities and preparations therefore. Mr. Haan's letter said in part: 'Information: Hirota . . . now the 'big stick' of the Black Dragon Society, in their Aug. 26 meeting, told of the news that War Minister Tojo has ordered a total war preparation to meet the armed forces of the United States in this Pacific emergency. Tojo is said to have told him of the Navy's full support of his policy against America. The most suitable time to wage war with America is December, 1941, or February, 1942.'"[72]

There was never any evidence that Emperor Hirohito was aware of, or read, Franklin Roosevelt's eleventh-hour plea to renew the talks between the two aggrieved nations. In fact, the Japanese government refused to acknowledge that they had even received it and, as with all diplomatic cables, it was supposed to be sent via the ambassador of record in a given country, in this case, Joseph Grew.[73] On Saturday the sixth, Grew was listening to a broadcast radio, out of San Francisco. The signal was so strong it could be heard all the way to the American embassy in Tokyo. Grew was startled to hear a news report about an important message sent to Hirohito from the president, which had been released to the American media, but knew nothing about it himself. He told his staff that the radio transmission from the State Department may have been deliberately interfered with.[74]

Had Hirohito received FDR's message the evening of December 6 and been moved by it, he certainly had it in his power to recall the fleet heading for Pearl Harbor. The Japanese people did not even know, for several hours after, of the attack by their country on American and British military forces. Around the time of the attack, a Tokyo radio station was broadcasting a lecture by a university professor on "Good Morals."[75]

Two days later, the text of the message from FDR to the Japanese emperor on December 6, which was nothing but solicitous, respectful, and worried, was released by Washington. It spoke of the long friendship between the two countries. Grace Tully said it had been drafted by Cordell Hull himself.[76]

Of course, it was pure State Departmentese, flowery, fulsome, excessive, and effusive when a little more plain and blunt talk might have caught the attention of Tokyo. American presidents had fought for years with the stuff churned out by the striped-pants set at the State Department, and FDR was no exception. He knew when it was time to be solicitous and time to hit an opponent over the head with a two by four. Still, there was never any evidence that Hirohito ever saw the missive; he had the same problem as FDR: too many meddlesome bureaucrats.

Washington was bracing for both Japan and Germany to widen the war quickly. In the Pacific, commercial vessels were warned to be on the lookout for Japanese ships, and mines littered the sea routes and harbors. In the North Atlantic, officials were expecting the Germans to step up operations there. "Official observers in the capital expect the Japanese action to be followed by an all-out German attack in the Atlantic, with German submarines operating near the United States coasts."[77]

The Optimists Club was appropriately meeting as scheduled at the Mayflower Hotel at 12:30 on December 9. They had much to consider.[78] Almost forgotten for a moment in America was the war raging on the European and African continents, so focused were Americans on the new war in the Pacific, where thousands of Japanese troops were landing daily at Manila and Japanese planes were conducting an unremitting bombing raid. A CBS correspondent there said it was a "bad dream." Midway Island was also still under attack as of the eighth, while Japanese radio was claiming they had taken Wake Island and Guam.[79]

Two days after the coordinated attack, the Axis power was still laying waste to the men and materiel of the American military. In Guam, a wire story said the Japanese had sunk the navy minesweeper *Penguin*, all 840 tons of her. There were survivors, but in the battle to take Guam, civilian employees of Pan-American Airways had been killed.[80] Guam's garrison was practically nonexistent, "virtually defenseless."[81] Guam had been discovered by Magellan in 1521, and under the Treaty of Paris ending the Spanish-American War in 1898, it became a U.S. possession.

An old American aircraft carrier, the *Langley*, was also rumored to have been attacked while in Philippine waters, but then it was later revealed that the ship had not been hit.[82] Japanese forces, though, had apparently landed on the Philippine island of Lubang. It was reported the invading force was assisted by Japanese fishermen.[83]

Thailand had already surrendered.[84] The Japanese were also prosecuting the war farther south, attacking Australian outposts, and had renewed their bombing of Singapore as well. Hong Kong was bombed twice on the eighth.[85] Japanese civilians in Singapore "gathered in leading . . . hotels and geisha houses and indulged in boisterous drinking parties," so excited at the looming Japanese bombing of the city.[86]

The newspapers were loaded with bad news from the Pacific. A foreign correspondent, Vincent Sheehan, who had just returned from the Far East, told an audience at Bryn Mawr College that America was staring at defeat. The United States, he said, will "have the greatest humiliation in its history" when the citizens learned of the "staggering number of . . . battleships lost" in the attack. "I'm telling you, responsible people in Washington expected last night that eastern cities would be bombed." A report was circulating that Germany was planning to attack the United States without a formal declaration of war.[87]

The postmortems on December 7 were starting to roll in, and they were uniformly bad for the U.S. military and especially Adm. Husband E. Kimmel, commander of the Pacific fleet at Pearl Harbor, and Gen. Walter Short, in charge of the army forces stationed in Hawaii. The country needed scapegoats and unfortunately for these two men with exemplary careers, it would fall to them to eventually take the blame, though they had been as caught in the dark as much as anyone else in the military or the civilian government.

On December 7 and 8, the media attention focused on Kimmel was universally positive. The *Baltimore Sun* called him "two-fisted . . . a reputation of being one of the toughest in the service." Kimmel, fifty-nine, had been appointed commander in chief of the Pacific Fleet on February 1, 1940. His commendable service record was there for all to see and no one in the hours after the attack said anything against him.[88] At least publicly. But this would change rapidly. Within hours and with no evidence, Congressman John Dingell of Detroit took to the floor of the House and called for his court martial.[89]

Dingell "proposed to demand that court-martial proceedings be instituted against . . . Lt. Gen. Walter C. Short . . . Maj. Gen. H.H. Arnold . . . Maj. Gen. George Brett . . . and Admiral Husband Kimmel, commander of the Pacific fleet."[90]

The halfcocked Dingell, after some vicious comments about the services, had to be reeled in and reprimanded by Congressman Alfred Lee Bulwinkle of North Carolina, who said, "It is the patriotic duty of every American, especially every congressman, to be guarded in his words in order not to give aid and comfort to the enemy." Bulwinkle was met with applause on the House floor, in violation of decorum.[91] Vague party lines were forming, with some Republicans defending Kimmel and some Democrats pummeling him.

But others in Congress were already asking navy personnel uncomfortable questions, including wanting them to "explain how Japanese penetrated

Hawaiian defenses."[92] The House Naval Affairs Committee requested that Adm. Harold Stark, chief of Naval Operations and navy secretary Frank Knox appear before a hearing on the tenth to discuss what happened in the Pacific. Stories that a "large portion of the Pacific fleet has been wiped out" floated across the nation's capital.[93] Conspiracy theories began to circulate among isolationists that FDR had let the attack happen to bring America into the war. Although now debunked by the facts, those theories persist to the present day. FDR's anguish at the attack seemed sincere enough; aides and confidants have since reported in their memoirs that the president pounded the table as he pored over Pearl Harbor damage assessments, agonizing over every loss, demanding to know how this could have happened to his beloved navy.

People wanted to know why planes were helplessly lined up wingtip to wingtip, making it easy for Japanese bombers and fighters to destroy en masse. Others wanted to know what had happened with the newfangled radar that had recently been installed on Oahu that was supposed to pick up large scale numbers of planes, or why the spotting stations failed to note the large numbers of Japanese planes, or how a flotilla of Japanese ships had crossed thousands of miles undetected.

Yet another postmortem delved into the psychology of attacking America on a Sunday, speculating it was a way in which to adversely affect American morale. Plus, it was the optimum time in which to attack, as "the custom of the American military services to grant as much leave as possible on Sundays and rest at ease in barracks or aboard ship."[94]

Some recounted the time of an earlier naval battle between the United States and Japan in 1863. An American sloop, the *Wyoming*, was approaching the coast of Japan. Three Japanese ships with superior firepower engaged the *Wyoming*, but due to the better marksmanship of the Americans, they won the contest.

Another take on the "Who shot John?" aspect of the new war came from the *New York Times*, a take more sympathetic to the Japanese point of view than the Grey Lady's readers probably shared: "Throughout this year the crisis developed, with Japan always reaching out farther. The United States froze all Japanese credits in this country, cut off her supplies of oil, scrap iron and other war materials, and stopped buying Japanese silk. Britain and the

Netherlands Indies followed suit. These economic measures were followed by military moves in which the country strengthened its forces in Hawaii, Manila and other Pacific bases, and the British sent a fleet to Singapore, with both countries shipping heavy strength in bombing planes to the Far East. As these measures tightened, Japan protested against economic strangulation and military encirclement."[95]

The Japanese had also signed the Tripartite Pact with the Axis powers in September of 1940, had invaded Manchuria in 1931, invaded East China in 1937, quit the League of Nations in 1933, signed the anti-Comintern pact with the Third Reich, sunk an American naval ship on the Yangtze River in 1937, engaged in a military buildup, occupied French Indochina, and through her fascist government had become increasingly hostile to the West.

It was becoming increasingly clear why the Japanese had struck, or some so thought. In short, the Japanese saw the American and British military presences in the Pacific and the Far East as threats to the desires for an empire that exceeded the home islands of Japan. It was also becoming clear that Japan, in the twentieth century, had never troubled herself with actually declaring war before attacking an opponent. In 1904, her navy attacked the Russian Fleet at Port Arthur before war was declared. In 1931 she struck at Manchuria, in 1932 at Shanghai, and in 1937 at Peiping without warning.

The details of Secretary of State Cordell Hull's meeting with Ambassador Kichisaburo Nomura and Special Envoy Saburo Kurusu of two days earlier were just beginning to be made clear to the American people, along with the documents they had handed him after Japan had attacked Pearl Harbor.

Hull, seventy, was a courtly gentleman, a career diplomat respected on both sides of the aisle for his acumen and calm demeanor. Not this time. The extraordinarily long "Memorandum" given Hull accused America of wanting war while Japan wanted "world peace." The duplicity and revisionism was astonishing. The document stated, "Ever since [the] China affair broke out owing to the failure on the part of China to comprehend Japan's true intentions . . ." In point of fact, Japan had invaded the sovereign country of China four years earlier, and in the process, had butchered thousands of innocent civilians. As far as the Chinese were concerned, there was no misunderstanding. They understood perfectly well what the Japanese military was up to. The Japanese accused Washington of "impractical principles" while applauding themselves for signing the Tripartite Pact with Germany and Italy in the interest of peace. They also criticized the United States for objecting "to settle international issues through military pressure" but rather attacked America for "pressure by economic power." Hull's frustration with Japan had been growing for months. Some afternoons he liked to relax over a game of croquet. But each time he hit his ball, he would yell "Japan" in frustration.[97]

Hull digested the long, mendacity-laden document and then exploded. "In all my 50 years of public service I have never seen a document that was more crowded with infamous falsehoods and distortions—infamous falsehoods and distortions on a scale so huge that I never imagined until today that any government on this planet was capable of uttering them."[98]

That was during the day of December 7. That evening, around 6:00 p.m., he blasted the Japanese again for the "treacherous and utterly unprovoked attack upon the United States."[99]

The details of the proposal Hull had made to the Japanese were also revealed; in exchange for withdrawal of their forces from China and Indochina and for signing a nonaggression pact with other Pacific powers, America would release frozen Japanese assets, sign a new trade agreement with the Japanese, and lift the trade embargo. The Japanese rejected the offer outright.[100]

And now eighty-eight years of an uneasy friendship that had existed between the two countries since Commodore Matthew Perry sailed into Tokyo harbor in 1853 was over. Before that historic meeting, Japan had been under self-imposed isolation for more than two hundred years, turning away all would-be suitors. Perry's hailed diplomacy was the beginning of an "Open Door Policy" and trade, and good relations had flourished between the two countries. When war broke out between Japan and Russia in 1904 (during which Japan also attacked without a declaration of war), America made favorable loans to Tokyo. And at the Portsmouth Peace Conference in 1905, President Theodore Roosevelt "was a strong factor in the favorable peace terms won by Japan."[101] Roosevelt later won the Nobel Peace Prize for his actions at Portsmouth.[102]

Along with Japanese nationals, German and Italian nationals came under greater government scrutiny. The Federal Bureau of Investigation announced the initial arrest of 350 "dangerous aliens," including 300 Germans and 50 Italians "listed for arrest."[103] Police in the Canal Zone began to detain Italians and Germans along with Japanese nationals.[104] In Alabama, seven individuals were deemed "dangerous aliens"; five Germans, one Italian, and one Japanese were arrested. The policy coming out of Washington was "that all aliens, especially Japanese, were under the strictest observation of government agents."[105]

Francis Biddle, the attorney general, declared "hearing boards"[106] would be arranged to consider the case of some Japanese picked up, but he also cautioned, "'Even in the present emergency, there are persons of Japanese extraction whose loyalty is unquestioned,' he added that it would therefore be 'a serious mistake' to take any action against these persons and asked State and local authorities not to take such action in their communities without consulting the Department of Justice."[107]

The FBI disclosed that by the ninth, "700 to 1,000 Japs [had been] locked up as 'dangerous to security.'" It was also revealed that 391 Japanese had been arrested in Hawaii, and 345 on the mainland had been arrested in the hours after the bombing of Pearl Harbor. They were placed in "temporary detention stations, principally on the West Coast."[108]

The Home Office in London also declared it was arresting Japanese nationals, starting with the staff members of Domei, the government-owned propaganda agency. Going further, the British issued an order for "all Japanese over the age of 16" to "report as soon as possible to the nearest police station" and produce "their registration certificates."[109]

In the United States, the Civil Aeronautics Authority ordered all commercial airlines to not allow Japanese nationals to purchase tickets or fly with them.[110]

In Los Angeles, as in every other major and minor city in America, efforts to deal with Japanese nationals accelerated. In that city alone, it was estimated there were some forty to fifty thousand Japanese. "A military quarantine was set up around Terminal Island, in Los Angeles Harbor, home of a large Japanese fishing fleet." Traffic was prohibited from entering or leaving the island, and fishing boats were ordered back to their docks, where government officials took control.[111] Maps, binoculars, and radios in the possession of Japanese were ordered confiscated. "Stop all Japanese" was the standing order.[112]

It was the same in San Francisco. The city instituted "a special squad of fifty extra policemen" to guard "the Japanese colony, which covers thirty-six square blocks and has about 7,000 residents. Agents of the FBI picked up a small group for questioning."[113] But one *New York Times* story suggested the FBI initially had a plan to incarcerate all Japanese living in America.[114]

Because of the heavy concentration of war industries in California, combined with the large Japanese population, officials worried about the possibility of sabotage, and extra security was ordered around all plants. Mrs. Roosevelt had already jumped into the whole issue of how Japanese, Italian, and German Americans would be treated, saying, "She saw absolutely no reason why Japanese with 'good' records—meaning 'no criminal nor anti-American record'—had anything to fear." Biddle did say, however, that the mass arrests of Japanese citizens in the Canal Zone and Hawaii were inevitable.[115]

Though large numbers of Japanese were rounded up nationwide, the government said it was interested in only a small number of potential threats to American security among the thousands. "The alien census last year listed about 92,000 Japanese, 90 percent of who live on the West Coast, and for months the F. B. I. has been preparing a list of those to be picked up immediately in the event of war." The Alien Census Act also provided for the fines, imprisonment, and deportation of any Japanese who failed to register. In 1941, Washington had far more powers to deal with Japanese than it did in 1917 to deal with Germans living in America.[116]

From corner to corner of the country, pledges of fidelity to the war effort came from labor groups, corporations, Filipinos in Los Angeles, "Americans of Korean descent," and the Japanese-American Citizens League.[117] The Japanese diplomats in many of the consulates in the United States were truly astonished at their country's actions, and many openly questioned their own government. The Japanese Consul General in San Francisco, Joshio Muto, called the attack "unimaginable."[118] Kenji Nakauchi, the general consul in Los Angeles, actually apologized for his country's actions. "What can I say except that I am quite sorry!" When asked about roundups and internment camps, he said he saw "no reason why thousands of Japanese should be imprisoned." Nakauchi pointed out that Germans and Italians in Vancouver were not imprisoned when Canada went to war with the Axis powers.[119]

Ashamed of his country's actions, one Japanese national attempted hari-kari by cutting himself with "a pocketknife and with a needle." Matsuabo Matushita told police, "My country has done wrong attacking the United States of America." It was reported, "[T]he wounds were slight."[120]

A news report in the *Evening Star* said, "It is extremely difficult for Americans to distinguish their enemy, the Japanese, from their friends, the Chinese," according to a Smithsonian anthropologist, Dr. Ales Hrdlicka. Only after a period of time, he said, can Anglos tell the difference by "facial expressions, mannerisms and ways of speech." He said they, along with Filipinos, "all came from the same Mongoloid stock and have the same general physical characteristics." Several Chinese in Washington had been embarrassed since the war started by being mistaken for being Japanese. A Chinese reporter arrived at the White House with a note pinned to his lapel that read, "Chinese reporters—not Japanese—please."[121]

In New York, Chinese-Americans received buttons to wear to distinguish them from Japanese nationals. The blue buttons were distributed by the United Chinese Relief and proclaimed, "Thumbs up for China." It was reported that "many Chinese, mistaken for Japanese, had been mishandled."[122] A full-page ad appeared, sponsored by United China Relief calling for the defeat of Japan. Officials of the organization included Pearl S. Buck, John D. Rockefeller III, David O. Selznick, Wendell L. Willkie, and Mrs. Franklin D. Roosevelt.[123]

The FBI seized the offices of Japan's Consulate General on Fifth Avenue to "begin impounding papers and records." Morito Morishima, head of the office, was interrogated by the agents and his possessions examined. In those, agents with the "alien and sabotage squads" found "twenty film negatives of scenes in New York and Washington," including "the Washington monument, bridges in Washington and New York, and the New York skyline . . . and one that appeared to be of a dam or reservoir."[124]

Attorney General Biddle, concerned over the "wholesale arrests" of Japanese aliens, issued a statement saying that only the FBI could make such arrests[125] and any suspicion of nefarious activities should be reported to the local FBI office. U.S. attorneys were instructed to pass the message along to state and local authorities to let the FBI handle the Japanese roundup.

Apparently the FBI had been making lists of Japanese aliens for months.

Across the country there was an outpouring of volunteers. Dozens of armed men showed up at the Hall of Justice in Los Angeles, reacting to an erroneous radio story that said the Civilian Defense Council asked them to come forward.[126] Units of the State Guard were activated, and the Armory in Los Angeles was put under twenty-four-hour guard.[127] The Motion Picture Producers Association "made available scores of studio trucks for the detail."[128] New York police were overrun when they put out a call for airplane spotters, and "40,000 civilian observers" went on "24-hour duty" in "13 East Coast States."[129] The acting mayor of New York, Newbold Morris, told listeners they could expect a "'token visit' from Axis bombers at any time."[130]

The navy's intelligence office in Los Angeles was sealed up tighter than a drum, and the uninvited were turned away, albeit politely. But down the hall were the navy's public relations offices, whose doors were wide open. "Well, after all, there is a difference between the Navy's intelligence office and its publicity bureaus," a reporter wryly noted.[131] However, with the new flood of enlistees, what the navy needed more than anything else were good typists.

The navy banned cables to and from Hawaii and the Philippines, and Uncle Sam banned outright the sending of any news whatsoever to Japan, Germany, Italy, and Finland.[132] The Service also asked the press to take care in stories given to them by the next of kin about servicemen who had been killed or wounded, or about the location of their current billet. And never were the names of ships to be published in connection with any sailor. "Voluntary censorship" was bandied about, but the government also warned of enforcing the 1918 Espionage Act.[133]

State and local agencies swung into service quickly, motivated as much by fear, anger, and disinformation as patriotism. Defense preparations were being organized in every city, town, village, and hamlet of America. Volunteer guards were placed around utilities. Judges and magistrates swore in citizens to pledge to defend America. Police stations were swarmed with volunteers.

A volunteer auxiliary police force was forming in Los Angeles, with thirty thousand citizens wanting to sign up.[134]

The dome to the state house in Sacramento was blacked out, and all forest lookout stations went on a 24/7 basis.[135] The Boulder Dam was also put under twenty-four-hour guard, and Route 93, which crossed over the dam, was closed to traffic.[136] New York mayor Fiorello LaGuardia, head of Washington's Civil Defense program, issued a six-point program for "civilians in areas subject to possible aerial bombing." Rule Number One was "Keep Cool. Above all, keep cool. Don't lose your head."[137] People stopped working to listen to war news, colleges let students out of class to listen to speeches by FDR, and pedestrians gathered around parked cars to listen to the radio. The war was everywhere and was quickly being injected deeply into the body politic of America.

And yet life went on. Hedda Hopper's Hollywood gossip columns appeared nationwide, Americans went to movies, went to work, went to church, went on with their lives, albeit with a shadow looming over all people and all activities.

"There's a war on!" was a refrain that was only beginning to be heard. Movie theatres began to paint over the upper lights of their marquees in order to lessen the chance of them being seen from the air. People were spending a lot more time looking up in the sky. Women's silk stockings—"a prized possession this year"—were still available at J.J. Haggarty Department Store in Los Angeles, but this wouldn't last.[138]

Nash was touting their newest car, claiming it would get "25 to 30 miles on a gallon!" and had air conditioning.[139] Marriage announcements and marriages and Christmas parties continued. Advice columns, such as "The Gentler Sex" by Malvina Lindsay, informed women readers of "the desperate wife who decides to have an affair because of her husband's infidelity."[140] It foreshadowed the sea change in sexual attitudes and activity on the home front, when men went off to war and left their wives and girlfriends behind. After the war, when confronted with pregnant wives, many returning GIs never properly did the math and assumed that the babies were theirs.

Meanwhile, frostbite sailing races were still being held on the Chesapeake, Christmas shopping went on, women still bought fashionable shoes, men bought pipes and trench coats and "snoots" at Macy's and jewelry for their wives at Garfinckel's department store, accidents happened involving drivers and pedestrians. The Women's Pages (later known in the post-war world as "Style" sections) carried new recipes and fashion tips. One advice columnist, Dorothy Dix, admonished her female readers, "Men are slaves to beauty, yet when they marry they pass looks up."[141] Babe Ruth signed a movie deal with Metro-Goldwyn Mayer to appear in a film about his former teammate, Lou Gehrig.[142]

Yet there would be a real and tangible and permanent change in America. "Textiles, wool and cotton goods will become scarce," cited the *Wall Street Journal*.[143] The paper noted that soon leather would also be in short supply.

The paper forecast what no one else in journalism had yet. A radical change in America was coming. "War with Japan means industrial revolution in the United States. The American productive machine will be reshaped with but one purpose—to produce the maximum of things needed to defeat the enemy. It will be a brutal process. It implies intense, almost fantastic stimulation for some industries; strict rationing for others; inevitable, complete liquidation for a few."[144]

Americans would also have to learn to do without or with less—or find another source or substitute—of products that had come in from the Far East. "Primarily, these are rubber and tin. Secondarily, there is coconut oil, tungsten, chromium, copra, tung oil, palm oil, manila hemp, jute, graphite. Sugar too.[145] Civilian use of Copper, Lead, Zinc and other vital metals to disappear."[146] The nonmilitary use of copper, as an example, was prohibited or severely curtailed for "building supplies and hardware, house furnishings and equipment: dress accessories: jewelry, gifts and novelties: burial equipment: automotive, trailer and tractor equipment, and a miscellaneous list which runs from fire-fighting apparatus, toys, beauty parlor equipment, barber shop supplies, bicycles, chimes, bells, keys, and a host of other items." Five hundred and fifty thousand tons of copper would be needed for shell casings and cartridges in 1942.[147]

Chrome would also shortly be curtailed. It was used for automobile bumpers, bun warmers, toasters, coffee thermoses, irons, and had dozens of other nonmilitary applications. Welders, who had threatened a strike, now called for burning their American Federation of Labor membership cards.[148]

American housewives tossed in the sponge when told there would be a severe curtailment of sponges. Not only would the war cause disruption in supply, but a blight in the Atlantic had wiped out whole beds. Back then, sponges were not made synthetically.

During the American embargo of Japan, the administration had decided not to include oil, as the country was wholly dependent upon oil imports from the United States and cutting it off might cause too much shock to the Japanese economy. All bets were off now, on that score, but no matter. Because of frugal policies, Japan had a stockpile, according to estimates, of up to a two-years' supply of the precious liquid.[149]

The shipping schedules for commercial ships were radically changed to suit the new priorities. First, they would no longer be published in the newspapers. Second, the war effort took priority. Also, because of the war conditions in the South Pacific, it would take twice as long for merchant ships to traverse the distance due to the presence of Japanese submarines. Also, the military expected a 50 percent reduction in the transport of nonmilitary items.[150] The government announced "secret plans" to secure defense factories from saboteurs under the Plant Protective Service.[151] Aviation fuel took a front seat to refined gas for the civilian population. Because of the high performance nature of aircraft engines, they required additional lead in the gas to prevent what could be dangerous engine knocking, which meant the American car driver could look forward to their engines knocking for the duration of the emergency.

The industrial might of America had been ramping up for the past year, due to Lend-Lease, but now it would be turned up several more notches. A beneficiary of American generosity was the Free French government led by Charles de Gaulle, which a day after everyone else declared war on Japan.[152]

Yet there was a spiritual change to the country as well. "The tentacles of a great crisis are reaching down into the hearts and minds of all the people. And the full measure of the impacts upon the nation can be determined only with realization that a great international crisis has come to force readjustments in the lives and thoughts of all individuals."[153]

The attack changed American attitudes and outlooks forever. Since the end of the Great War, America had become an increasing isolationist country, and it was reflected in her policies of high tariffs and tight immigration policies, as well as the Neutrality Acts of the 1930s. Americans told themselves that they were protected by two great oceans and nothing could ever befall their homeland. Columnist Walter Lippmann called the image of us sitting comfortably isolated and protected by the oceans a "deadly delusion."[154]

The war in Europe often seemed very far away, with little impact on the daily lives of American citizens. But now, there was a new unity in the land not seen in its history. The factionalism that had been a hallmark of Americanism had dissipated. "Behind this determination stand not alone the members of our government. Behind it, dedicated with them to the extirpation of the counterpart in the Pacific of the criminal architects of ruin, pillage and slaughter in Europe, stand a people united as never before."[155]

It was war. "This is the World War in the complete and literal meaning of the words—a war which can end only in our victory or in our defeat."[156]

Deep in some newspapers of America it was reported that German embassy officials in Washington were burning papers as "bits of charred paper floated down" to the street. A truck arrived to deliver brown wrapping paper. A "society reporter" visited the embassy, and the charge d'affaires, Hans Thomsen, said, "Have you come to say goodbye?" To which she replied, "Well, have I?" Thomsen demurred, only saying it was "a little premature."[157]

In Berlin, an official of the Third Reich told the Associated Press that his country was preparing to issue a "clarifying statement" on the war between the United States and the empire of Japan.[158] The spokesman said America had been the aggressor in the Pacific, and according to the terms of the Tri-Partite Pact, Germany and Italy were duty bound to come to the assistance of their ally. Secretary of State Cordell Hull jumped into the fray and said he, too, had heard rumors that Germany was about to declare war on America.[159] The White House announced that FDR was going to address not only the Pacific but Europe in his radio broadcast, including a "Nazi pattern." Elaborating, the *Washington Evening Star* reported, "There was a strong implication . . . that

Mr. Roosevelt's words tonight will be virtually a declaration of war against Nazi Germany."[160]

And then a reporter for NBC, David Anderson in Stockholm, broadcast a story in which he "predicted" Germany would declare war on the United States "within a few hours."[161] He elaborated, saying that American embassy officials in Berlin were already evacuating. And unconfirmed reports said a meeting was planned the next day in the Reichstag. A performance in the Kroll Opera House in Berlin was canceled because this was where the Reichstag met.[162]

CHAPTER 10

THE TENTH OF DECEMBER

"US Warships in Battle Off Manila, Berlin Says"

Sun

"Roosevelt Sees a Long, World-Wide War;
Japanese Invade Luzon, Fight in Manila;
2 Big British Warships Sunk, Tokyo Says"

New York Times

"Japs Sink Two British Dreadnaughts"

Birmingham News

Franklin Roosevelt appeared in good spirits and good health to the reporters who filed into the Oval Office. FDR was dressed in a grey suit, white shirt, black tie, and black armband for his mother, Sara, who'd died the previous September. "He was smoking a cigarete [*sic*] in an ivory holder . . . and he chatted smilingly with correspondents."[1] "He looks fine," one reporter whispered to another and it was noted "there were no haggard lines in his face. His color was good. There was about him a calm confidence." Another was heard to say, "He thrives on activity—and he has plenty of it now."[2]

He'd been confined to a wheelchair for years, only occasionally using the painful leg braces when in public. In all of his years in the presidency, he'd only been photographed in the wheelchair maybe three times. Secret Service men routinely confiscated photographs and negatives, and the White House press corps was in on the cover-up, berating new members not to photograph the crippled and confined president.[3]

The security around FDR had increased appreciably, as reporters were asked repeatedly to show their press credentials before being allowed into the briefing with the president.[4] Yet by that evening during a long radio broadcast, the wear and burden of the war and the long day showed in his face. The stress of the war years with its never-ending long days and long nights, combined with his endless smoking of Camel cigarettes, contributed mightily to FDR's decline in health. Several years into the war, a young reporter assigned to the White House beat was appalled during his first day on the job when he realized the haggard, sallow-skinned decrepit man sitting before him was the president of the United States.[5]

But at the dawn of the war, and flexing his new powers, FDR issued a proclamation saying that "all alien enemies are enjoined to preserve the peace . . . and to refrain from crime against the public safety and from violating the laws . . . and to refrain from actual hostility or giving aid or comfort to the enemies of the United States." It was also noted that "violators [would] be interned."[6] Japanese subjects were prohibited from leaving Hawaii, and local military commanders in the battle zones were given wide latitude to imprison those they deemed a threat.[7] Nationals from all three countries who were in America were "liable" as far as the government was concerned, especially Japanese because "an invasion had been perpetrated upon the territory of the United States by the Empire of Japan."[8]

The edict put a halt to the process for nearly 500,000 Japanese, German, and Italians wanting to live or stay in the United States. J. Edgar Hoover was keeping FDR apprised of the FBI's efforts, via Maj. Gen. Edwin M. Watson. "I thought it might be of interest to the President and you to have the inclosed [sic] charts before you, which show the number of Japanese, German and Italian aliens taken into custody by the FBI as of December 9. This gives the exact location of the number apprehended and places at which they were apprehended." The memo was accompanied by a detailed chart of the forty-eight states, denoting pickups.[9]

The administration was also getting ready to ask Congress for virtually unrestricted powers, including the ability to send arms and other support materiel to any country fighting the Axis powers and not just against Japan.[10] The White House was seeking nothing less than authoritarian powers in the conduct of war. It went even further.

With the help of the Federal Communications Commission and the War Department, the White House in essence nationalized the nation's radio industry. "President Roosevelt signed an executive order late today . . . to designate radio facilities for use, control or closure by the War or Navy Departments. . . . The effect of the order is to give the Government freedom to step in and supervise directly or make use of all radio facilities of the Nation."[11] The order also allowed "other agencies of the government" to step in and take control of private radio broadcasting facilities.[12]

FDR was drawing broad support from many corners. Gen. John J. "Black Jack" Pershing, America's only five-star general, still on the active duty roster at the age of eighty-one, sent the president a letter, offering his services. FDR responded kindly, calling him "magnificent. I am deeply grateful to you . . . under a wise law, you have never been placed on the retired list."[13]

A dispute among constitutional scholars broke out over exactly when America went to war with Japan, fueled by FDR's language proclaiming "a state of war has existed" even though Congress had not formally declared war on Japan at the time. Most agreed that a state of war did not come into actual existence until 4:10 p.m. on the eighth, when the president actually signed the proclamation of war. Whatever the variances, all agreed that the president's powers were now vastly expanded. "Statutes which operate in such periods authorize the President to take over transportation systems, industrial plants, radio stations, power facilities and ships, and place some controls on communications systems," reported the *New York Times*.[14]

The mobilization of the political and business class to fight a highly industrialized global war, combined with the concentration of power into the hands of the commander in chief, was profoundly changing what had once been Fortress America. It marked the beginning of what would later be known as the Imperial Presidency. The expansion of presidential powers in response to Pearl Harbor also presaged the postwar National Security State, in which civil liberties were sometimes curtailed. This was all to come. But in December 1941, it was already clear to ordinary and powerful citizens alike that a major shift in American society was under way and that the republic as originally envisioned by the Founding Fathers was giving way to something different.

A quote from Alexander Hamilton from *Federalist 74* was bandied about to support the contention that wartime conditions allowed for the expansion of executive powers: "The direction of war implies the direction of common strength; and the power of directing and employing the common strength forms an unusual and essential part in the definition of the executive authority."[15]

Most believed President Roosevelt now had enhanced and broaden powers not only over the military but the citizenry, the economy, and labor as well. One euphemistic new example: "The Secretary of War may rent any building in the District of Columbia."[16] In other words, the federal government now had the right to commandeer private property. Indeed, in his press conference, FDR suggested that a seven-day workweek in the war industries might be necessary and proposed convening a conference of business and labor to discuss the matter. The word *parley* was used, but in fact there would be little to discuss.[17] He also floated the idea of a "Conference on the Defense of [the] Western Hemisphere."[18] Also proposed was the notion of "enforced savings" of the average worker that would automatically deduct "10 to 15 percent of all income and wages."[19]

The issue of who exactly was an American also came up in debate. The law said Japanese could not become naturalized citizens "under provisions of the act of Feb 18, 1875 amending the act of July 14, 1870 limiting naturalization to white persons or those of African descent." Open to question was whether a child born in America, of Japanese parentage—*called "Nisei"*—was considered a naturalized American.[20]

The government was now monitoring or restricting the movements of over 1 million individuals, virtually all of Japanese, German, and Italian heritage. As of the tenth, the attorney general's office said they had now picked up over one thousand foreign nationals. FDR's proclamation instituting prohibitions on those still roaming free, including the ability to possess a firearm, "ammunition, bombs, explosives or material used in the manufacture of explosives; shortwave radio receiving sets; transmitting sets; signal devices; codes or ciphers; cameras; papers; documents or books in which there may be invisible writing; photograph, sketch, picture, drawing, map or graphical representation of any military or naval installations." The directive went on with even more specifics and restrictions.[21] Arrests continued. "A Japanese was seized near Oakland Airport and another was arrested near the scene of an early morning fire in Oakland."[22]

Hawaii had the same concerns, only magnified. The territorial governor, Joseph Poindexter, who'd been appointed by FDR, worried about "the conduct of Hawaii's 37,000 Japanese aliens and 100,000 American-born Japanese."[23]

Also open to question was how to deal with approximately fifty Japanese diplomats still in the country. Cordell Hull made an appeal to a neutral European country to act as the go-between involving the two warring countries.

American diplomats were still in Tokyo as well, including Ambassador Joseph Grew. There was also the matter of approximately five thousand Americans on Japanese soil. But there were only a few neutral countries in the world now, including Switzerland, Spain, Portugal, and Sweden.[24]

Tokyo meanwhile announced there were 1,270 Americans, British, Canadians, and Australian citizens in Japan.

In reply, the Japanese announced they would abide by the Geneva Convention and allow U.S., British, and Canadian diplomats safe passage to a neutral port of call.[25] But the Japanese government also announced it had arrested one hundred American and British nationals.[26] Thousands of other noncombatant Americans were spread throughout the War Zone, and the British government reminded the Japanese government of the Conventions and the Geneva Protocol of 1925 strictures against the use of chemical weapons.

Allies rounded up initially 25,000 Japanese in Davao in the Philippines and another 100,000 at Bilibid prison in Manila. In Davao, Japanese "have submitted peaceably. Some appeared voluntarily at concentration centers."[27]

Also worrisome for Washington was that while few of her naval officers spoke Japanese, "a vast number of [Japan's] military officers ... speak English. This is bound to give Nippon an edge in questioning war prisoners, translating intercepted messages and in obtaining information from material found on men fallen in action."[28]

The questions were why did it happen and how did it happen? Pearl Harbor had often been referred to by the navy as "the Gibraltar of the Pacific."[29] Just one day before the attack, Secretary of the Navy Frank Knox had issued a statement saying the navy was ready.[30] It was more than just being "backstabbers-in-the-dark," as the *Los Angeles Times* described the new enemy.[31] Senator Burton Wheeler of Montana said the Japanese "must have gone crazy."[32] Winston Churchill had warned for more than a month that the Pacific was a powder keg waiting to explode.

Pearl Harbor was a vitally important outpost for the American military and thus a direct threat to Japan's designs on an empire stretching up and down the Asian east coast and spreading into the Philippines and the Pacific. This answered some of the why, although it was far more complicated. After all, the Japanese had already invaded China, Manchuria, and French-Indo China, and many presumed America would also tolerate the invasion of Thailand. Deeper issues were involved.

Why did the Japanese attack America and Great Britain? One answer was the character of the military men running Japan. "These men are the most reactionary school. They have long been practically at grips with Emperor Hirohito, trying to divest him of actual state authority, reduce him to helpless isolation in the palace, and to restore an aristocratic regime tantamount to the old-time Shogunate under which for 250 years, ending around 1870, Japan was locked away from the outside world."[33]

The biggest fascist of all, Prime Minister Hideki Tojo, was the majordomo in all military and political affairs in his country. As a fascist, militarist, and overtly nationalistic, Tojo wasn't hard to figure out, as his defense for keeping troops in China was the positive affect it had on Japanese military morale. His nickname was "The Razor." When he became prime minister in

October 1941, he was assigned the task of evaluating the negotiations with the United States to see if peace was possible but within a matter of days signed off on the audacious plan to launch a sneak attack against America.

Why did the American military fail to see the threat posed? Why did American diplomats and politicians fail to remember that Japan, in her long history, had never actually declared war on an opponent before attacking that opponent? Why did American politicians and diplomats fail to recognize just who and what was running the show in Tokyo? "The real rulers of Japan have been a clique of army and navy officers whose thought processes, fanatical, mystical, belong in another age. They are a direct throwback to the Shoguns, Diamyos, and Samurai who ruled in ancient and medieval times. . . . They were Fascists before Mussolini, National Socialists before Hitler."[34]

But the Japanese people were also a proud and courageous race. They were unyielding and Tokyologists knew that, for the Japanese, "national suicide would be preferable to yielding."[35] The word *fanatical* to describe the Japanese was cropping up in more and more articles. The Japanese had often been poorly and cruelly portrayed in the political cartoons of American newspapers, but now it took an uglier, racist turn. A hated caricature was emerging of the average Japanese citizen and certainly the Japanese military. The president of Tufts University, Leonard Carmichael, accused the Japanese race of being "infected with madness."[36] Political cartoons routinely depicted the Japanese in the most vicious possible manner. Short, "bifocals and bamboo," squinty-eyed, often with a knife in the back of Uncle Sam, egged on by caricatures of Hitler and Mussolini.

Still, the bigger question on the minds of Americans and official Washington was how were the Japanese so successful in sneaking up on Hawaii? Sure, it was a big ocean, but it was also a big armada and should, some thought, have been spotted by navy or civilian ships or planes. Pan American flights over the Pacific were routine, and the military on Oahu did have planes and ships dedicated to be on the lookout for potential threats from the sea. Indeed, one that had landed in the middle of the battle over Oahu made its way safely back to San Francisco while another, along with twenty airline personnel, successfully escaped from Guam.

One expert said the navy suffered from "Scapa Flow." Scapa Flow was where the Germans surprised and sank the British Royal Oak in early

October of 1939, at a time when the Brits should have known better. The *Christian Science Monitor* acidly wrote, "Why the American Navy permitted itself to be surprised in the Pacific will take some major explaining from a command which almost at the same moment was declaring its marine forces 'second to none' in the world."[37]

The army, along with the navy, seemed confused as to its next step. The army oddly announced that it was not planning any type of offensive operations against the Japanese any time soon.[38] A White House source elaborated, saying nothing on the scale of the 2 million doughboys sent to Europe in 1917 was being contemplated. And while it was the Japanese who had attacked America, "the most formidable enemy still is Germany."[39] Stories circulated that Germany was planning on aiding the Japanese with military hardware. Adm. William D. Leahy supposedly told a journalist four years earlier that Japan needed to be corralled. In 1937, isolationists labeled him a "warmonger."[40]

The blame game and the "I knew it all along" parlor room nonsense were only beginning to gain a head of steam. Some of the headlines: "While Japan caught the United States Navy napping at Hawaii," "U.S. Learns Lesson in Attack,"[41] "U.S. Navy Caught Off Guard,"[42] and "Preparedness of Defenses is Questioned in Washington: Capital Hears Queries About Functions of Hawaii Off-Shore Patrol,"[43] Conclusions were being jumped to all over the place, and the navy was increasingly under attack by American politicians and editorialists and not just Japanese militarists. "Also heard in the rising uproar were proposals for a housecleaning of the Navy Department, beginning with the Secretary, Frank Knox."[44]

FDR was asked at his press conference the day before who was to blame and he bristled at the offending reporter. A reporter also complained that it seemed to him the War Department had clamped down on all information, but Roosevelt smiled and "told the correspondent his toes hadn't been stepped on."[45] "Asked if it would be the policy to make public no bad news, the President answered in the negative, but added that the rule of accuracy and determination not to aid the enemy would be the standard of measure." He also shot down the notion that some papers were unhappy with the policy, noting that he'd also "heard other reports where the shoe was on the other foot."[46]

Along with the finger-pointing, conspiracy theorists started coming out of the woodwork. Senator Guy Gillette, Democrat of Iowa, claimed he'd been told by a source that the State Department had been told by another source that the Japanese would attack America in either December 1941 or January of 1942.[47] No doubt there had been formal and informal warning about the Japanese, and the War Department's Enigma machine had decoded transmissions between Tokyo and their embassy in Washington, but nowhere in those transmissions was it explicit that Japan was going to war with the United States. The War Department had issued "war warnings" to the field commanders, including Admiral Kimmel and General Short, but none of those ever mentioned Hawaii.[48] Roosevelt himself had been given several top secret memos alerting him to the possibility the Japanese could attack the Philippines or Hawaii, but in the end, everybody just could not fathom it. All thought the Japanese's next target was Thailand. It was one of the greatest bait and switches in world history.

Experts on the Far East weighed in, saying the attack was to break up a suspected blockade of Japan, before the Allies and the United States could get it going in earnest. Others, including Kimmel, thought FDR was being deliberately provocative, when the president personally ordered the fleet moved from San Diego to Oahu early in 1941.[49] He also complained of being kept in the dark about the increasing diplomatic difficulties between Washington and Tokyo and implied that had he known, he would have taken steps to protect the fleet.

With perfect 20/20 hindsight, the *Washington Post* opened its lead editorial of December 8 saying, "The Japanese attack on Hawaii began precisely as many Navy and Army officers predicted it would." The editorial did not name these visionary individuals, and there was no reporting before December 7 in the *Post* or any paper in America for that matter about their warnings of a possible attack in the Pacific by Japan.[50] The paper, however, being located in the nation's capital, was marinated in the "as I said before" tuchas-covering culture of the town.

The *Post* also had an aggressively pro-Roosevelt, pro-interventionist editorial policy with a habit of patting itself on the back. "This paper has gone on that assumption since Hitler and the Italians leagued themselves with the Japanese" that war was inevitable and it would not be confined to the

European powers. In arguing for a swift entry into the war, it said, "This is our rendezvous with destiny."[51] Their crosstown rival, the *Washington Times-Herald*, was a vicious and bitter opponent of FDR, the New Deal, Lend-Lease, and internationalism. The paper was owned by newspaper mogul Col. Robert McCormick, whose opposition to FDR was reflected deeply in all his papers.

Adding to Americans' doubts about the world situation was the fact that while their government was telling them one thing, other sources were telling them something quite different. Network radio correspondents were reporting in great detail about destruction in Manila while the War Department was saying the Philippine base in question was operational—or saying nothing at all. "Continuing as it did, the silence created a growing possibility that the public would simply begin to believe all rumors, simply because no facts were made available to controvert them."[52] The Japanese were dropping propaganda leaflets by day and flares at night, to illuminate bombing targets. There was constant chatter going around that German pilots were participating in the attack, flying Japanese warplanes.[53]

Americans did not know of the six separate military targets successfully hit in Oahu by the Japanese, or of the near-complete destruction or disabling of twenty-one vessels in the American fleet, or that over three hundred first-line Air Corps and navy planes had been destroyed, or that three thousand of the fellow countrymen had been brutally killed only because they wore a uniform and happened to be in the wrong place at the wrong time.

There was no news coming out of Hawaii about the extent to which the Japanese had succeeded, including the murder of 1,177 sailors and marines assigned to the *Arizona*, which having taken a bomb into her magazine, exploded in a earth-shattering fireball and sank to the bottom of the harbor. Nearly the entire crew was lost.

Hawaii was under martial law, and retail stores were ordered closed so the civilian government could order an inventory of available food supplies. The White House said repairs on the damaged ships and planes were in effect and replacement planes were being "rushed" to Hawaii, but the fact was Pearl Harbor, Ford Island, and Hickam Field were only beginning to pick up the pieces. Dead and missing soldiers and sailors were still unaccounted for, and investigations hadn't even gotten underway. A sad epilogue to December 7 was that a squadron of six planes from the *Enterprise* was on approach to Pearl Harbor after a vain search for the Japanese ships, and despite being told repeatedly they were "friendlies," they were shot down by panicked U.S. sailors. Only one of the six planes landed safely.[54]

Honolulu wasn't completely caught unawares of Japanese intentions. For some time, residents of Oahu had been warned what to do in case of attack, to "lay in emergency food supplies," and warned they might have to evacuate to the mountains should war come to their island. "It is safe to say that no other American community was as well prepared for war as was Hawaii."[55] Ironic.

The risk was great after December 7 of another Japanese attack on Hawaii, so Americans thought. "Unless the naval patrol around Hawaii, and indeed around the fringe of American islands farther west can be made more effective, periodic harassing attacks on Hawaii are practically certain."[56] Secretary Hull said publicly he expected more surprise attacks on the part of the Japanese. And fresh claims by the Japanese included the sinking of a "mother ship" and the downing of an American plane near Hawaii.[57]

The Japanese were crowing now; what was left of the American fleet was no match for their intact fleet in the Pacific. "This force would be regarded as utterly inadequate to accomplish any successful outcome in an encounter with the thus-far-intact Japanese Fleet."[58]

As of the tenth, the war news only became more depressing. The Japanese sunk two huge British battleships, the thirty-five thousand ton *Prince of Wales* and the thirty-two thousand ton *Repulse*, in the same Pacific battle. Hundreds of men were lost, and the *Repulse* went down immediately after the torpedo and dive bomber planes had attacked. The ships, without air cover, were simply sitting ducks to air attack. Winston Churchill was truly stunned at the news. "In all the war, I never received a more direct shock." Churchill wrote in *The Grand Alliance*.[59]

He was down to only nineteen battleships. The Japanese claimed they'd also sunk the *King George V* battleship.[60] It was learned that two British islands in the Pacific, Nauru and Ocean, were under attack by the Japanese.[61] Both were small, but both were strategically important, as part of the Gilbert Island chain halfway between Hawaii and the Philippines. The Japanese had also apparently seized a British airfield located in the northern Malaya Peninsula area.

Japanese troops stormed ashore at Luzon in the Philippines. They were also "in force in Malaya," as reported from Singapore.[62] "Bitter fighting continued throughout the night and today."[63] The Japanese claimed they bombed Clark Field and Nichols in the Philippines again and shelled Midway Island again, as well as shooting down nine American planes over Wake Island. The Japanese navy had also captured over two hundred commercial ships of all countries, all in the waters off the China Coast and southward.

American fighters were off the ground in Manila and finally engaging the enemy, however there was respect for the Japanese fighters. One American flyer described the opposing planes as "plenty good and heavily armored."[64]

The Japanese took possession of the *President Harrison*, with a compliment of U.S. Marines on board.[65] They were tightening their grip on Thailand, sending in more troops, and tightening their grip on Bangkok.[66] Shanghai was also now safely in Japanese hands.[67]

FDR received classified daily reports from London on the situation in the rest of the world. The reports were frank and disheartening. In all world sectors, the Axis powers were on offense and the Allies were on defense. "Heavy air attacks . . . A small enemy force landed . . . German progress . . . Battle casualties . . . German . . . long range bombing force on Eastern Front is still being vigorously pursued . . . seriously damaged by bombs."[68]

New causality reports were coming in from Hawaii. Leading the latest list was Sergeant Walter R. French, twenty-nine, of Delphos, Ohio. He was in the Medical Corps. The War Department acknowledged a mistake, in that Wilbur Carr, nineteen, of Franklin, Ohio, was not dead as his parents had previously been told. Young Carr was alive and well.[69]

In New York, for the first time in thirty-five years, the huge lighted clock at the top of the Colgate-Palmolive-Peet building was darkened as a precaution.

Handbooks were issued to all the schools in New York City, outlining air-raid procedures for the children, teachers, and administrators.[70] The U.S. Capitol was darkened for the duration of the war and the flood lights, which had illuminated the great building for years, were turned off.[71]

In the face of depressing news came more depressing news. The thirty-first president had taken to the airwaves the night before from the Oval Room of the White House to give his fellow countrymen a more fulsome report on the attack on Pearl, the situation regarding the Japanese, and to generally buck up morale, but also to let the American media have it right between the eyes.

He might have started out looking crisp and alive that morning, but Roosevelt looked fatigued at the end of December 10, with dark circles under his eyes. He was still attired in a grey pinstripe suit but now looked baggy and loose. His remarks could be heard over most of the free world and parts of the non-free world, except Vichy France, which jammed the NBC transmission. The American radio audience was estimated to be 90 million citizens. In 1941, the population of the United States was 130 million.[72]

He opened, blasting Tokyo, saying, "The sudden criminal attacks perpetrated by the Japanese in the Pacific provide the climax of a decade of international immorality." Early in his remarks, he made a compelling case that the Japanese, Germans, and Italians were all the common enemy of the United States and that each of them was a threat. "It is all of a pattern," he said.[73]

Then, "We are now in this war. So far, the news has been all bad. We have suffered a serious setback in Hawaii. Our forces in the Philippines . . . are taking punishment but are defending themselves vigorously. The reports from Guan and Wake and Midway Islands are still confused, but we must be prepared for the announcement that all these three outposts have been seized. The casualty lists of these first few days will undoubtedly be large."[74]

He assured loved ones that the dead of family members would be made known to them as judiciously as possible and that "they will get news just as quickly as possible." Roosevelt turned his attention to all the disinformation being spread around. "Most urgently, I urge my countrymen to reject all rumors. These ugly little hints of complete disaster fly thick and fast in wartime. They have to be examined and appraised. As an example, I can tell you frankly that until further surveys are made, I have not sufficient information to state the exact damage which has been done to our naval vessels at Pearl Harbor. Admittedly the damage is serious."[75]

"I cite as another example a statement made on Sunday night that a Japanese carrier had been located and sunk off the Canal Zone. And when you hear statements that are attributed to what they call 'an authoritative source,' you can be reasonably sure from now on that under these war circumstance the 'authority source' is not any person in authority." Clearly, Roosevelt had become angry with all the innuendo and false information over the past several days and warned that a lot of the disinformation could be coming from the Japanese as a means of sapping American morale. "This is an old trick of propaganda which has been used innumerable times by the Nazis."[76] And then he took on the national media.

"To all newspapers and radio stations—all those who reach the eyes and ears of the American people—I say this: You have a most grave responsibility to the nation now and for the duration of this war. If you feel that your government is not disclosing enough of the truth, you have every right to say so." And then he dropped his anvil. "But—in the absence of all the facts, as revealed by official sources—you have no right in the ethics of patriotism to deal out unconfirmed reports in such a way as to make people believe they are the gospel truth. The lives of our soldiers and sailors—the whole future of this nation—depend upon the manner in which each and every one of us fulfills his obligation to our country."[77]

Then he swung into an impassioned defense of Lend-Lease, contending the program had bought the Allies time against the Axis powers. "Precious months were gained by sending vast quantities of our war materiel to the nations of the world still able to resist Axis aggression." FDR moved to the heart of his remarks, telling Americans what they had learned and what they must do. "I repeat that the United States can accept no result save victory, final and complete. We have learned that our ocean-girth hemisphere is not immune from severe attack." And finally, "We are now in the midst of a war, not for conquest, not for vengeance, but for a world in which this nation, all that this nation represents, will be safe for our children." He made no bones of his intentions, saying, "We expect to eliminate the danger of Japan, but it would serve us ill if we accomplished that and found that the rest of the world was dominated by Hitler and Mussolini."[78]

Concluding, Roosevelt said, "So we are going to win the war and we are going to win the peace that follows. And in the difficult hours of this day—and through dark days that may be yet to come—we will know that the vast majority of the members of the human race are on our side. Many of them are fighting with us. All of them are praying for us. For in representing our cause, we represent theirs as well—our hope and their hope for liberty under God."[79] The White House was flooded with letters and telegrams praising FDR, supporting his efforts. Many volunteered to do what they could do for the war effort.[80]

That evening FDR dined alone, went for a swim, and "went back to his desk, the war dispatches, phone and radio communiqués."[81]

Despite FDR's plea, the country was overrun with rumors. The day after the president lectured Americans about not engaging in unfounded gossip, it became clear the East Coast scare of planes about to bomb New York, Boston, and Washington of the day before was indeed a rumor that had raced out of control and was passed along by radio, government, and military sources. "The story grew from mouth to mouth. Newspapers and radio stations could not deny it. They could get no authentic information one way or another. The War Department's statement that it had not originated the report could not be interpreted as a denial."[82]

What began as an innocent phone call to Mitchel Field turned into confusion. A man had called the First Army Office in New York, innocently asking about "any truth in a report that bombers had been sighted. He said he had heard it in a radio broadcast from Washington." From there it went to the airfield commander to whom it was somehow announced that the War Department *had* an "enemy plane approaching the coast."[83]

This quickly metastasized into a "phony tip," which then set off a panic of wailing sirens and general confusion that affected millions along the East Coast, for no reason whatsoever. Panicky housewives called husbands at work, pleading for them to come home. Others called newspapers wanting to know where bomb shelters were located. Three hundred planes stationed at Mitchel Field on Long Island took to the air, looking for nonexistent enemy planes. On the fears of eminent attack, the stock market declined deeply. The War Department did not apologize for causing so much of the problem, but newspapers did print notices telling readers how to react in the future to air-raid warnings.[84]

The whole thing "at noon yesterday threw the Atlantic Coast from Portland, Maine to Norfolk into a confusion which, in some places, bordered on hysteria. Somehow somewhere—so the story went—an unidentified enemy airplane had been sighted over the sea. It was all an extraordinary comedy of errors superimposed on a people stunned by the events of the last two days into an exceptional state of suggestibility."[85]

The fallout over the supposed sighting of enemy planes over San Francisco continued. The army denied it was a dress rehearsal or a hoax, as those in New York, Boston, and Washington found out. In San Francisco, they stuck by their story.[86]

There, Gen. John J. Dewitt emphatically, loudly, and scarily berated the civilian population for not reacting sooner and with more alacrity to the warnings and air-raid sirens, going so far as to say that it would have been "a good thing" if some bombs had indeed dropped, as a way to awaken the populace. "He denounced as 'inane, idiotic and foolish' those who refused to believe there was real danger." He warned of "death and destruction." He told people to "get the hell out" if they didn't start to take things more seriously. He said he hoped for enemy bombings. "It might have awakened some of the fools in this community who refuse to realize this is a war." He said a bombing was "imminent." He told FDR the fact that there had been no sabotage by Japanese in San Francisco was evidence that it was coming soon. He favored the forced internment of all Japanese living in America.[87] Dewitt was widely praised. Dewitt was also a nutcase.

Congress was actively engaged in the war now. On the ninth, the Senate had passed a number of war-related bills and then adjourned at 2:08 that afternoon. But the House had their nose to the grindstone, passing bills and holding hearings until they adjourned at 4:47.[88] The Senate Naval Affairs committee met for over an hour behind closed doors where they learned more details about the coordinated attacks. Opinions, however, were out in the open. "Members left this session saying that they were 'stunned' by what they had heard. Though some committeemen had indicated that they went to the meeting prepared to criticize, they left pledging full cooperation in meeting new Navy demands.[89] Others were panicky, though. One senator advocated seizing every questionable piece of property in the Western Hemisphere such as French Guiana from which airplanes could be launched to bomb America.[90]

The House committee with oversight of the navy held a closed-door meeting but was scheduled to hold a hearing the next day as well. They were still trying to pin down Secretary Knox and Admiral Stark on a mutually agreeable time to testify.[91]

The issue of secrecy arose. Senator Charles Tobey of New Hampshire, who three days earlier had been an isolationist and a Republican and who was now an internationalist and a Republican, shocked his colleagues when he said, "But when a thing is a fait accompli, and when, as reported on the floor of the Senate in conversation today, a large part of the Pacific fleet is wiped out—and that is a fait accompli, the enemy certainly knows that—the American people and their representatives in Congress ought to know it." A colleague attempted to shush him, but Tobey kept flapping his gums.[92] Other members of Congress were just downright mad. Congressman Emanuel Celler lost his temper so badly, the House actually went into a brief recess until he cooled down. Celler was angrily calling for all isolationists to apologize to Roosevelt.[93]

With America's eyes on the Pacific, across the Atlantic, the Nazis were only beginning to employ their politics of hate. The pawn Vichy government, at the direction of Berlin, rounded up some eleven thousand communists and "Jews who entered France since January, 1936." The reason being, according to Vichy head Marshall Petain, they were to blame for the attacks on German officers in Paris. "Attacks against officers and soldiers of the armies of occupation constitute a national danger for France." Petain said investigations "have proven Jews, Communists and foreigners to be responsible." Petain went so far as to send Adolf Hitler a telegram, offering his "condolences" over the attacks on German officers by Parisians.[94]

But the real target was France's Jewish population. "The announcement also says that all Jews who have entered France . . . are to be either incorporated in working formations or confined in concentration camps. The measure is described as applying Jews in the occupied and unoccupied zones alike."[95]

This dispatch in the *New York Times* ended hopefully. "Despite the severity of these measures there is a strong feeling here tonight that the execution of hostages will not resume."[96]

The situation in Berlin continued to disintegrate rapidly. American journalists, some of whom the Third Reich had successfully feted over the past several years, convincing them of the superiority of the "Thousand Year Reich" and that National Socialism was the only way forward, now ordered these same scribes confined to their homes.

Throughout the 1930s and up to 1941, American journalists stationed in Paris and Berlin fed their newspapers back home a steady diet of stories, many of them puff pieces, about the fascist celebrities in their midst. The American public couldn't get enough "Hitlerania" from these reporters. Many of them were lazy and besotted hedonists, a little too enamored of café society. Others, such as William J. Shirer in Berlin, would go on to chronicle the rise and fall of Nazi Germany with brilliant distinction. But now, neither the hacks nor the professionals were allowed to go to their offices. German officials claimed it was a retaliatory strike because supposedly German reporters had been arrested in the United States.

Berlin also wasn't too fond of FDR's remarks of the previous evening.[97]

There had been no slackening or shortage of young men wanting to enlist, and in many areas even more young men turned out day after day. "All recruiting records of the nation's armed forces were shattered . . . as thousands of men attempted to enlist for combat duty in the Army, Navy, Marine Corps or Coast Guard."[98] It appeared that America would need every man possible for all the battles coming down the road.

Not just in the Pacific either but maybe in North Africa and Europe. It was reported that the American embassy in Rome was burning papers "in preparation for severance of American diplomatic relations with the Axis."[99]

CHAPTER 11

THE ELEVENTH OF DECEMBER

Germany and Italy Declare War on U.S. and Sign New Axis Alliance

The Evening Star

United States Declares War against Germany and Italy

The Robesonian

Naval Base, Air Depot at Manila Aflame after Merciless Attack

The Atlanta Constitution

T he formalities began on the morning of December 11, 1941, when German and Italian diplomats paid a call on Secretary of State Cordell Hull to advise him of their governments' decision to declare war on the United States of America, something Hull and the world already knew. Now the whole world would be completely aflame.

After declaring war on America, Adolf Hitler and his fascist factotum, Benito Mussolini, gave ranting speeches in their respective capitals to appreciative and cheering audiences.[1] Hitler announced that "the war would determine the history of the world for the next 500 to 1,000 years. This," he said, "has become the greatest year of decision by the German people." The Japanese ambassador was seated at the Hitler speech; their fates were now joined.[2]

The führer elaborated his reason for war with America, saying, "If anyone said the cultural values have been brought back from America to Europe, it was only the invention of a decayed Jewish mixture."[3] Hitler viewed America as too decadent and lazy to fight a global war effectively—certainly too weak to go up against the so-far unbeatable Wehrmacht. In Hitler's febrile mind, American society was rotted from within by a mongrel Jewish-Negroid race that was addicted to pleasure and the sort of jazz music that was now banned in Germany. Unbeknownst to him, German youth surreptitiously gathered in jazz-listening clubs at great personal risk to savor that same music in still-urbane places such as Berlin.

America was a paper tiger poised to fall; that was apparent to Hitler, who declared that Italy and Germany were now bound to Japan in a "death pact."[4] The strutting and hyper-macho Mussolini, in addressing a crowd of 150,000, simply called it a "steel pact."[5] Like Hitler, Mussolini also went after FDR. "One man, one man only, a real tyrannical Democrat, through a series of infantile provocations, betraying with a supreme fraud the population of his own country, wanted the war and had prepared for it day by day with diabolical obstinacy."[6] Hitler also threw back in Washington's face the leaked War Department document of several days before, which had claimed that the U.S. government was mobilizing for a conflict against Germany to begin in 1943.[7] Secretary of War Henry Stimson had prepared a document at FDR's request, outlining what it would take in terms of money, manpower, and materiel if the United States entered the war, but it was certainly not a declaration of war.[8]

Concluding, Hitler modestly remarked, "I am now the head of the strongest military force in the world, of the strongest air force and the most gallant navy. Behind me is the National Socialist Party with which I grew great and which grew great with me and by me. I thank the President and I thank God for the opportunity given me and the German nation that our generation, too, may write a page in the book of honor of German history."[9]

None of this was news to either Franklin Roosevelt or Cordell Hull. The speeches themselves happened about thirty minutes before the nations' diplomats arrived—and news, even then, traveled fast. Roosevelt and Hull had known this was in the offing and even wanted to get into the war to help Britain. In Our Country, Michael Barone wrote, "The United States entered

1941 with a president who was determined to bring the country to the defense of Britain. . . ."[10]

So, it was not surprising that Hull took the whole matter with a bit of nonchalance. He didn't even bother meeting with German first secretary Herbert von Strempel (who was suspected of funneling money to pro-Nazi groups in America)[11] and Chargé d'Affaires Hans Thomsen. They arrived at 8:30 a.m., thirty minutes after Hitler's announcement. Hull was not there, and the two diplomats waited an hour before meeting with Ray Atherton, chief of the European Division. Atherton took the note and said his acceptance of it was only the formalization of the undeclared war that had existed between the two countries since 1939—in retrospect, an astonishing statement. Hull then arrived, but through an aide he informed the two Germans that he was "too busy with important matters to see them."[12] Hull was frostier than the Washington weather, which was only in the low twenties. The *New York Times* reported the only excitement generated at the State Department was from the "correspondents and photographers seeking information and pictures."[13]

The message Hull refused to accept came from Foreign Minister Joachim von Ribbentrop, via their ambassador to America, the same as which von Ribbentrop had given personally in Berlin to the American representative, Leland Morris,[14] and Chargé d'Affaires George L. Brandt around the same time. America had not had an ambassador to Germany since 1938, when Hugh Wilson had been recalled for discussions and never returned.[15]

Like the Japanese declaration, the German avowal accused the United States of all manner of things including "having violated in the most flagrant manner and in ever-increasing measure all rules of neutrality in favor of the adversaries of Germany." The missive elaborated, saying, "Although Germany on her part has strictly adhered to the rules of international law in her relations with the United States during every period of the present war, the Government of the United States from initial violations of neutrality had finally proceeded to open acts of war against Germany. The Government of the United States has thereby virtually created a state of war." The statement concluded by breaking off diplomatic relations between the two countries and "as from today, considers herself as being in a state of war with the United States of America."[16]

The situation between Washington and Berlin had been deteriorating for several years, at least since the Munich Conference in 1938, when Roosevelt had publicly urged Hitler not to seek any more territory. In April 1939, FDR had actually offered Hitler economic assistance in exchange for Germany to abide by "10-year[s] of peace and disarmament."[17] By the fall of 1941, the two countries were at war in nearly all respects, at least on the high seas, with Hitler's "unrestricted warfare" directive on all American vessels,[18] both military and commercial.

Some slow-learning observers complained that Germany was in complete violation of the Versailles Treaty ending the Great War, but it was beyond moot at this point. A war machine of terrifying abilities had been assembled and was being led by a madman.

Later that morning, around 10:40 a.m., Italian Ambassador Prince Colonna arrived at the State Department but only delivered a verbal message of the Italian pronouncement of war on America. This time, only the lowly political adviser to Hull, James Dunn, granted an audience to the Italian. Dunn told Colonna, with all the contempt he could muster, that the United States "fully anticipated that Italy would follow obediently along" the lead of Germany.[19] Apparently Colonna had to be roused for the meeting. Earlier, reporters had banged on the door of the Italian embassy in Washington, only to be greeted by a servant wearing an apron who replied, "The boss is still in bed."[20] Following the formalities, all representatives agreed to surrender their diplomatic credentials, and all parties agreed to the safe and speedy passage of nationals to their respective countries as proscribed by the rules of international law.

Hard as it was to comprehend, the goal of the Geneva Conventions had been to civilize war.

That afternoon, Roosevelt sent a communiqué to the Hill, along with a request for resolutions of war against Germany and Italy. It said:

"On the morning of December 11, the Government of Germany, pursuing its course of world conquest, declared war against the United States," he said. "The long-known and long-expected has thus taken place. The forces endeavoring to enslave the entire world now are moving toward this hemisphere. Never before has there been a greater challenge to life, liberty and civilization. Delay invites great danger. Rapid and united effort by all the peoples of the world who are determined to remain free will insure a world victory of the forces of justice and of righteousness over the forces of savagery and of barbarism." Then concluding, FDR wrote, "Italy also has declared war against the United States. I therefore request the Congress to recognize a state of war between the United States and Germany and between the United States and Italy."[21]

The *New York Times* noted that while "all over the city the Stars and Stripes flew proudly from public buildings,"[22] the vote in Congress came amid a "grim mood."[23] But it was also a determined mood. Unlike the vote on war with Japan, Congress this time passed the declarations without opposition, as Congresswoman Jeannette Rankin squeakily voted, "present."[24] The people of Montana had been apoplectic over Rankin's vote several days earlier against war with Japan.[25] This time, the Senate voted 88–0 for war with Germany and 90-0 for war with Italy. Two members had been in *abstentia* but apparently in town for the vote on Germany but made it back in time for the vote on Italy. Those two were Democrats William Smathers of New Jersey and Charles Andrews of Florida who both "arrived in the Senate chamber just too late to vote for war against Germany, but were recorded in the Italian count."[26] Again, as with the vote on Japan, some members were missing but sent messages indicating they would have voted in the affirmative.

The silent galleries in the House were not filled to capacity as they were on the eighth, but present were British ambassador Lord Halifax and Archduke Otto of Austria.[27] Halifax had recently journeyed to Detroit, only to be pelted with eggs by isolationists there. He took it in stride at the time saying, "My, those people certainly were good shots."[28]

While there was nearly 100 percent unanimity in the country to going to war with the hated Japanese, Americans were somewhat more ambivalent about going to war with Germany and Italy, even as the Third Reich had just sneakily torpedoed American military and commercial vessels, much the same as the Japanese had at Pearl Harbor. There were many German Americans and many others who saw Hitler as anti-communist (but pro-socialist) and that knew he had revived the German country. This made some Americans more dubious about the European War. And by and large, Americans had never had anything against Italy. What's more, the East Coast cities of America teemed with their own "Little Italy" sections. Still, despite the ambivalence, not one newspaper of record editorialized against the declarations of war. From

Chicago to Minneapolis to Seattle to New Orleans, all praised FDR, all condemned the Axis, and all exhorted Americans to do their utmost to win.

With the two war resolutions in hand, the president first balanced his cigarette holder on the edge of his desk and then signed them, muttering, "Everything seems to come in threes." He then asked Senator Tom Connally for the time, and "with lips drawn back from clenched teeth," Roosevelt scribbled it on each piece of historic paper, along with his distinctive signature.[29] About a dozen members of Congress were there in the Oval Office, and the room was deadly silent. He signed the declaration of war against Germany at 3:05 p.m. and the declaration of war against Italy at 3:06 p.m. From the time his message had been read to Congress at 12:21 p.m. until he signed the resolutions passed by both houses of Congress, America had gone to war with two more countries in less than three hours.[30]

Congress also voted to take the handcuffs off the President. Quickly, they voted to allow U.S. troops to go beyond the constraints of the previous law that barred them from leaving the Western Hemisphere.[31] The House that morning had opened with a prayer by the chaplain, Rev. James S. Montgomery, "with an appeal for divine aid for the nation."[32]

Calls for a formal investigation into the attack on Pearl Harbor were growing louder. Senator Charles Tobey, Republican of New Hampshire, having earned headlines for himself the previous day with his unremitting attacks on the military and his near-leaking of sensitive military information to the press, called yet again for an inquiry and again let the world in on confidential information. "Senator Tobey asserted that the fleet's listening devices 'weren't working,' that the ships 'lay at anchor and no steam up' and that more ships were sunk than had been disclosed by Roosevelt." When asked by a colleague where he'd gotten his information, Tobey replied he'd gotten it from two other colleagues. Tobey told reporters, "I wouldn't want to tell all I've heard on the floor of the Senate." He blasted the navy for allowing a "disaster that's almost unspeakable."[33]

Democratic Senator Scott Lucas of Illinois rose to angrily challenge Tobey, warning him that it was "a serious thing to indict anyone until you know what you are talking about." He said Tobey "does not know what he is talking about and he admits he does not. You, Mr. Senator from New Hampshire, are no naval strategist." Lucas was just warming up, furiously and repeatedly attacking Tobey. When Tobey asked Lucas to yield—a cherished and time-honored senatorial privilege—Lucas refused to give him the floor.[34] Tobey was one of the most unpopular men in Washington.

Yet Tobey was not the only senator raising hell. It was bipartisan. Senator Frederick Van Nuys, Democrat of Indiana, charged the military with "criminal negligence." He said it was the responsibility of Congress to get to the bottom of the matter. But Van Nuys himself also trafficked in rumors, as he told reporters "he had heard reports the British military intelligence service had warned the American forces that an attack by the Japanese might be imminent."[35] Meanwhile, Frank Knox and Admiral Stark had still not appeared before any congressional committees.

In his syndicated column, "Washington Merry-Go-Round," Drew Pearson tsk-tsked, "Alibis cannot very well explain away how both Army and Navy Intelligence had their guard down so carelessly when Japanese planes swooped down out of the early morning sky at Hawaii on Monday." He then eviscerated navy intelligence as being dominated by "royalty," where family connections, breeding, and good table manners were more important than skills and, well, intelligence. Navy intelligence, Pearson charged, was dominated by "wealthy young blue-bloods. Only members of the best families can qualify for Military Intelligence, and how much they know about the life around a Japanese waterfront is questionable."[36]

Following Tobey's tirade, another Republican, Minority Leader Charles McNary, who had been Wendell Willkie's running mate in 1940, offered into the record a resolution of unanimous support for FDR by the GOP members.[37] Later that day, the chairmen of Republican and Democratic parties, Joseph Martin and Edward Flynn, respectively, exchanged telegrams in which they pledged to set aside partisan differences for the duration of the war. They also sent a telegram to the president, indicating their peace accord and then suggested that the headquarters for both parties in Washington be turned over to non-partisan activities to support the war effort. Roosevelt accepted their pledge and suggested the facilities be converted to civil defense.[38] Martin, said "Republicans will not permit politics to enter into national defense."[39] It would remain to be seen how durable this peace would be.

As politicians were making accusations and conjectures and suppositions about the attack on Pearl Harbor, other individuals were pointing out that the navy's patrol planes in the days leading up to December 7 went out each day, at exactly the same time and followed the same route, each day. The theory was the Japanese could have timed their approach and attack when the patrol planes were not in the area. One officer said, "You could set your watch by those flights."[40] Given the fact that the Japanese consulate was a stone's throw from the harbor on Oahu, and from which there was a considerable amount of spying going on, it was one of the saner theories.[41] Secretary of War Henry Stimson, much esteemed by all in Washington, stepped into the fray when he asked Congress not to investigate any dereliction of duty at Pearl Harbor and instead leave it to Roosevelt to get to the bottom of it and take action if deemed necessary. "We don't even know yet all the details of the fight in Hawaii," he sagely pointed out.[42]

Naval officers were still marveling at the accuracy of the Japanese attack at Pearl, but with little photographic evidence and shaky firsthand evidence, some guesstimated that the Japanese must have flown planes into the American and British ships. Another theory was the Japanese had developed some horrific new bombing technology, possibly based on a "magnetic principle" to account for their uncanny accuracy at Pearl.[43] Worse, the *New York Herald-Tribune* reported that "said "an informed source" said the Japanese were making plans to launch suicide bombers at the West Coast.[44]

Abruptly, all three congressional committees, which had begun preliminary investigations into "what happened in Hawaii," shut down. "The House Navy Affairs Committee abandoned an investigation," and its chairman, Carl Vinson, Democrat of Georgia, said there were no plans to reopen the nascent inquiry. Meanwhile, Senator Harry Truman, Democrat of Missouri, announced his Senate Defense Investigating Committee would cease any further inquiry in the surprise attack as would the Senate Naval Affairs Committee.[45] The wagons of the bureaucracy were being circled, and editorials across the nation applauded the decision to forestall any investigation.

Stimson would only concede that there had been a "heavy loss of planes" in Hawaii and then said oddly that the loss "is being made good at the present time."[46] The United States and Great Britain had adopted radically different methods in alerting the civilian population as to military reversals. Whereas Washington was under a near-standing order to stay mum on specifics of losses, Winston Churchill believed instead in hitting the British subjects right between the eyes, withholding nothing, reasoning this would rally the civilian population to greater resistance, as opposed to obfuscating. "No one can underrate the gravity of losses inflicted on the United States nor underrate the length of time it will take to marshall the great forces necessary in the Far East for victory," said the prime minister.[47] With the sinking of the *Repulse* and the *Prince of Wales*, Churchill immediately went to Parliament to tell the members in person and in detail. [48] With the loss of the two ships came the deaths of nearly 600 men and officers[49] including a personal favorite of the prime minister, Admiral Sir T. S. V. Phillips.[50]

Churchill was also forthcoming about reversals in North Africa. "The Libyan offensive did not take the course its authors expected, although it will reach the end at which they aimed," he said. Of course, England had several more years of experience in these matters than did the U.S., and it was harder to explain away German airplanes overhead bombing London than it was an attack 6,000 miles away in the middle of an ocean. Still, Churchill was stricken over the twin losses, according to correspondence with Roosevelt.[51] A survivor of the sinking of the *Repulse* was Cecil Brown of CBS, who'd been embedded on the ship.[52] Another embedded journalist, O.D. Gallagher of the International News Service, was on the *Prince of Wales* and found himself bobbing in a life preserver in shark-infested waters. Of the attack and his long hours waiting to be picked up, Gallagher wrote, "The physical hell created by the Japanese attack was matched by a psychological hell."[53] The British so embraced the hard truths that even the Christmas card put out by the Admiralty reflected on the loss of the two ships.[54]

In Washington, officials deliberated on the need for air-raid shelters and "pontoon bridges across the Potomac River and other emergency plans...."[55] Treasury officials discussed the possibility of higher taxes with members of

Congress.[56] And a plan to fingerprint and issue government identity cards was thrashed out in Congress "as a measure of protection against saboteurs and as a means of speedy identification of hostile agents."[57]

Moreover, in the nation's capital, the Office of Production Management announced that it was ordering Detroit to cut construction of automobiles scheduled for January of 1942 by 50 percent.[58] The *Washington Post* reported that the U.S. was making plans to issue an outright ban on the sale of new tires and would confiscate all imports in order to conserve rubber for the war effort. The government also announced that it might freeze tin stocks to prevent speculation.[59] The decree came from the Director of Priorities, which was a part of the Office of Production Management.[60] Only the orders for automobile from defense contractors would be processed. The government came down hard on tire manufacturers, warning them to surrender their inventories. They were told to "cough up" or else. Americans would have to learn how to patch and re-patch flat tires; used tires were exempt from the edict.

Washington bureaucrats also "ordered a 75 percent reduction in the manufacture of coin-operated gambling machines and juke boxes because the metal is needed for the war industries."[61]

A rumor going around D.C., promulgated by Eleanor Roosevelt, was that the president had met with a Japanese diplomat on December 7, but in fact there had been no such meeting. "Imagine the nerve of that man sitting with my husband in the White House when Japanese bombs were falling on our boys! And when I came in he got up and actually bowed and was full of smiles," she told audiences.[62] The First Lady had apparently been misinformed. Doris Kearns Goodwin, in her Pulitzer prize-winning, *No Ordinary Time*, explained that "the only explanation is that Eleanor mistook the Chinese ambassador, who had stopped by to see the president shortly after noon, for the Japanese ambassador."[63]

It also leaked out that there had been a contentious debate a year earlier over the oil embargo of Japan, with Harold Ickes, Robert Morganthau, and Frank Knox on one side, arguing for the embargo; and Cordell Hull on the other side, against it. FDR eventually sided with the pro-embargo faction in his cabinet, but only after Japan had stockpiled enough of the precious liquid to conduct extended war operations.[64]

The day before the war declaration by Germany and Italy, FDR had convened his "inner war cabinet" for an hour-and-a-half meeting at the White House beginning at noon. "Those present at the meeting . . . included . . . Hull and Stimson . . . the acting Secretary of the Navy, James V. Forrestal, Admiral Harold B. Stark . . . General George C. Marshall . . . and Sumner Welles, Under-Secretary of State." During this meeting, the final touches were being added to FDR's "battle room" in the West Wing of the White House.[65]

In addition to a flurry of memos about the disposition of the *Sea Cloud*, a yacht that had been requisitioned by the navy and owned by a wealthy individual, Roosevelt also had to put up with Harold Stark, who was a racist and a bootlick. "Dear Mr. President, You are not only the most important man to the United States today, but to the world. If anything should happen to you, it would be a catastrophe. I do not say this to you because of my own personal relationship, but as a cold-blooded fact. I have said if I were Hitler and were timing it, and he probably has timed it, that I would have ready a spectacular raid on the United States—Washington, New York, or somewhere. Please . . . let somebody provide . . . a place where, in case of an air raid or any other disturbance, not only your safety, but the precious hours of sleep which you need and which are probably too few, would be provided for against any disturbance of any kind." [66]

The news coming from the Philippines and the entire Pacific was becoming gloomier as the battle for Wake Island raged on, and the Japanese were advancing toward General Douglas MacArthur. The Japanese took the airport on Luzon by parachuting in thousands of troops. "More than 100 bombs were dropped in the first hour of the attack."[67] The Japanese were invading Luzon and inexorably driving towards Manila. Furthermore, Tokyo claimed to have sunk a U.S. battleship and submarine in the area, though neither was identified. Berlin radio reported that the Japanese had sunk an American aircraft carrier, the *Lexington*, which, if true, would have been a devastating blow. But both Tokyo and Berlin were schooled in psychological warfare and, in the days after December 7, flooded the airwaves with disinformation.

It also appeared that the British "Gibraltar of the Far East," Singapore, was about to fall to Tokyo.[68] The great fear among G.I.'s was falling captive into enemy hands. The Japanese believed no man should ever allow himself to be a captive of another man, and in their culture, it was better to die than to live with the shame of being a prisoner of war. Personal suicide had an honored place in the Japanese culture. Trouble was, they imposed this view onto their enemies, and it would shortly become known how monstrously cruel and cold-blooded the Japanese were towards American, British, and Australian POWs. Furthermore, what Americans did not realize how racist many of the Japanese military leadership were. They hated Anglos, Chinese, Koreans—anyone not of the Japanese race and culture.

The bad news kept coming. The Japanese took the American consulate in Hanoi and arrested the U.S. Representative there, O. Edmund Clubb, along with his staff.[69]

Americans could take some cheer in the sinking of a large 29,000 ton Japanese battleship, believed to be the *Haruna*.[70] But in a bombing raid on Manila and Cavite, the Japanese claimed they'd destroyed dozens of parked American planes. Cavite was aflame. Still, a spokesman for MacArthur told reporters, "'The situation is completely in hand' and that Japanese forces along the coast were being mopped up."[71] Roosevelt had once said of MacArthur, "never underestimate a man who overestimates himself."[72]

Roosevelt also once told a crony that Huey Long and MacArthur were the most dangerous men in America.[73] There was no doubt, though, that MacArthur was a national hero, an image fostered in part by his aggressive press staff. For example, the week of December 8, there was the general, heroically photographed on the cover of *Life* magazine with the caption, "Commander of the Far East."[74] The magazine effusively called him a "stickler for sartorial splendor." The fawning profile was written by Claire Boothe, wife of *Life* publisher Henry Luce.[75]

The U.S. Army continued to run print ads asking for recruits, but it was a waste of time. None of the branches could process the incoming deluge of applicants fast enough.

The first member of Congress to be called up was a young and lanky congressman from the Hill Country of Texas. An FDR and New Deal man through and through, Lyndon Baines Johnson, was ordered to report in San Francisco for active duty at the 12th Naval District, with the rank of Lieutenant Commander.[76] The day after FDR's address to Congress, Johnson went to see Admiral Chester Nimitz, also from the Hill Country of Texas, and ask Nimitz to sign the paperwork placing him on active duty.[77]

It wasn't as noble as it appeared. It was really about making himself look good to his constituents. Johnson successfully wheedled and schemed and pulled strings to keep himself out of the war zone and off any ship; ultimately, he only saw the most minimal of duty, sometimes seeming more like a tourist in the Pacific than a fighting man for the Navy. He and his aide, John Connally, found time to tour nightclubs in California and hire a Hollywood photographer to take pictures of them in their Navy dress uniforms.[78] After the war, the driven young congressman would prove his relentless ability to get what he wanted as senator and then president.

The sale of defense bonds quickened even as the newspapers were still hawking Christmas gifts. Suggestions for gifts that men could give their wives included diamond rings, going for as much as $29.00,[79] and "Barbizon gowns," elaborately designed slips and lingerie.[80] Also being hawked were fur coats from $59.95 up to $325.00 at J. Fred Johnson & Co. in Kingsport, New York.[81] Racial stereotypes also filled the newspapers. In the *Evening Star*, the D. L. Bromwell Co. was advertising the "Darkey Hitching Post," a racial caricature of a black lawn jockey in the form of a small yard statue.[82] Haley's Car Service ran an ad with a drawing of a Japanese man in the now-familiar distortion complete with oversized eye glasses, evil-looking eyebrows and a large and mean smile.[83] Other popular choices were Old Spice aftershave in an elaborate box set for men, and lingerie for women.

Approaching the holiday season, U.S. Agriculture officials assured American households that there was no need to worry about food scarcity, despite gossip going around. "They pointed to America's bulging granaries and well stocked pastures, and confidently seconded President Roosevelt's declaration that 'there is enough food for us all' and more left over to send abroad. Only in the case of spices . . . and some luxury items imported [from] the Far East is there the possibility of a restricted supply."[84] In California "alien Japanese"-grown vegetables were taken off the market even though there was plenty of demand. "At present, no transactions are being made and none are legal with alien Japanese," said a produce official. Also, there was fear of poisoned vegetables coming from alien Japanese farms making their way into stores there.[85]

Housewives were stocking up for the Christmas holidays and would need plenty of sugar for pastries. Sugar was fetching 15 cents for a two-pound bag, two cans of Del Monte Bartlett peaches were 29 cents, and "Flako" pie crust was 11 cents a package.[86] A quart of 90-proof rum was going for $1.99, though food prices had skyrocketed in the past year.[87]

Corn was emerging as a vitally important staple of the diet for civilians and G.I.'s, as well as important feed for livestock. From corn, scientists could extract oil, sugar, and starch along with "a multiplicity of chemicals used in everything from textile and drug manufacture to leather tanning and explosives."[88] Fortunately for the war effort, corn harvests for 1941 had gone through the roof, with billions of bushels generated.

At the McCord radio factory in Detroit, new helmets were being developed for the military. For over twenty years, American G.I.'s had still been using the old "doughboy" helmets of the Great War, which when turned upside down, looked like a chamber pot. The new helmet were stronger, more comfortable, and most importantly, provided more protection to the American soldier.[89]

The head of the Office of Production Management, William Knudsen, held a press conference in which he not only called for a doubling of the production of four-engine bombers, from 500 to 1,000 per month, but also for a "168-hour, 7-day work week." Industries that needed to be stepped up, he said, were "guns, planes, tanks, ammunition and shipbuilding." Plants for the construction of aircraft would be located inland, away from easy enemy air attacks.[90] Also in Detroit, the Nash-Kelvinator Company was churning out airplane propellers. A week earlier, Nash-Kelvinator had been making cars and appliances.[91] America's peacetime industrial might was rapidly becoming a wartime "Arsenal of Democracy."

America easily outstripped the Axis powers in the production of steel and in the mining of sulphur, which was needed for gunpowder. Indeed, up until December 7, much of the world's exports of sulphur came from the United States.

The newest casualty lists rolled in from the Pacific, and now death announcements were beginning to appear in local newspapers. War Department letters were arriving at the homes of grief-stricken parents and newly minted widows. In small-town America in 1941, there were few secrets; when someone learned of the loss of a beloved boy, within minutes neighbors knew and would come over to offer condolences. Shortly thereafter, the family minister or priest or rabbi was at the home to help console the suffering parents and forlorn family.

The local newspaper would invariably find out and write up a small story of the boy who'd died, giving his rank and service of record, along with a photo from the family (if possible) and a quote from the boy's high school football coach or scoutmaster. Headlines such as "Two Alabamians Die in fighting around Hawaii"[92] or, "Lynn, Hingham Youths Killed at Honolulu"[93] appeared in papers around the country.

After the initial gasping shock from the mailman—who painfully knew he was the unwilling messenger of death—came the realization that their son was never coming home again, never bounding into the kitchen again, asking what was for dinner. A boy who had left home, tousle-haired, full of adventure, freckle-faced, toothsome, the light of his parents' life, the joy of his grandparents, the secret love of the girl next door, was now dead. His Christian name had often been an afterthought. He was not John but "Johnny." He was not Edward but "Eddie." He was not Thomas but "Tommy." Or he might have had a nickname—Butch, Dutch, Mick, Duke, or Barney.

Now the boy would never know the love of a good woman or watch his son take his first step or have a catch with that son. He would never see the first time his son would put a razor to his face, watch a daughter go off to the prom, walk her down the aisle, or know the quiet pride of being a good man among the uncommon men of his country.

Grey hair would never be combed. His parents would never hold him again, hug him again, and dry his tears again, even as they could not stop their own. The pain and the feeling of emptiness and helplessness were unbear-able for the thousands of inconsolable parents and grandparents and brothers and sisters. Everybody had a sick, wrenching, and wretched feeling in the pits of their stomachs. Some filled theirs with alcohol to deaden the pain. Some mothers' hair went white in a matter of days. Some simply withdrew. None would ever get over the loss of their boy.

It was so final, so useless, so stupid, so heartrending. But it was also as necessary as it was tragic.

Private William T. Anderson of Quantico, Virginia, was first on the new lists of dead soldiers, though the names was not released in alphabetical order. His nearest relative was his now grief-incapacitated father, Herbert C. Anderson.[94] This roll call of the dead came from the army and announced eighty-seven more men killed in Hawaii. The list was of three officers and eighty-four enlisted men. Under the heading, "More Victims" a second list of eleven men killed was released, but it was also announced that Private Robert R. Niedzwiecki of Grand Rapids and Private Raymond C. Joiner, of Henderson, North Carolina, who had both been reported as killed, were in fact alive, much to the relief of their families.[95] The parents of Wilbur Carr of Franklin, Ohio, were also relieved to find that the reports of their son's death had been premature.[96]

Another tragic Pearl Harbor death was that of Rear Admiral Isaac Campbell Kidd, fifty-seven, the first flag officer to die in the Pacific. Kidd had reported for duty on Oahu in February of 1940. He was a chief of staff and an aide to the commander of a battleship group in Pearl Harbor, though the War Department did not release the name of the ship on which he lost his life on December 7.[97] (It was later learned that Kidd was on the bridge of the *Arizona* where he assumed command, trying vainly to get it up to battle stations. When the ship exploded, he was killed and his remains never recovered. For years, Kidd had warned to deaf ears to watch out for the Japanese and was regarded in the navy as an expert on the emerging enemy. His son, Isaac C. Kidd Jr., was scheduled to graduate the following week from the Naval Academy in Annapolis, just as his father had in 1906. Admiral "Captain Kidd" was later posthumously awarded the Medal of Honor.[98]

In unoccupied Vichy France, it was reported that, under the pretext of the charge of subversion, eleven Frenchmen were shot by Germans. Elaborating, the Associated Press story stated, "Reports from the occupied zone said police made mass arrests in southern France and ear-marked hundreds of Jews and 'Communists' for concentration camps."[99]

While diplomats in Berlin were going through the formalities, the Nazis were less formal and cordial to American journalists and citizens. In retaliation for the arrest of German nationals in America, the Third Reich arrested the precise same number of Americans residing in their country, including four Associated Press correspondents.[100] Tit for tat, the government there announced that for every German arrested in America, they would arrest an equal number of U.S. citizens.

As of the eleventh, U.S. Attorney General Francis Biddle announced that the Justice Department and the FBI had picked up "865 Germans, 147 Italians and 1,291 Japanese as enemy aliens."[101]

There was also the very real problem of what to do with the possessions of the Axis Powers that had fallen into American hands. After delivering the message of war from Mussolini, members of the Italian embassy were furiously trying to sell their cars. Embassy officials were also stocking up on American vitamins by having a delivery boy from a nearby pharmacy make repeated trips to and from the facility, loaded down with "boxes of vitamin pills."[102] Several days later, an exchange of journalists took place between Germany and the United States, although a New York Times reporter, Guido Enderis, was exempted by the Nazis and allowed to stay on in Berlin.[103]

A new government office, similar to the Alien Property Custodian agency set up during "World War I" was created in the U.S. to handle the property of the soon-to-be leaving foreign diplomats as revealed by the Washington Post. The Post's use of a numbered war was possibly the first iteration in print.[104]

The nation's capital was expanding its scope and realm of inquiry. "The Department of Justice turned its attention today to disloyal Americans," which the Boston Evening Globe referred to as "potential Benedict Arnolds."[105] The Los Angeles Times called them "quislings."[106]

The notion of Nazi spies let loose in America became a preoccupation of not just the FBI but also of popular culture. This was epitomized by the release of the farcical, "You Nazty Spy!", a Three Stooges short subject film, produced by Columbia Pictures in January 1941, in which the hapless ring-leader Moe Howard actually performed an astonishingly realistic imitation of the führer. As far as these three Jewish former vaudevillians were concerned, satire was the best way to answer the absurdities of Nazism.

Now that war was official, the movie moguls in Hollywood—the vast majority of them Jewish—eagerly embraced what they saw as their patriotic duty and shed any inhibitions they may have had about taking on Germany. These immigrants (mostly from poor provinces in Russia) also saw the war effort as their golden opportunity to prove their *bona fides* as assimilated American citizens. Americans were about to be inundated with a sea of flag-waving, patriotic celluloid, much of it stridently propagandistic.

The phrase "Fifth Columnists" kept coming up in news dispatches. The expression had its roots in the Spanish Civil War and referred to subversive elements inside a country who were working with outside agitators or revolutionaries. The worry in America was that Fifth Columnists were working clandestinely to help the Axis Powers through sabotage and subversion. But Biddle said that FBI Director J. Edgar Hoover had assured him there were no Fifth Columnists operating in the United States.[107] Yet in Miami, officials discovered a train trestle wired to explode with dynamite, its wires and batteries set to detonate.

The Justice Department contradicted itself and said that no lawful American could be arrested, though for what it was not specific.[108] It also decided to suspend the naturalization citizenship of over 450,000 Japanese, Germans, and Italians born in America.[109]

Tensions mounted in the country, and sometimes it seemed as if everyone was a suspect. Brush fires on the coast of Washington State were suspected by local police to be signal fires for approaching planes. "The fires were in the form of arrows" pointing to a naval base and Seattle.[110]

No one was yet using the word "paranoia" in describing Americans after December 7. After all they'd gone through in just a scant several days, their skittishness was understandable. The Navy Department announced it had mined the New York Harbor and warned commercial vessels to take care while approaching and departing the port.[111] It also announced that due to the constrictions of war, fallen sailors and marines would be temporarily buried "where they died . . . They will be buried with full military honors."[112]

The nation's capital was just as skittish. In addition to armed navy guards posted at all federal buildings, machine-gun nests went up around town as well, including on the Memorial Bridge, which connected the town to Arlington National Cemetery and Virginia. Civil-defense units were organized in all cities, big and small, all locales nationwide.[113] In Atlanta, "Immediate organization of an Atlanta Emergency Defense Corps, dedicated solely to the protection of the lives and properties of Atlantans" was urgently reported by the *Atlanta Constitution*.[114] To answer the propaganda campaigns being ginned up by Tokyo and Berlin, it was urged "that men trained in public relations and publicity work [could] constitute a counterforce against subversive propaganda."[115]

Though under martial law, military and civilian officials were incrementally loosening things in Hawaii. Stores had begun to open, and though the naval facilities of Ford Island and Hickam Field were smoldering still, there was only light damage to civilian areas. A phone call was even allowed from a man on the islands to his brother in California, but it was closely monitored by navy censors. "He was given permission to talk to his brother on condition that nothing was said about the weather, military conditions on the island, cables, letters, or the war in general."[116]

Following the scares of two days earlier, newspapers began publishing guidelines for the dos and don'ts of civilian defense. Helpful tips included "Don't believe or spread rumors . . . Don't mention air raids in the presence of small children . . . Don't rush into the street if an air raid should come."[117] A columnist for Baltimore's *The Sun* told readers, "Fear is one of the most contagious of diseases, and the individual should remember that, if he breaks down, the man next to him is very likely to follow suit."[118]

Other news stories contained helpful suggestions on "How to Teach Yourself to See Better in Blackouts." "Blackout seeing is practically the reverse of daylight seeing. It is done not only with a different part of the eye—but with a different and special set of nerve endings."[119] It was urged that children's energies be focused on "knitting and dishwashing."[120] And, "Don't expect all news to be good. We are at war. Mistakes and accidents are inevitable, some battles may be lost." At this point and for some time, all American military battles would be lost.[121]

Only four days into a great new world war, America was losing. Terribly.

So it was well-received news when the songwriters of America began churning out quickie songs to boost the national morale. "Tin Pan Alley's batteries, featuring saxophone and fiddle rather than bugle and drum, are ready to open fire on Japan." The papers reported that thousands of songwriters were flooding the offices of song publishers with tunes like, "You're a Sap, Mr. Jap" and "The Jap Won't Have a Chinaman's Chance" and "Good Bye Mama, We'll See You in Yokohama." The president of Broadcast Music, Inc., which put out the call, was Sam Lerner, who had a slightly more famous brother, Jay.[122]

Anti-Japanese sentiment was manifesting itself in other ways as well. The annual Japanese Cherry Blossom Festival in Washington was changed instead to the "Oriental Cherry Blossom Festival." Vandals also cut down four Japanese cherry trees, originally planted in 1912 as a gift from Tokyo, along the Tidal Basin in the nation's capital. Inscribed on the trees was "To Hell with the Japanese."[123] Two of the destroyed trees had been planted when Mrs. William Howard Taft attended the ceremonies commemorating the gift. When FDR ordered the building of the Jefferson Memorial in 1939, some outraged Washington women chained themselves to the trees one cold morning because some would have to be bulldozed before the memorial could be built. An enterprising government staffer took steaming pots of coffee to the tree huggers, who drank the proffered liquid happily and excessively. The staffer then waited for nature to take its course at which time the bulldozers moved in. [124]

Department stores across America were taking Japanese products off their shelves, "some of which were destroyed and the remainder placed in storage. Some merchants were rebuked by patrons for displaying 'Japanese' goods, which were, however, Chinese, as proved by the 'Made in China' label. Dance bands were not playing 'Japanese Sandman.' At the Freer Gallery of Art, Nipponese paintings, sculptures, and representations were removed. The gallery had been "world famous for its Oriental collection."[125]

G.C. Murphy, a national chain of five-and-dime stores, was one of the first to remove all their goods manufactured in Japan. At another, Woolworth's, a clerk laughed about burning up a Santa Claus made in Japan.[126]

Other welcome news that helped distract Americans was that Hollywood was continuing to churn out flicks. Walt Disney, a genius and true American original who had invented the color cartoon and feature-length cartoon, had just released *Dumbo* when his studio was commandeered by the military on December 8. (It was adjacent to the vital Lockheed air plant, and his site was needed as a primary defense station.) He halted most other work at his studio to finish his next feature-length cartoon *Bambi* before accepting a commission from the Naval Bureau of Aeronautics to make twenty animated training films. These were the first in a flood of Disney films in aid of the war effort (both live-action and cartoons).[127]

Greta Garbo and Melvin Douglas were starring in a new racy comedy, *Two-Faced Woman* (it proved to be a flop and Garbo's last movie),[128] and gossip columnists spotted Walter Pidgeon, Richard Ney, and Greer Garson taking a respite from the filming of their new British wartime movie, *Mrs. Miniver*.[129]

Baseball legend Babe Ruth was headed to Hollywood "to play in the Lou Gehrig picture [*Pride of the Yankees*]. It will be an enriching experience, no doubt," said the Bambino.[130] A new comedy was released, *Look Who's Laughing*, starring Edger Bergen, the famed ventriloquist and actor, and popular comedic actress Lucille Ball. Millions of Americans went to the movies each week to see cartoons, serials, newsreels, and feature presentations—in 1941, the greatest source of popular visual entertainment.

But these distractions did not negate the horrific reality unfolding across the globe. After announcing their "death pact," the three Axis allies strengthened their agreement by also announcing a "no separate pledge." In essence, "the agreement bound them not only to make war indissolubly together, but also to make peace after it in a common front."[131] FDR also made a pact, but with Chiang Kai-shek and his forces in China battling the occupying army of Japan. He told the generalissimo they had a "common enemy."[132]

The speculation that German planes had been used at Manila and in other battle zones was regularly dispelled now as experts began asking rational questions, including how the planes would have gotten to the Far East anyway, what with the British naval blockade and the very remote possibility they had been flown all the way from Germany to Japan. It was established shortly thereafter that no German planes or pilots had participated in any battle in the Pacific, nor had four-engine bombers been used at Pearl Harbor by the Japanese. The Germans weren't needed, as the Japanese seemed to be doing a thorough job all by themselves.

Manila, Luzon, and other parts of the Philippines were under sustained and numbing attack by round-the-clock Japanese bombing, despite the whistling-past-the-graveyard talk of "Dugout Doug" MacArthur.

The psyche of the country was badly battered. Since the morning of the seventh, all the news had been dire, except Roosevelt's spectacular declaration of war against Japan. The daily reports of Nazi gains, of British losses, of false alarms, of casualty reports, of rumors, innuendo, gossip, indecision, inaction, roundups, cancellations, and detentions, were wearing down a population that had been battered for over a decade since the onslaught of the Great Depression.

At the end of 1941, just when—for the first time since 1929, unemployment had dipped below 10 percent,[133] when war seemed a faraway proposition and when America had two oceans to protect her—an unwanted war had overrun the country. Now, even the White House was undergoing evening blackouts, and plans were made to move the original copies of the Declaration of Independence and the U.S. Constitution from display in the Library of Congress to a secure location in Maryland. The documents creating the very foundation of the government were put in hiding, as officials feared their destruction by bombs or saboteurs.[134] Hiding one's government was not cheery news. Mrs. Roosevelt hated the wartime precautions utilized in the White House, especially the long and dour blackout drapes.[135]

Apartment buildings on the East and West Coast were organizing their basements as bomb shelters, complete with stocked food and toys for children. The Seventh Wonder of the Modern World, the Panama Canal, was closed each evening.[136] Preparations were going forward for the construction of bomb shelters in the greater Los Angeles area. One proposal was for shelters to be no more than 300 feet apart from each other.[137] Yet another air-raid warning struck terror into Southern California. At night, unidentified planes flew over the entire coast was blacked out, and radio stations went off the air after announcing the raid. "Anti-aircraft and machine gunners scrambled to their weapons at Ft. MacArthur, which was promptly placed on an 'alert' basis."[138] The planes went unidentified and no bombs fell.[139]

During the state-wide blackout, car accidents were reported, and several drivers were killed as a result. Airplanes headed for Los Angeles were diverted to other cities, as the radio beam at the airport had been turned off. The fact that a noisy electrical storm happened along at precisely the wrong time did not help Southern Californians' jittery nerves.[140] New York had experienced three false air-raid warnings in just a couple of days, including one during rush hour on the morning of the tenth.[141] The city was still trying to clean up the mess and the confusion, even as hotels in the five boroughs were making their own plans for air raids.[142]

Across the country, Americans were asked to stay off the telephone line, so as to not tax the phone system. Far more stringent sacrifices and huge mistakes would follow shortly. Government officials in New England sheepishly announced that they had frankly botched the faux air-raid alert of several days earlier.[143] Citizen confidence in government was waning in some quarters.

The news of the war and the incompetence of America would get worse, much worse, before it got better.

CHAPTER 12

THE TWELFTH OF DECEMBER

Army Death List from Hawaii
Reaches 155, Still Incomplete
The Evening Star

Knox in Honolulu
The Atlanta Constitution

Plan Bared for Mobilizing Men, Women
The Boston Daily Globe

These early days of the war were among the very worst. As of the twelfth, Wake Island was still holding on—but just barely—and in a press conference, FDR praised the beleaguered marine garrison fighting there. The British conceded that operations were not going well in the Malaya-Thailand sector and that the Japanese "had dented British defense lines in the jungles. . . . Heavy fighting continued."[1] Hong Kong was closer to being occupied by Japanese troops, who were also coming ashore on the Philippine main island of Luzon, where most of the commerce and population were located. The Japanese claimed they had destroyed over two hundred Americans planes, the vast majority still on the ground. Also, "The Japanese attacked Olongapo, 50 miles west of Manila, one of the most important naval installations in the Philippines [and] the province of Batangas and Clark Field, 40 miles north of Manila."[2]

Some unconfirmed reports said Japanese pilots were flying their planes into American targets, and Admiral Thomas Hart, commander-in-chief of the Asiatic Fleet, said the Japanese inflicted "very great damage. There was a considerable loss of life, more among the civilians in the city of Cavite than among the naval personnel."[3] Whereas General MacArthur was confident, Hart could only muster a languid, "We shall do our best" statement.[4] For his part, Winston Churchill more confidently told Parliament, "We are all in this. Not only the British Empire now, but the United States are fighting for life. It would indeed bring shame upon our generation if we did not teach them a lesson which will not be forgotten in the records of 1000 years."[5] Churchill for his part had been jubilant about the Japanese attack on America. "Churchill regarded the Japanese attack as Britain's salvation. He recalled in his memoirs the emotion he felt at hearing the news: 'We had won the *war* . . . '"[6]

The night of the seventh, he was having a depressing dinner with Averill Harriman and American ambassador John Winant. A butler brought in a small radio, and Churchill fiddled with the dials, finally getting it turned on. When he heard the report, Churchill immediately called FDR via the trans-atlantic line. "What's this about Japan?" Roosevelt confirmed that Japan and America were now at war: 'We are all in the same boat now," FDR told the British prime minister.[7]

As of the twelfth, the Russians had still not decided if they would declare war on Japan. Joseph Stalin was locked in a fight to the death with Germany along a 1,800-mile front and was terrified that if he declared war on the Japanese, they would invade Siberia, opening a two-front war. The German offensive, Operation Barbarossa, involved 4.5 million German soldiers,[8] and Russia needed all the men they had in uniform to stave off the assault. Russia could barely muster the forces to withstand the German invasion, so it was open to question whether Russia could even send troops to meet the Japanese. As of December 1941, the outcome of the German offensive was still uncertain, and the smart money was on Hitler's army. However, it did appear as if Germany had slowed for the winter, unable to continue its assault because of the brutal Russian cold. But the army of the Third Reich remained in place, hunkered down, with Moscow still in sight.

Out of the midst of the war gloom was some somberly and disquietingly good news with the announcement of the first American hero of the "New War."[9] Captain Colin P. Kelly Jr. had been the pilot of the plane that had sunk the Japanese battleship *Haruna,* and his name had been released for radio and newspaper reports. Kelly's type of aircraft was unidentified in news reports as was the cause of his death, but it was made known he had scored "three direct hits on the Japanese capital ship."[10] Kelly's tragic heroics were a bit of good news in the morass of the unremitting bad reports and bulletins going around in America. But in this, the first naval battle between America's forces and the Japanese, other ships had slipped away, avoiding greater losses for the enemy. In addition to everything else, luck seemed to be on Tokyo's side.

Another little bit of heroic news was the report of the Pan Am Clipper that had escaped Guam, shot up by the imperial navy, but had managed to limp back to San Francisco with the passengers—all employees of the airline who had been stationed on the island—safe and unharmed. It was a story of great courage involving the pilot, who had to engage in some fancy flying to escape the war zone. Left behind at Guam were hundreds of civilians, though, as well as a handful of U.S Marines.[11]

Interestingly, commercial flights by Pan Am continued in the Pacific, although along new routes and with new passengers: military men. "No commercial passengers or private materials are accepted for the time being on the Pacific," the air service company said, although flights for private citizens would continue along the east and west coasts of the United States.[12]

The sad realization of another world war was beginning to settle in. Americans were stoic and resolved though, even as they were facing the unknown. President Roosevelt proclaimed, "The eleventh of December, 1941, will be recorded in history as the date marking the formal beginning of the Great War to preserve this world as a living space for free men. For Americans, there is a certain measure of comfort to be derived from the fact that we are formally at war . . . At long last we know where we stand and we know what has to be done."[13] Before the eleventh, America had only been at war with Japan, and it was still a matter of consternation for many Americans whether their country should get into the European war. The surprise declaration of war by Germany and Italy committed America to a wholly different kind of war, a completely "undiscovered country" of death and destruction.

Only days into the new world war, very few in America really knew yet what would have to be done, the sacrifices that would have to be made, the carnage and slaughter of millions of civilians by the Axis Powers, the untold millions of deaths of young men in uniform on both sides, and how this war would change the world—and their nation—for all time.

America's fighting men had already died in wartime since the attack on the seventh, and many more would die in the days, months, and years ahead in war zones around the world; but thousands of fighting men also died in accidents right here in America, and not a day went by that did not include bulletins of military airplanes crashing in Norfolk, Miami, and Texas, or accidental drownings or accidental shootings in and around the other hundreds of military installations. So many domestic military plane crashes occurred that guidelines were issued instructing civilians on how to help downed pilots escape from the craft and their harnesses. The sacrifice of these service men who were stateside was no less than those of their brothers in harm's way across the rest of the world.

Everybody was coming to understand the rationale behind the Japanese attacks. It was not insanity. The scheme was a blending of their own philosophy of attack first then declare war later. The goal, by utilizing the Nazi blitzkrieg—lightning war—had been a quick decapitation of the American military in the Far East with the hope that Washington, left virtually defenseless to an invasion of the West Coast, would sue for peace. Then the empire of Japan would have the entire western Pacific to itself, with its weak governments and rich natural resources.

Some Americans were also coming to recognize that the arrogance and braggadocio of the American Navy before December 7—that the U.S. Navy was superior to that of the Japanese—had been a myth. "The sea power of the United States and the sea power of Britain were inferior to Japanese sea power in the Pacific last week; they are still inferior, though even more so, today."[14]

The fact that many ships in the spring of 1941 had been repositioned to the Atlantic had further weakened the American naval presence in the Pacific. "The attack on Hawaii was a serious military defeat, bordering on a disaster. For a nation of less strength, it might have been an irretrievable disaster. This blunt fact cannot be concealed, even though full details have not been made ,public, for obvious military reasons."[15]

It had been five days since the attack on Pearl Harbor, and Americans still had few hard details of the attack, but they had heard rumors of additional attacks there. No photographs of the aftermath appeared in the nation's publications.

Other than the names of the battleships *West Virginia* and *Oklahoma*, which had appeared in early stories, no subsequent bulletin contained any details about the damage done at Pearl Harbor by the Japanese. "There probably is good reason for suppressing temporarily the Pearl Harbor statistics, since the Japanese can only guess at what damage they did—until they have time to hear from their spy system in the islands. But the whole story should be told reasonably soon," opined the *Los Angeles Times*.[16]

After being picked up in the shark-infested waters of the China Sea, war correspondent Cecil Brown filed a harrowing story of the head-shaking loss of the British ship *Repulse*.[17] "In [a] float, a young midshipman, with a hole in his side big enough to put a fist in sat silently, clenching his teeth. Some men had the skin scalded from their backs, but made no complaint."[18]

Japanese planes had first set the ship aflame, and then, like sharks smelling blood in the water, more planes swooped down. The ease with which the Japanese had sunk the giant battlewagon only added to the sense of vulnerability all Americans felt. Allies were also taken aback at the ferocity at which the enemy soldier waged war. Japanese society, with its emphasis on consensus, had subsumed the needs of the individual. Dying for the greater good of the group was honorable. This social value was the product of centuries of feudal warfare; after a long tradition of devastating civil war and the Way of the Shogun, the small and crowded island nation of Japan had learned to survive by placing great value on social peace and the sublimation of egoism. "They die with the same fervor in battle as the Mohammedan. . . . This national characteristic of the Japs may prove a great factor in the Pacific fight," said an expert on the Far East to a group of businessmen in Alabama.[19]

One newspaper, more blunt and concise in its assessment of Japan's edge in waging war, simply described the enemy as "short and sturdy."[20]

It was slowly dawning on Navy officials and an American public that had been weaned on the unsinkable-battleship theory that—after December 7 and the subsequent and apparently all-too-easy sinking of the *Repulse* and the *Prince of Wales*—the day of the mighty warship had passed. The airplane, whose development as a war weapon in the Great War had only scratched the surface, would rule this new war.

The old Spads and Fokkers and Nieuports of years earlier lumbered along at not much over 100-miles-per-hour and were weapons of short-range capability. They mostly fought each other. Now, the Japanese, the Germans, and the British all had superior fighter planes and bomber planes. They were equipped to take on other planes and targets on the ground and the high seas. These planes and their pilots had advanced training techniques, bombing sights, long-range capabilities, high altitudes, and, most importantly, speed. Some of the fighter planes of 1941 cruised at well over 320 miles per hour and in dives and dogfights could approach 340 miles per hour or more. America was developing the B-17 and other durable high-level bombers but was woefully behind on fighter planes. The navy in some cases was still flying biplanes.

Originally established as a part of the U.S. Army in 1907, America's aviation force in the years leading up to 1941 went by a number of different titles and was placed under various parts of the army. One of its most familiar titles, the U.S. Army Air Corps, was used from July 2, 1926 to June 20, 1941. The air corps fought during World War II as the Army Air Force. The service name that we all know today, the U.S. Air Force, didn't become its own service until after the war in 1947, gaining special strategic prominence in the post–World War II nuclear age.

But in 1941, Hermann Göring's mighty Luftwaffe ruled the skies. The British already had lost two aircraft carriers to German aerial assault, the

Courageous and the *Glorious*, though British planes had helped sink the great German battleship *Bismarck*. Of course, the Italian Navy, such as it was, had nearly been blown out of the water by British airplanes in the Mediterranean. One editorial bluntly and accurately said, "The war with Japan is an air war."[21]

In Europe, the Germans had perfected the use of military aircraft in their blitzkriegs across the European continent, and though they had mostly abandoned the Battle of Britain, the unremitting aerial assault might have succeeded had not Hitler abruptly changed the bombing targets from military to civilian out of a spiteful desire to demoralize the British populace. The bombing of the military targets was nearly wiping out Great Britain's ability to produce and get aloft her Spitfire and Hurricane fighter planes. By changing targets, Hitler gave the English a chance to rebuild their industrial plants and the bombing of civilians in London did nothing more than anger the stubborn and resolute British.

Understatedly, David Lawrence wrote in the *Evening Star*, "The bomber may decide this war."[22] The British were engaged in daytime bombing of German naval installations at Wilhelmshaven and Emden, but planes were also being used to observe German ship movement.[23] The fear was, with American and British ships now occupied in the Pacific, the Germans would step up their naval operations in the Atlantic.

A new idea was mulled over in Washington to expand a Selective Service for all able-bodied men *and* women from the ages of eighteen all the way up to sixty-five, even more all-encompassing than the British draft.[24] "We undoubtedly are soon going to consider the registration of women," said Brigadier General Louis B. Hershey, director of the Selective Service Administration. "He estimated there were about 20,000,000 who could serve in some way, either replacing men in factories, enlisting in civil defense or with the armed services in noncombatant capacities."[25] Then Congress introduced a bill to draft able-bodied men but the actual training would be of men ages nineteen to forty-five; however, Hershey said that a "boy of 19 would not be sent into combat service." He elaborated on an expansive draft. "This registration is necessary to get an overall picture of the manpower of the country."[26] Earlier notions about the drafting of women were set aside for the time being.

But, five days after Pearl Harbor, recruiting offices across the nation were still being mobbed. It wasn't just the quantity of the young men eager to enlist; it was the quality as well. Prior to the seventh of December, most of the enlistees were poor, unhealthy, and relatively uneducated country boys, looking frankly for a way to get off the farm, to get a bed, decent medical attention, and three squares a day. Get up at 6 a.m.? Big deal. These boys had been doing it all their young lives and for no pay from Daddy either. Being in the Army with clean uniforms, clean sheets, hot-water showers, and weekends off was like a vacation for a lot of these down-at-the-heels farm boys.

Now a new kind of young man was enlisting. The average recruit was twenty-one, had at least a high school diploma, and their health was considerably better than their country cousins. "The Army expects 50,000 volunteers in December, twice the November total. The more exacting Marine Corps has 4,000 in sight, also doubling last month."[27] At one recruiting station, a navy yeoman was admitting young men for enlistment when he was stunned to look up and see his own son signing.[28] The army also put out a call for 10,000 women to sign up as much-needed nurses, and the Red Cross issued an urgent alert for blood donors.[29]

Not everybody wanted to serve. "Dallas Thompson, 21, colored, was sentenced today to serve from one to three years in jail on a guilty plea of violating the Selective Service and Training Act of 1940. The presiding judge told him, "The Army doesn't need a fellow like you." According to the story, Thompson pretended he could not read or write when apparently he could do both perfectly well.[30]

That some black American men were reluctant to serve in the U.S. military was understandable. The military was still segregated, and black soldiers got the bum equipment, the bum food, the bum assignments, and were generally treated like bums. Their treatment in the Great War had not been forgotten. "Blacks had volunteered to serve in a segregated army for a segregated government, confident that after the war their sacrifices would be rewarded. When black veterans returned in 1919, the got a nice parade through Harlem and nothing else—no jobs, no challenges to segregation, no progress."[31]

Still, over the course of the new war, over 2.5 million black Americans registered to join in the fight, and those enlisting in South Carolina received Bibles courtesy of the American Bible Society.[32] The account of this new war would later be replete with stories of young African American men, overcoming the Germans, overcoming the Japanese, and overcoming their own country.

An eighteen-year-old boy quit his job at the engine house of the New Haven Railroad and left a note for his pals.

"To my buddies at the roundhouse. I was born in America. I enjoyed more privileges than any boy anywhere in the world. I had free speech; the right to chose my religion. I worked where I pleased and spent my money where I pleased. Yes, I did enjoy myself. I had liberty, fought and paid for with the blood of my forefathers. We all realize that this God-given liberty which we enjoy is in serious danger of being destroyed forever. But we know that it will never be destroyed while boys like you and I can prevent it. That is why I left my job here and enlisted in the United States Marines today. As our beloved President said last night, if I have to pay the supreme sacrifice to defend out liberty, I will consider it a privilege. So, until I see you again, have hope in us; we will not let you down."[33]

The letter was signed Tom Mahoney. Young Tom's father had served in the navy in the last war. Tom Mahoney would only have a short period of time to become a man. "One day at war in Manila had made tough, determined soldiers out of a good many American youngsters who only yesterday were just kids in soldiers' uniforms."[34]

Bond sales were high as Americans were rushing to banks and post offices and other locations to buy up the notes which lent to their government billions of dollars, to be paid back later with interest. At all levels and among all groups, everyone wanted to pitch in some way, somehow, for the war effort. Congress was also exploring new "war taxes," possibly totaling as much as $6.5 billion, to be paid in lump sums by businesses and individuals.[35] Every December, newspapers carried ads reminding citizens their taxes were due before the end of the year. The concept of "withholding" had yet to be introduced by the federal government and then adopted by those state governments that also imposed income taxes.

Volunteering for civil defense, which hundreds of thousands and possibly millions of Americans did, was not for the faint of heart or those lacking commitment. Long hours were spent training civilians on spotting and discerning enemy versus friendly planes, how to operate gas masks, crowd control, and potentially dangerous work. Over the course of the hostilities, thousands of civilians died in war work.

In Arlington, Virginia, "more than 1,000 volunteer air raid wardens were sworn in last night after sampling odors from four different types of gases available for present-day warfare and witnessing the extinguishing of an actual incendiary bomb."[36] Groups organized themselves in order to volunteer. Catholic women's groups, Boy and Girl Scouts, Jobs Daughters, Masons, Daughters of the Nile, Kiwanis Clubs, and Lions Clubs, these and more stepped forward. Everywhere CD (Civil Defense) workers scanned "the sky for enemy bombers."[37]

Construction began on a bomb shelter at the White House, between it and the Treasury Department in "the underground space" that once "housed the Treasury Department vaults." But Grace Tully could never understand why the bomb shelter—which FDR had resisted anyway—had "open sky above and it was never explained to me why the protective structure had this weakness."[38]

Boat owners on the Mississippi, on the coasts, and on the Potomac River also volunteered to guard bridges and report suspicious activities. The Coast Guard Auxiliary organized much of this work.[39] Snafus happened everywhere, but Americans were sincere in their desire to pitch in. New guidelines were published advising people how to deal with air raids, including how to protect their pets. If in a car, pull over and turn off your lights. If a pedestrian and no shelter were available, readers were advised to "Lie Down."[40]

Women's silk stockings were making their farewell appearance, as the important material was needed for parachutes. Replacing them, along with the cumbersome garter belts and hooks, were "Spunsters" made from nylon, a synthetic material. American men lamented the passing of the day when the wind would whip a woman's skirts up, revealing the sexy ensemble. Woodward and Lothrop Department Stores began hawking for all their female customers the new "bright little brief panties" that women skaters had used. Later, they became known as "panty hose."[41]

The national government claimed that the initial roundup of suspected aliens was nearly over, but "additional arrests may be announced during the next few days," the office of the Attorney General said. But the *Los Angeles Times* then reported a "Jap and Camera Held in Bay City"; the man had been taking photos of the city from Twin Peaks. And then another story appeared on how "two Japanese yesterday were taken into custody ... with maps of Los Angeles County and Japanese literature in their possession."[42]

Princess Stephanie Hohenlohe, a member of the Hungarian royal family visiting the United States, was picked up by the FBI. "Once reputed a friend of high Nazi officials and a colorful figure in European political intrigue ... the short, red-haired ... was sent to the United States Immigration Station at Gloucester, NJ." A Republican member of Congress urged the FBI to arrest prominent labor leader, Harry Bridges, along with other "dangerous aliens."[43]

A Chinese man, Samson Lee, recounted all the problems he had on a simple train trip from Hartford to New York and back and how ticket agents, conductors, and others demanded repeatedly he show proof that he was Chinese and not Japanese. Fortunately for Mr. Lee, he did have such proof. In frustration, he said, "Perhaps I should just wear a sign around my neck to say I am a Chinese." He had his own cultural observances of the differences between the Japanese and Chinese. "One great difference between the two people is in their manners. Japanese are very boorish compared to the polite Chinese gentlemen. Most other people do not like them so very much."[44]

Lee's troubles were nothing compared to the unidentified Chinese man whose body was found in Seattle, nearly decapitated. According to officials, he may have been mistaken for a Japanese "secret agent."[45] But in a case chalked up to "racial hatred," a Filipino man attacked a Japanese man with a knife as the two rode on a Pacific Electric Railroad car.[46]

In Washington, the State Department was also asking Americans to forgo serving on any "free movement" committees "or groups representing foreign countries whose activities are contrary to American policies."[47] Loosely translated, the government did not want Americans to get caught up in ethnic politics but instead pledge "100 percent unity" to America. The State Department went even further, saying "the government does not look with favor on any activities designed to divide the allegiance of any group of American residents between the United States and any foreign government in existence or in prospect."[48]

The government agencies also asked Americans to "rat out" their fellow citizens. "The Department of State is glad to be informed of the plans and proposed activities of . . . organizations representing such movements." The government was not going to tolerate any "split loyalty."[49] As if to buttress its point, the FBI in Los Angeles arrested Robert Noble, a "self-styled admirer of Hitler" and charged him with "making seditious and disloyal utterances in wartime. If convicted, Noble could go to jail for up to twenty years."[50] In Boston, a "radio transmitting set" and the owner, an "alien," were seized. In the Italian section of Beantown—the North End, once home to the likes of Paul Revere—a cache of "twenty shotguns and rifles and fifteen revolvers" was also taken by G-men, and the owner, an "Italian alien," was arrested. Those taken into custody could not meet with journalists, photographers, or "the general public."[51]

More and more, Washington, D. C., was becoming an armed camp, a city expecting to be under siege at any second. Atop the Commerce Department, citizens could plainly see machine-gun nests, and within days, the nests were atop all federal buildings. More "dry run" blackouts were planned for the town, and it was proposed that the front and back bumpers on all cars be painted white, along with white lines on roads and sidewalks, so as to guide pedestrians and drivers to air-raid shelters.[52]

The commander of the Coast Guard, Admiral Richard R. Waesche, warned Congress of the likelihood of disruption. "Enemy agents may start an epidemic of fires and explosions in vital defense centers at any time." The concern was of sabotage, the kind that had taken place during the last war.[53]

It was clear that this war was a new kind of war, one that would require new approaches. The War Department organized a "Battle Room" in the White House, complete with "telephones and other modern instruments of communication. . . . Army and Navy officers plotted movements on maps. . . . [It was] a unique communications center across the hall from [the president's] office at the White House." During the Spanish-American War, President McKinley had a war room, but it contained only maps.[54] With its communications tools, FDR's became a real nerve center. All this would cost a lot of money, and Congress passed a new appropriations bill totaling $10 billion. But this was only the beginning. General Motors had already begun retooling its operations under Lend-Lease and a $720 million contract from Washington to churn out machine guns, diesel engines for tanks, and "Allison" engines for aircraft.[55]

Some worried about FDR's expanded new powers, especially those over radio properties by government officials, and then it was subsequently announced by the Federal Communication Commission "that the Army and Navy would take over some facilities and close others. It was officially denied that this was censorship." The head of the FCC, James Branch Fly, got a bit testy and said "It does not mean any general taking over of radio is contemplated. . . ." The industry fell right into line, raising nary an objection. "On the heels of this action Neville Miller, president of the National Association of Broadcasters, urged all broadcasting stations to 'exercise unusually careful editorial judgment in selecting news.'"[56] The edict did not apply to newspapers though, and their independence was reasserted in a decision by the Supreme Court that upheld their right to criticize and comment on government.

Unlike most other papers, the *Washington Post*—which had generally been supportive of FDR—came out four square against government censorship. "The people . . . are adult . . . they are entitled to know what is going on. This newspaper . . . hopes that the President will entrust the information job to men who are wise and technically proficient rather than to officers who are neither."[57]

On the West Coast, a lower court had ruled that the *Los Angeles Times* could not comment on the proceedings of a trial there, but the upper court overruled it. It was a significant decision for a free press.[58] Even so, editorialists routinely applauded the government's new abilities. Said the *Birmingham News*, "We shall have to live, perhaps not literally but surely in spirit, as if we were under martial law—subordinating absolutely everything, as far as possible voluntarily, to the gigantic effort we must make in order to survive. The soft talkative days are gone, and the hardest days we have ever known since Valley Forge have begun."[59]

Indeed, just a few days later, the War Department rolled out new proposals "for prompt suspension of radio broadcasting operations when enemy air raids are threatened anywhere in Continental United States." It was put into effect immediately. "The orders apply to standard broadcast, high frequency, television and relay broadcast stations." Stations were even given scripts to read before going off the air. "At this time, ladies and gentlemen, radio station _____ is temporarily leaving the air in conformity with the national defense program. Keep your radio on so that upon resumption of our service we may bring you the latest information."[60]

Everywhere the word "sacrifice" was on everybody's lips. In Alabama, the "Add a Plate Club" was started to encourage families to invited enlisted men to dinner. The club hoped the goodwill would spread across the country.[61] And it did, for the most part—except in Paterson and Jersey City, New Jersey, where five men who operated a fraudulent charity for kids that took in over $290,000 and gave out a little more than $2,000 for "Crippled Kiddies" were sentenced to long prison stretches and heavy fines. But in New York City, the offices of the Civilian Defense Volunteer Committee were "flooded" with volunteers, up to 100 per hour.[62]

Others worried about a new kerfuffle involving Eleanor Roosevelt, when she somewhat facetiously advised that young American women learn how to drink so they could better adopt male roles on the home front. Temperance groups were not enamored of the advice of Mrs. Roosevelt, whose stance in this regard was ironic because she often frowned on her husband's favorite vice, cocktails promptly at 5:00 p.m., a cherished habit that the president referred to as "fivesies."[63] FDR, in need of temporarily forgetting the enormous burdens on his shoulders, would ebulliently mix drinks in the Oval Office and delight in swapping gossip with his staff. The puritanical Sara Delano Roosevelt, mother of the President, was known to have once remarked: "Franklin, haven't you had enough of your cocktails?"[64]

If power added to FDR's cares, it didn't stop him from accumulating it. He had switched roles, as the press described it, from "Doctor New Deal" to "Doctor Win the War." The United States was not the only representative form of government to have voluntarily given up power to the chief executive. Both Australia and Great Britain had done much the same, and the contradiction was lost on everyone. The Allies, to combat the dictatorial, militaristic regimes of the Axis Powers, had resorted to more authoritarian forms of government. A bill was offered in Congress to further expand the president's powers, including the ability to "redistribute the functions of the various government agencies" and also the ability to award no-bid contracts. But, "the most important [proposal] would allow censorship of communications by mail, cable or radio transmitted to any foreign country."[65]

Absent from Washington for several days had been Secretary of the Navy Frank Knox. He'd failed to respond to congressional inquiries (until they had been squashed) and did not appear in any news stories. He had been absent from the all-important meeting at the White House the day before, sending the "acting" Navy Secretary. It was then learned that Knox had covertly shown up in Hawaii to conduct his own investigation of what happened and to prepare a briefing and report for President Roosevelt. The navy chief had arrived in Hawaii the evening of the eleventh.[66]

By December 12, nearly all of the Pan-American countries had fallen into line behind the United States. From Argentina to Guatemala, most declared war on Japan, Germany, and Italy. This was important because it negated the chance of a power, friendly to the Axis, establishing military bases and harbors from which they could wage a harassing and easier war against the United States.

The war bureaucracy in Washington was growing exponentially. Congress, under its own assault of phone calls and visits and letters from worried constituents, voted an appropriation that would allow each senator to have an aide at the princely sum of $4,500 per annum.[67]

The war bureaucracy was also expanding its rule over the private sector. Previously, Washington had directed Detroit to cut production of new cars by 25 percent in December and by 50 percent in January 1942 because of the steel and rubber shortages. Buick had already begun its ad campaign in the *Saturday Evening Post* and other publications touting its new "automatic drive" under the slogan, "Better Buy Buick."[68]

Now the Office of Production Management (OPM)—another New Deal holdover—ordered Motor City to halt the production of new cars altogether by some plants. It stated that "a changeover to defense production would be accomplished as rapidly as possible after Government orders are received." General Motors was hit hard, and Chevrolet, Oldsmobile, Fleetwood, and Fisher body plants were shut down immediately. Chrysler also had to shut down its De Soto, Dodge, and Plymouth plants.[69] Indeed, war planners actively considered halting the production of all new cars by February of 1942.[70]

Ironically, as the government was ordering Ford, General Motors, and Chrysler to gin up seven-day-a-week production schedules to turn out war materiel, all the companies were engaged in immediate and massive layoffs of skilled car makers and assembly-line workers. Shortly, International Harvester and Bell Aircraft, along with dozens of other manufacturers, would go on seven day production schedules.[71] At the top of the list as ordered by OPM were anti-aircraft weapons. All through the years of the New Deal, officials of the OPM had used phrases like "oversupply" when referring to labor in America. No longer. Now the military had first dibs on all healthy young American males.

In a press conference on the twelfth, just five days after the attack, FDR had asked American newspapers not to publish the casualty lists from the Pacific anymore. He clarified his request by saying "that it might be permissible for individual papers to print individual stories that a person had been notified that a relative was a casualty." The *Evening Star* in Washington also reported, "The next of kin and dependents of naval casualties are being notified and are being asked not to divulge the name of ship or station to which the relative was attacked."[72] But Roosevelt's request was too late to stop the publication of the newest casualties in Hawaii announced by the army, losses that totaled 155 dead: 146 enlisted men and 9 officers. Wounded men were not announced, but the army made clear that many of these would not survive.[73]

At his meeting with reporters at the White House, the president went out of his way to single out Senator Charles Tobey for harsh criticism. Tobey had been on the warpath, engaged in a blame game of the military, especially of Admiral Kimmel. "President Roosevelt today joined in a bitter denunciation of uninformed criticism of the conduct of the Pacific fleet. 'He repeated somebody's gossip, he made it as a statement of fact which he had no right to do whatsoever,' the Chief Executive said."[74]

He also told the gathering that he thought, for the time being, the forty-hour-work-week would be sufficient. This was part of the deal the government had worked out with labor. In exchange for this from the government, labor would put a stop to all strikes during the emergency.[75]

Kimmel now issued his first public utterances since the attack on Pearl Harbor the previous Sunday, but rather than point fingers or attempt to explain what happened, he instead commended "the men of the Navy, Marine Corps and Army. We Americans can receive hard blows but we can deliver harder ones. In these days when we face the task that lies ahead with calm determination and unflinching resolve it is truly great to be an American. Instances of valor were so great in number that they are too many to enumerate. The same sort of selfless courage was displayed then that will win the war."[76]

The panic of the prior day over dynamite found on a train trestle in Miami was cleared up. As reported by the Associated Press, "A 38-year-old colored man confessed yesterday, the FBI announced, that he set a charge of dynamite on a Florida East Coast Railway trestle, then reported it to the police in the hope he would become a hero and receive a reward." Stokes McCreary was charged with the violation of the "anti-sabotage statute."[77]

Newspaper articles of the era routinely identified the race of African Americans as either "colored" or "negro" in reporting exploits both good and bad. Whites were never identified as white, and the papers almost never covered Hispanics. It wasn't just the newspapers that were segregated. So too was Washington, essentially a Jim Crow town. "Blacks looked out on city that was rigidly and thoroughly segregated. Throughout the city, [the] hotels, restaurants, movie theaters, libraries and taxicabs refused to serve blacks."[78]

The war and the military had swiftly become a deeply and tightly woven stitch in the American cultural fabric. There was virtually no place anyone could turn now and not be reminded of the war; even children, even on Santa's lap. In Atlanta, a department-store Santa Claus was entertaining kids, listening to their Christmas wishes, playing his role to perfection, when his mood suddenly changed, becoming somber and stoic. Stepping out of character, he began to read to the children a letter from one of his three sons, all of whom were in uniform.

"Dearest Dad,

There is a war on and I am now in it, but that must not be a cause for you to worry. Of course, there is danger and there will be more danger to come but if I am to die a soldier's death, so be it.... You must think of me as doing my duty to God and country. Be brave and show outward pride, that the mite of humanity you helped bring into the world is now a soldier doing his part of defending our great and wonderful country.... You must pray, not only for me and others in the Army, but for the innocent women and children who will have to endure untold suffering from this fight for freedom of religion, speech and democracy. I am not afraid to die for this....

Until then I remain and always,

Your Loving Son."[79]

The letter was not unique. Hundreds of thousands of mailboxes were filled each day with letters to and from G.I.'s, and within a matter of months, millions of mailboxes would be filled with long missives from sons and daughters in uniform in the far-flung regions of the globe. Uniformly, the letters were tender, funny, inquisitive, brave, confident, patriotic, self-deprecating, and well-written.

Public education in America in 1941 was the best in the world, and dedicated teachers led by rote, by repetition, and by discipline mixed with a healthy dose of tenderness and the knowledge that the hand that rocked the cradle truly ruled the world. A high-school diploma was a hard-earned document and those young Americans who received a diploma had language skills, writing skills, citizenship skills, geology, biology, physics, Latin, Greek, and an expansive list of books read. According to 1940 census only

24.5 percent of young Americans received a high-school diploma in 1941,[80] and less than 5 percent completed four years of college.[81] All in all, well-educated, even erudite and mannerly, young men and women came out of high school, ready to go out into the real world and contribute to society.

America in 1941 was a do-it-yourself enterprise, despite the welfare state created by the New Deal. People still looked to themselves to solve their own problems. Many schools still used the McGuffey Readers, which had worked so well for their parents and grandparents, to help young students expand their vocabularies. The "Palmer Method" of cursive writing was taught, over and over and over, and penmanship across the culture was generally excellent. Men and women took pride in their cursive script and their ability to write numerous letters each day. Because the rule was, if you got a letter, you had to send a letter. At three cents for a first-class stamp, letters were frankly practical as well. Long-distance phone calls were hugely expensive, car travel was for sensible reasons such as going to work, and flying on planes was for businessmen and G.I.'s, but not for the average citizen's pleasure. Taking a train or a bus trip was a big deal, and people dressed accordingly.

Letters were the standard form of personal communication for private citizens and government officials alike. The worst to receive, of course, was the telegram from Uncle Sam. "We regret to inform you that your son. . . ."

CHAPTER 13

THE THIRTEENTH OF DECEMBER

Saboteurs Light Flares in Blackout at Manila; Sentries 'Shoot to Kill'
Atlanta Constitution

4000 Japs Drown
Boston Evening Globe

Weather Bureau Halts Forecasts
Los Angeles Times

House Gets Bill to Register All Men 18 to 64
New York Times

A mid all the bad news in America emerged a small bit of comic relief. In San Francisco, the Japanese proprietors of dry cleaning establishments were apprehended, and all of their assets, financial and otherwise, were confiscated or frozen by government officials—including the clothing of their customers, who, predictably, got hot under the collar. "The United States attorney's office, besieged with irate demands for a ruling, said Washington would probably issue an order allowing persons to submit affidavits declaring that their pants—and coats and vests—were not Japanese assets."[1]

Clothing and closets were on the mind of other government pen pushers, especially the nosy officials of the Census Bureau. Originally mandated by the Constitution to count the population once every ten years as a means of apportioning congressional representation, bureaucrats had expanded the mission over the years into something considerably more intrusive: to gain demographic data on the American people. Incredibly, government poll takers in the 1940 census asked American men and women how many individual articles of clothing they owned and how many they purchased each year. "Census Bureau officials declare they have found the explanation for cluttered clothing closets in the American home; people just buy more than they need." Apparently the government thought that women who annually purchased: "Four dresses; 16 pairs of stockings; 4 pairs of shoes; 2 hats; one pair of gloves; 1 blouse; 1 apron or smock; 7 lingerie items; 1 sleeping garment" were buying too much.[2] The breakdown of men's clothing purchases was just as conservative as the women's, but they too got a lecture from meddlesome Census officials.

Americans accepted constitutional provisions to create armies and navies in order to protect them, their freedoms, and their livelihoods, but it was open to question how much Americans needed or wanted the government's sartorial advice or input on the condition of private closets. To civil libertarians, it was more worrisome than laughable.

Some of the wartime black humor coming from government was just in bad taste. A prankster at the Tennessee Department of Conservation asked for a requisition for 6,000,000 licenses at $2 apiece for hunting "Japs." The response from another bureaucrat was in equally bad taste: "Open season on 'Japs'—no license required."[3] Political correctness was still decades away.

Other government agencies reacted petulantly as well. The Maritime Commission changed the name of a large packet ship from the *Japan Mail* to the more palatable *China Mail*.[4] The merchant marines also "weeded out" Japanese, German, and Italian nationals from service, even taking those already on ships, off.[5] Of more immediate importance, the Attorney General's office made a new announcement that over 2,500 aliens had been arrested, not including those in the Canal Zone or the Philippines.[6] In the Canal Zone, dozens of Japanese civilians had been arrested, taken from their homes and placed in "quarantine stations, a tent city mushroomed to accommodate the aliens and alleged Axis sympathizers as roundups began."[7]

Also, forty-three Americans in Hawaii were "placed in custody," suspected of subversive activities against their country.[8]

American allies in Cuba, Nicaragua, and Mexico also began the roundup of Nazi diplomats and those alleged to be supporters of the Axis Powers, including Japanese fishermen on the west coast of Mexico who were "suspected of 'espionage.'" President Batista of Cuba seized all Axis possessions and was holding all Axis personnel on the Isle of Palms, some forty miles south of Cuba.[9]

In the "funny, dumb, and dangerous" category was the story of a housewife in Detroit. Mrs. Donald de Rusha had been walking along the shore of Lake St. Clair when she happened upon a "gadget." While she did not know what it was, she thought the fifty-pound object would make a nice doorstop. The object was an undetonated piece of military ordinance.[10] Luckily, her error was pointed out in time, and no one was hurt.

Even as war and enemies—real or imagined—dominated the thoughts of the citizenry, they still enjoyed distractions to take their minds off the crisis. A long running "soap opera" was the ongoing private/public tale of poor little rich girl, Gloria Vanderbilt, thin, pretty, inheritress, and hugely controversial as the granddaughter of a robber baron and the daughter of two supremely narcissistic and unbalanced parents.

Gloria herself was a bad news buffet. At only seventeen years of age, she was in the newspapers constantly, photographed in skimpy cocktail dresses at nightclubs in New York and Los Angeles. On the twelfth, it was announced that she was going to marry a man fifteen years her elder, Pasquale Di Cicco, who had already been married, divorced, and, as a Hollywood agent, romantically linked to a number of other women—none of whom stood to inherit another $4 million when they turned twenty-one, however.[11]

Poor Gloria's life had already been a mess-and-a-half. Her mother had been declared unfit when Gloria was a child, and the court remanded her to an aunt. Gloria's life up to that point had been a movable feast of wine, men, and scandal. Americans, by and large, followed her car wreck of a life with salacious and prurient *schadenfreude*. It was all outrageous stuff in 1941, a time when society regarded the low brow hijinks of high society with an almost Victorian sense of propriety.

In the *Atlanta Constitution*, as in many other newspapers around the country, there were listed the "Downtown Theatres," "Night Spots," "Neighborhood Theatres," and "Colored Theatres." The movies shown at the theatres for black Americans were generally low budget, little known, or had already been shown first in the "whites only" movie houses. These included *Wyoming Wildcat, Buck Benny Rides Again* (starring Jack Benny and his manservant, Eddie "Rochester" Anderson), *Beat Me Daddy*, which was the name of an Andrews Sisters song, and *White Eagle*, of cowboys-and-Indians genre. In the heart of Dixie—Atlanta—one of the most popular black movie houses was named the "Lincoln."[12]

Besides celebrity scandals and movies, another pastime available to Americans, and indeed the world, was the Geminids meteor shower which appears every December and promised to be especially brilliant this time around. Some theologians thought this meteor shower was what led three kings to a small manager one thousand nine hundred and forty-one years earlier.

Newsreels detailing the December 7 attacks were beginning to hit America's movie houses. "War took the play in all newsreels on programs opening yesterday at movie theatres."[13] No actual footage of Pearl Harbor was shown for obvious reasons, and most of the news shorts dealt with the history of the relationship between the United States and the Japan. The "March of Time" newsreel was judged to be among the better of those shown, but Fox also produced some that were informative. However, in each case, only the shots of civilians in action in Honolulu were shown, almost nothing about the navy or the Air Corps.

Of course, none of the newsreels reported on the *Arizona*. It was nearly a week after the attack when the name of the ship finally appeared in the newspapers, though it was a wire story of a London report of a Japanese propaganda claim. American editors ran the item, but some ran it with headlines that doubted its veracity. "Reuters today quoted a Japanese naval communiqué broadcast from Tokyo as saying that the 32,000-ton United States battleship *Arizona* had been sunk in action in Hawaii. The *Arizona* was launched in 1915, and its normal complement is about 1,359 men."[14]

But the story, fourth-hand, was generally treated as an unfounded rumor except by the *Boston Globe*, the *LA Times* and the *New York Times*, all of which gave the Japanese claim a bit more veracity. As the *Birmingham News* noted, "It has been an Axis technique to make spectacular war claims, especially naval, in hopes of learning the true results of attacks from its adversaries' denials."[15]

The Japanese also claimed they had hit Honolulu again at the same time that Secretary of the Navy Frank Knox was conducting his investigation. But this was, like so much other radio traffic, chalked up to propaganda. Still another rumor was going around Washington that "as long ago as November 15 Government officials had received confidential and reliable information from Tokyo pointing out that Japan had definitely decided to wage war on the United States, even before it sent Saburo Kurusu with a badly camouflaged peace dove to Washington." But this conspiracy theory had it that Japan's Black Dragon Society was behind the attack on America.[16] The attack had been planned for months, but the Japanese fleet did not leave the home waters until November 26.

Finger-pointing was continuing in Washington, albeit it in softer tones now. The last refuge of patriotism had cloaked any meaningful questions about culpability in either the civilian government or the War Department about the attack on Pearl Harbor. The War Department was still sticking to its story that only one destroyer had been sunk and one battleship "capsized" at Pearl Harbor, but even after almost a week had passed, less information, not more, was forthcoming. The old adage, "the first casualty of war is truth," was proving true enough.

After a quick trip to Oahu to meet with navy officials there and to inspect the damage, Knox returned to Washington. He ducked reporters, who clamored for a comment, only saying, "I will not have statements to release until after a conference with the President."[17] The weather in Washington was a bit harsher than what Knox had left behind in Hawaii, where it was always clear and sunny. On the thirteenth, Washington was paralyzed by a cold rain, snow, sleet, and freezing temperatures that forced government workers to keep their cars at home and call cabs. Problem was, for every cab there were dozens of impatient federal workers.[18]

In Knox's absence, President Roosevelt was meeting daily—even hourly—with his military planners and leaders. At his request, Congress authorized a huge boost in the navy's budget to allow an increase in the surface fleet by 30 percent—a tip-off to the unspoken damage done at Pearl Harbor. He'd also sent to Congress a report on the history of U.S.–Japanese relations and the progress of Lend-Lease.[19]

Planned additions to the navy included at least seven new battleships, six new aircraft carriers, twenty-seven new cruisers, eighty new destroyers, and forty-seven new submarines.[20] All told, the new complement of ships would add some 900,000 tons to the fleet.[21]

For the first time, the gates to the once-accessible White House were closed. The wrought iron fence that had gone up some years earlier with its large gates had always remained open, until the twelfth when they were permanently shut. Now anyone wanting to get into the White House complex had better show a "pass with picture engraved on it" to be admitted. And no longer would "cabs, private cars, delivery wagons" be allowed to enter.[22]

FDR was thirty-five minutes late to his weekly Friday gabfest with reporters, something he normally was on time for. But he did have a country at war to run.[23] FDR enjoyed an easy repartee with reporters; he was a smooth pro at manipulating the Washington press corps with humor and flattery. His powers of obfuscation were truly impressive. He could charm the pants off "the boys" of the Fourth Estate, who eagerly scribbled down his insouciant witticisms, while at the same time telling them absolutely nothing of substance. FDR was widely revered at the time, but certainly not by everyone. Regardless of ideological viewpoint, one fact was clear, throughout the Depression and now on the cusp of global war, Roosevelt's energetic activism, his irrepressible confidence, and his effervescent charm reassured a frightened nation when it needed it most.

His totalitarian counterparts overseas starkly reflected the sort of leadership that America could have born when the economic system collapsed in the 1930s. Now that total war had broken out among the great powers, a tale was making the rounds that Hitler and Stalin were engaged in a deal which would halt the Nazi invasion and they would sign a peace accord. Some wondered how true it was and if it was a factor in Stalin's still not declaring war against the Japanese, as all other Allies had already done. But the Nazis were still pounding the British in North Africa, claiming to have downed seven planes and that "British troops were bombed and shelled successfully."[24]

The air-raid drills had not gone well in Los Angeles. In fact, they were an unmitigated disaster. Glitch followed glitch. Mistake followed mistake. There were car accidents in which people were killed because of the doused street lights but no clear rules on operating cars at night without headlights. Rather than reassure the civilian population, all the practice blackouts did was add to a sense of "hysteria." The general in command, W. A. Ryan, frustrated, said any future blackouts would "be ordered only when danger from air attack was actual."[25] The county fire warden complained that the sirens on his fire apparatus had worn out because they had been overused.[26]

The newest panic in Los Angeles had begun when a flashing yellow light had been misinterpreted to mean "Raiding party on the way." The yellow light was only supposed to mean "alert," while a blue light would signal "blackout." Everybody was thoroughly confused. Half the city responded poorly, and the other half didn't know what to do. Civilians were ordered off of beaches, and then the order was rescinded. Proprietors of commercial establishments saw their lights smashed by law enforcement officials if they were not turned off within the prescribed three minutes given. In some cases, the broken lights increased the risk of fire. Huge fines and jail time of up to 180 days were proposed for those who violated the rules, whatever they were. In one instance, the only arrest made was that of a drunken man.[27] It was never really a blackout; the street lights remained on because they operated on 800 different timers strewn across the city. As no one had been forewarned of the practice blackout, no one was available to turn off the timers. Because of the strict rules against driving in some areas, work crews could not get to municipal lights to turn them off. The owners of billboards also were never told of the blackout drill.

It wasn't that the citizenry didn't want to cooperate. It was the politicians and the military that could not coordinate their actions, especially since they were still attempting to devise a uniform code for alerting the public. Rules would also have to be established for doctors making house calls during blackouts and air raids.[28]

In Long Beach, factory workers began the long process of painting thousands of windows black to help facilitate round-the-clock production.[29] A system of lights, bells, whistles, and horns was eventually established and then never used. But the coast guard issued new regulations "to prevent aliens from escaping on vessels leaving Los Angeles Harbor."[30]

The blackout in California went from the coast to 100 miles inland. Yet a fourth blackout was imposed on the City by the Bay and this one did not go any better than the previous ones. It too was marred by accidents, "violence," and of course, new rumors of unidentified enemy planes.[31] It was finally decided that to avoid any confusion, all vehicular traffic had to pull off the road and stop for the duration of air raids and blackouts.[32] Fines and jail time were imposed on violators.

All told, eight ports of call were designated "defensive sea areas" by an executive order from President Roosevelt. This meant they were closed for the duration of the war. The three on the West Coast were San Francisco, San Diego, and Puget Sound. On the East Coast: Portland, Maine; Portsmouth, New Hampshire; Boston; and Narragansett Bay, Rhode Island, were all closed to commercial boat traffic that did not have the proper authority.[33] The San Francisco Bay was closed to all boat traffic except military vessels. "Any ship entering the bay will do so at its own risk. No non-government vessel may enter or navigate on these waters without specific permission from the Government," reported the *San Francisco Chronicle*.[34]

Baltimore city fathers saw the silliness over blackout drills taking place in other cities around the country and wisely announced their own practice, but ten days in advance, giving all enough time to prepare.[35]

San Diegans went through their own panicky air-raid warning when "something" was sighted "out there" off the coast.[36] Whatever "something" was, something disappeared, unidentified. Yet another air-raid drill in New England had also gone poorly and several motorists were badly injured from driving their cars with the headlights off.[37] Blackouts were also risky because not everyone played nice when they did occur, especially thieves. The owners of jewelry and fur stores in New York were advised to remove their merchandise during the blackouts, as theft had been a common occurrence in London during the raids.[38] The city also issued a brochure with verbiage that seemed terrifyingly prescient, even visionary. The title of the pamphlet was "If It Comes" and read in part: "New York City is in little danger of attack from airplanes. But such an air attack is not impossible. New York, as the nerve center of the nation, presents a tempting target which might justify an enemy in taking great risks. We must prepare now against this possibility of aerial attack."[39]

In another security measure, the United States Weather Bureau announced it would suspend public announcements of weather forecasts. "This action is being taken to prevent the flow of valuable data to enemy analysts." The Service did say, however, it would release weather data on the weekend for "winter sports conditions."[40] Newspapers no longer would contain any specific data, and radio certainly would not broadcast any specifics on weather forecasts.

For many though, the war had gotten out of control when it was announced that New Orleans had cancelled its annual Mardi Gras. Soberly, city officials said the massive street party "would not be consistent with the present state of the nation."[41] The bacchanalia of the Big Easy was now a bust.

Meanwhile, churches in New York were preparing for bombing attacks. Different religious denominations had differing guidelines for clergy and parishioners alike. The chancery of the New York Catholic Church said that in the event of an air raid, congregants were excused from completing Mass but priests were not. The priests had to complete their services, even if bombs were raining down from the heavens.[42]

New York, like Los Angeles, had been pretty much of a disaster in its practice drills. The irony was that the head of the nation's civil defense program, Fiorello La Guardia, was also the mayor of New York. A later blackout drill in New York proved to be more organized. "Brightly lit marquees and lobbies of theatres along West Forty-fifth Street—in the heart of the city's Great White Way—[were] blacked out." Ten theatres were holding plays that night while the blackout occurred , even as the audiences were in their seats and the performers were on stage. On their own, the shrines of the American theatre on their own established their own guidelines for air raids and black-out drills, just as the churches of New York had.[43]

Some were speculating that the unidentified planes spotted earlier in the week over Los Angeles and San Francisco were scout planes for the Japanese, but it remained a mystery with some speculation that the planes were American aircraft from one of the many military airfields on the West Coast. Some ludicrously suggested that, in remote regions of the United States, there existed "secret airfields" that the enemy was using.[44] And there was also a considerable amount of disinformation still out about the raid on Hawaii.

New reports said there were six separate attacks at Pearl Harbor, the first at 7:55 a.m. and the last two at 7:15 p.m. and 9:10 p.m.[45] The Japanese gov-ernment also told their populace that they'd bombed New York City. Twice.[46]

Battery powered radios were now being pitched as Christmas gifts touting their ability to get the latest news on air raids, even if the electricity went out. To accommodate holiday shoppers, street parking was banned all throughout the downtown areas of Washington including "both sides of F Street, NW from Sixth to Fourteenth Street."[47]

It was also decided to go ahead with the annual Christmas tree lighting on the South Lawn of the White House, presided over by the First Lady and the president with a twist: "The tree-lightening [sic] ceremony will fol-low a patriotic theme.[48] The invocation will be offered by the Most Reverend Joseph M. Corrigan, rector of Catholic University, while the benediction will be given by the Reverend Oscar F. Blackwelder, president of the Washington Federation of Churches. The carols to be heard would include 'Joy to the World,' 'Adeste Fideles,' 'It Came Upon the Midnight Clear,' and 'Silent Night, Holy Night.'" It would be just too crushing to American morale to have the symbol of Christianity doused by the enemies of Christianity. Events were planned throughout the city for men in uniform, so as to ensure that none of these young men would be alone if possible. Outdoor Christmas lighting for private residences and businesses in Washington was banned however.[49]

Mrs. Roosevelt, meanwhile, was on a West Coast tour, discussing civil defense, meeting with Red Cross officials, and meeting with defense council officials in San Diego. While there, she visited her son John and his wife.[50]

The unanimity across the country in support of war against the Axis Powers was no less than astonishing. From July 4, 1776, to December 6, 1941, the country had been more or less divided over all matter of things, and compromise was the glue that held together America.

Compromise as a watchword, though, had been replaced by compel. The American people were compelled mostly by their own free will (along with a generous amount of peer pressure) to support their president and their government as never before. The *New York Times* sent reporters all over the city to sample opinion, and what they discovered was no less than amazing. "There was no disunity; there was a fusing of people of all groups, all classes, all nationalities, all races, into a feeling of national solidarity. There was no panic; there was the quiet refrain, 'They started it; we'll finish it.' There was no hysteria; there was the cold-voiced slogan, 'Remember Pearl Harbor.' There was no more isolationism or pacifism; there was a united people, ready and willing to back up the President of the United States and the armed forces to the limit."[51]

The president of the Life Underwriters Association of New York, Miss Beatrice Jones, said "the Jap attack was the something that had to happen to bring the American people up with a sharp turn . . . to impress on them the soft days are over."[52] A pacifist group, the Mothers of American Sons, voted to disband and turn their assets over for the purchase of war bonds.[53] And General Robert Wood, national chairman of the America First Committee, announced its formal dissolution once and for all by an act of its committee. Wood issued a statement urging all Americans to get behind the war effort, something not thought possible a week before in anybody's worst nightmare.[54] Adding to this was the unity among the twenty-one countries of the Western Hemisphere. They were 100 percent unified in opposition to the Axis.[55]

Deeper into the polyglot culture of urban America, some wondered about the attitudes of Italian Americans and German Americans. Generally speaking, the Italian Americans in New York's Little Italy and Harlem professed their loyalty to America, denounced Mussolini, and took his picture down or turned it to the wall. German Americans by and large were supportive of their adopted country as well, but some "dyed-in-the-wool Nazi types sullenly said nothing but looked daggers at American inquirers." Visitors to New York, where a great many Germans Americans lived, discovered that while most German Americans applauded the United States, they did not do so with the same vehemence as the Italian Americans.[56]

To underscore the observations of the reporters, a nest of German spies, including several women in New York, had been caught some weeks earlier and convicted by the government for passing along state secrets to Berlin. The case was thin, and it may have even involved entrapment by the FBI. The presiding judge may have tipped his hand of the flimsiness of the government's case when he advised the jury, "men are not sent to jail for their opinions in this country. A man is entitled to believe that the German race is a superior race . . . that the world was created in order that the German race might dominate it. So long as he does nothing to carry those views into effect to the detriment of the United States."[57]

The jury deliberated for eight hours before convicting all fourteen on both counts of conspiracy.[58]

Private pilots had been grounded since the seventh, and the Civil Aeronautics Board began background checks on the 94,000 licensed pilots in America, investigating their "character and loyalty to the United States."[59] The Civil Aeronautics Administration (CAA) slowly began lifting restrictions on those whose backgrounds checked out, but it limited recreational flying to a "ten-mile radius of the base of operations" and mandated that any distance flying must first be approved and a strict flight plan filed and obeyed. The CAA also reserved the right to confiscate any plane "piloted by an alien or suspected alien."[60]

Government officials were moving in other directions as well to prevent sabotage. In Massachusetts, guards were placed around drinking water supplies and plans were made for the inspection of milk pasteurization facilities.[61] Civilians were warned that if water supplies, were interrupted due to poisoning or bombing, they would have to get by on three pints a day. Under the state and local committees on public safety, new precautions were being instituted daily. "Crack Army Crews" were at the ready, manning antiaircraft batteries and searchlights twenty-four hours a day, seven days a week.[62] Atop many buildings in the greater Boston area could be seen the antiaircraft guns and men assigned to them, and were "secret storage places for ammunition within speedy delivery distance of the anti-aircraft gun establishments."[63]

Cameras were banned at the East Boston Airport after someone was spotted taking pictures of government planes there.[64] The Navy also announced that all navigational lighting and radio beacons along the Eastern Seaboard might be turned off for the duration of the national emergency. Boston, like Washington and other locales in America, was quickly becoming an armed camp. "Sights, sounds and smells of the Army have become a part of the daily life for city dweller and suburbanite alike."[65]

Civilian Defense insignias began to sprout up across the Boston area and around the country on armbands and helmets, on posters and public buildings, all showing what would become the iconic simple letters "CD" inside a equilateral triangle inside a circle. Other patches designated specialties such as "Auxiliary Police," "Auxiliary Fireman," "Bomb Squad," "Fire Watcher." The insignias began in Massachusetts but spread quickly across the country, along with the specified duties and ranks of the volunteer arm of government.

Sober Bostonians were relieved to see a Guinness beer advertisement touting beer's healthful benefits because of its "barley, hops ... yeasts."[66] Others were curious as to what the pacifist Norman Thomas planned to say at Harvard, which was still examining what the war meant to Harvard.[67] Sophisticates descended from the *Mayflower* exhibited their own form of nativism when the Museum of Fine Arts closed to the public its "Jap art treasures ... for the duration of the emergency" according to the *Boston Evening Globe*.[68]

Some miles away on Cape Cod, the Selectmen who governed Provincetown voted to shut off the light at Pilgrim Tower. The monument had been dedicated some years earlier by Teddy Roosevelt. A couple of townsfolk complained that the light at the top of the monument was weak, while the North Truro lighthouse was enormously powerful. But it was turned off, even as the Truro light was kept on.[69]

As if to underscore the danger involved, the famed insurance company, Lloyd's of London, cancelled its policy of insuring American property.[70] Also, a black market for the sale of automobile tires was emerging, and Justice Department officials were busy keeping track of this. A rationing system was hastily arranged.

Although Washington had ordered the "fixing" of many goods and services in the economy, a federal judge nonetheless ordered fines against he "Big Three": Reynolds Tobacco, Liggett and Myers Tobacco, and American Tobacco for "price fixing," conspiracy, and monopoly of the cigarette market in America. In each instance, the fine against each company was $5,000.[71] The government also fixed the prices of most oils and lubricants, but not butter, salad dressing, or shortening.[72]

Local officials in California had originally blocked the vegetables produced by local Japanese farmers from being shipped to market for fear of poisoning. But Uncle Sam jumped in and gave these very same farmers a pass to continue operating and shipping their products to market. There were just too many military bases in the Golden State that were dependent on the farmers for fruits and vegetables: "to put them all out of business would interfere with the normal economy of the region . . . the Treasury . . . issued an order exempting them from the restrictions which now apply to all other Japanese aliens." The Treasury Department also issued an order allowing the Japanese access to their frozen bank accounts—but only $100 per month.[73]

In New York, the FBI, based on a "telephone tip from a man who spoke in broken English with what seemed to be an Italian accent," was looking for some WPA workers who had been overheard by the tipster, plotting to blow up the Coney Island Police Station.[74]

There were newspapers in America in 1941, and there were tabloids in America in 1941. The *Washington Post*, the *New York Times*, the *Wall Street Journal*, the *Evening Star*, the *Christian Science Monitor* were for the most part sober, serious, and down-to-earth papers that more calmly reported the facts of the war and the government—their editorial policies notwithstanding. Then there were the tabloids such as the *Boston Daily Globe*, the *San Francisco Chronicle*, the *Los Angeles Times* and the *Chicago Tribune*, which tended toward screaming headlines and stories that were thin on facts, but long on hyperbole. To examine the San Francisco or Los Angeles tabloids on December 13 would convince the reader that America and the Allies were winning, that all was calm and well. In reality, while the Americans still held Wake Island and the Philippines, it was only a matter of time before the superior numbers of the Japanese military would overwhelm these two territories as well as others in the western Pacific.

More honest observers knew and reported the reality: just days in and America was losing the war. "American armed forces battled Japanese attacks on three sides of Luzon Island." It was also reported the Japanese were on the offensive in the jungles of Malay, their tanks rolling.[75]

The stock and commodities markets were slapdash. There were so many factors including: price controls on some commodities, production controls on others, plus the unsettling war news, along with new announcements coming out of Washington. It was not a good time to be in the market. A chart of the market from 1914 to 1941, showing the index of industrial production, demonstrated a steady gain over three decades, even with the big dip at the onslaught of the Great Depression. Industrial stock prices for the same period, however, showed a huge peak in 1929 and then a precipitous decline all through the 1930s. Even with production up from 1937 on, stocks still fell. Airplane stocks were flat too. Eastern Airlines, Western Airlines, Trans World Airlines, American Airlines, United, all showed minimal growth.

Smoking was allowed on all flights, in all sections, at all times. Some preferred "Kool" cigarettes: its advertising said an overwhelming majority of smokers—83.2 percent—agreed that the menthol brand eliminated "smoker's hack!"[76] Others preferred to give cartons of Phillip Morris as gifts wrapped in "gay Holiday packings,"[77] while others still thought a carton of Old Gold's in the "gay, NEW . . . YULETIDE CARTON," which offered "New Smoking Happiness," looked just fine in Santa's holiday sack.[78] The best slogan of the season may have been for the Proctor toaster: "Merry Crispness."[79]

But the best ads artistically were still the Coca-Cola seasonal featuring a hale and hearty Santa enjoying a bottle of the world-famous drink. Their longtime slogan was, "The pause that refreshes."[80]

There could be no pause in the war as the navy conceded that Guam was "probably taken" by the Japanese. "The Navy announced today it was unable to communicate with the Pacific island of Guam by either radio or cable and added that the capture of Guam by the Japanese was probable."[81] Some 400 navy men and around 155 marines were left to defend the garrison on the island. The loss of the small but strategically important island was devastating. "Similarly, Wake and Midway may fall despite heroic resistance. The Navy had already reported that in one 48-hour period, the Japanese attacked Wake four times by air and once by naval units, and that during the latter assault, a Japanese light cruiser and destroyer were sunk by aerial counterattack by the Wake Marine garrison." Wake was nothing but a little "V-shaped" island in the middle of the Pacific, 2,400 miles west of Hawaii. Strategically, it was anything but nothing.[82] Palmyra, only hundreds of miles south of Hawaii, was also an attractive target for the Japanese.

The frankness of the navy was uncharacteristic of how the military was handling setbacks, publicly.

During the previous evening, Japanese night bombing had obliterated parts of Manila around Clark Field. At first report, 75 civilians were killed and another 300 wounded. The U.S. Army continued to issue bulletins claiming that the Japanese landings north of Manila on Luzon had been repelled and that American G.I.'s were once again "mopping up" the area.[83] The Japanese claimed otherwise, saying publicly that their forces were making their way inland on the big island of Luzon towards Manila.

The British, more experienced in global war and hence a bit more frank than the Americans, admitted that operations were not going well in the Hong Kong sector, that the Japanese were on the offense, and that the Brits were withering under the pounding. The Japanese agreed. "Japanese Army headquarters declared the fall of British crown colony of Hong Kong was imminent following complete Japanese occupation of Kowloon whose 4-mile-long and supposedly impregnable defenses have been battered down."[84] The Japanese littered the area with propaganda dropped from airplanes designed to inflame racial tensions between the Chinese and the British.

It was announced, however, that Dutch submarines had sighted and sunk four Japanese troop transports on the east coast of Borneo. Torpedoes were fired, and 4,000 Japanese troops were sent to the bottom of the Pacific.[85] In an "exclusive" story for the *Boston Evening Globe*, the "Jap Naval Attache at Vichy" denied that pilots for his country were using the planes as "human torpedoes" calling it a "myth." The paper also claimed that neither Washington nor London was pressuring Moscow to get into the fight against the Japanese.[86] The same day, however, the *Washington Post* ran a story saying "Tokyo admits using 'human torpedoes.'"[87] It was the war's first confirmation of kamikaze pilots.

Reporters caught up with the widow of Captain Colin P. Kelly Jr., the twenty-six-year-old West Point grad and pilot who was credited with the sinking of the *Haruna*. Mrs. Marion Kelly was calm, saying "I know he's happy," of her now-deceased husband. Photographed on her lap was one-and-a-half-year-old Colin P. Kelly III, nicknamed "Corky." His mother bravely, if also forlornly, continued, "And Corky will be proud too." The mother and son had little choice as the most important man in their lives was dead. There was little left in the emptiness except pride and pain, a Gold Star in a window to replace the Blue Star that had previously been displayed, and, under the improved pension legislation for war widows, $42.50 a month for the rest of Mrs. Kelly's life or until that time as she remarried, from a grateful government.[88] But the curly headed, handsome young pilot with the wide-set eyes would never walk through the door of his home again, never again throw his arms around his wife, never again have a son bound up into a warm embrace.

Unfortunately, the Kelly's would be one of the first of many who would bravely tell reporters how "proud" they were of the men in their family who had fallen in the new war.[89] The first Gold Star of World War II had already been awarded to the mother of Private Joseph G. Moser by Mrs. Mathilda Burling, president of the Gold Star Mothers of America.[90]

A tradition of the first war had been revived. Blue stars in the front windows of American homes denoted a family member in the service. Silver stars were for a family member who'd been wounded. And then there were the Gold Stars. So many more sad stories were yet to come of dead soldiers and sailors.

In war, it always seems that the women and the children are the ones who suffer the most.

CHAPTER 14

THE FOURTEENTH OF DECEMBER

Civil Service Law Bars Aliens from Federal Payroll
Boston Sunday Globe

San Francisco's Women Get Ready to Fight
San Francisco Chronicle

U.S. Flyers Battle Japs in Manila Raid
The Sunday Star

Japanese Report Fate of Hong Kong Sealed
Los Angeles Times

Seven days after the surprise Japanese attack on Pearl Harbor, 836 days after the surprise German attack on Poland, and three days after Nazi Germany and fascist Italy declared war on the United States, an observer needed a scorecard to tell who, around the globe, was at war with whom. The Associated Press went so far as to use a sports metaphor in calling it a "lineup."[1]

At war with Germany, Italy and Japan: *the United States, Great Britain, Canada, China, Free France, the Netherlands, Netherland Indies, New*

Zealand, Poland, union of South Africa, Costa Rica, Cuba, Nicaragua, Dominican Republic, Honduras, Haiti, El Salvador, Guatemala, and Panama.

At war with Germany, Italy, and their European allies only: *Soviet Russia, Belgium, Czechoslovakia, Ethiopia, Greece, Luxembourg, Norway, Yugoslavia.*

At war with the United States, Britain, and Russia: *Germany, Italy, Slovakia, Rumania.*

At war only with Russia and Britain: *Finland, Hungary.*

At war only with the United States and Britain: *Japan, Manchukuo, Bulgaria.*

Broken relations with Germany, Italy, and Japan: *Mexico.*

Broken relations with Japan only: *Colombia.*

Broken relations with the United States: *Hungary.*

Expressing "solidarity" with the United States: *Argentina, Brazil, Bolivia, Chile, Ecuador, Paraguay, Peru, Uruguay, Venezuela.*[2]

Not mentioned were Ireland and Vichy France, which was little more than a hand-puppet for Berlin, although there were some in the West still under the illusion that the Marshal Petain government could or would stand up to the Axis Powers. Joseph Stalin still had not decided to declare war on Japan, still looked out for his country's own interests, and still demanded Lend-Lease help from America. He was angry that, despite his country's enormous sacrifices in staving off Hitler's Operation Barbarossa, he seemed to be getting little help in return from America and the Brits. A delusional paranoiac by nature, Stalin began to suspect that the Allies intended to let his country bleed at the hands of the Nazis. After all, in Stalin's mind, his partners of convenience—America and Britain—were capitalists and, as such, could not be trusted. Indeed, one of his greatest fears was that FDR and Churchill would eventually make common cause with Hitler, and all three would then pursue him. Stalin trusted no one, as reflected by his incessant, murderous purges of millions of innocent people. Meanwhile, the Irish, blinded by an age-old hatred of the English, could not see that the Third Reich was their enemy too. The island of Eire remained neutral.[3]

Argentina, though expressing solidarity with the United States, was thought among the knowledgeable in Washington circles to have strong Nazi leanings.[4] To be sure, South America was riddled with Nazi spies and sympathizers, making that region a prime surveillance target for both the FBI and FDR's brand-new foreign spy agency, the Office of Strategic Services (OSS), the precursor to the CIA.

What with countries at war and with all of the borders and bureaucrats and bribes needed to get from locale to location, noncombatants and civilians queued up in ports of call and airports, in terminals and in train stations. They waited interminable hour upon interminable day upon interminable week, without transit visas, trying to get out, get in, get going, get back, get home. "Lisbon has been crowded for many months with persons who have gone there in the hopes of getting transportation to America via the Pan American clippers or ships of the American Export Line."[5] Somewhere, Bogie and Bacall were stuck too, and time went by.

Just hours after the German army said it was hunkering down for the long Russian winter and awaiting spring to renew its offensive operations, came fresh stories declaring the Russian army now had the Nazis on the run, at least outside of Moscow. But, as much of the reporting came secondhand from Stalin's propaganda machine, it was unknown what was true and to what extent it was an exaggeration. "The German high command said early this week that with the settling in of winter, Nazi troops had entrenched themselves and that Moscow and Leningrad could not be taken before spring."[6] The New York Times accurately digested the Russian propaganda and said, "It seems unlikely that the Germans have suffered real disaster the red Army avers." Hitler claimed the German army would regain the offensive after the winter snow melted.[7]

The Nazis were continuing their purges in other occupied areas, such as in Vichy, where resistance members were shot for possessing guns or holding a different political view or simply being of another race—basically, anyone who wasn't a Nazi. "In the unoccupied zone, roundups of Jews, Communists and 'terrorists' generally continue day by day."[8]

It was later revealed that over a hundred non-Aryans were lined up and shot by the Nazis. The occupying Nazi General, Otto von Steuelpnagel, signed an order levying fines of one billion French Francs "exclusively" against Jews in Vichy. The order never elaborated what the fine was for, although bulletins pasted all over Paris made clear, the Nazis were not done with the matter—they were on the hunt for more "anarchists." Also, by von Steuelpnagel's order, "A large number of criminal Judeo-Bolshevik elements will be deported to hard labor in the eastern territories. Other deportations of still greater numbers will follow."[9]

The Nazis also began registering Americans in Germany, but oddly, only those over the age of fifty and under the age of fifteen.[10]

Yet another American pilot emerged as an early hero of the war. This one was John G. Magee Jr., a pilot/poet in the best tradition of Antoine de Saint-Exupery. He was the son of a rector of St. John's Episcopal Church in Washington. Impatient to get into the fight, young Magee had joined the Royal Canadian Air Force months earlier, and while the details of his death were not revealed, he too had "slipped the surly bonds of Earth . . . and, touched the face of God."[11]

Curiously, as one city after another had stumbled and bumbled its way through air-raid drills and blackout drills, the nation's capital had yet to complete a first, true dress rehearsal. As of the thirteenth, one was not planned for several weeks, even though the head of the local civil defense warned that without complete cooperation, "failure . . . may mean the blasting out of life or property."[12]

The city had good reason to protect property, and not just the public property of the government either. Many private insurance companies had stopped writing policies or cancelled policies on "war risk" homes and businesses located in Washington. "The majority of the reputable companies closed their books with the first rain of bombs on Hawaii."[13] Consequently, the federal government took $100 million and created a "nation-wide war insurance system to pay the private owners of homes, farms or factories in the Continental United States for damage or destruction resulting from enemy aircraft."[14] The new government bureau, the War Insurance Corporation, also covered crops and fruit orchards.

The federal city for years had been a sleepy, fevered, malarial swamp, appallingly humid and hot in the summer. It was situated on the Potomac River, which had become a slow-moving cesspool. Sewage was dumped in from homes upstream: from Georgetown, whose sewage drained right into the river; from the Army base at Ft. McNair; and from the Anacostia River, which fed into the larger Potomac. Until a WPA project built the Tidal Basin to control the river, it often overflowed its banks, sometimes even as far as the White House, and everything reeked. Between the New Deal, Lend-Lease, and now a new war, the town had changed radically.

David Brinkley memorably wrote in *Washington Goes to War*, "A languid Southern town with a pace so slow that much of it simply closed down for the summer grew almost overnight into a crowded, harried, almost frantic metropolis struggling desperately to assume the mantle of global power, moving halting and haphazardly and only partially successfully to changing itself into the capital of the free world."[15] Because of the advent of air conditioning, it was at least tolerable in the summer months now. But on this Sunday, December 14, it was doused by heavy sleet that knocked down the phone lines.

British diplomats had so hated being posted to Washington that they were paid extra, the same as if they were assigned to a war zone.[16] Now, Washington was ground zero for a world war zone. The town was radically altered, forevermore.

The town took soldiers and sailors, not only of America, but of America's allies, to its bosom. British and Australian enlistees were truly amazed at how hospitable Washington was. "Decent, that's what these people are. Why, there are more conveniences for service men here than I've ever found anywhere."[17]

There were canteens where men in uniform could listen to music, write letters, put their feet up. There were dances at churches and civic centers, there were of course bars on every corner, but there were also lectures and concerts, historic tours and church services. At the Botanic Gardens, there was a poinsettia display, and a variety show at the Washington Hebrew Congregation.[18] The cities of America, and especially Washington, had transformed into one big "R and R" station for men in uniform. The town bristled with a military presence, and the navy's PBY's routinely took off and landed on the Anacostia and Potomac Rivers.

The war had radically changed life in the military and aboard ship as well, especially in a combat zone. Censorship was widely employed in letters to and from sailors. It was not at all unusual for gobs and swabs to open their "V-Mail," only to find it already read by navy censors. Sensitive information such as the names of cities and ships, as well as details about other sailors, were neatly cut out of the letter with scissors. The same treatment went double for outbound letters. In a letter home, a sailor wrote, "We hear on the radio that the U.S.S. was sunk. We couldn't send out any message because it would give our position away to the Japs."[19] Wives and girlfriends were advised not to put multiple lipstick kisses on the outside of letters as it could be interpreted to be code.[20]

As a consequence of rumors, the postmaster general had to go so far as to issue a statement saying there would be no censorship of in-country mail.[21]

Civilians were also admonished to be careful what they said and to whom, especially "ship movements or other information which might be valuable to the enemy. You are violating the security of the United States and endangering the lives of your fellow Americans if you fail to observe . . . precautions." A Five Point Plan was released, all of it urging civilians in each of the points: "Don't discuss . . . . concentrations . . . movements . . . new weapons . . . naval personnel."[22]

In other words, shut up.

But, curiously, newspapers were still publishing the billeting and deployment of individual G.I.'s, naming names and destinations.

More guidelines were issued for blackouts. "Matches and cigarettes used on open streets are easily spotted by rooftop watchers." Eleanor Roosevelt advised Americans that the government was worried about poison gas attacks, implying that the Japanese had used gas against the Chinese. She also suggested that in order to keep children calm, parents should teach them "war is a game."[23] Long stories appeared advising people on how to deal with a gas attack by the

Japanese. Evacuation plans were developed, and Congress debated the bill to fund gas masks for the civilian population. Initially, the government wanted to distribute 38 million gas masks along the East and West Coasts.[24]

Bombing chitchat continued endlessly. In the militarily unimportant area of San Joaquin Valley, a mass exodus of farmers and farm workers ensued after rumors spread that they were about to be bombed.[25] Still, there was reason to be concerned. Law enforcement officials found evidence of attempted sabotage at dams in both California and Maryland. Advice columnists and veterans of the London bombings urged Americans that work was the best therapy for getting over the bombing jitters. When asked by the Gallup polling organization, a plurality of Americans on both coasts believed they might be bombed.[26] Stories appeared in newspapers on the "dos and don'ts for handling fire bombs," giving readers tips on what to do should one fall in a backyard undetonated. "Suppose an incendiary bomb fell in your vicinity, what would you do?"[27] Some training sessions to teach civilians how to handle undetonated bombs were called by the dubious moniker, "skull practice."[28]

The president's eldest son, James, went on active duty for the marines. In short order, all four Roosevelt boys would be in uniform, John, Elliot, and Franklin Jr. The recruiting offices of the country were still being inundated with applicants, some who had been sent away more than once due to the outpouring. "Boys" and "white-haired men" continued to show up.[29]

One young man in New York was so deeply moved by the war and the sacrifices of his fellow Americans that he changed his status from conscientious objector to 1-A. "In the face of this dastardly inhuman attack . . . I feel my stand as a conscientious objector in untenable. I feel proud to admit that I have made a mistake in taking the impractical stand of pacifism and repudiate it without the slightest reservation or hesitation. I stand ready to serve!" The wire story did not release the name of the young man for obvious reasons.[30]

In newspapers throughout the country, stories of young men (and some women) in the war zone or in flight school or gunnery school or boot camp or nursing school began to appear, generated by proud parents and other family members.

And more were turning up dead. A headline in the *Atlanta Constitution* read, "Georgian Killed in Hawaii Attack." It told of Lt. Ralph Hollis of the Navy.[31] On the front page of the *Birmingham News* was another headline, "Lauderdale Negro Killed in Naval Engagement," its story telling of twenty-three-year-old Anthony Hawkins Jr. who had "died in action" in Hawaii.[32]

In Lynn, Massachusetts, the parents of Army Private Leo E. A. Gagne were making plans for his mass. He'd been killed at Hickam Field in Hawaii. The outpouring of friends and strangers, like everyplace else in America, was awe inspiring. "Members of his grief-stricken family had hardly made announcement of their plans to have a mass celebrated in the hero's memory when veterans of World War I offered to join them by paying military honors." Also, the local Veterans of Foreign Wars and the American Legion, along with community groups, came out to pay tribute and console the grieving family. The burial would not be anytime soon however. "The body will not be returned to this country until hostilities have ended, according to the War Department."[33]

High school students were assembling stretchers and first-aid chests for carrying bandages and medicines.[34] In Miami, a blind man offered his services and those of his seeing-eye dog to help people in blackouts.[35] Boy Scouts were distributing 5 million air-raid posters.[36] Yet another newspaper account told of a senior class deferring the $37.50 collected for a trip to the purchase of war bonds instead.[37] Meanwhile, school kids in New York could be heard singing, "Hi-ho, hi-ho, we're off for Tokyo, to bomb each Jap, right off the map, hi-ho, hi-ho."[38] Such stories appeared by the thousands.

Civic mindedness was deep in the culture now. While not necessarily the clean-living model, a nonetheless patriotic group of strippers at the Follies Theatre in Los Angeles, led by Miss Dorothy Darling, pledged they would purchase $500 worth of war bonds each week.[39]

Nationally, the American Automobile Association organized an effort to drive women and children to and from military bases while also transporting soldiers and sailors to their new duty stations.[40] Virtually everyone was supporting the war effort now.

The final nail was driven in the coffin for the America First Committee. They'd already folded their tent, but not before the storefront of its New York office was besieged with "junior clerks, office boys and stenographers [who] made it a point to pass by the . . . office during the lunch hour and by, shouted remarks and finger postures added to the discomfiture of the staff." A "for rent" sign was hung in the window.[41]

A week earlier, the organization had bragged about setting up shop in every congressional district in the country, as a means of pressuring federal candidates into adopting their nonintervention agenda. Now the organization was deader than a doornail, and the former head of the organization, General Robert E. Wood, offered his services as a former military commander to President Roosevelt.[42] Wood was a highly decorated and much-esteemed veteran of the Great War.

Congress was nearing passage of a new Selective Service Act, the word "selective" being, by and large, window dressing. The aim was to scoop up as many males as possible. The 1-A classification referred to all able-bodied young, male American citizens between the ages of eighteen and forty-four years of age. The classification of 2-A was reserved for men whose work was considered essential, including many professional baseball players after January of 1942. The classification of 2-B was for men working in war industries, and 3-A was for married men.[43]

Government officials made it plain, however, that any jobs in the private sector filled by women would be vacated for men once they returned from combat.[44] But a federal circuit court of appeals made clear that there was no college deferment for studies or athletics. A football player at Gonzaga University sought to defer being drafted until he finished his gridiron career, but the court threw him for a loss.[45] Also, the U.S. Golf Association and the PGA mulled over suspension of the pro links tour for the duration of the war, and military leaders called for cancelling the Rose Bowl.[46]

The PGA considered a suspension, in part because of tour crowds on the West Coast. "Japanese planes have been seen reconnoitering over San Francisco. Machine gunners and bombers have a fondness for targets of that nature," reported the *Sunday Star*.[47] The amateur and professional tennis tours made no indication of cancelling their seasons. Bobby Riggs was the number one ranked player in the world.[48]

Movie director Frank Capra was anxiously awaiting his orders. His *Meet John Doe* had premiered in May. On the twelfth, five days after Pearl Harbor, he'd accepted a commission as major in the *Army Signal Corps*, and on the thirteenth he'd wrapped principal photography on *Arsenic and Old Lace* with Cary Grant and Priscilla Lane; only editing remained.[49] Capra had already served in "World War I" (as the *Los Angeles Times* called it) as a math instructor at Ft. Scott in San Francisco.[50]

Soon, General George C. Marshall would give the talented young filmmaker a vital assignment: to create a documentary series called *Why We Fight* that explained to Americans the stakes involved in this world war, outlining the differences between American democracy and the totalitarian systems overseas.[51] Meanwhile, in case anyone in Tinseltown didn't get the message, big prints ads were purchased telling readers that, "All theatres are open and operating as usual! Even during Blackouts the show goes on as usual, with outside lighting curtailed in cooperation with the Citizens Defense Committee."[52]

War work was proving deadly, and not just for those in uniform. At a munitions plant in Iowa, a massive explosion killed nine and badly injured twenty.[53] Over the course of the war, thousands of civilians would be killed in the war industry or because of new procedures. In Los Angeles, a man fell into a culvert and drowned during a blackout.[54] With many of the ships in the sea lanes running without lights, a collision involving a commercial vessel, the *Oregon*, and an unnamed navy ship off of Nantucket resulted in the death of seventeen sailors.[55] Risk came with the territory for all Americans nowadays.

If American sacrifices and rationing were austere, Canada's were downright Scrooge-like. The country rationed gasoline and prohibited the manufacturing of "bicycles, tricycles, children's metal wagons, ice skates, roller skates, beds and furniture and appliances of every sort made of metal, such as electric broilers, fans, grills, irons, electric tea kettles and a host of other metal objects of everyday use are not to be manufactured except by permit."[56]

While Americans would not experience gasoline rationing (not yet anyway), the quality of their gasoline would go down. The anti-knocking ingredient—tetraethyl lead—that gave gasoline the octane so needed for automobiles was considerably more essential for the high performance engines of American airplanes. It would also mean that miles per gallon would drop, significantly.[57]

Questions arose again, about food and food supplies. During the Great War, American housewives had experienced food shortages and "to a housewife, a world war is a world war." Government officials cooed that this time it would be different. Supplies were high, sugar could be expected to continue arriving from Hawaii, and new oils, to replace coconut and palm oil from the Far East, could be acquired from South American countries. Also, foodstuffs would not be shipped overseas in the quantities of the last war. Still, this did not stop the rush of food buying, especially of flour, canned vegetables, and sugar (with good reason). Soap manufactures and sugar producers were rationing sales to wholesalers, in the hopes of stopping hoarders.[58] The Office of Production Management moved in and banned sugar-hoarding outright.[59] Then the government moved in and curbed the shipment of sugar altogether. Rationing began. "The federal restrictions are aimed chiefly at candy and soft drink manufacturers and bakeries."[60]

War was also costly. It would be financed with bonds and taxes and bank loans. The nation's banks as of the tenth had assets of $3.8 billion: "This indicated that the banks still have vast idle funds for financing the war."[61] And yet every day there were fresh stories in the papers about the young and old, the poor and rich, black and white, male and female, all purchasing defense bonds, some with their last few dollars.

Now, on a war footing, the country was divided into nine regions in order to facilitate military and civilians responses to possible attacks. The country was not divided on the economy however. By a better than 2-1 margin, Americans supported wage and price controls as a means of combating inflation as well as "war profiteering."[62]

The cost of living had been rising, doubling in less than six months with no compelling argument other than government control offered.[63]

In New York, bulldozers moved in to knock down the last of the 1939 World's Fair exhibits, including a pavilion created by the Japanese government to symbolize the eternal friendship of the American and the Japanese people.[64] The World's Fair had showcased many technological marvels and was enormously popular. It was at this venue that Radio Corporation of America (RCA) introduced television to the American public, an astounding invention that had to wait until war's end to come to fruition.[65] In 1941, the Fair's disintegrating remnants stood as a poignant reminder of a more peaceful and productive direction that the world could have taken, but didn't.

Even a week after the attack on Pearl, public information about the health and well-being of men and women in uniform only trickled out. In one case, a happy family received a telegram announcing that not only was their son-in-law safe, but he and their daughter—stationed in Oahu—had had a healthy baby boy.

The parents of Myrtle M. Miller of Baltimore were also delighted, as Myrtle, an army lieutenant and nurse stationed in Hawaii, was also "well, safe." There was no doubt that young American men bore the brunt of the fight, but a goodly number of women, too, had been at the scene of the battle. Myrtle's father said that his daughter stated, "If war should come, I will follow the boys. They will need help, and I feel it is my duty to do whatever is in my power to do."[66] Miss Miller's words were not just those of a woman or a nurse or a member of the army, but those also of an American.

The names of some of the army pilots who managed to get their planes into the air on December 7 were released by General Walter Short, who was still in charge of the army post in Hawaii. Head of the list was Lt. George Welch, twenty-three, a native of Delaware, who managed to shoot down four Japanese planes, one number short of making him an "ace." The photos of half a dozen army pilots, including Welch, who had fought Japanese in the skies over Oahu, were widely reprinted. "Lt. Louis M. Sanders . . . engaged Japanese plane and shot it down. Second Lt. Kenneth M. Taylor attacked six Japanese planes; shot down two. . . . Lt. Gordon H. Sterling, Jr., Second Lt. Phillip M. Rasmussen, Second Lt. Harry W. Brown . . . ." All were cited for "Spectacular Heroism."[67]

All were handsome young men with full heads of hair, square-jawed, all-American, each with a Tom Sawyer-glint of mischievousness in his eye.

Indeed, the Sunday papers were filled with pro-Allied stories, as if the government had done an information dump of positive news in order to buck up American morale. Stories told of how Americans flyers downed a handful of planes in dogfights over Pearl on the seventh, how American forces had supposedly hurled Japanese invaders back into the sea from their assault on the Philippines, and how British and Dutch forces were supposedly mounting counteroffensives against the Japanese and Germans. The articles were so glowingly positive about the Allies counteroffensive and bravery one could have been excused for thinking Japan would sue for peace within a matter of days.

The women's pages of the papers all featured energetic women volunteering, stepping forward for civic work, helping in their communities. In Georgia, dozens of women patiently took classes to learn Morse Code, tapping out dots and dashes, or more accurately, "dit's" and "da's." The women attending were described as "busy housewives" and "women" who "ranged from sweatered and socked school-age youngsters to grey-haired matrons." Classes had been pulled together by the American Women's Volunteer Service.[68]

This World, the Sunday magazine section of the *San Francisco Chronicle*, simply reprinted on its cover the first Associated Press alert on the attack at Pearl. "Bulletin Honolulu, Dec. 7—(AP)—At Least Two Japanese Bombers, Their Wings Bearing the Insignia of the Rising Sun, Appeared over Honolulu at about 7:35 a.m. (Honolulu Time) Today and Dropped Bombs."[69]

The ever-so-popular comic strips of America—many newspapers carried up to four pages daily—were the last to reflect the war culture. Cartoonists often drew their strips weeks in advance, so it was difficult to take advantage of current events to build into their storylines. So, while war was on everybody's else's lips, in "Wash Tubbs," "Boots and Her Buddies," "Superman," and "Joe Palooka," all the heroes and heroines of the comics went about their lives, fighting bandits, shady Hollywood directors, and other scofflaws. Cartoonists had not used their strips to promote a political agenda; though within a short time, they would be fighting Nazis and Japanese spies, especially in "Captain America," whose very creation was as a result of the war.

Theodor Seuss Geisel—who later became know as the gentle and kindly favorite of kids, "Dr. Seuss"—was drawing some of the toughest and most vicious anti-Nazi and anti-Japanese cartoons in the country.[70]

Roosevelt was getting a clearer picture of the damage at Pearl Harbor, as Frank Knox explained in a confidential, nineteen-page memo to FDR. Scribbled at the top was a note by Roosevelt: "Given me by F.K. 10p.m. Dec 14 when he landed here from Hawaii. FDR." The memo also went into some graphic explanations over the poor response of the navy and the poor displacement of aircraft. "At neither Army or Navy fields were planes dispersed." Of the few Japanese planes shot down, "American radio and other American built equipment was recovered from the wreckage." And, "The *Arizona* is a total wreck, her forward magazine having exploded after she had been damaged by both torpedoes and bombs."[71]

One week after the seventh, all the Sunday papers contained retrospectives and analyses of the attack, the war, and the future conflict. Many of them were pure spitball, and others still didn't have the full details of the war and the attack at Pearl Harbor. Several newspapers ran profiles of Admiral Yamamoto, not altogether unfavorably. One story noted he "does without the eye-glasses that mark most Japanese."[72]

The *Los Angeles Times* reported that Japanese radio was claiming that Admiral Kimmel had been killed at Pearl Harbor while aboard the *Pennsylvania*, which, according to the Japanese, had also met its demise.[73] Kimmel was alive and kicking, but the fact that the Japanese knew the *Pennsylvania* was the admiral's flagship, demonstrated how much they knew about the American Navy.

Some pieces accurately reviewed the importance of the tiny specks of islands in the Pacific to the war for both sides. The vast majority of Americans had never traversed the Pacific, and it was hard to describe or comprehend its massiveness. It was half again the size of the Atlantic, and planes, ships, and submarines could not roam with impunity. They needed to be refueled, and the men needed time to get their feet on dry land at periodic breaks. If the United States was overlaid over the Pacific, it would stretch only from the Philippines to the Marshall Islands.

Islands that Americans had never heard of before, such as Guam and Johnston, and Palmyra, were all of a sudden known and vitally important. "At the war's start naval bases were being constructed on Midway, Wake, Johnston and Palmyra Islands. Channels were being cut through the coral reefs and coral heads were being taken out of lagoons to provide take-off areas for fully loaded planes."[74] Japan controlled many islands in the Western Pacific and was now attempting to run America off the central Pacific islands. There was concern they would also seize the Aleutian Islands in the cold North Pacific and, from there, establish bases close to the West Coast of America.

The *Boston Sunday Globe* featured a column by Owen Scott who, without quoting an authoritative source on the record or on background, said that the country could not possibly begin to engage the enemy in any meaningful way before 1943. Also, "it will be in 1945 before the United States has its Navy operating in a two-ocean basis with full strength in both." He furthermore claimed the war would be won with technology and manpower.[75] American Exceptionalists would have begged to differ.

Yet other stories delved into how America would administer an occupied Europe, once the war was won. Considering how badly things were actually going, this was as astonishing as it was presumptuous. Still, not a soul in the country believed that the United States would not win in the end.

Newspaper and magazine ads for Christmas gifts included toy airplanes for boys and "pajama dolls" for girls.[76] There were ads selling military uniforms, ads pitching washing machines, pianos, tile for concrete floors, and sewing machines; ads for church services and social events and lectures and field trips filled the papers too. Men were urged to please their wives by taking dance lessons at the Arthur Murray Studios.[77] They were also urged to purchase "gift nylons."[78] Birth announcements and marriage license applications filled newspapers as did the ads for "naughty Can-Can"[79] underwear for women.

Debutante balls went forward, and the Elks, the Knights of Columbus, the Eastern Star, and the Colored Masons all met, elected officers, and stepped up their charitable works. The V.F.W. and the American Legion nationwide made their impressive pool of military talents available to civil defense.

The book review sections of all Sunday papers were eagerly read. John Steinbeck's newest novel, *Sea of Cortez*, was favorably reviewed in many, as were *Wolf in the Fold* by Nellise Child and *The Young Churchill* by Stanley Nott. The new novel *Storm*, by George R. Stewart, was reviewed but not altogether favorably. The best-selling novel was *The Keys of the Kingdom* by A.J. Cronin, and the best-selling nonfiction book was William Shirer's *Berlin Diary*.[80]

At the President Hotel in Atlantic City, rooms for the Christmas season were going for $4.50 for a single and $7.00 for a couple, per night.[81] All the Sunday broadsheets had extensive travel sections featuring resorts and hotels and articles on voyages and destinations.

The top ten movies of 1941 were announced. *Citizen Kane* topped the critics's list, but every film on the list would soon become a classic, from *The Philadelphia Story* to *The Maltese Falcon*.[82] Hollywood and the U.S. government had already begun recruiting and organizing "Bond Drives."

Some of the first actors and actresses to sign up for the bond drives were Mickey Rooney, Clark Gable, Bette Davis, Spencer Tracy, Bing Crosby, Judy Garland, and Jimmy Cagney. Also a young, up-and-coming actor, Ronald Reagan, though in the army reserves, had been turned away three times for active duty because of his extremely poor eyesight. It was so bad upon testing that, without contacts or glasses, he could not distinguish a tank unless it was less than seven feet from him.

Slowly, the references to the Great War as "World War I" were beginning to seep into news reporting. No one in Washington ever sent out a memo, but over time, all were coming to see that the "War to End All Wars" had simply been a prelude to a new world war. A columnist for the *San Francisco Chronicle*, Carolyn Anspacher opened her piece by penning, "Eternities ago, during a conflict now designated as World War I."[83] But Blair Bolles opened his Sunday piece by calling this the "119th week of World War II," making the case it had begun with the invasion of Poland in September of 1939, which of course was true.[84]

The fourteenth of December also marked 142 years to the day since the greatest and most indomitable American ever, George Washington, had passed away. Neither Washington nor his country would or could ever be denied. As the British had learned beginning in 1776—and the Axis Powers would in the near future—the American spirit was an indomitable thing.

CHAPTER 15

THE FIFTEENTH OF DECEMBER

Knox Reveals Six U.S. Warships Lost in Hawaii Attack

The Yuma Daily Sun

Japanese Pounding Hong Kong

Evening Star

United States Lend–Lease Aid
Now Totals $1,202,000,000

The Lethbridge Herald

2,727 Officers, Men Killed 'Not on Alert,' Secretary Declares

The Evening Star

I n Lisbon, the port was a madhouse of clamoring humanity, with thousands trying to flee Nazism. The last ship of the American Export Line was about to set sail for the United States before the harbor closed. Only Americans and British subjects with passports and transit visas were allowed aboard. No Germans were allowed, even if they opposed Hitler, and all those German citizens in Portugal wanted nothing to do with the Third Reich. The "pitch blackness of Nazified Europe" was what they now faced.[1]

Still, with their Aryan features, they had a chance to survive in Germany or on the European continent, provided they used their wits. For others, the prospects were terrifying. "Many refugees from Germany were affected. Some 600 Jewish refugees from various countries now in Portugal feared that new developments might cut them off from escape from Europe."[2] The tales of those left behind ripped at the heartstrings: the elderly couple who had hitchhiked for seventeen days, hiding in cellars, in haymows; fathers trying desperately to get their children and wives to safe passage. Left behind were "kings and dukes, ministers of state, and men of letters, businessmen and just ordinary people, some fleeing because their lives were in danger; others because they shared in the panic that was in the air. There was tragedy and despair, generosity and kindliness, mixed unhappily with selfishness. Lisbon has become just another trap from which, this time, there may be no escape."[3]

As the last ship sailed over the Western horizon, "It is hard to imagine the tragedy of the moment for many thousands of human beings from all over Europe. At any moment, the fate of thousands of helpless fugitives from the Nazi 'New Order' in Europe may be sealed."[4]

Also behind enemy lines (or soon to be) were American Christian missionaries throughout the Far East. The Catholic Church had by far the most, with nearly 1,300 priests, brothers, sisters, and scholastics scattered across the region. There were also a couple hundred Baptist missionaries.[5] Prayers were offered for their safe return.

Despite their early successes, General Tojo warned the Japanese people at a public rally of a long and brutal war with the Americans. In America, *Life* magazine opined, "Close observers of Japan have said for years that if that country ever found itself in a hopeless corner it was capable of committing national hari-kari by flinging itself at the throat of its mightiest enemy. Japan has found itself in just such a corner . . . Japan's daring was matched only by its barefaced duplicity."[6] But Tojo also bragged to the Japanese Diet that the American and British fleets in the Pacific had been "crushed."[7]

Midway Island was still in U.S. hands as of Monday, the fifteenth, but FDR had already cautioned the American people that all of the central Pacific islands—save the Hawaiian Islands—and all those of the Far East could fall to the Japanese. In his way, he too was warning his people of a long and brutal conflict and that the news would get worse before it got better. Guam had already fallen, and with it, the fates of 155 marines and 400 navy men were now in the hands of their captors, who did not have a good track record when it came to POWs.[8]

Across America, the refrain "Remember Pearl Harbor!" was heard more and more. It followed in the tradition of other American battle cries: "Give me liberty or give me death!" from Patrick Henry; "Don't give up the ship!" from Captain James Lawrence in the War of 1812; "Remember the Alamo!" from General Sam Houston, before the 1836 decisive battle of San Jacinto in the Texas War of Independence; and "Remember the *Maine!*" which found its origins in a gin mill in New York in 1898, shortly after the explosion of the ship in Havana harbor, which sparked American eagerness for the Spanish-American War. (Whether or not the Spanish or their allies had planted a bomb on the *Maine* was open to question, as it was not unusual for ships of the day to see faulty boilers explode, but for men like William Randolph Hearst, the propaganda value was too attractive to quibble over details such as welders' seams or the efficacy of iron bolts.)

Time magazine observed that never had the people of America ever been this united. "What would the people . . . say in the face of the mightiest event of their time? What they said—tens of thousands them—was: 'Why, the yellow bastards!'"[9] December 7 had become indelible.

Everybody knew where they were on December 7 when they heard the news of Pearl Harbor. There were but a few dates in American history for which someone could say, "I remember where I was when I heard . . . ."

December 7, 1941, was at the top of the list.

FDR had yet to meet with navy head Frank Knox, but rumor out of Washington had it that the navy thought it might be possible to refloat and refit some of those ships hit by the Japanese. Because the harbor was relatively shallow and because the Japanese bombers had ignored the dry docks, the damaged and sunken ships would not have to be towed the 3,000-or-so miles to San Diego.

Still, the fact that repairs were being discussed and that the president had met with Admiral Samuel Robinson—head of the Navy's Bureau of Ships, which was responsible for construction and maintenance—was confirmation to the casual observer that severe damage had occurred at Hawaii.[10]

All major publications had done profiles of the military brass including Admiral Ernest "Rey" King, Admiral Harold "Betty" Stark and Admiral Husband "Kim" Kimmel. Kimmel had been featured on the cover of *Time* magazine the second week of December.[11] Stark had picked up his nickname while an underclassman at Annapolis.[12] *Time* wasn't afraid of controversy, even as it had a tendency to shill often, for the Roosevelt Administration. Its reporting could be terse, mincing few words. In their November 10 issue, they referred to the *New Republic* magazine as "pinko," suggesting the publication was soft on communism.[13]

Life and *Time* magazines took up Kimmel's cause but they were only two of a very few, to do so. Defending the increasingly beleaguered navy man, *Life* wrote "Admiral Kimmel had not been given enough patrol planes to spot enemy carriers a night's steaming away."[14] Still, "there was speculation whether Knox's investigation would lead to changes in either army or navy command in the Hawaiian area."[15]

On Sunday evening, the fourteenth, Knox—upon his return from Hawaii—gave his report to Roosevelt in a short meeting of thirty minutes. FDR studied it into the evening.[16] Knox's return to Washington was not announced until after he left the White House that evening. Then on Monday, eight days after the attack, some of the brutal truth was revealed to the American people.

President Roosevelt sent a report to Congress on Monday detailing that Japanese submarines had been used, something not previously confirmed. Elaborating he said, "The actual air and submarine attack on the Hawaiian Islands began at 1:20 p.m. Washington time on Dec. 7." Enraged, he said that it was well over three hours after the attack before U.S. ambassador Joseph Grew was notified by the Japanese that they had declared war on America. He also observed that "Japan . . . accepted the German thesis of racial superiority and extreme nationalism." Japan, he noted, had proclaimed herself in 1937 to be of a superior race when compared to any other country "of the Orient."[17]

The document Roosevelt sent to the Hill was essentially a recitation of the steady decline of the relations between the two countries, brought on by

Japan's growing militarism. News reports described the president's tone in the document as "bitter." The climax of the FDR's communiqué exclaimed that "there is the record, for all history to read in amazement, in sorrow, in horror, in disgust!"[18]

The report had been sent in part to placate some in Congress who had been agitating for more details. However, those Congressmen knew they had to tread lightly in their criticism. Senator Charles Tobey of New Hampshire, who just a few days earlier had created a scene on the floor of the Senate over the attack by calling for the heads of everybody in the military, was publicly rebuked by the American Legion of his own state, who called on him "to demonstrate undivided allegiance to our country . . . by supporting the proper civil and military authorities of this country."[19]

Knox huddled again that morning with the president for "two hours and 25 minutes" before meeting in a room packed with reporters and photographers. "Knox looked pale and haggard as he talked to the press in his office."[20] The report was startling. The massacre was widespread. FDR called it "barbaric aggression."[21] Americans were prepared to hear of a couple hundred killed. They were not prepared for thousands. "The casualties crept from rumor into uglier-rumor: hundreds on hundreds of Americans had died bomb-quick, or were dying, bed-slow."[22]

The bottom line was that far more men had been killed or wounded than previously thought and far more ships had been destroyed or damaged than previously reported. Knox's report only dealt with the navy's losses and only mentioned the army planes and hangers destroyed, although he did say that "army losses were severe."[23]

Knox told reporters that six American warships had been destroyed in the attack. He "declared that the Navy was not on the alert . . . that the Pacific fleet lost the battleship *Arizona*, three destroyers and two lesser craft . . . . Knox disclosed for the first time that the Navy had suffered 3,385 casualties in the Hawaiian attacks—2,729 officers and men killed and 656 wounded—fatalities in the sudden attack." He elaborated, saying, "Officers 91 dead and 20 wounded: enlisted men 2,638 dead and 636 wounded."[24]

Still, all the details would not be revealed to the American people, "and no complete report is promised."[25] The other capital ship he named besides the *Arizona* was the *Oklahoma*, along with four smaller ships; the *Cassin*, the *Shaw*, the *Downes*, and the *Oglala*. Not revealed was the number of civilians killed by the Japanese.[26]

Knox did say the *Arizona* was lost due to a direct hit by the enemy, and he dispelled the rumors that the Japanese had any kind of secret weapon or that they had used anything other than single-engine aircraft. Knox said the American forces destroyed three Japanese submarines and forty-one planes. He also claimed that the remaining American ships were at sea, searching out the enemy.[27]

Unpromisingly, he told reporters, "We are entitled to know if (a) there was any error of judgment which contributed to the surprise [and] (b) if there was any dereliction of duty prior to the attack."[28]

The Secretary of the Navy also made it clear that Japanese espionage had played a significant role in the attack, feeding the imperial navy constantly with updated information on targets and movements.

He finished the grim report by saying, "In the Navy's gravest hour of peril, the officers and men of the fleet exhibited magnificent courage and resourcefulness during the treacherous Japanese assault on Pearl Harbor. The real story of Pearl Harbor is not one of individual heroism, although there were many such cases. It lies in the splendid manner in which all hands did their job as long as they were able, not only under fire but while fighting the flames afterwards and immediately starting salvage work and reorganization."[29]

Knox paid tribute to an unnamed young seaman who, on his own, manned a machine gun and fired the first shots of America in the new war against Japan, "even before general quarters was sounded." He also paid tribute to the unnamed captain of a battleship who stayed at his post even as "his stomach was laid completely open by shrapnel burst."[30]

Before departing, Knox told the reporters there would be an investigation into the military leadership in Hawaii instigated immediately by the president.[31]

December 15 was "Bill of Rights Day," a national holiday commemorating the first Ten Amendments to the U.S. Constitution. Individual rights and freedoms took on a new meaning this time around, however, and President Roosevelt gave a one hour address, broadcast live from 10 p.m. to 11 p.m. on all radio networks. FDR, concerned about the agitated state of Americans, used his remarks to warn against "inflamed or hysterical action."[32] CBS Radio also broadcast a special entitled, "We Hold These Truths" starring Lionel Barrymore, Walter Huston, and Edward G. Robinson. Always on the lookout to promote young starlets, a Hollywood studio depicted Gene Tierney in a low-cut white dress, holding an oversized version of the document. Constitution meet Cheesecake. More seriously, concerned about the agitated state of Americans, FDR used his remarks to warn against "inflamed or hysterical action."[33]

The year 1941 was also significant as it was the 150th anniversary of the ratification of the Constitution by the Commonwealth of Virginia, in 1791, "which completed the necessary action on the Bill of Rights and gave it the full force and effect of the Constitution." Celebrations of the day were far and wide, involving public and private schools and towns and communities. Vice President Henry Wallace laid a wreath at the grave of George Mason, the Father of the Bill of Rights, at the Founding Father's home in Gunston, Virginia. The governor of Virginia, James Price, also spoke, and a ceremony took place at the tomb of the newspaper editor, John Peter Zenger, "the editor whose trial established the freedom of the press." The Librarian of Congress, Archibald MacLeish, was the mastermind behind the big day.[34]

The original Bill of Rights contained twelve amendments, but the two regulating the pay and the size of Congress were thrown out. As for the ten amendments that formed the final Bill of Rights, in light of current events, few if any people openly commented on which of those were effectively overlooked by the war effort.

A new document was also signed, but among Allies of a different sort. Together, America, Great Britain, the Netherlands, Russia, Free China, and others met in London and signed a mutual war pact declaring that none of the signers would embark on a separate peace agreement with any of the Axis Powers.[35]

On both sides now, it was all-for-one-and-one-for-all war, as representatives of the Axis Powers met in Berlin to map out *their* war strategies.[36] In Syracuse, New York, representatives of the Six Nations of the Iroquois Confederacy met as well to decide their next move. These six independent nations had declared war on Germany in 1917 and were gathering once again to determine if they as a group would declare war on the Axis Powers.[37]

Eight days after the attack, the White House was in a full lockdown. Papers and passes were demanded. Cops and military police roamed ubiquitously, stopping everyone, guns bristling. "Soldiers with sub-machine guns," the *Los Angeles Times* bluntly noted.[38] On the White House grounds, guard towers had been built and one-inch steel cables ran every which way, controlling the flow of foot traffic.

Security measures continued unabated. In Santa Barbara, miles and miles of federal parklands were closed to the public, including the Santa Ynez River locale. "Public entry is not to be permitted until the close of the war."[39] Entry to the Chesapeake Bay was tightly restricted by navy vessels. "Boats ordered to stop shall comply immediately on pain of being fired on."[40]

The New York state government announced that, in order to save steel, motorists would only be required to have license tags on the back of their vehicles, thus saving annually two thousand tons of the important metal. However, there would be no corresponding reduction in licensing fees.[41] It was enough to drive any man to drink, except for German nationals in New York. These "Nazi Citizens," as the *New York Times* called them, were prohibited by the state of New York from owning liquor licenses.[42]

In short order, the federal government ordered a halt to the manufacture of all new pots and pans and kitchen appliances made of iron or steel, and the industry "discontinue the use of brightwork or trim containing copper, nickel or aluminum."[43] However, a "war train" of sorts—but really called the "Defense Special"—was already touring the country, showing businessmen what the military needed to have manufactured. On the train, organized by the Office of Production Management, were blueprints and prototypes of fashioned metal parts.[44]

The culture had changed so deeply that *Time* magazine devoted a long article to the advantages of arc welding in the building of planes and ships.[45]

Washington was seizing an increased number of neutral or civilian ships, including those of allies, under the nautical rules of "angary." Maritime Law provided for a nation, during wartime, to take any and all vessels in order to defend itself. Still, the oceans would shortly be crammed with American-made ships. In anticipation of all that new construction, the industry estimated it would have to recruit over a million workers within a year to meet the military and commercial needs of the country.[46] The demand for shipyard workers was such that agriculture officials anticipated a farm labor shortage.

The navy began awarding what would become their famous "E" flags to civilian industries—and not just shipbuilding—denoting their "Excellent" work. Workers and management alike took real pride in flying these flags at the front of their plants.[47] The growing patriotism in America was such that, at the Hatfield Wire and Cable Company in New Jersey, during the morning Pledge of Allegiance, two of the 350 employees refused to salute Old Glory. Three hundred and forty-eight employees went on strike as a result and said that, unless the two were fired, they would not go to work. The two (who cited religious stipulations) were dismissed.[48]

Sunday also found 80 percent of General Electric employees at their posts, working yet another full day. The employees of the big corporation had already voted to work a six-day-week but here they were, on the seventh day, working hard in Schenectady, Bridgeport, Philadelphia, and dozens of other locations around the nation. The company employed 125,000 workers.[49]

The war industry continued to be dangerous for civilians and would be, throughout the years. At a plant in New Jersey, an explosion "blew an employee to bits" and injured forty others. The FBI and the navy opened an investigation to see if sabotage had been the cause of the blast.[50]

After a call for donors, the Red Cross was awash in the blood of American civilians. Local chapters were overrun with so many people walking in, they were asked to call ahead and make an appointment.[51]

America of 1941 was all slang, all the time. In the patois of the era, Americans had not "washed out" nor had they made a "hash" of things. Carl Sandberg once famously said, "Slang is language that takes off its coat, spits on its hands, and gets to work."[52] Coffee was "Joe"; and breakfast, lunch, and dinner were "three squares." Sailors were "swabs" and "gobs" and soldiers were "dogfaces" and marines were "jarheads." "When one soldier tells another 'our bean-gun grub was shrapnel, cream on a shingle, and ink with side arms,' he's merely saying the meal from the rolling field kitchen included baked beans, creamed beef on toast and coffee with cream and sugar."[53] An unknown or pushy girl was "sister."

Among civilians, "patch my pantywaist" meant being amazed, and "hoy-toytoy" was a good time. "Futzing around" was wasting time, and "dig me?" was do you understand? A "yum yum type" was a good looking individual, and "shove in your clutch" meant get going.[54] A "G.I." of course was slang for "government issue." Later, as the massive war effort generated its inevitable moments of chaos and confusion, harsher slang would emerge that had currency for many years, such as SNAFU (Situation Normal, All F—ed Up).

Many G.I.'s were going to get their Christmas furloughs after all. For those who were not released, the individual bases and the local USOs would do their best to ensure the young men a modicum of a Merry Christmas: after all, they were expecting packages from home, many of those packages containing cartons of cigarettes.

Cigarettes of every style, brand, and packaging were available to every civilian and G.I. in America. The refrain, "Smoke' em' if you've got 'em" became an unofficial military slogan, as superior officers would bark this refrain to enlistees when they went on break. Because cigarettes were included in rations and readily available in military PX commissaries, the federal government all but recommended, encouraged, and endorsed cigarette smoking by men and women in the military. One brand with their own pitch was "Juleps," which contained a "hint of miracle-mint."

Advertising encouraged "chain smoking" of Juleps for those who thought they smoked too much of another brand. They were also recommended for "the boys at camp." Spud cigarettes also billed themselves as good for a sore throat. So did Regent cigarettes.[55] And Philip Morris.

There was never a general outbreak of violence against Japanese Americans, Italian Americans, and German Americans, but the Japanese Americans living loyally in the United States had more to fear and thus more to lose than the others for obvious reasons. There were the occasional stories such as the Japanese man in California who showed up dead in a canal in his car, either because of an accident or foul play.[56] Still, U.S. Attorney General Francis Biddle, concerned that the civilian American population would take out their ire on the wrong people, issued an important statement on the matter: "The United States is now at war. Every American will share in the task of defending our country. It is essential that we keep our heads, keep our tempers—above all, that we keep clearly in mind what we are defending. The enemy has attacked more than the soil of America. He has attacked our institutions, our freedoms, the principles on which this nation was founded and has grown to greatness. It therefore behooves us to guard these principles most zealously at home.[57]

Biddle reminded Americans that "aliens form 3½ percent of our population," while restating that only those aliens with malice in their plans need fear the federal government.[58]

Japanese-Americans in Los Angeles opened up their own pro-American storefronts and announced they would rat out any Japanese they thought "who by word or act consort[s] with the enemies." They also came up with their own loyalty pledge.[59] Little Tokyo in Los Angeles was a ghost town; shops had been forcibly closed as the Treasury Department had ordered Japanese citizens to stay off the streets. Christian Japanese groups formed support groups. Japanese had some reason to be bitter towards the United States. Since 1924, with the passage of the Japanese Exclusion Act, only 100 Japanese individuals per year were allowed U.S. citizenship.[60]

For the eighth day in a row, the Japanese pounded both Hong Kong and the Philippines. In Manila, General MacArthur had the added problem of subversive elements on the island facilitating the Japanese offensive, as well as problems with some of the local native tribes and anarchist groups. The Japanese were attempting to incite a riot against the American military. Japan's propaganda agencies claimed their military was making progress in both battles, as well as all of Malaya where they were advancing toward Singapore.[61]

Even the stiffest upper lipped Brit was not hopeful about the outcome in either Hong Kong or Singapore, even though the Free Chinese were waging a furious battle against the Japanese. The *Christian Science Monitor* reported, "British troops admittedly were withdrawing from Kowloon. . . . Britain admitted that Japanese troops once again had gained ground in . . . North Malaya. . . . Britain admitted that its garrison at Victoria, southeastern Burma, was withdrawn following Japanese landings. . . ." According to London officials, the withdrawal from Kowloon was "according to plan."[62] It was a somber forty-sixth birthday for King George VI, who marked it with his wife, Queen Elizabeth, and his daughters, Princess Elizabeth and Princess Margaret.[63]

MacArthur issued yet another statement saying the situation was "well in hand both on the ground and in the air."[64] In fact, the conditions in Manila had deteriorated so critically that the national legislature was meeting in a basement and the Japanese had established three different beachheads on the main island of Luzon. The only encouraging news was that Filipino troops had won a fight against Japanese parachutists in the hills outside of Manila. The Allies had already declared Thailand as a lost cause, and Shanghai had fallen quickly.[65]

In the European sector, the German bombing of London had ground to a halt. Whereas London was bombed some 19,000 times in the month of September 1940, by September 1941 it had "only" been assailed from the air about 1500 times. Nazi air marshall Hermann Goering had once said that if Germans failed in the Battle of Britain, the German people could call him "Meyer."[66] The anti-Semitic slur was obvious.

The Allies did get some good news from North Africa, where the Brits had regained the offensive against Rommel, aided in part by Indian troops, which must have been particularly galling to the racist Hitler. "The Indians captured 21 Axis officers and 350 men. . . ."[67] Also, American planes had mounted a small counteroffensive in the China Sea, apparently hitting several Japanese ships.[68]

Deep in the hills of Yugoslavia, Serbian guerrillas were also giving the Germans fits, staving off division after division totaling several hundred thousand troops. Eighteen total by December of 1941, who were completely stymied by Draja Mihilovic, the heroic Serb general who commanded a force of less than 80,000 men.[69]

Greek guerrillas were also wreaking havoc with Germany's plans for their country, and despite their best efforts, the German Army and Italian Army could not dislodge them, in the face of widespread food and arms shortages. The Greek people were starving and, by estimates, receiving only around 250 calories a day whereas, before the war, they were getting "between 3,000 and 4,000 daily."[70]

After meeting with Knox, FDR had lunch with his 1940 Republican opponent, Wendell Willkie.[71] No eyebrows were raised whatsoever. FDR's press secretary, Stephen Early, joined them. The Indiana businessman had run a personality campaign in 1940; no one could ever out-personality Roosevelt. The Republican Party of the era was a confusing mishmash of internationalists and minimalists, New Dealers, and the like. It had no coherent organizing philosophy and thus was more akin to a loyal half opposition. The Democratic Party in 1941 was all over the feeble and flaccid GOP.

Willkie lost decisively even as FDR was seeking a third consecutive term, something no previous occupant of the White House had probably ever really considered and certainly not sought. (Ulysses S. Grant had sought a third term, though not consecutively.) Willkie was a Republican New Dealer and fervent internationalist who often spoke up in favor of Roosevelt; many wondered if he'd wandered into the wrong political headquarters as a young man. Willkie later penned a best-selling book, *One World*, which stood as one of the great exhortations ever written for a coming-together of humanity—or just a big collectivist secular humanistic world. Take your pick.

Willkie was recruited to supervise a labor-business conference called by the White House for the following week, but it leaked out that he might take on even bigger responsibilities.[72] The fact was, FDR and Willkie genuinely liked and respected each other.

As with all his days now, Monday was another busy one for Roosevelt as he announced that Lend-Lease to the Allies would continue now that America was officially in the war. He also nominated twenty-five army men to "temporary appointment" as generals. The Senate would have to approve these promotions, including that of Col. Theodore Roosevelt, son of Teddy Roosevelt and a distant cousin of FDR's.[73] Eleanor Roosevelt wrapped up her extended West Coast tour, traveled by train to Portland, and met with civil defense officials the day before. All this was recorded in her widely syndicated column, "My Day."[74] She arrived back at the White House just after 2:00 p.m. on the fifteenth.[75]

The Honolulu that Knox had left behind had changed a great deal in a very short period of time. A once happy, open, casual, and relaxed town was now paranoid, closed, and insecure. A curfew kept everybody off the streets at sundown. Movies theaters and restaurants stopped their businesses in time for patrons to leave and get home. Bars were closed; people did their drinking at home. Trenches were everywhere, as were barbed wire and barricades. Guards patrolled the streets, and "the use of a pocket flashlight or a match is likely to bring a bullet." Dinner parties and cocktail parties were a thing of the past, unless the host and hostess were willing to put up their guest overnight; cars were not allowed on the roads after sunset. Even so, many owners had painted over their headlights. Daytime driving was allowed, but gas sales were limited to half a tank, and the radio kept telling listeners to cut their driving to the bare minimum.[76] However, limited service on Pan American airlines began again between Honolulu and the West Coast, and for the first time in two weeks, the radio station KGU, a part of the NBC empire, returned to the airwaves.[77]

San Francisco was just as panicky as Honolulu. Constant air-raid warnings, blackouts, and rumors of enemy planes and ships had about frazzled the nerves of the average San Franciscan. So, when flares appeared in the night sky, they were rumored to have dropped from enemy aircraft. It was just one more headache they did not need. City fathers cancelled the annual East-West Bowl game, one of the biggest college football games of the year. Los Angles also cancelled the Rose Bowl and the Rose Bowl Parade. The Rose Bowl was moved to the East Coast and would be play at Duke University on January 1.[78] Still, the NCAA saw its role become more important, as the distraction of athletic competition would be helpful to the nation's morale.

The U.S. Maritime Commission announced that heretofore, ships would no longer be launched with any sort of pomp or ceremony. No pretty girls breaking champagne over the bow, no glitzy send-off. Ships would just roll off into the water for immediate sea duty, when finished.[79]

There was a war on, you know.

The gloomy news continued unabated from the Pacific. Washingtonians learned of two more of their young men killed. A navy pharmacist, Robert E. Arnott, twenty-one, who had married Loretta Houser of Silver Springs, Maryland, just the previous May; and Lt. Albert Gates of the navy, who was a native of the District and had once been an instructor at Annapolis.[80]

For the tiny town of Canton, Mississippi, population 6,500, it was even worse. In all of "the first World War," the town had lost but one son. On December 7, it lost three sons at Pearl Harbor. The town's eight churches dedicated their services to Eugene Denson, twenty-two, Keith Joyner Jr., twenty-four, and James Everett, twenty-nine. All were U.S. Army soldiers.[81]

Slowly, a new point of view on the attack was advanced in political and diplomatic circles around the country. The first was the damage could have been far worse. All the first-line carriers were at sea and so escaped unharmed. The Japanese never bombed the fuel and ammo dumps, and many of the ships hit could be repaired as it turned out. If the Japanese had caught the fleet flat-footed at sea, some speculated, the loss could have been 30,000 men and not 3,000 men.

Many in the military political and diplomatic classes also believed that America would have to join the fight sooner or later. What better way to get into a war than with the civilian populace completely united, ready to make any sacrifice, and with the moral high ground of indignation? The Japanese attacked without the decency of the government declaring war on America, first? America was a victim, was angry, knew it was a morally superior country to the Axis Powers, and knew what must be done to win the thing.

If there was ever such a thing as a "Good War," then this war met that definition. Said the respected journalist David Lawrence, "It was a stiff price to pay—but unity came that way. Thus someday the historians of the present epoch will speak of last week's events. For it is difficult to realize what a profound change the Japanese attack on Hawaii has made in American policy and American attitude toward things outside the United States."[82]

The Allies were a force for moral good in the world, and the Axis Powers were a force for evil. The eternal struggle between good and evil had taken on a new form. Rarely could a conflict of such carnage be labeled a "Good War," but this was one of them.

The Nazis weren't merely a conquering national power—they were a warning from history, a lesson as to the human potential for evil brutality. In 1941, not even the worst cynic could possibly imagine just how brutal the war would turn out to be.

CHAPTER 16

THE SIXTEENTH OF DECEMBER

Wandering Jews

Time

New Powers Voted for President

The Yuma Daily Sun

Yamamoto Planned Assault; Seeks to Take White House

The Christian Science Monitor

Buried on page sixty-seven of *Time* magazine was an article meanly entitled "Wandering Jews," covering the release of a 151-page report issued by Manhattan's Institute of Jewish Affairs. The document was horrendous in its content. "Not a Jew is left in Memel and Danzig. The number of Jews in Greater Germany has dropped from 760,000 to about 250,000 since the Nazis came to power. Warsaw's ghetto had more than ten times as many deaths (4,290) as births (396) last June. In all Poland, Jewish deaths since the start of World War II have been five times the normal rate—300,000 in two years."[1]

According to the magazine, "The volume covers 8,500,000 Jews in 16 countries tots up the first full balance sheet on what remains of Jewish life on the Continent." Italy had passed racial segregation laws in 1938, forcing many Jews to change their religion to Christianity in the hopes of emigrating to Central or South America. "Rumania's five-day pogrom last January was featured by 'kosher butchery,' a monstrous parody of the Jewish ritual for killing animals by throat-slitting. All Jewish men from 18 to 50 years of age have been drafted for forced labor. Their daily food ration is one-eighth of that provided for a Rumanian soldier." In Czecho-Slovakia, the report noted there had been "no Jewish problem . . . prior to Munich. Afterwards, the Nazis' Aryanized an estimated $1,000,000,000 worth of Jewish property."[2] *Aryanized* in this case was a euphemism for *stolen.*

The startling report went on to detail how, under Chancellor Hitler, the number of physicians and attorneys in Berlin and Vienna had declined from more than half to nearly non-existent. "Today there are no Jewish business enterprises in Germany, no Jewish lawyers, craftsmen, actors or musicians. . . . With the exception of the manual labor which they perform upon a virtual slave basis, the Jews have been completely eliminated from the economic life of greater Germany. Nearly a million European Jews had to flee their homes between 1933 and 1940. Most had gone into the Soviet Union and the United States had only allowed in 135,000 over that seven year timeframe."[3]

There in black-and-white, was the documentation of the systemic elimination of Jews from Europe. There was no "Jewish question." Anybody with half a brain knew what was happening to the Jews of Europe.

Other countries including those in Central and South America had changed their policies, halting Jewish immigration, walling them into Hitler's clutches. Official Washington and London "have creaked and groaned in the long-winded process of turning out their passports to freedom."[4] The port of Lisbon, the last chance for those escaping Hitler, had closed, and Gestapo agents roamed the city. Some Jews committed suicide rather than fall into the hands of the vile Third Reich. "Scenes at the Portugal frontier were indescribable. Piled up . . . a dirge of human mass pressing to get through. Some went back home, trusting in the promises of Nazi agents."[5]

Neither *Time* magazine nor possibly any other publication of note in America took any editorial position on the atrocious, unspeakable, revolting, repellant, and heartbreaking document. It was duly noted and then dropped out of sight. The relative silence of the rest of world was not lost on Hitler, who interpreted it as tacit approval of his genocidal "Final Solution."

The city of Boston had finally installed air-raid sirens on the roof of the Tower Building where the police headquarters was located. But almost nobody around town could hear the four big speakers. Later, more were added at strategic points around the city. Stores across the nation were reporting a brisk business for "blackout cloth," which homeowners used to cover windows from inside. As a result of the big demand, supplies ran short.[6] Also, a "booming" business in the construction of cheap fallout shelters in people's basements was emerging. For a couple hundred dollars, companies would pour two thick cement walls in your very own basement.[7]

It could have been a moot point as many municipalities changed their policies on air raids and children in school. Several weeks earlier, they were encouraging parents to retrieve their children during an air raid, and now they were telling them schools would be locked down and children kept until the danger had passed. Officials were also recommending that adults seek the nearest basement and not try to make it home.[8]

Astonishingly, the federal government was making plans to "register" children as part "of a program being worked out by the United States Children's Bureau and the Office of Civilian Defense for the protection of youngsters in American cities in event of air raids and especially if it should become necessary to evacuate them." Katherine Lenroot, the director of the effort, said it was in response in part to a school that told children to "go hide in the woods" during an air-raid test. She was confident that parents could be "reassured," even if children were removed, because the government would take care of all their needs.[9]

And yet it didn't stop there. Boston Harbor was essentially closed. All-night boat traffic was banned, and daytime coming and going was severely restricted. Fishing boats were tightly regulated, and space along the piers from which they sold fresh fish was all but eliminated.[10] As on the West Coast, the Weather Bureau on the East Coast announced that atmospheric reports were now a "war secret."[11]

Boston's brouhahas went beyond the war; one major fight was over the attempts by some, including doctors, to legalize the "dissemination of birth-control information."[12] William Cardinal O'Connell, Archbishop of Boston, was mounting a loud campaign against changing the law. Another controversy was how to deal with Boston's long-festering South Side. After "generations of neglect," government officials said the crime-infested area was "heading toward ruin because of congestion, deterioration and bad living conditions." A report was shot through with "overcrowding, disorder, litter." Part of the recommendation for cleaning up "Southie" included a "need for fewer saloons."[13]

Even louder than any of these controversies and certainly the ineffectual air-raid sirens was a big rally for Russia held in the Boston Arena. Ten thousand people turned out to pony up $35,000 in cash to aid the collectivist state. Guest speakers were Joseph Davies, former Ambassador to Russia, and Ivy Litvinoff, wife of Russian Ambassador Maxim Litvinoff. She told the throng, "I wish Mr. Stalin could see it."[14]

Davies, in a burst of exuberant class-warfare candor, said, "God bless you cold-hearted Boston people. . . . You may be the home of the Cabots and the Lodges but we know . . . beneath their capitalistic hearts were people who believed in democracy and liberty, freedom and courage."[15]

At the time, many on the American left were quite naïve about the real nature of the Soviet state. Many liberals and intellectuals, who should have known better, perceived it as a worker's paradise; it was only after the war that the true horrors of Stalin's repressive regime truly came to light. The muckraking journalist, Lincoln Steffens, famously asserted, after visiting communist Russia: "I have seen the future, and it works."[16] The ordinarily perceptive Steffens could not have been more mistaken. But in 1941, with Stalin's Red Army serving as the bulwark against the Nazi onslaught, the prize-winning reporter wasn't alone in his delusions. Even FDR viewed Stalin as an avuncular fellow with whom he could do business with, referring to the murderous dictator as "Uncle Joe." The ugly realities of the Gulag would eventually emerge for the entire world to see.

Meanwhile, outside of Beantown, a class of sixty volunteer women graduated from fire school. Upon receiving their diplomas, they gave a demonstration in which they practiced jumping "into nets from second-story windows, carrying hose lines up fire ladders and smothering 'bomb' fires, the women demonstrated what they had learned in the six weeks' course in all forms of fire-fighting."[17]

Just up the road from "the Hub," Dartmouth College announced it was contracting its academic schedule, cancelling the Christmas and Spring Break vacations so graduating seniors could enlist five weeks earlier. Nearly all college campuses were hotbeds of patriotism and volunteerism.[18] The president of the University of Alabama told his students, "We have an intelligent, patriotic government in Washington. . . . My appeal is to stick by the government, the President and Congress."[19] Yale University passed a resolution supporting the war.[20] The municipal colleges of New York City—Queens, City, Hunter, and Brooklyn—all reported a tremendous upswing in volunteerism and in war bond and war stamp purchases.[21] A coed at the University of Georgia wrote a sweet and patriotic poem that was reprinted in many newspapers. From the last stanza:

> So this Christmas I'm not asking for a brand-new car,
> NOT even champagne nor caviar,
> I'll be perfectly frank and play my hand
> All I want is a brand-new man.[22]

The weather across America had turned cold, and even in the Deep South temperatures were dipping into the twenties.

In preparation for the winter, the city of Washington instituted its annual snow removal plan, requiring citizens to move their cars off of all major thoroughfares—about eighty-five miles, all told—from 2 a.m. to 8 a.m. The city's Refuse Department was hopeful that its snow removal this time around would be an improvement over previous years. "The city is better equipped this year than previously to meet a snow emergency."[23]

In the face of the indifference by American leaders, a large gathering was announced for later in the month organized by American Jewish groups to take place in Madison Square Garden. A leader of the event said, "The Garden rally also will respond to a moving call recently received by American and British Jewry from Jews in the Soviet Union . . . . [T]he troubled experiences of racial and religious minorities at the hands of Hitler has been brought home to all of us by the events of the past few days."[24]

Rallies and prayer vigils were increasing across the country. The day before, 3,000 people of varying faiths came together at the National Cathedral in Washington to pray for "victory and peace."[25] Speakers included priests, ministers, and rabbis. The Right Reverend James Freeman broke down crying, as he quoted a sonnet written by Washington native, John Magee Jr., a pilot who had been killed the week before while flying for the R.A.F. Young Magee's father was also a minister with a congregation in the nation's capital, though he did not speak.[26] A Catholic church in Los Angeles had been holding a prayer vigil ever since the attack, serving communion each day.[27]

But not all men of the cloth were supportive. In New York City, a minister resigned his position because he would not "use his ministry to 'bless, sanction or support war.'" The Reverend John Haynes Holmes who was "a director of the American Civil Liberties Union . . . asserted that the American people were not guiltless in a war."[28] Meanwhile in Germany, Dr. Hans Kerrl, the Nazi minister of religious affairs, died unexpectedly. He expired, out of favor with Hitler, as he'd been unable to stop Catholic and Presbyterian criticism of the Third Reich.[29]

One nagging question involved the soon-to-be-passed draft registration act before Congress. Would the government really draft, for military service, men in their forties and even older? Government officials stepped forward to say that it was unlikely that anyone under the age of twenty-one or over the age of thirty-five would be taken in for active duty service. Eighteen-year-olds would not be drafted, but they were free to register and shortly become active-duty members of the military.[30]

Officials said that the government would register all men between the ages of eighteen and sixty-four so they could have a handle on how many men were available for potential military service. In any case, special training had to be added to the navy's boot camp because more than 10 percent of inductees did not know how to swim. Instructors basically taught the landlubbers a rudimentary dog-paddle stroke, but the real goal was to teach how to stay afloat for long durations without life preservers. Sinking was not an option.[31]

Recruiting offices continued to be heavily patronized by eager young men, and in some cases men more eager than young. In New York, a father and son appeared together to enlist. They were both accepted and were sent into the service together.[32] However, the policy of allowing family members to serve on the same ship or in the same unit would change shortly.

An unexpected—but certainly welcomed—enlistee was Clarke H. Kawakami, who'd been the Washington correspondent for *Domei*, the Japanese state-run media agency. He resigned his position in protest, calling the attack "the blackest and most shameful page in page in Japanese history."[33] The War Department played his story way up, seeing the propaganda value of young Kawakimi joining the U.S. Army, despite his having attended Harvard.[34]

New York, Illinois, Pennsylvania, and Ohio were leading the way with new enlistees, but the sons of all states were doing their level best to get into the military. As tens of thousands of young men were streaming into the army, a two-year veteran was leaving, thanks to being ratted out by his own mother. At the age of fourteen, Lynn Vinson had somehow conned the military and enlisted. Two years later, his mother went to the commandant of Camp Robinson in Arkansas with the proof that her son was underage. Vinson was given an honorable discharge but vowed to get back in as soon as he could.[35]

In spite of the national emergency, over 500,000 men in uniform would be granted a furlough to go home for Christmas and sample their mother's cooking and their father's advice.[36]

Many for the last time.

Publications across the country were crammed with notices and announcements for civilians, particularly for defense rallies and classes in such subjects as "incendiary and explosive bomb demolition" and "poison gas analysis."[37] In cities with tall buildings, there was a real fear that flying glass in a bombing raid could maim dozens, if not hundreds.

Food and transportation were always issues, and many stocked up on canned goods, just in case. Families made their own plans on what to do in case of an attack. Along with the men and women of America, children barely into their teens also stepped forward. In New York City, "250 boys and girls between the ages of 13 and 17 assembled . . . in Queens . . . to be instructed on the requirements of junior air wardens." Right off the bat, the seriousness was made clear when an instructor told them that, "if any of you are here seeking telephone numbers or dates go right home and remain there. We don't want you. This is not a social affair but the grim business of war."[38]

Around the country, more and more factories and plants were operated on a more rapid schedule. At many, the workers voted to "donate" their Sundays to the government and work for nothing. In Massachusetts, textile plants sought approval from the state to allow women to work past 10 p.m., and in New Hampshire, the governor waived the ruled forbidding women and children from working more than 48 hours per week, as long as they worked in a war-related industry.[39] Even the Eureka vacuum cleaner company had switched over to defense manufacturing.[40]

The Red Cross, the police, all the federal, state, and local agencies that dealt with volunteerism, the private organizations such as the Legion, women's groups, the Boy and Girl Scouts—all reported a tremendous upswing in Americans stepping forward. The Grand Exalted Ruler of the Benevolent and Protective Order of Elks, John McClelland, sent Roosevelt a telegram pledging that 500,000 Elks would take up activities to protect America.[41] It was assumed the Moose Lodges of America would also stampede into volunteer offices.

All the activities were duly reported in the nation's periodicals. Page after page after page of the papers also covered both the war front and the home front. And yet again, a newspaper noted the death of a sailor at Pearl Harbor. The New York Times reported that "45-year-old" Edwin J. Hill, chief boatswain "was killed during the Japanese attack." Hill left behind a wife and three children.[42]

Over the weekend, a bravely forlorn message was issued by the Department of the Navy: "Wake and Midway Continue to Resist." The two tiny islands—little more than lumps of coral atolls rising a few feet out of the ocean—had been shelled and bombarded for days by Japanese planes and ships. The battling marines of Wake were referred to as the "Devil Dogs" in the papers. A radio transmission was sent to Honolulu by the tough marines. When asked if there was anything the beleaguered men needed, the reply came, "Send us some more Japs."[43]

Rumors continued to swirl of a "shakeup" in the navy's high command in the Pacific, and no less an authority than the *Army and Navy Register*, an influential journal, speculated that the American ambassador to Vichy, Admiral William Leahy, was the top dog to take over from Admiral Kimmel.[44]

San Franciscans suffered through yet another blackout as the military claimed again that enemy planes had been spotted over the city. There was still confusion in California about headlights, cars, and driving during blackouts. Some drivers thought it was okay to drive if they covered their headlights with blue tint and others if they turned off the headlights, so the rule had to be clarified, yet again: no driving during blackouts.[45] Period.

With much of the Far East and Europe cut off from the rest of the world due to war, shortwave radio took on a new importance. As Americans listened to NBC or CBS or Mutual broadcasts, often the announcer would source their reports as "Berlin radio" or "Stockholm radio" as the networks had set up "listening posts" along the East and West Coast of America. "Today, these listening posts with their batteries of radio receivers listening to the short wave transmissions of the world are proving extremely valuable now that the fact of belligerency with all the Axis Powers has cut of the American sources of news."[46]

The war effort would cost much more than what taxpayers were kicking in, but as of December, economists estimated that only 20 percent of the economy was devoted to that purpose[47]; unlike Great Britain, where more than 50 percent of the national economy was used for their national purpose.[48] Still, America's economy was much larger than that of England's and certainly larger than Germany's or Japan's. Like a large ship, a large economy could not be turned on a dime, yet even so, the rapid revamping of the country's industrial complex and the redirecting of resources were impressive.

Private and commercial aircraft were increasingly recruited for the war effort. American Airlines took out ads in publications in the Northeast including the *New York Times* to advise travelers that flights to "Syracuse, Rochester and Buffalo" as well as other cities, had been cancelled or postponed. "The airplanes usually utilized for the operation of these flights have been assigned to the performance of an administrative mission for the transportation of national defense supplies."[49]

Much of the war effort would come from higher taxes; therefore, articles began popping up cautioning taxpayers to set aside enough money to comply and to make their once-a-year lump sum payment or quarterly payment. "Now is the time to figure your tax and begin putting away a little money each week to pay it," it was advised. The policy of the government was to collect taxes on March 15 of each year. The marginal tax rate began at $750 per year for single individuals and $1,500 for married couples. If the wife made less than $750, it was still mandated that the income be reported. The government figured to bring in around $1 billion on March 15, but taxpayers had a choice to file their taxes on the calendar year or, if they were a small businessperson, on their own fiscal year.[50] The government was not only coming down hard on taxpayers, it was also coming down hard on people who disagreed with it under the old Anti-Sedition Acts of 1917. G-Men picked up a Kansas City lawyer, Herman D. Kissenger, charging him with being a "long time sympathizer" of the fascist governments of Germany and Japan. He'd written a letter to Congressman John Dingell, Democrat of Michigan, in which he advocated the impeachment and court-martialing of Congress and the president. The U.S. attorney for the area said a federal grand jury would be assembled to consider the government's case against nutty letter-writing.[51]

In Chicago, when Roosevelt appeared on the screen in a movie house newsreel, Edward A. Loss Jr. booed him and was fined $200 by a municipal court judge, "the maximum" for disorderly conduct.[52] In Topeka, a mother was sentenced to one year in prison "because of the alleged failure of her two young sons to salute the American flag in school. The boys, Clinton and John H., were made wards of the court by Juvenile Court Judge Roy N. McCue, who said [Lucille] Meyer 'was guilty of encouraging the children in the contributing to their delinquency.'"[53]

The government was moving to seize a billion dollars worth of Axis property in America. The attorney general's office created "a special force of G-men . . . to impound the enemy owned property".[54] Much of the impounded property was eventually liquidated, but the government still had property seized in 1917 and had yet to release it because it lacked the authority, even after the Armistice.

There existed a real threat to America from spies and Fifth Columnists. Federal agents raided and seized the offices of the German American Bund, the German American Business League, and the newspapers they published in New York. A notice was posted on the door: "This property is under the control of the United States Government. All persons are hereby prohibited from entering the premises under penalty of law. H. Morgenthau, Jr., Secretary of the Treasury."[55]

Roosevelt received a short, contradictory memo on the matter of spies operating inside the United States. It said, on the one hand, that Frank Knox was overblown in his public allegations but, on the other hand, that 'considerable danger of sabotage to strategic points [was] left unguarded.'"[56]

In California, a German baron, Ernest Frolich de Meyer, was arrested wearing the uniform of a U.S. Army officer. When federal agents raided his apartment in Hollywood, they found navy and Marine Corps uniforms, "a short wave radio set and what appeared to be data on coast defenses."[57]

Government bureaucrats, in order to control supply and demand, debated full-blown wage and price controls and "consumer rationing cards," but these were ruled out for the time being.[58] Still, the Brookings Institute, which was advising the government on such matters, said the country could not have rationing without price controls, and it could not have price controls without rationing. Brookings advocated both.[59]

The federal government could also be inadvertently dangerous and often clumsy, even scary. In Los Angeles, a man awakened to find a live antiaircraft shell weighing fifteen pounds in his back yard, undetonated.[60]

The government was, in addition, nearly omnipotent. On final passage, Congress, by voice vote, approved new legislation granting FDR all the war powers given Woodrow Wilson in World War I. Plus, FDR could now issue noncompetitive contracts and reorganize the government as he saw fit and without the approval of the courts or Congress. He could regulate all the transactions of the government, and he could censor just about anybody and anything.[61]

The irony was lost on the citizenry that Roosevelt now wielded more power over the American people than King George III ever dreamed of, on his best days.

That evening, FDR and Eleanor dined with Henry Stimson, Grace Tully, and actor Melvyn Douglas at 7:30 p.m. Douglas excused himself at 9:15 p.m., and the Roosevelts turned in at 12:15 a.m. Throughout the month, though, Roosevelt dined or met, often alone, with women: "Miss Margaret Suckley" on the nineteenth, "Mrs. Mary Eben" on the eighteenth, "Mrs. Dorothy Brady" on the twenty-first, "Crown Princess Martha of Norway" on the tenth and again on the fourteenth. Unescorted women, both married and single, were also frequent guests in the private residence of the White House in the month of December 1941.[62]

American and Chinese pilots began airlifting civilians out of Hong Kong, as the prospects for holding the city dimmed in the face of the continued onslaughts. The Japanese had mounted an all-out assault by land, sea, and air to take the prized British possession once and for all. "The Japanese opened a general . . . offensive against Hong Kong . . . to take the British crown colony . . . the fate of the colony would be decided in a matter of days."[63] The Japanese also claimed that they'd wiped out an entire British mechanized division; it "had been destroyed" on the Malayan peninsula.[64] The news was equally bad in other Far East sectors of which London had control; Churchill's government hinted that some could fall. British resistance in Hong Kong was crumbling.

Meanwhile, "Japanese forces operating on Luzon are advancing according to plan, 'crushing enemy resistance at every point,' army imperial headquarters said today. Bombers which attacked air bases on central Luzon Saturday destroyed forty United States bombers and fighters on the ground and set fire to three other aircraft, it asserted. Barracks, the announcement continued, were destroyed in a raid on United States military headquarters."[65] American resistance in the Philippines was crumbling.

Adding insult to injury, Tokyo announced it had seized 225 American and British merchant ships. They also claimed that twenty-one American and British naval vessels had either been destroyed or badly disabled since the opening of the war, less than two weeks past.[66]

Plans for a supreme Allied War Council were moving ahead. FDR had met with representatives of all the Allied Powers at this point to work out the broad outline of such an organization. Roosevelt had already discussed it by transatlantic telephone with Churchill and had met with the Lord Privy Seal, Major Clement Attlee, to flesh out the concept. Problem was, Russia was still dillydallying about actually declaring war on Japan. The best Moscow could say was the Allies "could reasonably look forward" to Russia jumping into the Pacific war.[67]

The Russians for their part had successfully mounted a drive to push back the dug-in German Army from just outside Moscow and Leningrad. Initial news reports closely resembled the propaganda coming from Stalin's government, but as more independent sources confirmed, it became clear the Russians had gained an offensive. However, it was important to remember the Russians were still fighting on their own terrain and the Germans had driven hundreds of miles deep inside Mother Russia.

A British attempt to mount a counteroffensive in Thailand was repulsed by the Japanese, and the Japanese claimed to have sunk another British ship, though the name was not released.[68] Also, Vichy France announced it was intending to halt diplomatic relations with the United States, as a result of the seizure of several of its ships in American ports.[69]

On the more hopeful side, American forces were claiming to have sunk four Japanese troop transports operating near the Philippines, but again no details were released.[70] Admiral Yamamoto seemed unconcerned. He'd written a letter sometime earlier to a friend, which the Japanese state propaganda agency, *Domei*, released. In it he said, "Any time war breaks out between Japan and the United States I shall not be content merely to capture Guam and the Philippines and occupy Hawaii and San Francisco. I am looking forward to dictating peace to the United States in the White House in Washington."[71]

Lofty ambition, that.

Even before the war had begun in earnest, a ground of educators had met in Riverside, California, to plan for world peace. Organized by the Institute of World Affairs, they sponsored a weeklong series of talks, roundtable discussions, and panels. Nothing was concluded except that an "international governing commission" would be necessary to run postwar Germany, if only because "Germany must be humiliated and made to realize it mustn't molest people," according to one participating academic. Another educator observed that "while Germany may have foisted upon the world its 'Jewish . . . problem, the world must realize that it has a German problem to solve."[72]

One thing at a time.

Roosevelt was right when he warned the country that the news would become bleaker before it became brighter.

CHAPTER 17

THE SEVENTEENTH
OF DECEMBER

Women Demand to Be Drafted

Christian Science Monitor

Japanese Ships Shell Two Hawaiian Islands

New York Times

*Widows to Be Given Adequate
Support from U.S. in New War*

Birmingham News

Speed War Output President Demands

Evening Star

Justice Roberts Heads Pearl Harbor Inquiry Board

Washington Post

A Penny a Plane Club formed in Marshall, Texas. City fathers asked the residents if they would donate one penny for every enemy plane downed by the Americans. The club had started in Argentina and was wildly successful. There, residents of the country amassed a membership of 50,000 and "made possible the purchase for the British of a fighter plane costing $75,000 each month." The chief organizer of the American effort, Harry Adams, had been told of the success of the Argentineans and thought it could spread throughout the United States.[1]

Money seemed to be flying out of the pockets of the American citizenry, seemingly all for the war effort. Some banks actually ran out of government bonds because demand was so high. Nonetheless, a goal of $1 billion a month in bond sales was announced by the government. Three businessmen in Connecticut began a New *Arizona* Fund to raise money to build a new battleship to replace the one sunk by the Japanese.[2]

The city of Washington was awash in letters, all containing contributions to "Uncle Sam" from patriotic Americans. Some envelopes contained a penny. Others contained up to $200. Written on many of the envelopes was "Remember Pearl Harbor!" Children sent letters, businessmen sent letters, housewives sent letters, families and local clubs sent letters. An elderly man sent $25.00 with a note regretting that he was too old to fight. A woman sent $5.00, saying if it purchased just one bolt for an airplane, it would make her happy. Hairdressers sent their tip money, as did waiters and waitresses. Treasury officials said there were too many letters, making it impossible to count how much money had been received.[3]

Within America, a deep wellspring of charity had always existed. It was just one of the many qualities that made it unique among countries throughout the history of the world. But this outpouring had been unmatched in the history of the republic. The pain and anger of the citizenry had been channeled into positive actions, and perhaps Christmastime helped season the era with the kindness, love, and brotherhood demonstrated by a Jewish carpenter one thousand nine hundred and forty-one years earlier.

A little girl sent a letter to Santa asking that he forgo toys for her this year, and instead, make "every country free."[4] A dying man left his estate to an aeronautical library for young boys so that books could be "loaned to anyone by mail, without charge."[5] Even Congress—at least the House—got in the spirit of giving and sacrifice as Speaker Sam Rayburn, Democrat of Texas, announced there would be no Christmas vacation for the members—not even the three-day recess usually granted.[6]

Money was also flying into the pockets of some of Washington's biggest lobbyists. Tommy "The Cork" Corcoran had just steered a $21 million dollar loan to a new business "syndicate formed to produce manganese," from the Reconstruction Finance Corporation, or RFC, for which he pocketed a handsome fee of $65,000, a fee that was more than the vast majority of Americans would make in their life time. He told the Truman Investigating Committee that he'd picked up over $100,000 in lobbying fees over the past year.[7]

It was never really suggested that Corcoran had any special pull in Washington simply because he was part of the FDR Brain Trust,[8] and for a time he actually resided at 1600 Pennsylvania Avenue, NW; moreover, he said the fact that he was once counsel to RFC had nothing to do with the loan he'd secured for his client.[9]

Later, Truman learned to despise Corcoran as much as FDR loved him.

Charles West, another close adviser to Roosevelt, was suing a company for $700,000. He claimed they had rooked him out of his fees after he had arranged for federal business for them.[10] Most other Americans were less selfish.

Heavyweight champ Joe Louis and challenger Buddy Baer agreed to a title fight under the condition that the proceeds would go to the Navy Relief Fund. They raised thousands. They then met in a second bout and donated those proceeds to the relief fund as well, approximately $90,000 from both contests.[11] In gratitude, the Internal Revenue Service, for years after the war, pursued Louis claiming the donated money had been income to him.[12]

In Los Angeles, star pro football running back, Jackie Robinson, was thrilling fans of the Los Angeles Bulldogs. The Bulldogs were one of the many flimsy professional gridiron teams that had sprung up around the West and the South in the late '30s and early '40s, and Robinson, in an athletic class of his own, ran roughshod over opponents. Robinson would later switch games and break the color barrier in Major League Baseball after the war.

By 1942, Louis, Baer, and Robinson were all in uniform.

Clark Griffith, the owner of the Washington Senators, announced that he wasn't going to make an announcement about some important news regarding his baseball team because of the war. "In another week or so, we'll be veterans in the war and people will want to look at the sports pages as a change." Fans hoped whatever change was coming would be on the mound, as only the pitiable Philadelphia Athletics and the even more pathetic St. Louis Browns had worse pitching.[13]

The annual East-West Shrine college game held in San Francisco had been moved to New Orleans because of the apparent risk under which the West Coast was still operating.[14] As a result, other high school, college, and professional sports events were also cancelled or moved. With the baseball season over, the son of San Francisco, Joe DiMaggio, the "Yankee Clipper," was voted Outstanding Male Athlete of 1941, besting Ted Williams, the "Splendid Splinter." The winner the previous year had been Tom Harmon, "Old Number 99," the famous end of the Michigan football team.[15]

But the big unanswered question was whether or not Major League Baseball should be cancelled during the national emergency. The owners had already met in Chicago with no decision reached, preferring instead to see what Washington said. "End of major league baseball for the duration is being feared . . . as a result of what already has happened to the sports programs on the Pacific Coast," the *Boston Globe* observed.[16] In 1917, the game had been confronted with the same problem, but the government told owners to keep playing as it was too important to the nation's morale. Even so, a month was sliced off the schedules during that war. If the 1942 baseball season went forward, the minor leagues figured to take a hit, what with so many of their players young, single, and 1-A healthy. There were vague reports about future meetings between baseball leaders and governmental leaders.

The news from the world of sports that Americans did not get through newspaper or magazines, they could get from radio. Radio was simply the most dominant cultural force in America, even more than the movies, magazines, or the broadsheets. The role of radio as a form of news and entertainment in the American home could not be overstated. Radios were in the living room, the bedroom, and the kitchen. Radios were in cars and restaurants. They were simply everywhere, and everybody listened, especially now.

Radio had been the main form of entertainment for Americans since the early days of the Great Depression and even before. Many was the lonely pensioner who got by each night listening to Bob Hope or the "Texaco Hour" or "Our Miss Brooks" or the orchestra dance music, broadcast from a hotel in any given city in America. Only one's imagination limited what a radio show could do; the creative men and women could make the kids sitting around the living room believe Superman was really flying or ghouls were really at their door, or Little Orphan Annie was really meeting with the president.

Yet the entertainment side of the radio shied away from the war until *Fibber McGee and Molly* took up the subject. Fibber wanted to buy a globe, and Molly warned him to buy it with Japan still on it, before the Allies bombed it into smithereens. Bob Hope then jumped into the fray, telling audiences, "We may have to black out our lights, but we will never black out our sense of humor." Another was a bad routine between Jack Benny and Dennis Day. That did it. By mid-December 1941, radio, like everybody else in America, had gone to war.[17]

Congress passed a law that would provide for six months' salary and give life-time pensions to the families of the soldiers and sailors killed at Pearl Harbor. The salary was straightforward, but the pension was a more complicated system, based on widows, their age, and how many and how old the servicemen's orphans were.[18]

It ranged from a low of $30 per month to a high of $83 per month. It was a part of the Soldiers and Sailors Relief Act, but some additional laws also kept men in uniform from being harassed by collection agencies and lawsuits, and under circumstances prevented a war widow from being evicted if behind in her rent.[19]

Mr. and Mrs. Max Mueller of Omaha were notified that two of their sons, Henry, nineteen, and Erwin, seventeen, had both been killed at Pearl Harbor. The last the parents knew, both boys were assigned to the *Arizona*.[20]

More details were slowly being released from Hawaii, including the recovery of a "suicide submarine," one of three suspected subs thought to have participated in the attack at Pearl Harbor. A "midget submarine," it carried a two-man crew and ran on batteries. Its range was so limited that it could not make it back to a safe port. The three subs and crews who were believed to have engaged in the attack on Pearl Harbor knew they were on a one-way mission from which they, in all likelihood, would not return alive. A photo of the recovered sub that had washed ashore appeared in the papers.[21]

Submarines had been an important part of the story of the North Atlantic for some time. German "wolf pack" U-boats had been sinking everything in sight; however, subs had not yet become important in the fight for the Pacific, except when the story was bad. That day, a confidential memo from the Secretary of the Navy to FDR advised the president that the American naval sub presence in Manila was now tenuous. "How much longer the submarines can base at Manila is problematical."[22]

Also, the American Asiatic fleet was down to "one patrol bomber squadron . . . 2 cruisers, 8 destroyers, 3 gunboats, several minesweepers . . . surface vessel lack fighter aircraft defense, and cannot operate in areas where dominated by enemy aircraft strength."[23]

This story line would eventually change. For the first time since the beginning of the war, American naval forces reported sea action by American submarines in the western Pacific, adding that they had performed well enough but had little to no support from American planes or surface ships. The overall news from the region continued to be nearly all bad for America.

"Japan's assault on the Philippines slacked off . . . but defense forces regard the respite as only temporary. Most observers said the letup probably meant that the Japanese were moving additional forces and supplies into position off the island coasts, resting pilots, overhauling planes and marshaling gasoline, bombs and ammunition for new and powerful attacks." The situation was anything but "well in hand."[24]

The British were "having difficulty in Borneo, Malaya, and Hong Kong, and the American possessions of Johnston and Maui Islands in the Hawaiian area were shelled by Japanese naval craft." Also, "Wake Island and Midway were reportedly raided again . . . [S]evere fighting continued in northern Malaya, where Japanese troops continued to push southward toward Singapore, now using one man tanks. At Hong Kong, Japanese naval vessels were reported . . . to have joined the attack on the British Colony. The Japanese claimed they had sunk one gun boat and six torpedo boats and damaged a destroyer and three other vessels in Hong Kong waters."[25]

Lord Beaverbook, the British ambassador to the United States, said of Hong Kong, "We must be prepared for its fall" and proclaimed that it had no military value.[26]

Apparently, the attack on Maui had only been some Japanese torpedoes that hit the loading docks of a pineapple company; but still, Maui was part of the Hawaiian chain and only a hundred miles southeast of Honolulu. Also, a military airfield and "fleet anchorage" were located at Lahaina Roads there.[27] It was the first attack on the Hawaiian Islands since the seventh, and that alone made it terrifying. Johnston Island was described by navy officials as being hit much harder than Maui, and more importantly, that was the first time it had been bombed. Johnston Island was "discovered" by the British ship *Cornwallis* in 1807.[28] Some speculated that the Japanese were hitting many different locations in hopes of sending the navy off on a wild-goose chase.

The British were doing their utmost to hold onto Singapore, but this hold seemed more tenuous by the day. A knowledgeable source said, "British lack of naval superiority has changed the entire situation in Northern Malaya."[29] If Singapore was taken, it would be catastrophic to the cause of the Allies. If Singapore went, the rest of the Western Pacific could fall like dominos into Japanese possession.

There was a growing suspicion that the Roosevelt Administration, being heavily influenced by Winston Churchill, was more interested in first investing resources in the Atlantic and Europe and that the Pacific would have to wait. Two days later in an unsigned White House memo dated December 19, titled "First Priority of Military Strategy, the answer came in the next line: The Defense of the Atlantic Area between the United States and the United Kingdom." Both Africa and "the Pacific area" were noted as "secondary areas."[30] The condition of the Pacific was described as "bleak."[31]

Meanwhile the governments of Turkey and Ireland restated their decision to stay neutral. Ireland also refused to allow the Allies to use its ports. Vichy France also claimed to be neutral, although with hundreds of thousands of

German troops in the country and Marshal Petain at Hitler's beck and call, it was a joke. Conversely, Free French forces in Morocco, Algeria, and other locations were bravely working against the Germans, who were tightening their grip on the region. An underground movement in France was growing. Audaciously, they had detonated a bomb in Paris, killing six Gestapo agents and one German general. New reprisals came in the form of rounding up as many as 4,000 suspects including, of course, Jews. "This group included some of most influential and wealthiest Jews in Paris."[32]

Halfway around the world, another courageous group was fighting the odds. A small assembly of twelve Indians led by one British lieutenant furiously fought off a much larger force of Japanese in Kota Bhara, in Malaya, before finally succumbing.[33] The civilian evacuation of Malaya had already begun. "There definitely is danger—a real threat to Singapore by land," a British dispatch read.[34]

Meanwhile, it was rumored that Hitler had come close to suffering a nervous breakdown, frustrated with the lack of progress on the Eastern Front. His doctors told him to go to Berchtesgaden, his spectacularly scenic mountain retreat in Bavaria, for rest.[35] There, the would-be ruler of the world would gaze at the soaring peaks and become lost in reveries of his own megalomania. Meanwhile, in the field, his soldiers were behaving with characteristic thuggery. Three precious Russian shrines, the home of Tolstoy, the cottage of Anton Chekov, and a museum dedicated to Tchaikovsky, were sacked by Nazi troops.[36] In a confidential memo to Roosevelt from the British Embassy, the document said the Germans generals had decided to "try to stabilize their Russian front." The document also pointed out that the Russian air force had gained air superiority over the Germans, in part because they knew more about handling equipment in the freezing cold than did the Germans.[37]

There was no rest for the Poles under the heel of Nazi governor Hans Frank, an eager and enthusiastic supporter of Hitler's genocidal policies. While grinding Poland into the ground under his iniquitous administration, "hundreds of children between the ages of 14 and 16 have been executed for their political activities, including membership, in the Boy Scouts. A Polish official said in one town, 100 Scouts were executed in the central square and a nine-year-old boy was shot because he destroyed a Nazi propaganda poster."[38]

Secretary Knox had not been entirely forthcoming in his report on the damage at Pearl Harbor, but he had said all along he wasn't going to reveal everything, in the name of security. The *New York Times* said his report was "undoubtedly an understatement of the damage done."[39] The Japanese of course were claiming much more damage at Pearl Harbor and in the Philippines than Washington was, but this time, the Japanese estimates were closer to the truth than the American revelations.[40]

The casualty report was as accurate as could be expected in those days after the attack, but Knox said at the time the government would not release all that they knew, and now, once again, some members of Congress were agitating for a full inquiry. Knox also did not release the names of any of the deceased, but he did meet with key congressional representatives in secret. His report was long on heroics but short on specifics, such as the story of the four ensigns who, when their captain went down, supposedly guided their destroyer out of the harbor in an attempt to track down the enemy.[41]

Capitol Hill was sharply divided, with some members eviscerating Knox. One said that America needed a new Secretary of the Navy. Supporters of the White House had hinted for several days that Roosevelt would soon order an investigation. Others members of congress said if they went forward, they would not ask Knox to testify about his own findings. But another, Senator David Walsh, Democrat of Massachusetts, said they might have to "investigate the investigation."[42] Walsh had been a bitter opponent of Lend-Lease and was a fervent isolationist—until December 7. The call for a congressional inquiry had been safely bottled up for over a week, but it was beginning to escalate again. Knox had also claimed that the navy was at sea looking for the Japanese; that was true in only the barest sense.[43]

The chairman of the Senate Foreign Relations Committee, Senator Tom Connally, Democrat of Texas, was not satisfied in the least with Knox's limited report. "The statement . . . that neither the Navy nor the Army was on the alert at Hawaii when it was attacked by the Japanese is amazing. It is astounding. It is almost unbelievable. The Navy of John Paul Jones and that of Dewey must wear crepe. The old Army must carry an arm band. The loss of life is staggering."[44]

At the same time, photos of B-17s on the ground, aflame, at Hickam Field on Oahu were appearing in the newspapers. Photos of other damage done at

Pearl began appearing, but nearly all were of civilian centers and homes. Only a few photos of damaged planes were released and no photos of ships.

It was also revealed that a Japanese pilot on that day had landed his troubled plane on the island of Niihau, two hundred miles northwest of Oahu. Without phones or radios, these islanders knew nothing of the morning's attack. There the pilot encountered a native islander, Benny Kanahele. After being shot by the pilot three times, the large Hawaiian grabbed the pilot and rammed his head into a stone wall, killing him.[45] "The pilot shot me . . . in the ribs, hip and groin. And then I got mad. I threw him against a stone wall."[46]

Benny was, for the record, a woman.

So as to head off any congressional investigations into the attack at Pearl Harbor and to control the controversy, FDR went ahead and appointed his own Joint Inquiry Board, a blue ribbon commission made up of five men.[47]

They were to take the preliminary (and to many, unsatisfactory) findings by Knox numerous steps further and take the heat off the administration. A justice of the U.S. Supreme Court, Owen J. Roberts, would chair the panel, and he immediately promised there would be no "whitewash" of the events or those responsible. The other four members were all respected career military men.[48] They included retired Admiral William Standley, who was the former Chief of Naval Operations, retired Rear Admiral Joseph Reeves, retired Major General Frank McCoy and Brigadier General Joseph McNarney, who served with the Army Air Corps.[49] Admiral James Richardson was expected to be one of the appointed; however, he was in hot water with FDR after telling the president it was a mistake to move the fleet from San Diego to Hawaii.[50] Roberts had a distinguished career including his prosecution of Teapot Dome while he served as a federal attorney. Yet even with their careers of accomplishment, having been appointed by FDR, they were his men, beholden to him. "The membership of the Board satisfied Administration leaders in Congress, for it was announced that any Congressional action would be delayed until the Board had had any opportunity to study and act."[51]

At his press conference, announcing the board of inquiry, the president spent considerable time speculating about espionage activities in Honolulu prior to December 7. Roosevelt had met with General George Marshall and Secretary of War Henry Stimson as well as other military brass, just that day, to come up with the board; these men were described as "gloomy" when spotted leaving the Oval Office.[52]

The move by FDR, however, did not satisfy those on the Hill who did not consider themselves "administration leaders," but there was little they could do. Congressman Martin Dies, Democrat of Texas and Chairman of the House Committee on Un-American Activities, squawked that his own investigation into subversive Japanese elements operating in the United States had been shut down at the request of Roosevelt and Cordell Hull, the previous September.[53] He said that "his committee had information which 'clearly indicated a planned attack on Manila and Pearl Harbor.'"[54]

Heading off a congressional probe was exactly what the administration and the military wanted. Two items of immediate concern to investigate would be (1) a fresh claim by Hull that he notified government officials in late November of his concerns that events in the Pacific would take a turn for the worse and (2) that, apparently, several radio stations in Hawaii had continued to broadcast in Japanese, even as the last planes were departing Oahu and headed back to the six Japanese carriers.[55]

At the business and labor conference that had convened, FDR told both sides that all strikes must cease for the duration of the war. Even with the new laws on the book, there had been wildcats strikes around the country. He also called for round-the-clock production. The country, he said, has "got to do perfectly unheard of things."[56]

The longshoremen sent FDR a telegram pledging not to strike during the emergency.[57] Yet what got everybody talking was the olive branch offered to the American Federation of Labor by the Congress of Industrial Organizations. Jaws dropped throughout the labor community. The two collective bargaining agents had been feuding for years, but because of the emergency, a slight thaw had developed in their previously frosty relations.

Washington also announced an extension of the new tire ban, to be made permanent starting January 4. No new tires or tubes could be manufactured for civilian use; only to fill those orders coming in from the military.[58] Additional articles appeared in the papers advising consumers how to protect their tires, how to make them last, and how to make effective repairs. More government directives were forthcoming about the whole matter of tires and tire maintenance.

As the towns and cities of America struggled to perfect their blackouts and air-raid drills, advice was offered on protecting the family animals from falling bombs. The American Red Star Animal Relief organization sent out notices regarding horses, dogs, and cats. It informed owners that animals were important to morale and that there was no need to kill them, as many in England had done by the thousands with their own animals in the early days of the Blitz.[59]

Inland waterways were not overlooked when it came to security. Officials in the Empire State instituted tight navigation polices over the St. Lawrence Seaway. New York City seemed to have outpaced the other cities when it came to organizing its air-raid policies. First, the city worked with the newspapers to get the stories right once and for all, including the rules. Second, the drills were announced well ahead of time. "A test of the most powerful siren in the city, the steam-driven device on top of the Consolidated Edison Company's plant at First Avenue . . . will be made at 4 o'clock this afternoon and will be followed at 4:15 p.m. by the testing of two of the seventy new 'sirodrones' acquired by the city this week for air-raid alarms." Specific details followed, and the boxed item ran on the front of newspapers.[60]

On the West Coast, the mystery plane puzzle had still not been solved, but as the days grew shorter, the issue of instituting a form of "daylight savings" was debated, especially in Los Angeles where the Board of Supervisors decided to implement it for the county. It would allow citizens to get to work and back home during daylight hours. Hollywood studios had already implemented their own work schedule, which began the workday sooner but ended it sooner too.[61]

With FDR's new authority under the War Powers Act granted him by Congress, some Americans may not have agreed altogether with the new policies, but they understood the sentiment of their Allies down under. The headline in the *Christian Science Monitor* said it all: "Australians Give up Liberty to Assure Defense of Liberty." The story detailed how Aussie citizens were giving up all their basic rights for the war and doing so happily. "Australians have now been asked by their Government to throw their own freedom to the winds until victory has been won."[62]

The *New York Times* said Congress had conferred "on President Roosevelt almost unlimited powers to regulate the nation's emergency effort at home."[63] President Roosevelt's new agency for dealing with censorship said its mission was "partly mandatory, partly voluntary."[64] FDR announced the Censorship Bureau at a press conference, ironically, but he made no bones or apologies about the goals of the new agency. "It is necessary that prohibitions of some types of information contained in long existing statutes be rigidly enforced." He also called on "a patriotic press and radio"; and the new head of the department, Byron Price, a former executive with the Associated Press, made clear his initial target was the U.S. Mail—specifically, letters written by private citizens going outside the country.[65]

FDR appeared well, dressed in a gray tweed suit and black tie, but the dark circles under his eyes were noticeable to reporters. There was some light banter with a radio reporter over the rumor that Roosevelt had called the Japanese "dirty yellow bastards." Roosevelt cautioned the reporter to be careful with his consonants, and everybody laughed. When asked, he said he felt "fit as a fiddle."[66] Only the president's doctor knew that FDR was a very sick man. A longtime sufferer of polio, he was plagued with dangerously high blood pressure that went largely unaddressed. The toll of stress and illness were starting to show in his gray pallor and bouts of fatigue. To the rest of the world, though, he seemed as cheerful and vigorous as ever with his trademark cigarette holder stuck in his mouth at the usual jaunty angle. It was one of the greatest deceptions, in a war full of them.

"When he traveled by car, he was lifted in and out of the back seat away from public view. News photographers understood that they were not to photograph the president sitting in his wheelchair or being carried, and when anyone violated that rule the Secret Service confiscated the film," said David Brinkley.[67]

In the face of the new government crackdown on communications, the Justice Department announced that local officials had been going too far in arresting people under the Sedition Act and warned that in the future they must consult with Washington before moving ahead with any apprehensions.[68]

At the same time, the final Selective Service Bill was passed by Congress. While all men ages eighteen to sixty-four would be registered, only men ages twenty-one to forty-five would be drafted. But eighteen-year-olds could enlist with their parents' permission. The War Department estimated this new bill would produce an army of 8,000,000 men.[69]

The administration was also moving ahead with a war council among the Allies, to better coordinate land, sea, and air offensive operations and counteroffenses against the Axis Powers. FDR hinted that what might be needed was an "Allied General Staff" to blend together the military leadership of all the countries opposing the Axis Powers. That evening he ate late and then worked into the night reviewing documents, talking on the phone, and issuing dispatches.[70]

Bills were flying out of Congress. Money for the military, money for more military and defense related-housing, money for civil defense, "increasing the authorized tonnage of the Navy," another granting the navy access to every shipyard in America, publicly owned—or not.[71] A bill was offered to empower the government to take over the machinery in private plants, "an action now forbidden by the Property Seizure Act."[72] The government was now spending money at a rate of roughly $20 billion a year, with approximately 72 percent devoted to the military. With all the spending for the New Deal, Lend-Lease, and the war, the national debt soared to over $55 billion.[73]

New regulations also flew out of Washington dealing with the weight of bicycles, the manufacture of new radios, and even one proposal to essentially nationalize all industry in America. The Treasury Department was looking at a plan "for centralized government control over the flow of capital and the financial conduct of industry."[74] Regardless, a new aviation company saw a bright horizon, and private stock purchases were offered in the Cessna Aircraft Co.

The results of the public spending and the national will were already tangible. The B-17 "Flying Fortress"[75] bomber had been developed only several years earlier, but North American Aviation and the Glenn Martin Aircraft

Co., with plants in Tulsa and Kansas City, announced that two entirely new bombers would begin rolling off the assembly line in early January—only one month after the attack on Pearl Harbor.

These two planes, the B-24 "Liberator" and the B-25 "Mitchell" were being fabricated entirely from automobile parts supplied by the Ford Motor Company, Chrysler, Goodyear, and the Fischer Auto Body Co.[76] The thirty-one-day turnabout from peacetime manufacturing to an Arsenal of Democracy was no less than astonishing.

American Exceptionalism was a wondrous thing.

CHAPTER 18

THE EIGHTEENTH
OF DECEMBER

Hawaii Army, Navy Chiefs Ousted; Nimitz Replaces Kimmel

Los Angeles Times

Japs in Borneo Peril Singapore

Washington Post

Rationing of Tires to Start on Jan. 4

New York Times

Jap Victim's Father Tries to Join Navy

Los Angeles Times

Flag sales were up, but morale was down as it became known of the lonely and modest burials taking place daily near Pearl Harbor.

The demand for American flags was nothing like it had been on the eve of America's entrance into the First World War when sales skyrocketed 100 percent. In the days after Pearl Harbor, flag sales were up, by industry estimates, some 15 to 25 percent, which was impressive, yet also a bit less than expected.[1] Because of the demand for cotton, muslin, wool, and silk for the military, flags were being made out of rayon, but even these synthetic flags were scarce. The bottom line: there was a pent up demand, just not much supply. Among those dealers who had stocked up before December 7, they had sold out in a matter of hours.

In Hawaii, the young men who had fallen for that flag were buried. Each afternoon, on the island of Oahu, a group of marines trooped out to a grave site and fired a salute to yet another fallen American soldier or sailor. "A tight lipped group of six-foot marines in olive-drab uniforms raise their rifles and fire three volleys over the fresh earth as nightfall approaches fast. A bugle sounds taps."[2]

These forlorn memorials had begun on December 8 and had been going on for days. "They have been laid to rest on green hills overlooking the sea—there to remain until a peaceful time when the bodies might be returned to their native soil."[3] There were no family members, no politicians, no crowds. Only the brief discharge of guns, the trumpet, and the murmured prayers by men of the cloth punctuated the silence.

Nuuanu Cemetery was initially used for the first of the Pearl Harbor dead. The cemetery overlooked the sea. Then, when all the spaces had been taken, graves were dug on Red Hill, which overlooked Pearl Harbor. "Day after day, just before sunset, with simple dignity befitting the gallantry with which they died for their country, America's finest have been buried at Honolulu."[4]

Each burial observance was accompanied by Navy Chaplain Captain William Maguire and a black-robed priest. The priest blessed the ground with "holy water," and Maguire recited a committal prayer. On the decks of many of the navy vessels, Sunday church services were routine, some beginning at 8 a.m. None took place on December 7. Now prayers were offered every day. "Don't say we buried with sorrow," Captain Maguire said. "Say we buried with conviction. Our men died manfully and we will wipe out the treachery come what may. The spirit of these men lives on. I can feel it."[5]

Each grave was adorned with a floral bouquet, Hawaiian-style, all picked from nearby homes. "Each grave is marked and each body carefully identified for shipment back to the mainland after the war is fought and won—back to home towns." Maguire said he was proud of the sacrifices of these sacred dead. He said, "And while all this heroism was going on, those Japs were still machine-gunning. . . ."[6]

He told of men with arms ripped off, begging to get back into the fight. Men burned, nearly naked, screaming, "I want to get back to my ship. I want to get back to my gun." Other wounded men said, "For God's sake, I am alright."[7] They weren't.

Americans, Maguire said, "would glow if they could see how our boys died. If every American had seen how quietly, yes, quietly men suffered, how gallantly they died, how courageously they thought about the next man, they would glow. They would swear our front line will never give."[8]

In the towns and villages of America, because there were not bodies to bury, many internment ceremonies went forward anyway, as at Georgetown University with "flag draped catafalque symbolizing the bier of Ensign George Anderson Wolfe who died at Pearl Harbor"[9] Also among the fallen was Billie McCary, seventeen, of Shades Mountain, Alabama. He was on the *Arizona* as a member of the band, for which he played the tuba and the coronet. Just weeks earlier, the band from the *Arizona* had competed with sixteen others in Hawaii, and Billie and his band, came away with the gold cup.[10]

The first "white" resident of Birmingham—as noted by the *Birmingham News*—to die at Pearl Harbor was James Mark Lewis, twenty-one, seaman second class. Again the inevitable telegram: "The Navy Department regrets to inform you . . ." Concluding, it said, "The Department extends to you its sincerest sympathy in your great loss. To prevent possible aid to our enemies, please do not divulge the name of his ship. . . . Rear Admiral C.W. Nimitz, chief of Bureau of Navigation." James's dream was to be a navy chaplain, combining his love of boats as a child and his devotion to the Birmingham Tabernacle Gospel. His mother, age sixty, told the paper that, if she could, she would put on a uniform and go fight. The boy's father, "aged . . . sitting in the sun on his back steps his face cupped in his hands said only, 'they stabbed him in the back . . . he didn't have a chance.'" Seaman Lewis's remains had not yet been recovered.[11]

Julius Ellsberry was the first "Negro" resident of Birmingham to be killed at Pearl Harbor, again as noted by the Birmingham paper. "First to be notified here that a son had given his life for his country was a Negro family in Inglenook." Ellsberry, twenty, was a "mess attendant aboard a warship."[12] The paper featured an editorial headlined, "Julius Ellsberry. All Birmingham, white and colored, honors his name." The family got the identical telegram that the McCary family and the Lewis families had received.[13] The U.S. military may have been segregated, but death was color-blind.

In dying for their country, the boys, Julius, Billie, and James, were not separate but were equal. The price of war kept going up. It was a price equally shared by all social and economic classes. Everyone had a stake in the war; America was experiencing a social cohesion that had not been witnessed before.

In a marvelous public relations stunt, Roosevelt wrote a letter to another president: he wrote a letter to whoever would be president in 1956, recommending that the eighteen-month-old son of downed pilot/hero Captain Colin P. Kelly Jr. for appointment to West Point, fifteen years hence. "In the conviction that the service and example of Captain Colin P. Kelly, Jr. will be long remembered, I ask for this consideration in behalf of Colin P. Kelly, III."[14]

Nominations to U.S. military service academies such as West Point (for the army) were competitive. While some applicants may be eligible for a presidential nomination by virtue of a parent's service, all U.S. citizens were eligible to compete for a nomination from his congressional representative and senators. A nomination from FDR himself certainly constituted an amazing "trump card." Indeed, the president of the United States in 1956 offered "Corky" a.k.a. Colin P. Kelly III an appointment to the United States Military Academy at West Point, but in true hero fashion, the young Kelly refused, wanting to compete with everybody else for a place; and he did so, graduating from "The Point" in 1963. The president of the United States in 1956 was Dwight David Eisenhower, who in 1941 was an obscure, chain-smoking aide in the office of Army Chief of Staff George C. Marshall and who only months before had been promoted to the rank of general. Before that, he was a clerk for General Douglas MacArthur. Roosevelt loved being president, MacArthur wanted to be president, and Eisenhower hadn't even given it a thought.

The shake-up in the Pacific command finally came, oddly, before FDR's Board of Inquiry had even met to investigate what had actually happened at Pearl Harbor and whether or not anyone really was to blame. Indeed, the board was given the task of finding facts in search of a theory. "They will seek to fix the responsibility for the fact that the armed services were 'not on the alert' on Dec 7."[15]

Admiral Chester W. Nimitz, fifty-six, was named to replace Admiral Husband E. Kimmel, fifty-nine, who was unceremoniously removed as commander-in-chief of the United States Fleet and as commander of the Pacific Fleet. The position as chief of the navy was a fairly meaningless title, but the position of head of the Pacific fleet was where the rubber met the road. Nimitz would become commander of the Pacific fleet but not "Commander-in-Chief" of the navy itself. Also removed and replaced were General Walter C. Short, sixty-one, commander of the army garrison in Hawaii, and Major General Frederick L. Martin, fifty-nine, commander of the Army Air Corps there.

Stepping in for Short was Lieutenant General D.C. Emmons, fifty-two, and replacing Martin was Brigadier General C.L. Tucker. "The shifts were the direct result of the surprise Japanese attack on Pearl Harbor, December 7, in which the Hawaiian defense forces were caught off guard."[16]

Douglas MacArthur, who could have also been removed because he'd had some warning of an imminent attack, unlike Kimmel and Short, escaped unscathed because he was still fighting a battle in the Philippines, because he got better "press" back home than did the others, and because he was a personal favorite of Roosevelt's, despite their political differences. They were kindred spirits in that they were royalty in America. MacArthur was the scion of a famous military family. His father had won the Congressional Medal of Honor for action in the Civil War, and Roosevelt, of course, was the scion of a famous political family. They had worked together before, and there was a friendship, though based on society and not ideology.

In 1932, the Bonus Marchers of the Great War, had descended on Washington in the depths of the Great Depression to ask the government to pay early a bonus promised to the doughboys who had answered their country's call. The bonuses had been issued in 1924 but would not come due until 1945; however, many of these heroes who went over there were out of work, starving, and wanted the government to pay ahead of time, even if it meant forgoing the interest. FDR refused and directed MacArthur to rid Washington of the marchers. MacArthur used harsh actions to clean the city of the thousands of Bonus Marchers and their families. In 1936, when

Roosevelt had still not solved the Depression, the Democratically-controlled Congress, over the president's objections, paid the Bonus Marchers.[17]

Kimmel and Short were not American royalty, were frankly scapegoats—sacrificial lambs who had done everything by the book, had not been given all the facts by Washington, and now were being punished for it.[18] They had been as astonished by the attack as anyone else in the world, but had they been given the decoded Japanese communications between Tokyo and their embassy in Washington that the War Department and the White House were intercepting, Kimmel and Short may have had a chance to change or at least alter the course of history. Even the night before the seventh, when shown the next to last segment of the thirteen-part Japanese communiqué that presented the Japanese ultimatum, FDR read it and said, "This means war."[19]

That was never communicated to any of the field commanders in the military, especially in the Pacific, who had more than a passing interest in the intent of Prime Minister Tojo and his government.

Adding to this, the War Department and the navy had been tracking a large convoy of Japanese ships including six aircraft carriers just days earlier, but when the armada turned eastward, U.S. military strategists lost track of it. This too was never communicated to Kimmel or Short. All they ever got were oblique and confusing messages from Washington, reinterpreting the secret coded information going back and forth between Washington and Tokyo. The administration had believed that war was imminent between Japan and the United States, but they wanted Tokyo to commit the "first overt act of war" so a moral case for participation in the war could be made to the American people and the world community.[20]

The Roosevelt administration had successfully squashed any congressional investigation and had gained control of the matter by naming its own board of inquiry. Even so, it was obvious the blame was either going to Roosevelt, Cordell Hull, Henry Stimson, George C. Marshall, Harold Stark, Frank Knox, and the rest of the military and political leadership in Washington, or it was going to two competent, if politically naïve, men who were 6,000 miles away, without access to the press to tell their side of the story or defend themselves. The outcome of this was easy to see. The lead in *The Baltimore Sun* reported, "Without waiting for any more information on the contributing causes of the Pearl Harbor disaster," the men were humiliatingly dumped.[21]

Washington had seen the old "hang 'em out to dry" gambit a thousand times before. Someone had to take the blame, and the master politicians in Washington made sure it was going to be Kimmel and Short, and not themselves. The history of the country was marked with not only heroes but also scapegoats. "Sources" in Washington let it out that Short and Kimmel had not been "on the alert."[22] An unflattering photo of Kimmel was made available to the newspapers. This was all orchestrated: the War Department and the Secretary of the Navy made the announcement simultaneously. Secretary of War Stimson bluntly said his thinking was in line with Secretary of the Navy Knox regarding the "unpreparedness of the situation of December 7th . . . and to expedite the reorganization of the air defenses in the (Hawaiian) islands."[23]

Their demotion was the headline of every newspaper in America, and nearly all used the word "ousted."[24] It was humiliating, especially since Kimmel's new assignment was to stay in Hawaii on "temporary duty." The final humiliation was that he would have to stay to watch Nimitz replace him.

Nimitz, as head of navy personnel, only days before was signing the telegrams notifying the next of kin of the death of their sons. But he'd also seen plenty of sea action in war and peace. Now he would get a chance to lead the friends and brothers and teammates of those fallen at Pearl Harbor into battle. He met that day for an hour in private conference with President Roosevelt.[25]

Chester Nimitz, with a two-jump-up in rank to a full admiral, was being pushed to the center stage of history. Kimmel and Short, having been demoted both then left the military in early 1942 and faded into the mist of cruel and unjust history.

The bad news from Malaya continued. The Japanese were driving hard down the peninsula towards Singapore; and British troops were not only on defense, but London was beginning to withdraw some of its troops, which was tantamount to an admission that all was lost there. Events were not faring any better in Hong Kong, where the Japanese demanded the British surrender, but the British refused. The Chinese were attempting a counteroffensive to aid the British, who had received an impossible order from London to "hold on."[26] The Japanese also seized the strategically important Penang Island.[27] And things worsened in the Philippines as well; the Japanese continued moving towards Manila, and it was reported they were using buses to transport the invasion forces.

American forces in Manila did, however, destroy twenty-six Japanese planes. America's first ace of the war, First Lieutenant Boyd D. "Buzz" Wagner, had shot down five enemy planes in the air and was credited with the destruction of many of those twenty-six planes on the ground.[28]

Japanese troops made landfall on the island of North Borneo and Sarawak, both under British protection, both rich in oil, rubber, sugar, coffee, iron, coal, spices, and other treasures of the Earth.[29] Sarawak had an unusual history to say the least. One hundred years earlier, Sir James Brooke, an English officer, had helped the Sultan of Brunei fight off an insurrection. In gratitude, the Sultan gave Brooke the territory of Sarawak, and his descendants still ruled the area as of the beginning of the Second World War.

Later, the "White Rajah"—Anthony Robert Brooke, son of Sir James— penned an agreement with England to provide protection for his country. When war broke out, the island had been celebrating the centennial of "White Man's Rule."[30] Japanese forces were also invading Dutch-owned islands in the region.

Just north of Sarawak, an earthquake of huge dimensions shook Formosa, China, and Japan; and hundreds were killed. Yet another earthquake hit Turkey, with similar deadly results. Both were a reminder that while war was waged, the forces of nature went on unimpeded.

The eighteenth of December was not a day of gigantic news, unless one counted the ouster of Kimmel and Short, which was huge as it was the biggest shakeup in the military leadership since the Civil War, but many, it seemed, had expected that Kimmel and Short would be relieved of their commands sooner or later. It had been rumored in the papers and in political and military circles for days, and everybody took it in stride. Some members of Congress had demanded that Kimmel and Short be impeached. They had become marked men who, after December 7, were simply marking time, waiting for their sentencing without first being charged or even receiving a fair trial.

The American people had become used to temporary and sudden changes over the past several weeks. The 1940s were looking different than the 1930s, when little seemed to change. Now there appeared to be a point where Americans settled into a routine that involved change on a daily, if not hourly, basis. No announcement, no event, no pronouncement, no decision, no news was outside the realm of possibility, except one saying they would lose the war. No one in America believed that. A new reality had settled across America, and upheaval seemed the new normal.

In the realm of the new reality, the U.S government seized a half million pounds of tin, legally owned, that was being stored in a warehouse in New York City. It was needed for the war effort. No one blinked or protested.

Then the Office of Production Management announced it was "freezing" all tin supplies in the United States.[31] Tin would now be controlled by the Director of Priorities of the Metals Reserve Corporation, a subsidiary of the Reconstruction Finance Corporation, which eventually developed eight separate subsidiary corporations for the war effort. Washington also announced that, from now on, it would coordinate all air-raid drills and blackout drills. Americans for the first time were being urged to save scrap metal.

Announcements were made. The federal government announced it was hiring shipbuilders and metalworkers for operations in Pearl Harbor. The government also announced that fishing in New England would be limited to clear days only; the government announced it was, well, nationalizing the oil industry in California, citing national security.[32] And "the laundry machine manufacturing industry is going to be called on to fill war orders aggregating millions of dollars."[33]

"Eating habits may be changed a little because of the Jap war," said the *Wall Street Journal*. "All canned pineapple come from Hawaii. Supplies may be cut down due to shipping difficulties. Tuna and sardines for canning and other fish caught off the west coast will be harder to get due to naval regulations and risks to fishermen. Japanese canned crab meat is out."[34]

Airmail to the Pacific was halted for a time, but that came as little surprise. Also, "Northern California was battered by the winter's worst storm the first of this week but until today it was a military secret." The navy and

Weather Bureau brass had withheld the news until it was old enough to not do the Japanese any good.[35]

With the government's edict to limit rubber to almost exclusive military use, Price Administrator Leon Henderson caused a near riot when he said that production of such non-essential items as golf balls and tennis balls might be eliminated. Duffers and strokers swarmed into department stores and sporting goods stores, such as Abercrombie and Fitch, and cleaned them out in a matter of minutes.[36]

The NFL's annual Pro Bowl game, involving the winner of the NFL title and a team of all-stars from the other nine teams, was moved from Los Angeles, where it had always been, to New York.[37] Again, security.

The first refugee ship since the outbreak of formal hostilities between the Axis and the United States arrived in Jersey City. One hundred and ninety-one passengers breathed the air of freedom.[38] Reports from the Russian Front and North Africa were good for the Allies. The Russians finally appeared to be pushing the Germans back, while the British were also making headway in Libya. However, some analysts thought the Germans were simply reassessing and would mount a strike against Russia, farther south.

A navy bomber carrying six men crashed in Norfolk, killing all aboard,[39] and a plane carrying a general on a seemingly routine flight from New York to California disappeared,[40] but these noncombat-related crashes were now commonplace. There wasn't a day that went by without a report on a crash of a military plane. Meanwhile, civilian pilots now had to carry photo identification, something previously unheard of. Yet another rumored attack on the West Coast was reported, but this time it was a submarine and not a mystery plane.[41]

In FDR's confidential papers that day, was no mention of Kimmel or Short, or Nimitz for that matter. Some of the documents dealt with the deficient number of airplanes at the disposal of the navy: "The Navy has on hand an even 100 Douglas torpedo bombers known as TBD. This number is barely sufficient to meet minimum operating requirements."[42] A second memo noted that the navy only had 768 "aircraft torpedoes." Complicating things, "unfortunately, there is no such thing as a universal torpedo." Hopefully, it was noted that "a new Government torpedo plant is being erected in Chicago by the American Can Company, but this factory will not be in production until the end of 1942."[43]

Cubans uncovered a Gestapo plot to set up a signaling system in a mountain range overlooking the Atlantic. Two arrested operatives of Nazi Germany were found with charts and plans detailing the plot.[44] Nazi agents were also foiled in an attempt to blow up railway tracks in Bolivia that were used to ship tin and lead to the United States. Mexican officials discovered Japanese operatives attempting to install a radio transmitter. With all the attempts by the Axis Powers to commit sabotage in Central and South America, a conference representing all the Americas was announced for January 15 in Rio. Part of the approved agenda was to "curb the activities of 'undesirable aliens' in the Western Hemisphere."[45]

Sales of the "series E" bond—known as the "people's bond"—continued to skyrocket, up 146 percent over the previous week.[46]

All the government mandates to Detroit were bound to have an effect on employment in the car industry. Not only were up to 1 million assembly line workers affected, but also 44,000 new-car dealers, showroom managers, car salesmen, secretaries, swab boys, mechanics, tire salesmen, advertising and marketing executives . . . the list of those affected went on and on. At the end of 1941, when it became known that no new cars would be made for the foreseeable future, new car dealers did a land office business but it was only temporary. "Backbone of the dealer's business is the sale of new cars and trucks and such accessories as tires and tubes, radios, heaters, etc. Production of nearly all such goods, for the market in which he sells, is being severely restricted where not eliminated entirely."[47]

Some workers in Detroit would be rehired as the factories were retooling for the war, but many others would not. "Vastly increased output of military trucks and tanks, warplanes and aircraft fuselages and engines, marine motors, guns and shells and hundreds of other industry-made munitions will create jobs practically immediately for tens of thousands of laid off automotive workers. By late next year—possibly sooner in some cases—the serious unemployment problem now facing automotive centers should be wholly or largely solved," said the *Wall Street Journal*.[48]

The disposition of the thousands of "enemy aliens" who had been picked up by G-men in the hours and days after the attack at Pearl Harbor had still not been settled. The wheels of justice were turning especially slowly in this regard, and one of the first hearings for the thirty-six Japanese, German, and Italian nationals being held at, among other locations, the East Boston Immigration Detention Center would not take place until Monday, December 22.[49] In New York, some were being held at—ironically—Ellis Island.[50]

The port of embarkation had been closed for fifteen years, but now it was being used for something altogether different.[51] "Although no specific charge had been disclosed, presidential warrants for their arrest were based on a blanket allegation that their liberty was 'dangerous to the public peace and safety of the United States.'"[52]

Even if not being held in detention, "enemy aliens" could not "have in his possession firearms or other implements of war; short-wave receiving or transmitting or signal devices, codes or ciphers, cameras, and documents in which there may be invisible writing. Photographs, sketches, pictures, drawings, or maps or any military or naval equipment are also banned." An order came down actually telling the "enemy aliens" to surrender these items.[53]

The U.S. attorney for Massachusetts, Edmund J. Brandon, said, "While enemy aliens are not criminals' in the ordinary sense of the word, neither are they entitled to the rights set forth in the Bill of Rights. The latter applies only to citizens and aliens of countries other than enemy countries."[54] Brandon elaborated that the disposition of the alien enemies in captivity was entirely the prerogative of the president and that any American citizens who turned in a suspected alien enemy who was working to undermine the United States would receive the full protection of the Department of Justice.[55]

In Canada, all Japanese were being registered, regardless of status.[56] The national government in Vancouver alone had confiscated 1,035 Japanese fishing boats.[57]

Acting on a tip, the Chicago office of the FBI arrested the head of the consulate there, Kiagachiro Ohmori. The consulate office there was shut down and sealed. They also arrested an Austrian inventor, Dr. Fritz Hansgirg, who was working at a magnesium plant in California. The FBI did not elaborate on why Dr. Hansgrig was arrested.[58]

Still unresolved were the diplomats of the Japanese and German legations in Washington. The Japanese, it was known, were drinking heavily, as witnessed by the chauffeur for the widow Mrs. William Howard Taft, who accidently got himself stuck for a time in the Japanese embassy on Massachusetts Avenue in Washington. According to David Brinkley in *Washington Goes to War*, the Japanese envoys were drinking heavily the night of December 6, which accounted in part for the slowness in transcribing the last of the thirteen-part message for delivery to Cordell Hull on the day of December 7. The "embassy staff had been drinking Scotch whiskey all night and the translators were still drunk the next morning."[59]

American diplomats in Berlin had already been moved out of the city to a "comfortable hotel" until an exchange could be worked out, and the United States responded in kind, taking the German diplomats to an equally "comfortable hotel."[60] Switzerland was now representing the interests of the United States "in all belligerent countries."[61]

While men rushed to enlist, the need to bolster the ranks was great enough to discuss the possibility of drafting married men.[62] "The Government will become hard-boiled about drafting husbands whose wives are self-supporting, the Senate was told today, as military leaders made known their view that this country must have an Army much larger than 4,000,000 men."[63] Allowance would be made, but General Lewis B. Hershey, head of the Selective Service, said that a four–million-man army in that era was not practical. He explained to the Senate that the army "may have to go to the bottom of its manpower." He compared it to the Civil War, during which more than 2 million soldiers were twenty-one or younger, more than 1 million were eighteen or under, more than 800,000 were seventeen and below, and two dozen or so were just ten years of age. Germany, said Hershey, had a standing army of 8,000,000.[64]

The University of Kentucky announced that it would grant college credit to any of its underclassmen who either enlisted or were drafted for military service.[65] Not waiting to be drafted into the army, Japanese American brothers Benjamin and Fred Kuroki, of Grand Island, Nebraska, enlisted in the U.S. Navy. The story of two Japanese brothers enlisting ran on all the wire services.[66]

The women who wanted to serve finally got their wish when it was announced the military needed 50,000 nurses immediately. The army had 6,811 nurses on active duty, and the navy had only 828 trained nurses. Initially, the new nurses would serve as part of the Red Cross, but the idea was floated again of drafting women directly into the military.[67] Thousands of women had already stepped forward to volunteer their skills.

Eastman Kodak Company had developed "color prints direct from color negatives, the latest Eastman contribution to the progress of color photography for the masses." It was called "Kodacolor" and came in rolls that, once exposed, were sent for developing to the Kodak plant in Rochester, New York, and then sent back to the customer. It was a revolutionary development.[68]

But not every invention caught on immediately. With only several days left until Christmas, toy manufacturers were working overtime to fill orders for what was shaping up to be one of the biggest gift-buying seasons in years. "Plastic toys have not attracted the buying public, so far," said a spokesman for the Milton Bradley Company. He said "it takes a new idea a little while to make itself felt in the market and also because plastics . . . are expensive."[69]

CHAPTER 19

THE NINETEENTH OF DECEMBER

Enemy Aliens Will Be Kept in Camps in the Southwest

Christian Science Monitor

British-Canadian Garrison Is Still Holding Hong Kong

Lethbridge Herald

Japanese Bomb Panay Island in Philippines

Washington Post

resident Roosevelt's new proposal for an Allied Grand Council bringing together all the countries of the Allied Powers ran into headwinds: he wanted it based in Washington, but Winston Churchill wanted it nearer the front, in London. America had been in the war a little over a week, American troops hadn't even set foot on the European continent, and already there was intramural squabbling among the Allies. FDR would only say the discussions on the Grand Council were "in progress" and that they had been conferring for a week, but he would not elaborate beyond that at his press conference.[1] Nevertheless, the first meeting took place in . . . London.

A draft of a Memorandum of Agreement" for a Supreme War Council was prepared for Winston Churchill, FDR, Stalin, and the "Generalissimo of the Armies of the National Government of the Republic of China . . ."[2] Chiang Kai-Shek, who had already had a fabled career.

The document was very specific on theaters of operation, unity efforts, a "common agreement" not to make peace with any enemy until all the Allied Powers made peace with that enemy, and so forth.[3] Curiously, the Allies could never get it straight on what to call the operation.

The day before, President Roosevelt held a ninety-minute meeting with his American "war council," including new member Admiral Chester Nimitz. Nimitz was anxious to get to his new command but told reporters, "I am very sensible to the fact that I am being entrusted with a very great responsibility which I intend to discharge to the utmost of my ability."[4] Nimitz's wife, Catherine, could not join her husband right away, as she was at their vacation home in Wellfleet, on Cape Cod.

Roosevelt spent another long day, mostly at his desk, in meetings and "hacking away at the mound of memos and reports in the big wire basket on his desk."[5]

The government finally made a decision on the thousands of enemy aliens it was holding in various locations around the country. The plan was announced to build internment camps in the remote deserts of the American Southwest, but the War Department refused to reveal their exact locations. It did leak out, though, that a handful of enemy aliens were also being shipped to Montana.[6]

"Thousands of enemy aliens in the United States, ordered interned, after hearings held by the Justice and War Departments, will be sent to permanent concentration camps to be constructed in the Southwestern States, it was announced today."[7] Initially, three camps were planned for construction, and the aliens, already held at various army and civilian locations around the country, would be shipped there for holding for the duration of the war.

Just days after December 7, Attorney General Francis Biddle said the bulk of the arrests of aliens was over, but a mere two weeks after he made that statement, the arrests continued unabated. "Under special wartime powers the Federal Government is continuing the summary arrest and detention of any Japanese, Germans and Italians above the age of 14 who may have been deemed 'dangerous to the public peace or safety of the United States,' by the Attorney General or the Secretary of War." Nearly 500 "axis aliens" had been picked up in the Los Angeles area alone. FBI officials pointed out that "there are hundreds of dangerous aliens who came to this country as agents of sabotage and destruction, awaiting the day when, behind the lines, they could strike a blow for Japan, Germany or Italy."[8]

The internees were dressed in old army uniforms and given three square meals a day, but little else.[9] So as to avoid confusion and "embarrassment," Chinese Americans nationwide began wearing lapel pins and buttons bearing American and Chinese flags, distributed by the Chinese consul general's office in New York.

The diplomats representing the Axis Powers had it better. Germany's 145 attachés and nationals were being held in a posh resort hotel in White Sulphur Springs, West Virginia, and the Japanese envoys were holed up at a posh resort hotel in Hot Springs, Virginia. Rumors had it that both groups of diplomats were drinking heavily.[10]

Laura Ingalls, a popular, petite, and pretty aviatrix of the 1930s, was, it turned out, a Nazi stooge. Winner of many speed races and records, the thirty-eight-year-old was arrested and incarcerated in Washington on charges of being on the payroll of the Nazis without reporting either the money or her work. The FBI had her dead to rights as taking money over the years from agents of the Third Reich. She'd been a familiar sight to Washingtonians, having flown her silver low wing plane over the capital and "bombarded the city with peace pamphlets."[11]

What looked like altruism at the time may have been just another ploy by the Germans to keep Americans out of the European conflict. At the time, she was the head of the "Woman's National Campaign to Keep [the] United States out of War." Ingalls had spoken often at America First gatherings.[12]

The fight for the Philippines was rapidly deteriorating for the Americans, even as General MacArthur and Admiral Thomas Hart put up a brave front, claiming battle victories. But it was noticed that navy documents were being burned in an incinerator, a sure sign that things were not going well for the American side.[13] Some Filipino troops were battling the onslaught with only sharpened bamboo poles and knives.[14] Heavy bombing was reported over Manila in what was described as "hit and run "tactics"[15] and the Japanese claimed that U.S. forces were "in retreat." Three waves of Japanese planes hit the island of Panay especially hard, including a religious school located there. Civilians were killed, and a great deal of property was damaged on the sugar-producing island.[16]

The situation in Hong Kong was even worse, as Tokyo had gained a strong forward-command position, cutting off communication between the British forces there and the outside world. No one knew if the British garrison was still holding on and, if so, how long it could hold. "The Japanese made landings at several places thus making the dispersal of the British forces necessary to cope with the various assaulting parties." However, "the Anglo-Canadian garrison on the island is comparatively small with a considerable area to defend." The Japanese propaganda agencies "claimed that British resistance in Hong Kong was collapsing and that the capture of the crown colony, which they described as already half-conquered, was only a matter of hours."[17]

The word "claim" was liberally used in the public relations war between the Allies and the Axis. Winning or the perception of winning was important for the military, the politicians, and the citizenry. Morale was everything to all involved, and both sides were guilty of putting things in the best light or minimizing the damage done by the enemy. There was no question that the Allies were far more honest with their citizens than the Axis, perhaps because part of the glue that holds democracies together is the truth, while part of the glue that holds despotic governments together is lies. Lying comes easily for those whose aspiration is to control other people.

Wake Island was holding by its fingernails, subjected to round-the-clock bombing from warships and airplanes. Japanese ships, troops, and bombers were carrying out widespread offensive campaigns against American and British military outposts, while opening up new fronts in Dutch New Guinea and advancing toward the Burma Road. Supply lines were becoming an issue for the Allies. "Imperial Tokyo headquarters . . . asserted that Japanese troops operating from Aparri, 250 miles north of Manila, had seized a U.S. Army base and were driving southward. The Tokyo high command claimed furthermore that the Philippines air defenses had been virtually knocked out as a result of Japanese bombing attacks on flying fields. Britain's struggle to halt the Japanese drive toward Singapore took a darkening turn as British and Indian troops were acknowledged to have withdrawn below the southern border . . . apparently yielding the 115-mile-long Malayan Peninsula state to the Japanese."[18] The *New York Times* reported that the Japanese troops fought with a "fanatical disregard . . . of a constantly high death toll. "[19]

Frantically, a private naval message marked "Secret" ended up on Roosevelt's desk, pleading "there is no time to lose. We must at all costs hold Singapore. Hailed in the press are largely illusory. Due to the events of the past week, there is a dangerous undercurrent in certain powerful official circles which deprecates American and English prestige and our ability to win this war. That it is already too late is even being said by some."[20]

A source in London confirmed that British troops were evacuating the island of Penang, an "important . . . base . . . one of Singapore's major outer defense posts." American troops had been dispatched to Singapore to help the Brits hold on to the vitally important outpost, but the Americans had their own hands full.[21] Wake Island was bombed yet again; there was nothing to the little atoll, and it was a miracle anything was left of it. Some reports in the United States said there had been a lull in the fighting in the Far East, but you could not tell that to a flyer or an infantryman or the marines on Wake. Apparently an American submarine had sunk a Japanese troop transport in the region, while an American fighter pilot, Lieutenant Samuel H. Merett, his plane shot up, flew it and himself into the side of a Japanese transport.[22]

The British navy was faring better in the Mediterranean than in the Far East. They were literally blowing Italian warships out of the water on what seemed to be a daily basis. On the eighteenth alone, the Italians had lost 1 destroyer, 2 cruisers and 5,000 men.[23] The carnage was such that the Germans restarted their airplane attacks on British ships operating there.

The seasonal rains had begun, complicating the situation for the American troops in the Far East. The Japanese were accustomed to jungle fighting, mud, and guerilla warfare. The Americans were not. A news report said the Japanese had attempted a landing at New Guinea, which, if true, meant they were opening yet another front in the Western Pacific. The Japanese were cunning and knew exactly what they were doing. Strike fast before the Allies could effectively respond and then attack everywhere, as they had the advantage of position. Then bleed the Allies dry of men and materiel before London and Washington could effectively reply and rearm. After seizing the territory, fortify it and make it impossible for the Allies to regain possession. Their plan was working beautifully.

Concern was so high over the Japanese game plan of permanent offense that some started to speculate that the Panama Canal was also vulnerable. Knocking out the canal would add thousands of miles to any journey of an American naval vessel from the East Coast to the West Coast. Plus navigating the Straits of Magellan at the bottom of South America meant traversing some of the worst waters on the face of the earth. Locations along the Straits were named "Fatal Bay, Fury Island, Last Wreck Point, [and] Isolation Harbor."[24] Security around the Canal increased many-fold.

Roosevelt temporarily promoted MacArthur to a full general, "a rank customarily reserved for the chief of staff of the army." There was also some talk around Washington about MacArthur, having just received his fourth star, being awarded the rank of supreme commander of the allied forces in the Far East."[25] The promotion was warmly endorsed by many editorial pages, including those of the *Washington Post*.[26]

War was hell in the air, on the ground, and at sea. A British bomber had ditched in the North Atlantic, and the crew floated for days with little water or food. To make bad matters worse, they were harassed by sharks: "One of the sailors had a large chunk taken from his chest and died five minutes later. All of them had a bad case of sun poisoning and were blistered. Their bodies were swollen."[27]

The armies of the world had taught soldiers how to fight; their faiths told them how to die; and doctors helped them with their wounds; but no one taught or prepared them how to survive. Survival was as important to war as any other aspect, and yet it had been completely overlooked by the planners and tacticians and strategists. Survival equipment was nonexistent, but new drugs were coming on line that would save the lives of many wounded men. Among them were anti-bacterial "sulfa" drugs that were the precursors to penicillin. The production and sales of sulfa drugs grew rapidly after their discovery in 1935. By 1941, more than 15 million people were treated with sulfa drugs every year.[28] They proved a godsend on the battlefield.

On the domestic side, just as government officials were telling the American people that there was no cause for alarm and there would be plenty of food for the citizenry during the crisis, stories began to appear suggesting otherwise, that change might come in just a few months. "It's true those old meatless days, motorless Sundays, one lump sugar and weaker coffee are not in prospect now. Tea, pepper, tapioca and possibly soap will be scarce." It was also noted that meats, canned goods, and cigarettes would be available, but more expensive. Christmas turkeys were going up in cost.[29] Reports said that Italians Americans, French Americans, and other "hyphenated Americans" had no worries as there were plenty of Christmas "eels" available for their dinner tables.[30]

New tires and new cars were out, as were new radios, new vacuum cleaners, new kitchen appliances, and most other household goods. Gas rationing on the East Coast was forecast for the spring, and Washington was still deliberating across the board controls over prices. It was already controlling the price of grains. Civilians were also asked to stay off the long-distance phone lines or at least keep their calls brief. War was one thing and sacrifices were expected, but it tried men's souls when the flow of wines and liqueurs from the occupied countries of Europe "dried up."[31]

Not all the citizens who volunteered or made sacrifices or went without for the war effort had the best of intentions. In Los Angeles, "marauding gangs of self-appointed air-raid wardens who molest citizens on the pretense that they are 'aiding defense'" were a problem in the city of not-all-angels.[32] On the other hand, in San Diego, a "Minuteman" group of "crack marksmen" was formed with the help of local law enforcement. The job of the volunteer riflemen was to "crush any attempts at local sabotage."[33] Many were affiliated with local gun clubs and the National Rifle Association.

More and more death notices from the Pacific, including the Philippines, were appearing in the broadsheets. And more stories appeared of grief-stricken parents, fathers enlisting or trying to enlist, and mothers joining the volunteer cause. In order to help boost morale for the American citizenry, the

War Department produced the first motivational poster for the American effort. It was, at best, mediocre. The placard depicted five "ape-like figures in German uniform singing the Horst Wessel song."[34] Better though, was the reemergence of syndicated columnist Ernie Pyle after a four-month sabbatical. His wife had been ailing, and he had taken time off to care for her. Now one of America's famous scribes came roaring back, and millions of readers were delighted.

A recruiting office in New York held a poster competition. The first prize was a full, one-year scholarship to the Art Student League of New York City. The winning poster was excellent, creative, "portraying the undercarriage of an Army pursuit plane striking a tarmac" with the banner headline reading, "Be a U.S. Army Aviation Cadet." The private sector was always more creative than the public sector, and excellent submissions came from "children, housewives, doctors, lawyers, green grocers, students, and salesmen."[35]

The concept of a "just war" had been a difficult notion for religious leaders and for people who had been taught and who believed that all violence was against the laws of God and man: peace was always the way. However, these were new and horrific enemies of all that was decent, and they were equipped with instruments of mass destruction.

Pacifism was one thing, but letting evil win the Earth was quite another, especially when good had the means to fight back. The military announced it needed thousands more chaplains in order to minister to the spiritual needs of the American fighting man. Robert Paterson, undersecretary of war said that a soldier needed two things: "a firm faith in his country's cause and spiritual strength. The comforts the chaplains give the soldiers are beyond any reckoning."[36]

The Catholic Bishops of America, following in the footsteps of Pope Pius XII, endorsed the American efforts as a "war for peace" and promised to work with the U.S. government without becoming political in an earthly fashion. The Catholics said it was their mission "to try to help, as becomes churchmen, our Government in being the instrument of Almighty God for the setting up of a new era in which human rights, human dignity, human freedoms, and a sane human solidarity will offer to all peoples prosperity and a chance for the pursuit of happiness."[37]

In reflection, several writers were somberly remembering the millions in aid the United States had given to the Japanese people during the devastating earthquake of 1923. "In the United States, more than fifteen million yen was raised for relief work. The United States Army contributed several million dollars worth of supplies, the United States Navy two million dollars worth. Of course, the flyers who bombed Hawaii did not pause to think of the ancient and profoundly honorable duty of gratitude."[38]

Criticism continued over the dishonorable lobbying activities and the egregious fees received by former Roosevelt associates, Tommy Corcoran and Charles West. The report from Senator Harry Truman's investigating committee "demolishes the theory that New Deal reformers are any different really than their brethren of the old Deal."[39]

Another lobbyist, with an elixir that would have made ancient alchemists green with envy, turned a $42,000 investment into $34,000,000 in war contracts. Queried by tough-as-nails Truman about how this was possible, Frank Cohen, the beneficiary of his own largesse replied, "We were just good natured damned fools, that's all."[40] Unfortunately, noted some editorialists, there were almost no regulations dealing with the access-selling industry which was flourishing in Washington.

America went forward anyway. The new movie for children, _Dumbo_, was a big hit, as was the performance of Corporal Jimmy Stewart, who in a national radio broadcast several days earlier had commemorated the Bill of Rights. Stewart had enlisted a year earlier, was assigned to Moffett Field around San Francisco, and had been out of the Hollywood spotlight for months. Stewart had been drafted in 1940 but was rejected because he weighed too little. After working out with a Hollywood trainer, he put on enough weight to be accepted into the Army Air Corps. Flying and music, not acting, were always Stewart's first loves, even as he received the best actor award for his performance in the marvelous 1941 screwball comedy about social manners, _The Philadelphia Story_. An actor with a quintessentially American screen persona,

Stewart was able to take time off from his duties to participate with other actors and actresses in commemorating the Bill of Rights. He spent hours writing his own script, demonstrating a deep knowledge and appreciation of American history.

Upon hearing it, Spencer Tracy said, "One of the most deeply-moving patriotic deliveries I ever heard. If that's Army training maybe a lot of us who think we can act ought to join up," to Hollywood columnist, Harold Heffernan.[41] Captain Stewart ended up flying numerous bombing missions over Germany and was awarded a DFC, a high French commendation, and other medals. Stewart was a decades-long film star, a family man, religious, successful, an American hero, and finally the iconic everyday man. A wonderful life, indeed.

The *Wall Street Journal* calculated the odds of a young American male being drafted. If you were twenty-one to twenty-eight years of age, classified 1-A, and had not yet been called, guess what? Your number was up, and you would be drafted. It was a 100 percent certitude. If you had dependents, the odds were 1 in 7 of being called. If your work was classified as "essential," the odds were 1 in 4 that you would still be drafted. Except if you were a "farm boy." The army, inducted 1,000 of these young men then released them to go back to their work on the farm because their fathers needed them. Up in the air were boys who were still aged nineteen to twenty-one years of age. Roosevelt had wanted them drafted, but many in Congress only wanted them registered at this time.[42]

Then Secretary of War Henry Stimson abruptly announced that army enlistments would soon cease.[43] The patriotic outpouring since the seventh of young men wanting to sign up—such as "farm boys"—was depriving many war industries of skilled workers. The army would depend on the Selective Service to weed out the 1-A's from the 4-F's. The Selective Service had over a dozen different designations, including Conscientious Objectors (1-A-O) to 4-A, for the sole surviving son of a family. Such a designation would be employed more than once in this new war.

New laws were also passed to make it difficult for creditors and banks to get at the men in uniform and for those not in the military. When not thinking about the war or volunteerism or things of immediate concern, the men in uniform were thinking about the economy and their own situation. The country was going through one massive dislocation as it was switching almost instantaneously from a peacetime to a wartime economy. Before the seventh, the stock market had been unreliable, up and down. Housing starts were down massively in November, and many small businesses were barely holding on. No doubt war was good for economies, as Lend-Lease had breathed life into the torpid American economy, but it came with a price. As men and women were hired for war work, men and women were fired because of war work. The Secretary of War put out an all-points-bulletin hiring an "unlimited number" of "men and women stenographers." They were needed immediately, though it was open to question how many men were in the workforce who knew how to type, write shorthand, and take dictation.[44] And 300,000 auto workers had already been laid off in Detroit.[45] Until the economy could actually grow and consume on a large scale, creating a demand for goods and services, the economic situation would be tenuous.

The nineteenth was the Friday before Christmas, and because many G.I.'s could not make it home, the towns and villages and families of America took the young men in uniform to their bosom. Parties were organized, dances, meals, music, gifts. In Fayetteville, North Carolina, the main drag of the town was closed to traffic, and a massive street party was held for "the boys." Sixty-two thousand soldiers descended for a barbecue feast.[46] It was the same at Camp Blanding, in Florida where the locals laid out a massive spread for the soldiers; the same story was repeated all over the country. Churches in Baltimore were also feting thousands of soldiers. And the old hero of the First World War, Alvin York, was on a morale tour of American military installations.[47]

Roosevelt and the First Lady wanted the White House Christmas—despite the presence of antiaircraft guns throughout the area—to go forward as normally as possible. The massive spruce tree had been placed inside the fence on the South Lawn, as opposed to its usual location on the Ellipse, for security reasons. Nonetheless, the plan was to open up the White House lawn on Christmas Eve to 30,000 well-wishers and carolers and to enjoy a performance by the Marine Band. FDR was scheduled to speak just after 4 p.m., and then he and Mrs. Roosevelt would attend services at Foundry Methodist Church.[48] A White House staff party was also in the works for Christmas Eve.

Christmas was tough at the home of J.E. Ingraham of Eastaboga, Alabama, as he mourned the loss of his son, George. George Ingraham had been killed the morning of the seventh—just after mailing his father a Christmas card.[49]

Despite the war, or perhaps because of it, meetings in Washington on the future of the new medium, television, were going forward. Few in America had a television, but some government officials and executives with the National Broadcasting Co. saw its potential, primarily as a learning device and tool to alert many people on war developments. "The current discussions by N.B.C. are based on three main points: Increased use of television as a training device through programs dealing with air-raid precautions, fire control, first aid, etc; large screen television to be used in public auditoriums for civilian defense programs; and entertainment."[50]

The government considered moving nonessential agencies out of Washington to accommodate all the new military personnel and war industry civilians flooding into the city. Officials were also making plans to evict—forcibly if necessary—private companies from their places of business as well. To meet the needs of the navy alone, huge temporary buildings made out of aluminum were constructed on the mall, row after row of them. They looked like giant mobile homes and were horrendously ugly. The temporary buildings were still on the Mall twenty-eight years later when President Richard Nixon ordered them dismantled, as they should have been at the end of the war.

FDR "asked" the governors of the forty-eight states to consolidate all their public employment services "under the federal government" so as to "facilitate the rapid recruiting of defense workers." Yet a new agency, the State and Territorial Employment Services, was set up immediately. FDR said that a meeting in Washington to discuss the matter was "waste motion."[51] In essence, Roosevelt was federalizing the states' labor forces.

His new Bureau of Censorship began to flex its muscles, but the more it did so, the more some civil libertarians questioned the wisdom of such an agency. On the one hand, FDR abhorred censorship and said so. On the other, he saw the usefulness in chilling leakers and potential leakers, while putting a fright into anyone who might step over the line and communicate too much information from the government, on the radio or via a private letter. Congress was going one step further though. A bill that would "permit President Roosevelt to take control of telephone and telegraph facilities" was approved by the Interstate Commerce Committee. Potentially, it meant FDR could also control the "transmitting equipment of press services."[52] The Associated Press and United Press were the lifeblood of hundreds of newspapers around the country, and without the wires, their newspapers would be reduced to covering only farm reports and social doings.

Congress was still considering a plan to make Daylight Savings Time the law of the nation in order to ameliorate many problems associated with blackouts and air raids, while at the same time lengthening the workday.[53] Also under active consideration were federal laws enforcing and taking control of the blackouts in all the states.[54]

The head of the federal office of Civil Defense, New York Mayor Fiorello La Guardia, was under fire. "Responsible sources reported that high official White House circles were displeased over the Mayor's handling of the civil defense problem." Specifically, "under criticism were the false air raid alarms in New York last week, the air raid drill staged for newsreels in Times Square . . . and the complete failure . . . of the well-advertised test of a giant siren that proved virtually inaudible."[55] These were just three of the hundreds of expensive mistakes going on in the country.

Even at its most efficient, war is nothing if not expensive. The cost of war kept spiraling upwards. It was calculated that in December 1941, it cost the country an appalling $729 per second, but by 1942, it would be up to an astounding $1,400 per second.[56]

Some in academia had been slow to join the war effort. Two weeks after the declaration of war, the presidents of Wesleyan College, Colby College, and other schools pleaded with their undergraduate males to stay with their studies and get their degrees (and continue paying their tuitions) while others, including Harvard, finally got into the swing of things.

The president of Harvard said third-year law students could receive "war degrees" on a case-by-case basis with an abbreviated last year. Smith College organized an Ambulance Corps, Brown University added "14 military courses," Yale was offering degrees in three years, and Simmons College in Massachusetts was holding evening courses in national defense.[57]

By the afternoon of Friday, December 19, the Japanese were claiming to have taken Hong Kong, in spite of the claims of the British military. If the Japanese claim were true, it would be devastating. Just hours earlier, Secretary of the Navy Frank Knox spoke to the 1942 graduating class of Annapolis, whose graduation had been accelerated by six months because of the war. He told the 547 graduates that the army and the navy had repulsed a third attack by the Japanese at Pearl Harbor, but this was false as there had been no third attack. He also asserted that with thirty minutes notice, the Japanese air invasion would have been blown out of the sky. "There is no question at all, in light of what transpired, that half an hour's warning of the approach of the Japanese planes would have made all the difference."[58] Who knew?

However, Knox also told the young men in white dress uniforms what was becoming obvious to all now: the Japanese had by far the largest naval force in the Western Pacific.

"By far."[59]

Top left: ARM2/C Ellsworth Abbott "Barney" Shirley, USN. Killed in Action January 1945.

Top right: President Roosevelt signs the Declaration of War with Japan on December 8, 1941.

Bottom: Sugar rationing creates long lines at home.

The attack on Pearl Harbor

December 7, 1941

IF YOU CAN'T GO ★ BUY WAR BONDS

THIS HOTEL PLEDGES A 100% PAYROLL

OUR BONDS ARE THEIR SECURITY !!

SERVICE ON THE HOME FRONT

★ CITIZENS DEFENSE CORPS
★ CITIZENS SERVICE CORPS
★ AMERICAN UNITY
★ SALVAGE PROGRAM
★ VICTORY GARDENS

WPA

There's a job for every Pennsylvanian in these CIVILIAN DEFENSE EFFORTS

PENNSYLVANIA STATE COUNCIL OF DEFENSE
CAPITOL BUILDING, HARRISBURG, PENNA.

AIR RAID PRECAUTIONS

KEEP COOL

DON'T RUN

DON'T SCREAM

PREVENT DISORDER

OBEY ALL INSTRUCTIONS

PENNA ART W.P.A.

FEDERAL USA WORK WPA THEATRE

IF YE BREAK FAITH

BE CAREFUL
NEAR MACHINERY

help US
PRESERVE
your
SURPLUS... FOOD

JOIN UP NOW AT
615 REAL ESTATE TRUST BLDG
PENNYPACKER 5718
RUTH G. H. STRAWBRIDGE
CHAIRMAN

COMMUNITY FOOD CONSERVATION INC.
COOPERATING WITH

PHILADELPHIA COUNCIL OF DEFENSE   PENNSYLVANIA STATE COLLEGE
CHURCH ORGANIZATIONS   WORK PROJECTS ADMINISTRATION
GARDEN CLUB   NAVY LEAGUE SERVICE

"CENSORED"

FREE

Pvt. John Doe
U.S. Army.

EXAMINED BY 42

Mrs. John Doe
1000 Silence St.
New Orleans, La.
U.S.A.

LET'S CENSOR
OUR CONVERSATION
About the WAR

WPA WAR SERVICES of LA

Do with less—
so they'll have
enough !

RATIONING GIVES YOU YOUR FAIR SHARE

STOP
AND GET YOUR FREE FAG BAG

careless matches aid

WAR WORKERS!
ARE YOU LOOKING FOR A—
HOUSE?
APARTMENT?
ROOM?
WE CAN HELP YOU—
A FREE SERVICE

PHILADELPHIA
MES
ATION OFFICES

COME TO
NICETOWN BRANCH OFFICE
POLICE STATION
22nd & HUNTING PARK AVE.

OFFICE HOURS
10 A. M. TO 6 P. M. MONDAY TO FRIDAY
10 A. M. TO 3 P. M. SATURDAY

SAVE SCRAP
FOR VICTORY!
Save METALS
Save PAPER
Save RUBBER
Save RAGS

for disposal
call Salvage **LOC 7866**

PHILADELPHIA SALVAGE COMMITTEE

...we here highly resolve that these dead shall not have died in vain...

REMEMBER DEC. 7th!

Americans aid the war effort by collecting shoes, stockings, and cooking grease.

PLEASE DRIVE CAREFULLY
MY BUMPERS ARE ON THE SCRAP HEAP

Top: Actress Rita Hayworth participates in the scrap metal recycling campaign by donating her car's bumper in response to the call for bumpers and other non-essential metal car parts for the war effort in Hollywood, CA, Oct. 4, 1942.

Bottom: Women enter vocational schools to learn war work.

CHAPTER 20

THE TWENTIETH
OF DECEMBER

U.S. Reveals Foe Operating Subs off East Coast

Birmingham News

Hong Kong Defenders Staging Last Ditch Fight

Yuma Daily World

12 U. S. Agencies, 10,000 Leaving D.C.

Washington Post

Heavy Philippine Battle Rages; Japs Land Anew

The Sun

A s news days go in a new war, Saturday the twentieth was a relatively measured one even as planes were downed, ships were sunk,
soldiers were killed, and civilians were marched off to their own
extermination. A measured march was working inexorably against America
and the Allies.

The war news—such as it was—was getting worse for the Allies. The
newspapers began using phrases like "bad news from the East" and "heavy raid
reported close to London." A headline in the *Boston Evening Globe* screamed,

"Hong Kong Doomed."[1] The Saturday evening edition of Baltimore's *Sun* newspaper reported as if Hong Kong had already fallen, but in fact, the British garrison was fighting on, holding on, hanging on.

Winston Churchill once said that the only thing inevitable in war was disappointment. Power of an air force is terrific when there is nothing to oppose it..[2] To illustrate Churchill's point: for years a man had flown Christmas gifts to lonely lighthouse keepers and their families up and down the New England coast, but the navy grounded the "Flying Santa," fearing he might be mistaken for an enemy plane and shot down.[3] So much for Christmas spirit.

Still, Americans could take heart and draw on their own history for inspiration and resolve. After all, the twentieth was also the 164th anniversary of another beleaguered time in American history: when George Washington and his ragged and demoralized men straggled into Valley Forge, Pennsylvania, to make camp. Among his troops was Private Henry Cone of Lyme, Connecticut.

Congress was moving toward a break, even after a pledge by Speaker Sam Rayburn that the House would not go out of session because of the war. The plan now was to go into recess until January 5.

Since the attack at Pearl Harbor, the national legislature had moved with lightning speed over long days to declare war on three nations, appropriate billions of dollars for defense, grant the president unprecedented war powers, create a restructured Selective Service bill which was finally headed to President Roosevelt for his signature, and hold hearings on all sorts of war-related matters including corruption.

The head of the Selective Service, General Louis B. Hershey, sent Roosevelt a memo outlining his concerns that men in war-related industries should stay put and not be allowed to join the armed forces. "In many instances they are men of skills who should stay in war production or vital civilian activities." He advocated that recruiting stop and that the military depend instead on a draft.[4] Memos Roosevelt reviewed that day dealt with the disposition of loyal Japanese on the West Coast[5] (authored again by John Franklin Carter) memos on the Dutch East Indies,[6] memos on Russia,[7] and